DECEPTION

AND

REALITY

LIVING THROUGH THE MISSING
PAGES OF HISTORY

KELE D. GABOR

Copyright & ISBN

Deception and Reality - Living Through the Missing Pages of History
Copyright © 2016, 2017 by Kele D. Gabor. All rights reserved.

No part of this publication may be reproduced, stored in a retrieval system or transmitted in any way by any means, electronic, mechanical, photocopy, recording or otherwise without the prior permission of the author except as provided by USA copyright law.

This book is designed to provide accurate and authoritative information with regard to the subject matter covered.
Book design copyright © 2016, 2017. All rights reserved.

Soft Cover Print Edition

ISBN: 9780998885018
1. Biography & Autobiography / Personal Memoirs
2. Biography & Autobiography / Cultural Heritage
                                        13th March 2017

KELE D. GABOR

Prologue

An eyewitness account of events from the Heart of Europe during and after World War II.

Hungary is located in the geographical center of the European Continent. The Carpathian Mountains form a ring and the borderline around the Hungarian kingdom. This geological formation resembling a heart and the importance of this region played in commerce, power, and history of Europe were the reasons some scholars referred to the Hungarian kingdom as the Heart of Europe …

DECEPTION AND REALITY- LIVING THROUGH THE MISSING PAGES OF HISTORY

Contents

Prelude	5
Introduction	6
Three Good Friends	8
The Nazi Squeeze	21
Tent Village	40
Homeless	63
Experiencing the Unbelievable	88
Road to Recovery from WWII.	120
Hungary..	144
Communist Takeover	157
Somewhere in Russia	174
Existence under Communist Control	199
Amateur Detectives	226
First Arrest	247
New Experiences and Perspectives	272
Glimpse of the Traitor	311
Setting the Trap	337
Getting Some Evidence	352
The Evidence	385
Dangerous Game	406
Three Is My Limit	432
Aftermath	467
Conclusions	490
Journaling & Notes	496
Book Reviews	498

Kele D. Gabor

Prelude

The Dalai Lama always wanted to come to the Heart of Europe. When the Soviet type of Communism lost its grip on Central Europe and the Iron Curtain lifted, he was finally free to visit the Carpathian Basin. Here he told the Hungarian people, paraphrased, "This is the place where the seed of the awakening and rebirth of the New World will sprout."

Let the content of this book represent the first few green leaves on the emerging seedlings from our land.

DECEPTION AND REALITY- LIVING THROUGH THE MISSING PAGES OF HISTORY

Introduction

Have you ever wondered how the Jews became the most influential people and why they are not more popular, but economically, financially and professionally the most successful and powerful group in the world? How the Hungarian First Armor Division saved more Jewish people from Nazi concentration camps than the rest of the world combined?

Why was the over one-thousand-year-old Hungarian nation mutilated by the Treaty of Trianon (Versailles) after WWI and again after WWII?

Why has America won the wars, but typically lost the peace?

How to find out what your life purpose should be?

If you want to know about these topics above and learn even more, please read on.

To make peace between the world and us, we must share the whole truth. However, many events described here were purposefully left out of historical books.

By hiding the truth, we have a hard time keeping the peace at home or in the world.

This book is dedicated to many courageous Hungarians who were sacrificed by Western (double) agents and to the millions of people who died as freedom-fighters or were forced to live under the yoke of foreign or evil governments or religious extremists.

After the World Wars, when the victors divide the spoils, political borders change. New nations are then formed and others removed from the maps, which create sufferings for all the adversely affected people. Most of these "forced unions" were at the expense of the over one-thousand -year old Hungarian kingdom in Central Europe. These unions of incompatible nationalities, religious groups, or minorities will fall apart, like the Czech and Slovak Republics or Yugoslavia. Typically, new wars start when the ill-willed peace treaty is drawn up by greedy or ignorant diplomats, just like after WWII when the Cold Wars began.

There are no communist nations! The correct labeling is "socialist states with totalitarian leaders protected by the Marxist or communist ideology."

However, in my writing I'll use this erroneous term communist instead of socialist, just for ease of reading and understanding.

Kele D. Gabor

The writer believes most misunderstanding, hatred, racism, and animosity among peoples are either the result of misinformation or ignorance.

Much of the misinformation and ignorance was spread purposely to justify or to cover up grave errors or injustices committed by the world powers and conquerors when dividing and/or creating new countries in Central Europe, the Middle East, and around the world. Current problems and sufferings, mostly unreported, will continue until these regions are properly restored and stabilized.

The stories in this book are based on actual events. I will tell you what I have learned, seen, and experienced. I will describe historical events from a closer perspective, from experiences of my own or others, but I have changed the settings or characters to protect the innocent. Some chapters are fictionalized; however, the texts will be peppered with actual names, places, and dates just to give more credence to the facts in cases where collateral damage is unlikely.

Since I'm an American, I can write freely without observing the rules of international diplomacy or protocol, political correctness, and without favor to religion, gender, ethnicity, ruling classes, or governments. However, I still have to be mindful of the numerous relatives and friends still living in Hungary and neighboring countries that may be harassed, worse yet arrested, deported, tortured, or even killed.

Emotionally, it was very difficult and painful to recall the things I have wanted to forget. I hope the readers will understand and appreciate it.

So, read on and travel with me while I recount some of my pleasant and unwanted adventures.

These writings include many historical events that may be contrary to what you have learned. However, these facts should be known so as to have a better understanding and perception about the current conflicts all around the world. One must know the past in order to appreciate the present, and the present is the basis for the future! I also believe there is no public opinion; there are only published opinions. Some of my writings include purposely covered up historical events to put the winners in a better light or to make the losers look worse. I believe the losers would write a more truthful history than the victorious nations.

"Those who do not remember the past are condemned to repeat it."
—George Santayana.

Three Good Friends

We watched as the sun played hide-and-seek with the clouds. The three large windows of the living room faced to the west. It was mid-afternoon.

I was convinced the heavens were sending secret messages when short and long light pulses came from the sun as the clouds passed between us in quick succession. I tried decoding them, but the resulting Morse code made no sense.

A deep, dark cloud appeared, covering the sun. The entire room, including the shiny furniture, turned a grayish-blue tint. The weather front must have come from the north, as the most southerly window on the left, that had the most cracks from the earlier bombing, was the last to light up. The room was large, about seven by seven meters. Along the windows, from left to right, was the grand piano. Nearby was a beautifully carved and inlayed late eighteenth century round table, where three men sat playing cards.

Even though the tabletop was light enough to see the three players and the outline of the cards, the faces could only be made out when the sun rays poked through the thin white curtains.

The three men were all in their mid fifties. They originally met about forty years earlier, spending eight years close together in the gymnasium (high school) in the city of Udvar, in the eastern part of Hungary.

This region is also known as Transylvania. Udvar was the region for the Székelys, settled in Transylvania for over fifteen hundred years.

The three friends went to the same school during the same years and in the same way— on scholarships. They were bright and capable students, and they all came from different parts of Hungary.

I was fortunate to attend the same school, in the same classroom, and may have sat on the same bench as my father did forty years earlier. This particular Hungarian school was fairly old, close to five hundred years.

It first opened its doors in the second half of the sixteenth century. This school is still a "gimnázium" (comparable to a junior and senior high school combined) and currently serves a large area, as most other Hungarian schools and universities were forcibly closed by the Romanian government after 1948.

Kele D. Gabor

The host, Vajk, my father, was originally from the territory of Nyitra, located northeast of Pozsony. Pozsony is now the capital city of Slovakia and has been renamed to Bratislava. Ironically, Pozsony was the coronation city for most of the Hungarian kings for about six hundred years.

Sketch of My Father, Vajk (1943)

Deception and Reality - Living Through the Missing Pages of History

The three close friends came from old Hungarian families with a history of high standards, hard work, and fairness. They all had a strong belief in the basic human rights: freedom, independence, and equal rights for all.

I became the lucky recipient of some of the three good friends' wisdom, knowledge, teaching, and mentoring. I owe thanks and appreciation for their patience with me, ultimately helping me to overcome the many difficult life-threatening situations and survive the onslaught of foreign occupations, socialism, and communism without sacrificing my principles.

Álmos, the man in military uniform, with a rank of a colonel, came from Banya, an old Hungarian gold mining town in eastern Hungary, also in Transylvania. This old Hungarian City was part of the "giveaway" by Stalin to appease the Romanians for his taking a large part of Moldavia after WWII.

Father Tibor, the tallest one, was from the city of Zombor, believed to be in the area where Attila the Hun first established his headquarters in the fifth century. Now the fifteen hundred-year-old Hungarian settlement is located in Vojvodina in Serbia (ex-Yugoslavia).

The three men's friendship lasted all these years, and they understood each other very well. They were apart a few times, during WWI and the ensuing years while Austrian, Czech, Communist, French, Russian, Romanian, or Serb forces occupied parts of their homeland. During the early part of WWII, they also had to go their separate ways. But in September 1944, a few months after the German invasion and Nazi occupation of Hungary, all three of them met again, miraculously, in the city of Zala. They stayed in even closer contact with each other from this point on.

Usually, they met at our home every Sunday afternoon. If, for some reason, one of them could not attend, the other two played chess instead of cards.

While they waited for one another, they would tell stories and I eagerly listened. In retrospect, I found those vivid stories more entertaining and informative than some of the best movies from Hollywood. There was no TV at that time; extracurricular learning came primarily from books, parents, and friends—that is, if we wanted to learn more than was taught in schools. Also, it was learning not limited by a director's view, but only by our own imagination; every story could be visualized in full color, in real time, and one could become a part of it.

Vajk, the politician and also the host, was slightly darker in complexion and had dark eyes, hair, and skin. He was wearing his formal Sunday suit with striped gray pants, white long-sleeved shirt, and maroon necktie already loosened at the neck and his black silk vest. He had taken off his black jacket and hung it in the wardrobe. Vajk looked the oldest, with his dark mustache and slick black hair that had begun to turn white at the edges. His distinguished features were his high forehead, aristocratic nose, his demeanor, but most of all, his intense eyes. His eyes were dark and warm but bright; he could look into you, around you, through you. His eyes seemed to speak. With just a glance, he could set you at ease, make you examine your conscience, make you smile, make you laugh, or make you cry. But be aware when he raised his eyebrows! With his searching glance, he could always find good in people, even in his enemies. His body was strong, but his walk was easy and light. His height was average, but when he appeared, spoke, or smiled, he became much taller. His warm, baritone voice was always friendly, and he treated everyone equally. In spite of his high position in government, his many achievements, education, awards, recognitions, responsibilities, and title, he was kind, helpful, considerate, and generous to everyone.

I remember well when the man delivering coal for the winter was running late; my father helped him unload the heavy cargo to ensure he could get home before dark, as carrying a light on the wagon was illegal because of the frequent air raids.

One time, this coal deliveryman pulling a heavy load stopped his horses beside me as I was walking home from school. He jumped off the wagon, and with a big smile, he said, "Don't believe the Nazi officials or Nazi controlled newspapers. Your father is a very good man, and you are lucky to be his son." At that time, it didn't mean much coming from this man. I knew what he said was true, and I loved and respected my father very much. However, a similar incident occurred four years later, except that the comment began, "Don't believe the Communists or their newspapers."

The second man at the table, Álmos, was a veterinarian with the rank of colonel. He sat in the corner and looked quite different than the host, with light-blue eyes, fair skin, and a bald head. When the sun shone on his head, it looked bigger and brighter; the sun's reflection created a small, shiny halo on top of his head. He looked the most professional in his fancy gold-braided military officer's uniform. He wore a military khaki jacket with a black velvet collar that was unbuttoned at the top and black trousers with red stripes and very shiny black boots. His black gold-braided military shako was left on the small table in the hallway. The colonel looked smart in his uniform, although he was heavier than the other two men.

His blue eyes were bright; he had rosy cheeks, a small nose, and a perfectly round head. To my surprise, he didn't wear a mustache, even though one would expect it of an ex-hussar (cavalryman). This was the last time I saw him in his military uniform.

The colonel was always clean and looked like a well-dressed mannequin without a toupee. Every time I saw him, I recalled my grandmother's line about modern men, "Man without facial hair is like a cake without icing."

She must have been aware of what some of the helpful features were on men, as she was a very attractive woman, even at her older age. She married again in her late fifties for the fourth time to a physical-education teacher ten years younger than she was. She lost her first husband at the beginning of WWI, the second toward the end, the third, my favorite, died of lung infection after running a marathon race on a cold, rainy day.

Don't be misled by Álmos's baby face; he could be tough— very tough. I saw him once in a military review. You could say he either didn't know the meaning of or refused to believe in the word of excuse. His comportment toward women was just the opposite; he was kind, considerate, and loving; an officer and a gentleman. He was popular at parties, as he was an excellent dancer, good singer and composer, and an accomplished self-taught violin player. When one asked why he picked such a difficult instrument to play, the answer was always the same: "There is no other musical instrument with better sound to depict and describe the mood, curves, and shapes of beautiful women, and it can laugh, cry, or be happy or sad."

His wise remarks did not always make sense at the time, but later many of his statements became clear. One prominent thing still stands out in my mind, the way he described the love of country that can truly blossom only through military service.

He said, "Everyone should go through a basic military training, like in Switzerland, as only this type of service gives you the real intimacy needed between you and your country. While you're learning to actively defend your country, your appreciation and love will grow for it. This feeling of intimacy will develop in the service, which is seldom obtained through civilian or political jobs. When you serve your country, it affords the feeling of the lover's touch. Loving your country without serving first in the armed forces is like being with your lover but unable to touch."

Only after I served my country in the US military could I truly appreciate his wisdom, and this is what I have learned:

It is a soldier, not the government
        Who gives your country independence.
It is the soldier, not the justice system
        Who gives you freedom and equality.
It is the soldier, not the poets
        Who gives you the freedom of speech.
It is the soldier, not the politicians
        Who gives you the right to vote.
It is the soldier, not the reporter
        Who gives you the freedom of the press.

Colonel Álmos usually ended up at center stage at every party. In his free time, he would build violins or dabble in military strategy. His reason for the constant work was that we must learn more, improve, and set an example of how to be a better human being, but definitely not to be the so-called civilized man. According to Colonel Álmos, civilizations did more harm than good to all God's creations. They started wholesale colonization, slavery, the slave trade, mass executions, mass deportations, and inhuman political prisons like the French Devil's Island in Guiana. They tortured men and animals, burned witches, destroyed forests, fisheries, and wildlife. In the name of progress and civilization, they polluted water, soil, and air, conquering nations that could not defend themselves, spreading diseases and fear wherever they went, robbing and killing the natives while blinding the people with so-called new religion.

These so-called civilized Western nations are also responsible for most of the ills in Central Europe and the world, including the starving of prisoners in the concentration camps. According to Álmos' information, Western spies knew about the concentration camps and reported their findings, but the Allies refused to do anything about it, except for not bombing them. It was sad to see every time we drove by Western embassies, thousands of people were waiting in line to obtain visas, mostly Jews trying to escape the Nazi concentration camps. Sweden was the first country to act in a humanitarian way and opened the borders, helping more than forty-three thousand Jews all from Hungary to survive the Holocaust.

England finally started to issue visas, but only for children. The USA never helped or accepted Jewish refugees, not even their children. Even the Red Cross was approached to help feed the prisoners, but the Allies would not permit it. The Hungarian government under Regent Horthy's leadership saved more Jews than the rest of the world combined.

The threesome even predicted that the wrong people will be blamed for all the atrocities Stalin and Hitler committed, while the Western Allies wash their hands. I hope that one day the truth will surface and the Western Powers will have the courage to admit and apologize for their gross miscalculations and failures. It was sad to see the Warsaw massacre by both the Germans and the Russians. Similar incidents were repeated by the Allies— like bombing the city of Dresden, which was internationally declared as the City of Peace reserved for the injured, women, and children.

The three good friends knew the fact that the Christian churches, our people, and our government did more to save people from deportation and the concentration camps than the entire free world combined.

For Colonel Álmos, being a highly respected veterinarian had its advantages. He knew every general and all the chiefs of staff. They all had a favorite horse, dog, or other animal needing his expert and special care.

Everybody trusted him, including the new general staff that was put in place in 1942 through 1943 by the Nazi high command, made up exclusively of newly promoted officers of German descent. Years later, I worked for retired Colonel Álmos one summer to help treat animals. He was even more skillful in treating animals than being a party man.

The third man, Father Tibor, a priest and a professor, was thinner, taller, and sharing some of the features from each of the other two friends. He had dark hair, tanned skin, with big sky-blue eyes and a small bald spot on top of his head.

On this occasion, Father Tibor wore a casual civilian outfit; dark pants, light-gray shirt with a black-and-white circular collar with a loose black leather jacket that was at least one size too big. He definitely looked better and more distinguished when he wore his priestly habit. His constant companion, a charcoal gray umbrella, was hanging in the hallway. Father Tibor had a distinguished look about him; he was tall, well-built, soft-spoken, and always in control. From his posture and the way he carried himself, one could guess he had some military background, but no one would have suspected he was an expert swordsman and a well- decorated cavalry captain during WWI. He had a thin face, thick lips, long nose, and big blue eyes with dark, bushy eyebrows. All his facial features were very masculine but pleasantly arranged on his face. I often wondered how he became a priest and remained single with his debonair good looks, soft voice, and excellent humor. In mixed company, women surrounded him, and they always demanded some entertaining stories of his archaeological excursions to India, China, Mongolia, Egypt, and the Holy Land.

Since he was versed in many ancient languages, he had done a great deal of translations in his spare time. It was a pleasure to hear him talk; he made the stories come alive. He taught history and archaeology. What a combination! He could usually "dig up" the truth, regardless of what the current government approved or what was politically correct text written in history books.

I have never forgotten when Father Tibor brought me a wooden puzzle from China. He knew I loved to solve them. Typically, I took them apart in a paper bag so as not to see how the pieces fit together. This way, it was more challenging to reassemble them. However, this particular puzzle of the pagoda was so tricky that after several failed attempts, I got angry and swept the pieces from the tabletop, yelling out, "I'm a failure." Father Tibor, witnessing my quick temper, instead of scolding me, started to address me formally as "sir." This infuriated me, and I was ready to explode. Then with a calm voice, he said, "There are no failures in life. You must treat each 'failure' as a wonderful educational experience and with the same respect as your best teacher, as that is the way we learn the most." Later in life, I would remember his words, and they saved me from a lot of frustrations and disappointments.

We saw Father Tibor with some regularity but lost contact with him for about a year after my father's death. However, good fortune followed me everywhere, and I saw Father Tibor again many years later. I was assigned as a young engineer to help frame an archeological site southwest of the city Csaba on the border between the mutilated Hungary and the newly created and enlarged Serbia. The lead archeological expert was my father's old friend, Father Tibor. At that time, he would review with me some of the artifacts found, their placements in the graves, and their significance. It was truly an eye-opening experience.

However, this is a separate story that I'll tell in later chapters on how historical events are falsified for the benefit of people in power. Now I only respect teachers of history who have at least limited background in archeology or can read, write, and understand at least one foreign language.

Since the three experienced and well-educated good friends' professions and expertise were so different, when they all agreed on future events in the field of world politics, religion, or military issues, they were right on, confident, and absolute. It was sometimes uncanny how they were able to predict the moves of Hitler and Stalin, and sometimes Churchill and Roosevelt, including the prediction of the Nazi coup to replace Hungarian Regent Horthy and Prime Minister Kállay, who despised Hitler and refused shipping "enemies" of the Third Reich to Germany. They were also correct in assessing potential problems between Eisenhower and Montgomery. They also predicted the removal of Patton and the repeated assassination attempts on Hitler. I recall the discussions on consequences of a successful assassination of Hitler. The threesome predicted many benefits worldwide after Hitler's death. As they stated, "The German occupying army would be removed, and we could conclude all peace treaties and get Hungary out of WWII."

After WWII, they expressed concern about General Patton's safety (the latter assassination of General Patton was never revealed to the American public. The newspapers never reported that there were two consecutive and separate accidents, and a third in the ready, and each with progressively larger and heavier Russian military vehicles within minutes of each other).

Probably the most troubling puzzle for the three good friends was the Allies' failure to stop the flow of Romanian oil to the German military.

The Allies knew that WWII was entirely fueled by Romanian oil, and without it, there could be no war fought by the Germans. Even today, the historians, reporters, or politicians fail to document that fact. The English made a faint attempt to blow up the oil fields and refineries in Romania, but without proper planning and necessary resolve. The three good friends labeled the English attempt a joke and the Allies' biggest failure to shorten the war. Much later, the American bombers had to stop the flow of fuel to the German Army by destroying the refineries in Polesti, Romania, with great sacrifices.

The other issue, which they could not come to an agreement on, was why the Allies did not want to save the Jews from concentration camps.

The USA, England, France, Russia, and the rest of the free nations denied visas to all the enemies of the Third Reich, which included most of the Jews.

Yet all the leaders knew that war is expensive and the means to finance the war for Germany was to take it from the richest class of people— the Jews.

Of the three gentlemen, only Vajk served as an advisor to Regent Horthy, but the country would have benefited more if all three friends had been a part of the cabinet.

The men were playing ulti, or also, which is an entertaining and challenging card game for three players. The easiest way to describe the game, it is a cross between bridge and pinochle.

Regardless of the challenging nature and the complexities of the game, the game itself was inconsequential to the players on this occasion.

There was a lot to celebrate after being apart for most of WWII and then together again for the last few months. The mood of the players resembled the dark and the light game the clouds were playing with the sun. When one would speak of pleasant things that all felt thankful for, it would be followed by sighs of concerns about the future. It was a very unusual yin and yang day. Typically, but not this day, the conversation would be about world issues, each describing the same events and consequences from their own perspective. Eventually, they came to an agreement on what course of action nations or leaders would or should pursue.

It was the first Sunday of March in 1945. The small remnants of the German occupying forces were still withdrawing, leaving nothing behind.

What they could not take with them, they would destroy. The Germans rounded up thousands of cattle and hundreds of horses, put them into wagons, and waited for the locomotives to take them to their own starving country. Somehow, they always found a way to take the pigs, as they needed their fat (glycerin) to make explosives. The wagons were locked and guarded. They waited and waited for a locomotive until the crying of the thirsty and hungry animals drove most of the guards away. Fortunately, some of the guards cared enough to open the doors and let the thirsty and hungry animals out before they deserted them. Horses escaped, but the cattle were dumb or stupefied, as they stayed around the abandoned train stations looking for food and water. Not much was to be found. I still have this vivid memory of the hundreds of starving and thirsty animals, some already dead, left behind by the Nazis close to railroad stations.

In the meantime, the Russian Red Army was pushing West at a steady space; they already occupied about half of Hungary. The "liberating" first wave of battle-hardened Russian soldiers just wanted to find and kill Hitler (they pronounced it Gitler) and Nazis (they called Nyemetski) and also to steal watches to take home (most languages in Eastern Europe referred to Germans as "Nemet," meaning "dumb," as they were the only nationality settling Eastward that would not learn to speak the regional languages).

However, the next wave of the Russian soldiers and the occupying forces were a different story. Some lucky people fortunate enough to escape told terrible and unbelievable stories about the Russians. They told stories of the brutality, ignorance, and primitive behavior and of the dirt and the filth. Later, we were to experience the "unbelievable."

The three continued with their card game, although halfheartedly. They were in no mood to celebrate the great things and the miracles of the past few months. These stories were instead shared quietly among them earlier while my mother prepared the food. Regretfully, I could not be there on this day to listen to the shared good news or stories recited among them, as it was my turn to split wood for the cooking stove. When the meal was served, they ate as though they had never eaten before. They ate ravenously, even chewing the liquid part, savoring every bite. It was the first soup they had eaten in many months with real meat in it. The second course was everyone's favorite. It consisted of a large platter of diced boiled meat, rice flavored with carrots, brown mushrooms and yellow and white root vegetables, all mixed together. It was beautiful with tantalizing aroma, and the taste was perfect. The rice was very difficult to come by, but a few days earlier, it was received in a trade from a defecting soldier who exchanged it for some civilian clothes.

The meal was pleasant and comfortable; everyone was satisfied with full stomachs, but not necessarily in a good mood. We should have been very happy and content with the good meal. We gave the Lord our thanks for a good meal and all the good things. However, in spite of the blessings, the adults seemed preoccupied. In retrospect, I realize and understand deep down they were concerned about the uncertain future and what it would bring. They did not have the heart to share their earlier experiences during the Communist takeover in 1919. They knew, but would not say, that the terrible Nazi occupation under Hitler's leadership may have been child's play compared to the horror yet to come after the Communist takeover under Stalin's paranoid dictatorship.

I still remember the thanksgiving prayer led by Father Tibor after the noon meal. It began, "God, who gave us the food and drink, blessed be thy name…" Then, he looked toward us at the end of the long table and asked us to give thanks to the Lord one by one. I recall what the grown-ups and I said. My father, Vajk, turned toward my mother, his second wife, who was almost twenty years younger, and nodded.

She spoke next. "My dear God, there are so many things to thank you for the past year, but I want to say a special thanks for freeing my husband from the Nazi execution squad and helping my children and me to escape from the holding place for the concentration camp."

Next, my father turned toward Álmos, so the colonel spoke. "God, I thank you for the good news that, after all, my only son may still be alive somewhere in Russia. God, help him and bring him back alive and in good health."

My father spoke next. "God Almighty, thank You for returning my family from the internment camp, saving my family from the Romanian soldiers, and letting us unite again. Also, thank You for finding my two close friends again."

I recall giving thanks to the Lord for our family and friends not getting hurt by the falling bricks when exploding bombs nearby shook them loose from the cellar ceiling.

When every child finished, Father Tibor added, "Thank you, God, for the American bomb that killed the horse that gave us the meat, which we just ate. Amen."

Kele D. Gabor

The Nazi Squeeze

The card game among the good friends continued after dinner, and before it came to a conclusion my brothers and I went outside to catch some of the warming rays from the sun.

The courtyard in the center of the structures was large enough for parking several big trucks with trailers, and it still had room for us to run around to our hearts' content. It was rectangular, and it was only accessible through the covered main gate facing north. The main structure where we lived was L-shaped and ran on the south and the west sides of the compound. The entry to our living area faced the main gate. When one passed through the entry into a hallway, the door on the left led to the dining room, and the one across the hallway led to the large family room.

The door just right of the entryway led to the hallway. The first door led to the formal sitting room, where guests were typically entertained. Past the guest room, next to the sitting room, was another bathroom, followed by four other bedrooms.

Left of the main gate, on the north side of the courtyard, was another structure stretching eastward containing two large apartments, each with three bedrooms. The first apartment housed a middle-aged couple who seldom spent time outside. They preferred to stay within their own space, not socializing at all. Later, I understood their reservations to mingle; they were ashamed their only son signed up for the German Youth Group at age sixteen and left the country for training in Germany. Two lovely ladies, a mother and a daughter, occupied the second apartment. The lessee of this apartment mysteriously disappeared in 1942, after he made a public denouncement of German-descent settlers who supported the Nazis, leaving behind his beautiful wife and a very attractive nineteen year-old daughter. In spite of his anti-Nazi sentiments, his young, beautiful daughter fell in love with a German officer. Now she was seven to eight months pregnant.

On the east side of our compound, there was a garage, a woodshed, and a coal shed, an unused outhouse. Immediately beyond this structure was the compost hole where all the greenery went for composting. The only live vegetation that could be found inside the courtyard was in small, narrow flowerbeds alongside and close to buildings on the north and south side. This time of the year, only violets, tulips, and a few lilies of the valley were blooming. On the south side, there was a tall fence meeting the east end of the kitchen walls of the main building. Across the fence on the other side was the local police station, also with a good-sized courtyard.

One never knows what new things could be discovered until one explores. We found a place to climb over the tall fence to visit the now abandoned police building with an easy access through a broken window. An entire large piece of glass had fallen into the captain's office when a bomb hit nearby. It was easy to reach in and open the second window and climb through. This place became our play area and hiding place. It was filled with lots of weapons, several uniforms of many kinds, and letter-size paper by the clerk's desk, neatly stacked, that we used for making paper airplanes.

It seemed like the men left behind everything that would identify them as uniformed servants of the country or that would incriminate them in some way after the war. The clothing consisted of uniforms for police, military, border guard, porter, Navy, Air Force, bus driver, and others that we could not identify. We even came across German officer and Schutzstaffel (SS) uniforms. It was a few weeks prior to our discovery of access to the building when most of the uniformed men tried to change into civilian clothes.

I assumed most of them went home to their families or into hiding.

It took us only one afternoon to pry open the locked door behind the captain's office. It was full of treasures, metal headgear, and belts with an assortment of military buckles, sabers, knives, and bayonets with sheaths.

Now that we had a cache of weapons, we were ready for anything. In retrospect, it was our good fortune we all had fencing lessons, enabling us to respect those weapons and do no harm even during the mock battles and duels among us. One of our favorite games was to re-enact freeing my father from the Nazis— one of the many miracles we experienced during and after WWII.

On one occasion, our sisters joined us in the re-enactment of the locals freeing my father from certain death. The entire scope of the game changed. Our sisters first had to set the scene describing the events leading to the arrest of my father and recite the litany of sins with which my father was charged by the Nazis. To do it according to our sisters' wishes, they brought over and read articles cut out from the local Nazi-controlled newspapers. I distinctly recall the first few charges as we repeated them, as the German translator did to the people gathered around to watch the scheduled public hanging.

The first charge was "lover and hider of Jews" and "traitor" because of his refusal to leave Hungary to take his newly assigned post in Germany. Next was "spying and trying to negotiate with enemies of the Third Reich." This meant countries such as England, Soviet Union, and America. The irony of these charges was that the Communists replayed a similar scenario just three years later. The difference in the charges was that Vajk "protected the enemy of the state," such as businessmen, instead of the Jews, the clergy, and ex-Nazis, but the "spying for the West" charge remained the same.

Our sister, who had the role of translator, announced the charges; we picked up our swords and with a battle cry started to hit a Nazi officer's uniform we had stuffed earlier with straw. We could not replicate the actual noise level and the yelling of the thousands of people who had gathered, not to witness a hanging, but to free my father from the Nazi Germans.

The Nazis miscalculated by notifying the press about the upcoming public execution. They had not anticipated my father's popularity in the region. People gathered with homemade weapons hidden under their coats. When the announcement was translated, the entire group yelled and ran up the hill close to the church to free him. The five Germans, one officer and four prison guards, ran in the opposite direction. Even the local locksmith was there to help remove the cuffs from my father's wrist.

It took a long time to quiet the victorious crowd so that Vajk could thank them for his life and freedom.

The problem with Admiral Horthy, the regent of Hungary in the late 1930s and the early 1940s, according to some of his critics, was that he believed in or trusted Hitler longer than justifiable. However, that is not the case.

Horthy was a conservative, Royalist, Restoration Protestant who served as a decorated navy admiral under the Austro-

Hungarian dual monarchy in WWI and sought to re-establish Hungary as an independent kingdom.

Everything in interwar Hungary under Horthy was known as the royal institution, such as the Royal Hungarian Air Force, Army, and Navy, just as in Britain. As an Anglophile, he sought alliance with Britain and only reluctantly sided with Germany in the war after 1941, when the Nazis threatened his two sons' lives and the Soviet Air Force bombed our large city of Kassa located in the northeast part of Hungary.

The regent did everything humanly possible to keep Hungary independent of Nazi Germany. For example: in early 1943, Horthy appealed again to the Allies to help Hungary leave the Axis powers. I found out much later that this letter of appeal, currently in the English Foreign Office library filed under F.O.371/34498./C.120351, was rejected.

During the ensuing discussion of the request, Professor Haimer appeared, representing the Jews, and objected to any assistance, as he was concerned about the life of eight hundred thousand Jews still relatively safe in Hungary. He reasoned that Hungary's exit from the Axis would prompt an immediate German Army occupation of the country. It happened anyway less than a year later. There is no justification why over fifteen million Hungarians were made slaves, hundreds of thousands killed or taken to concentration camps, and the entire country was sacrificed for about four hundred thousand Jews the Germans took in late 1944, out of which ninety-one thousand never returned. It is also beyond common sense and logic why the Jews refer to Horthy as Fascist and still demand compensations and apologies from the Hungarian people when it should be the other way around!

After the Allies declined to help Hungary leave the Axis powers, Regent Horthy arranged to have his son fly to England as a special emissary to have the Allies reconsider their initial negative response. Unfortunately, Istvan Horthy died in a plane crash right after take-off in Russia, during his last scheduled sortie and just before his prearranged flight to England (later in America, I found out from the ex-head of the Hungarian counter espionage agency that the Nazis found out about the secret peace mission and sabotaged his plane to kill him. Horthy's younger son, Miklos Jr., was more fortunate, as the Americans freed him from the concentration camp just before he was supposed to be hung).

Horthy's Hungary was one of the safest places in Central Europe for the persecuted, as it provided refuge for escaped Polish prisoners of war and officers and many displaced persons fleeing from the Nazis, including the Jews.

After repeated unsuccessful attempts at negotiating with French and English diplomats to revise and reinstate old Hungarian territories unjustly taken in 1920, Regent Horthy still refused Hitler's request to a simultaneous attack of Czechoslovakia at the meeting in Kiel in 1938.

Regent Horthy and his cabinet's decision to reject Hitler's plan cost us dearly, as Germany no longer supported Hungary's claim for all the lost territories. In fact, Hitler vetoed the already widely supported return of Northern Hungary to re-establish the one-thousand-year-old common border with Poland.

The same scenario and punishment by Hitler was replayed when claiming the eastern part of Hungary, where again he only supported the return of half of Transylvania. Hitler also let us know that without further cooperation with his government, we could not count on his support, regardless of how much justification was offered for any other claims. From the time of the Kiel disagreement and the regent's unwillingness to declare war on the Soviet Union in 1941 until the Russians bombed our city, Hitler never supported our efforts to reinstate our thousand-year borders. Uniting with Hitler at that time would have ensured the return of all our unjustly taken Hungarian lands. Instead, Regent Horthy did everything humanly possible to turn toward England to preserve independence from the undesired German or Russian influence!

I remember some of the Hungarian diplomats' frustrations in trying to protect the mistreated Hungarian population that were forced to live in the newly created neighboring countries. The borders were changed to punish Austria and its allies for starting WWI. Unfortunately, the treaty primarily penalized Hungarians instead of Austrians because Western diplomats had very limited knowledge about the history of Central Europe and the over one-thousand-year-old Hungarian kingdom.

Since 1922, the number of Hungarian minorities decreased steadily, according to the neighboring countries' statistics, and more and more crimes were committed against our people. Our universities, schools, libraries, and churches were closed down, property was confiscated, and false charges were brought against Hungarians. They lost their jobs and suffered forced displacement of entire families and individuals.

Both the French and the British repeatedly rebuffed our diplomats' requests for help. The British asked us instead to form a block with the Czechoslovaks and the Austrians against the steadily growing military might of Germany and Italy. Our delegates, who were trying to negotiate with these countries' representatives, practically cried about the extreme ignorance of the Western diplomats. How could a mutilated country stand up against an already powerful Germany without having defendable borders and a well-equipped army? Even requests to strengthen our army to protect us from potential Czech, Romanian, and later German and Russian expansions were refused by both countries. Even requests for returning territories where the Hungarian population exceeded ninety eight percent were denied.

In 1940, the Nazis, and especially Hitler, were extremely upset about Hungary letting the remaining Polish Army escape after their successful "blitzkrieg" (lightning war) on Poland.

I stood by the window, watching as the long lines of Polish soldiers marched past our home in Parkány, Hungary. Parkány is now in Slovakia.

Every time they passed a house with a Hungarian flag on it, such as our home, the leading Polish officers ordered the appropriate right or left face so they could salute the displayed Hungarian flag while marching by in formal steps.

Kele D. Gabor

In spring of 1941, reports appeared on Regent Horthy's desk about the mysterious death of the highly respected Prime Minister Teleki. Count Teleki resisted any kind of German influence in Hungary. Less than a month after his public announcement that Hungary would stay neutral and would not permit any German influence or support of the Third Reich, Count Teleki died under suspicious circumstances. I know Regent Horthy received several conflicting reports, one of which contained the following information:

After the alarm early in the morning, I was the first person on the scene and I found the following situation and facts:

1. The victim's head had bullet holes that had entered from the left front temple.
2. The bullet holes closely matched and probably were the same .22 caliber as his personal pistol that was placed in his right hand.
3. His pistol was clean with an empty magazine and apparently had not been fired for a long time.
4. The victim was right handed.

The signature on the report was Géza Dezsô, head of the investigating team.

This report was enough for Horthy, and most of the government officials not to accept the suicide theory and to consider publicly denouncing the Gestapo-style assassination and getting involved in Hungary's internal affairs, but without the French and English support, the defiance would have been suicidal. The French, English, and American governments would not help even the fleeing Jewish population. Tens of thousands of Jews were trying to escape the Nazi concentration camps, but receiving visas from these free countries was nearly impossible. Most of the Jewish children who were accepted by a few western nations never saw their parents again.

Later, Géza Dezsô became one of Regent Horthy's most trusted confidants. It was Mr. Dezsô, who a year after the made up "suicide" story about the prime minister exposed the successful Nazi plot to control internal affairs by infiltrating the Hungarian military high command and most of the government offices. During the reading of the report about the Nazi plot, Regent Horthy visibly cried.

Some historians, like Father Tibor, knew that standing up against the

Nazis would have been impossible with our miniscule and ill-equipped army. The Germans would have rolled over Hungary ten times faster than Poland and they did it later, in 1944.

Germany needed supply of some critical raw materials, especially aluminum for the Luftwaffe (Air Force). They also needed access to the eastern front through a less hostile country, such as Hungary, in the center of Europe. Germany had no bauxite mines, and Hungary had fifty one percent of the entire aluminum deposits of Europe. There could be no Luftwaffe without Hungary's bauxite mines, and there would have been no WWII without the Romanian oil to fuel the German tanks and trucks. Hungary's defense capability was too weak to resist any foreign invasion, as the size of their military force had been reduced to less than five percent of what was needed to defend the country.

The Treaty of Trianon at Versailles, drafted in 1918, forced on us this weak military of thirty-five thousand personnel, including officers. What country could have survived a Nazi attack with an ill-equipped army of thirty five thousand men? Countries that had the military power to resist the Nazis, such as Czechoslovakia and Romania, let the Nazis have their way rather than fight. These newly created countries had a combined force that was ten times greater than Hungary's. They were much better equipped, supplied, and supervised by the French generals.

The Treaty of Trianon reduced the Hungarian military as follows:

1. The infantry could not have heavy machine guns, mortars, or artillery. The Artillery units were limited in the number, size, caliber, and number of shells they can carry. For example, the maximum caliber gun was around ten cm, and the number of shells allowed was one hundred and five, for mortars, the limit was seventy pieces.
2. The cavalry was limited to horse and bicycle units. No tanks, heavy armor, airplanes, or anti-aircraft guns were allowed.
3. No chief of staff organization was allowed.
4. The Hungarian Royal Navy had to be dismantled.
5. The Hungarian Royal Air Force also had to be disbanded.

It is easy to point fingers at world leaders like Great Britain, and primarily France, for their short-sightedness and ignorance in creating intolerable conditions after WWI that led to an unstable Central Europe and provided the incentives to start WWII (to understand part of the devastation of the Versailles Peace Treaty for Central Europe, please read "The Economic Consequences of the Peace", by John Maynard Keynes).

Father Tibor used to say Hitler was born of Western ignorance by the imposition of intolerable conditions after WWI set by the French dictator of peace, Georges Clemenceau, and his dishonest advisors. Many wars begin when the peace treaty is signed, as world powers typically want to conquer by dividing. Look at Kurdistan, disappeared from the map and divided amongst three countries: Turkey, Iraq, and Syria.

The Treaty of Trianon (Versailles) was engineered by the Frenchman Clemenceau, with the help of the dishonest Czech advisers Messrs. Benes and Masaryk. They didn't just subdivide Central Europe but created unbelievable suffering for all other people living in the Carpathian basin and making the native Hungarians one of the largest minorities in Europe. Stanley Baldwin, the English prime minister, said, "The European peace ended on the day the Trianon treaty took effect."

Each new country formed, such as Czecho-Slovakia, Enlarged Romania, or Yugoslavia, inherited many minorities, including over seven million Hungarians, which represented serious problems and some threats for the new, inexperienced governments. For example, the Czechs suddenly inherited a large Slovak, Hungarian, and German population who were feared or considered to be second-class citizens. Romania also did not know how to deal with its minorities, especially the better-educated Hungarians, but the Ruthenian and Ukrainian population were also mistreated. Yugoslavia had its share of minorities, which mistrusted and, at times, even hated each other. The Bosnians, Croatians, Hungarians, and Slovenians despised the Serbian-controlled army and government. All these new countries established after WWI, at the expense of an over thousand-year-old Hungary, acquired territories far beyond their wildest expectations, but they also inherited nationalities, minorities, class, and economic problems, which they didn't know how to deal with.

The subdivision of Hungary was based on false statistics provided primarily by Edward Benes, who often contradicted even himself.

Lloyd George, the English prime minister, said in his speech on October 7, 1929, "All documents provided to us during the peace conference (Trianon) were deceptive and lying."

Herbert Henry Asguit, English prime minister, said in 1925, "This peace treaty is not the work of Statesmen, but the result of grave and fatal mistakes."

J. L. Garvin, English press agent, wrote in 1926, "From all the conquered nations the talented, superior quality Hungarian people were given the worst deal."

The people responsible for the division of Central Europe knew the terrible sufferings, injustices, and cruel deeds committed against all the people of the Carpathian basin. Many statesmen objected and predicted dire consequences. The most outspoken European leaders and statesmen who openly criticized the injustices committed against the people in Central Europe included Lloyd George, Francisco Nitti, Rene Dupuis, Andre de Hevesy, Henry Pozzi, and Charles Tisseyre.

Here are a few more issues worth mentioning:

Archibald Cary Coolidge (1866–1928), a professor knowledgeable about Central Europe, gave the following report to President Wilson on January 19, 1919, in regard to the Trianon Peace Treaty, objecting to the subdivision of Hungary and the forced separation of Transylvania. "Brutally forcing and compelling acceptance of such an arrangement in this treaty as final on a thousand-year-old unified country will bring hate, resentment, war, discord, and military confrontation within a foreseeable future." (He left out human sufferings, but all his warnings were ignored.)

President Woodrow Wilson had the foresight to create the League of Nations, a precursor to the United Nations, to oversee and to correct injustices against nations, people, and minorities, but the American Congress would never ratify or accept his vision of world peace. This raises the following question: if con is the opposite of pro, is congress the opposite of progress?

British diplomats and politicians knew very little about Europe, as they never considered themselves to be a part of it, so when the vengeful French statesmen decided to carve up Central Europe, they approved the massacre or enslavement of millions of innocent people and the huge reparations payments to ensure long-lasting economical suffering in Central Europe. These French and English diplomats gave too much credence to one Georges Clemenceau and his cohorts, who dictated the most unfair peace treaty in modern history.

Kele D. Gabor

The Germans knew the Hungarian alliance was shaky, so they infiltrated the government. The infiltration was accomplished similarly as in the United States by the Russians and by the Communist sympathizers during and after WWII. The Russians benefited from Communist sympathizers in the Roosevelt administration at such high levels as the assistant to the secretary of treasury and the NSA. Other advisers to Roosevelt often persuaded him to side with Stalin instead of Churchill.

The Nazis also knew Hungary had fought long and hard throughout history against any intruders, but especially the German attempts to conquer it. It started as early as the seventh and eighth centuries, when the Avars, like Magyars before them, settled in what was known as Avaria; hence, the new name Bavaria. Here the struggle began between the Hungarians, or Magyars, and Germans. The fight continued in the ninth and tenth centuries and was revived in the seventeenth, nineteenth, and twentieth centuries. The only times the Germans succeeded was when Hungary was weakened by protecting Western Europe from Tartars or the Turks or when the Germans received help from Russia.

After the Austrian army helped push out the Turks in 1686, they stayed as an occupational force and attempted to control Hungary. After one hundred and fifty years of fighting against the Turks to protect Western Europe, Hungary had to fight again to free themselves from the Austrians, who were the new oppressors for two hundred years. Under the leadership of Rákóczy, the Kuruc (Hungarian) and Labanc (Austrians) wars began. Hungary was successfully beating the Labanc until the Austrians got help from other nations, so in 1710 Hungary was forced to capitulate. In spite of the Hungarian loss against the Austrians, Ferenc Rákóczy[1] became a legend and a revered hero of the Hungarian people, like George Washington for the Americans.

The freedom fight from Austrian rule started up again in the

---
[1] If you enjoy inspiring music, listen to the "Rakoczy March" by Berlioz

middle of the nineteenth century. In 1849, Hungary had successfully freed itself from the Austrian Germans by defeating their army, but once again with the Russians' help, Austrians were able to prevail. The only benefit achieved was a little more independence negotiated in 1867, but not the complete freedom the people of the Carpathian basin had fought for.

However, at this time, the new Hungarian parliament was formed with voting rights and involvement in decisions affecting both countries. The Austrians, unfortunately, ignored the Hungarian votes against starting up WWI. Austria felt compelled to start the war because of the assassination of the Austrian prince, totally disregarding the Hungarian objections.

Under Hungarian law in the Hungarian kingdom, the Serbian assassin could not be executed because of his young age (seventeen), which further infuriated the Habsburgs.

The Nazis wanted to put their own man in control, as Regent Horthy would not permit German-style concentration camps for the enemies of the Third Reich. The Nazis knew that there were plenty of sympathizers, especially among the German settlers in Southern Hungary (similarly in the United States, many German immigrants supported the Nazi movements just as the American Jews support Israel).

By 1941, the Hungarian leaders were convinced about the road to disaster with Hitler. However, since military resistance was futile, the Regent Horthy preceded with peace negotiations behind the Nazis' backs, ignoring earlier threats against the lives of his two sons. The German Army was ready to occupy Hungary, and they had already placed Nazi agents in many key positions. The Gestapo arrested, killed, or abducted almost every individual who was involved with or attempted negotiation either with England or Russia. In early 1942, the Hungarian Army chief of staff secretly went to see Hitler and took the oath to serve the German Third Reich behind the regent's back. However, the struggle continued between the Hungarians and the Nazis on a different front. That front not only included Wallenberg (the Swedish diplomat helping the Jews), Regent Horthy, and Colonel Koszorus, but also the ex-military officers who had been dismissed from the German sympathizer chief of staff, the clergy, and most Hungarians.

Here are quotes from the Congressional Record article 1 of 4 (page E1109), dated Thursday, May 26, 1994:

Mr. Lantos, Mr. Speaker, this year marks the fiftieth anniversary of the Hungarian holocaust. I rise today to recognize one of the great heroes of the Hungarian holocaust, Ferenc Koszorus, who at great personal sacrifice to his own life, saved thousands of Hungarian Jews from deportation to Nazi death camps.

During the turbulent time in the summer of 1944, advancing Allied forces were closing in on Berlin while Hitler was racing to implement the final solution, the destruction of the Jewish race.

There were many acts of heroic compassion and humanitarianism during this period. I would like to recount the story of Col. Ferenc Koszorus, one of the most remarkable examples of bravery and courage of the time.

Ferenc Koszorus was a colonel in the Hungarian Army in charge of the First Magyar Armored Division, stationed in and around Budapest. He learned that Laszlo Baky, secretary of state and director of all security forces, with the exception of the army, had planned a coup d'etat to install a police force completely subservient to the Nazis. They would see to it that Hungary was purged of all remaining Jews.

By June 1944, the Nazis had incarcerated and liquidated most of the Jewish population of Europe. In the capital of Hungary, Budapest, there remained approximately two hundred and fifty thousand Jews still alive.

Budapest was still under the control of the Hungarian police force. The Nazis believed that this force was not ruthless and brutal enough to deal adequately with the complete destruction of the large remaining Jewish population of Budapest.

With the help of the Gestapo, Baky formed several battalions of gendarmerie forces loyal to him. Orders from the Regent (Horthy) to disband the gendarmerie went unheeded. Colonel Koszorus controlled the last remaining active army unit in Hungary. At the time when few others would stand up to the Nazi occupation, Colonel Koszorus took the initiative to resist.

Realizing the severity of the situation, Colonel Koszorus consulted with the Regent and began preparation on his own to stop Baky and the gendarmerie battalions. On July 5, 1944, at eleven-thirty p.m., Colonel Koszorus ordered the units of the 1st armored division to take up positions at strategic points in Budapest, sealing off all the roads leading into the city. By seven a.m. on July 6, 1944, all the units were in place and Colonel Koszorus informed Baky that if his gendarmerie did not leave and disband, they would be destroyed. On July 7, 1944, Baky capitulated and evacuated his forces.

Colonel Koszorus' unparalleled action was the only case known in which an Axis power used military force for the purpose of preventing the deportation of the Jews. As a result of his extraordinarily brave efforts, taking a great risk in an extremely volatile situation, the eventual takeover of Budapest by the Nazis was delayed by three and a half months. This hiatus allowed thousand of Jews to seek safety in Budapest, thus sparing them from certain execution.

It also permitted the famous Raul Wallenberg, who arrived in Budapest on July 9, 1944, to coordinate his successful and effective rescue mission.

In October 1944, after the Germans had taken Budapest, Colonel Koszorus was forced into hiding to avoid certain execution by the Gestapo. While alive, Colonel Koszorus never received recognition of his action. In 1991, Ferenc Koszorus was posthumously promoted to the rank of general by the Hungarian Government.

His memory is honored with a plaque placed in the famous Dohany Street Synagogue, in Budapest.

Therefore, it is with great honor and pride that I rise today in recognition of the valiant, patriotic efforts of Ferenc Koszorus.

Many thousands of families are alive today as a result of the heroic actions of one man who stood up for his beliefs in a very uncertain and dangerous time. His loyalty to his country and love of humanity are an inspiration to all who struggle against oppression and the vile bigotry of racism.

Too often, the efforts of those who struggle against the Nazi oppression go unrecognized. This year, the fiftieth anniversary of Hungarian holocaust, the world reflects on the lesson learned. I am proud to honor Colonel Koszorus, a patriot, a humanitarian, and a hero."

This speech is representative of the historical events that took place during and toward the end of WWII. It also falls in line with the politically correct and acceptable "historical" lines. However, it leaves off some very important facts, such as that Colonel Koszorus directly reported to Regent Horthy and the First Magyar Mechanized Division was in charge of protecting the Hungarian government, including the Regent himself, to prevent the complete Nazi takeover of Hungary.

The reason that this and many other similar facts are not made clear in the speech is so they could label Regent Horthy a fascist. Can you imagine the far-reaching consequences of making the regent also a well-deserved hero of the Holocaust? The entire subdivision and mutilation of Hungary could not be justified. It was easier to falsely accuse and blame Regent Horthy for selling out to the Nazis in order to gain back some of the historical territories where the majority of populations were still Hungarian in spite of relentless persecution and displacement of the indigenous Magyar population.

Other important facts are also left out, such as that more Jews survived the Holocaust in Hungary than in the rest of the German-controlled or -occupied territories combined. As a result, Hungary has the highest percentage of Jews in Europe. The speech conveniently left out also that Colonel Koszorus was put in a Communist prison after WWII by the Jewish-run secret police for his military service. The real tragedy was that from the close to four hundred thousand Jews taken to concentration camps, about ninety-one thousand never returned to Hungary, and many of them might have perished in Nazi captivity.

Contemporary historians know Hitler, like Saddam Hussein,

was a student and follower of Stalin. Most decisions Hitler made in policy were copycat moves of Stalin's methods, which had been proven to work. The concentration and forced labor camps, like gulags for the dissidents, the Gestapo, the SS, the youth groups, the public relations, the propaganda, and others, were all first tried and proven to work by Stalin. The Nazi Party (National Socialist German Workers Party) was set up and operated as the National Russian Communist Workers Party under Stalin's leadership. We refer to the German version as Fascist, but not to the Russian Communists.

Fascism simply means "authority," originating from the word author. Most governments use the label more freely than they should.

The use of fasces (fascio in Italian) comes from the Romans, implying powers (delegated or acquired), and it is symbolized by an ax in a bundle. The derived meaning for fascism implies the misuse of power, force, command, and control. This extrapolated meaning makes sense; however, using this definition, socialism and communism as practiced by Stalin were definitely more fascist than the Nazis. Fascism is also used to designate governments who eliminate all opposition, as Stalin did. Hitler was just copying his teacher, Stalin, when his opposition was eliminated. At least Hitler waited to eliminate his opposition until they openly turned against him. Stalin, on the other hand, only needed his suspicion or just a feeling of insecurity in order to eliminate his perceived enemies.

The secret police, led by Beria, Lavrenty Pavlovich and controlled by Stalin, eliminated anyone suspected to be a threat, starting with Lenin and Trotsky. They built concentration and forced labor camps (gulag), primarily in Siberia, to hold the millions of deported mostly Christians on false charges and labeled them the "enemy of the people." Nobel Prize winner Alexander Solzhenitsyn, who spent eight years in Communist prisons, wrote most extensively about the evils committed by Stalin, Beria, and his gang in the book 'The Gulag Archipelago'. He wrote, "The Gulag Archipelago informed an incredulous world the blood-maddened Jewish terrorists had murdered sixty-six million victims in Russia from 1918 to 1957!" He also cited Cheka Order No.10, issued on January 8, 1921: "To intensify the repression of the bourgeoisie."

Stalin (a name he adopted in 1913, meaning "steel") was known as Josif Visarionovich Dzhugashvili. Stalin planned the assassination of Lenin when he found out that Trotsky was selected as the successor to Lenin. In his last will, Lenin advised his followers to remove Stalin from any leadership position of the party, as Stalin was rude and inclined to abuse power.

Stalin even saw Russian generals who were victorious over the German Army and then became popular with the Russian people as a threat and had them eliminated.

It seems that Western leaders and politicians have problem dealing with immoral acts of "allies," as they close their eyes to the wrongdoings of their partners, regardless of how evil they are. That may be why the assassinations of General Patton and Lenin by the direct commands of Stalin are not publicized. General Patton was the only American officer who openly expressed his dislike of Stalin and his totalitarian system.

More examples of Stalin's paranoia are the atrocities committed against Ukrainians, Chechens, Poles, Hungarians and other ethnic groups, just because they tried to break away from the forced union of the Soviet states.

The ex-leader of the Russian KGB admitted to the elimination of at least fifty million of their own people (one of the greatest genocides and holocausts known), but they could only prove the killing of thirty-six million of them, as many of the original documents conveniently disappeared.

These numbers do not include POWs or crime-related executions or the execution of thousands of Polish and German officers.

People who believe Hitler was the most evil man in the twentieth century are either uninformed or misinformed by individuals who want to cover up the much greater atrocities committed by Stalin and Mao!

Deception and Reality - Living Through the Missing Pages of History

In the fall of 1944, Regent Horthy was arrested and taken to Bavaria to be under house arrest, guarded by the Gestapo, after his attempt to seek peace with the Allies, including Stalin. The Americans finally freed Regent Horthy from the Nazi captivity in Germany and his only remaining son, Miklos Jr., in Italy in 1945.

It is interesting to read The Secret Notes of Horthy, ironically, first published by the Communists in 1949. It is fascinating how the Germans removed the railroad ties on a short segment of the rail in front of Regent Horthy's green Turan fast train so he was forced to transfer to another train that was controlled by the Nazis. Once the Nazis had Horthy, they arrested him and took him to Germany.

Labeling Regent Horthy as fascist is erroneous, yet it found its way into some of the American history textbooks. The claim that Horthy joined the Nazis for payment of regained Hungarian territories is also false. Based on the League of Nations charter, Hungarians living in the Carpathian basin had strongly objected and protested the unfair division of its land and of its people since 1920. The Polish and German borders were readjusted, and Austria was saved from total financial collapse. Hungary would have been next to correct the similar injustices and mistakes as early as 1922 and 1923. Unfortunately, the internal disorder and discord in the League of Nations created by the French invading and occupying the Ruhr in order to enforce payments for reparation, and by Mussolini occupying Corfu, set an end to the process and caused a ten-year delay in minimal readjustment of some of the borders for Hungary.

The erroneous designation for Regent Horthy, who would not permit the Nazi-style concentration camps in Hungary, might have come about from the Communist Czech leader Benes, who befriended the Americans, the English, and the Russians to cover up the Slovakian crimes against the Jews. Or was it just Communist propaganda made believable by the Western-sympathizing liberal media?

My father would come home very frustrated after getting the reports from the American and English representatives. He would say, "They just refuse to understand that we have already experienced the Communist takeover in 1919 and we really know what we are talking about." General Patton seemed to be the only Western military commander who had knowledge of European history and the Communist atrocities.

My father and his two good friends also agreed that the United

Kele D. Gabor

States would win the war, but based on their inexperience in foreign politics, they would lose the peace again, just like after WWI. History has proved this. French, English, and American ignorance, inexperience, and self- serving foreign policies caused the loss of many lives of Hungarians, Polish, and Ukrainian people in Europe, including the pain and suffering of so many that continue to this day.

After the world wars, many new countries were created out of ignorance or revenge. It is beyond my comprehension why the United States' policy is to keep these borders intact. Why prevent or delay of the breakup of these countries? The people inside these borders want freedom and independence.

Hasn't there been enough killing and enslavement of minorities or ethnic groups?

Tent Village

Infiltration of the Hungarian government by German and Nazi sympathizers began as early as March 19, 1941. After full German control and military occupation of our country in 1944, the Hungarian government had a difficult time protecting Jews from the Nazi-style concentration camps or any other people considered to be the enemy of the Third Reich. While the Slovak Tiso and the Croatian Pavell governments actively supported the Nazi effort to deport all the Jews into Auschwitz or other camps, Regent Horthy and Prime Minister Kállay of Hungary opposed this and were able to prevent the deportation until the German military took control. This is the reason that more Jewish people survived in Hungary than any place else controlled or occupied by the Nazis.

The Nazis altered the Hungarian government by installing Nazi sympathizers in key positions, like the military chief of staff, in 1942. On October 16, 1944, the Nazi coup, led by Obersturmführer Skorzeny, took over the Royal Palace and eventually helped the Germans capture the regent and the prime minister as prisoners of the Third Reich. They also kidnapped Regent Horthy's last living son, Miklos Horthy Jr., by drugging, wrapping him in, and smuggling him out in, a Persian rug; and later transporting him to a concentration camp in Germany. After the Nazis captured Miklos Jr. they moved him, to be far away from his father, to an Italian concentration camp where he was sentenced to death by hanging. However, before carrying out the sentence, the American Army liberated the camp so Miklos Jr. survived. During that time his father, Regent Horthy, was under house arrest in Bavaria. He didn't know the fate of his son until after being liberated from German captivity in Bavaria.

The Germans installed their own puppet government, replacing the Hungarian leadership. The new Nazi leaders were Salosján (changing his name to Szálasi to sound Hungarian) and Prime Minister Kugel (who also changed his German name to Gömbös to sound Hungarian).

With the new Nazi puppet government, the Germans had a free rein to deport anybody, including approximately four hundred thousand Jews, in spite of the objections of many Hungarian officials and the

KELE D. GABOR

Vatican.

I remember when the ambassador from the Vatican appealed to the new Nazi puppet government in Hungary and asked Szálasi to stop any further deportation. To the best of my recollection, the message the Pope sent was, "The Pope and the Vatican expect the same vigor in protecting the Jews and preventing the deportation process as the previous administration ."

We all know the message was ignored and the deportation process began. The nations that had the power and the means to slow down or stop Hitler and Stalin's atrocities chose to ignore it. Once the Allies won the war, they were able to rewrite history to suit the victors. According to many reports and eyewitness accounts, the American and English officers were shocked by what they saw in the liberated concentration camps.

The high-ranking officers even knew about the Siberian prison camps, the gulag. However, as Father Tibor put it, "It was too difficult, if not impossible, to drum up international support for saving the Jews, as even the international efforts to save the more admired and liked noble Indian race have failed a century earlier."

After the atrocities were made public about the concentration camps, the Western powers had to accept and support the new Israel. The fact that most people in the world didn't know what was going on in the Nazi or Russian-run camps should have been made clear so no one could collectively blame or keep the people and nations responsible for the evil deeds that were purposely hidden from them!

In October, my father had refused to join the fleeing Nazi sympathizers or other high government officials who were ordered to leave for Germany. His refusal to follow the order of the Nazi-controlled government marked our family for deportation and concentration camps.

My father was arrested in his office. Our family didn't know about it until his secretary stopped by late that afternoon with the devastating news. We prayed hard for his safe return that night and every night thereafter. The next day, we were told we had two hours to pack about ten kilograms of personal goods per individual; children were allowed only five kilograms. We didn't have many valuables left. Most of our valued possessions had been traded or sold for things that were needed to survive. Our beautiful family heirlooms, the jewelry, one of the grand pianos, Persian rugs, many of the guns and rifles, china, crystal, and our favorite toys, were replaced by survival needs— cooking lard, salt, honey or sugar, bread, warm clothing, boots, homemade soaps, pocket knives, and other basic goods.

After the ten o'clock curfew, a low-ranking Nazi officer politely woke us up. The officer and two guards gave us fifteen minutes to get ready to leave our house. We walked in the dark, so no one could see us, straight to the railroad station about two kilometers away. Now we understood how entire families disappeared without a trace. We had no problem with the short notice of fifteen minutes, as we were already prepared and slept in our clothes. The two guards positioned themselves, one in the front and one in the back. We were not allowed to talk; my sister sneezed, and the leading guard immediately reprimanded her. She cried quietly the rest of the way to the station.

We were happy to see other families at the station, just to know we were not alone. We thought we might have a better chance to survive and to resist if all of us stuck together. Families had no adult male members, except for a few grandfathers. All the families seemed to be quiet and kept to themselves, as if they were afraid to reach out. They were told not to socialize and to keep quiet. The Nazis had parked the open wagons some distance from the station; in case of a bombing attack, they would less likely be killed. The station had been bombed many times before, and now it was barely standing. The roof and all the large glass windows were gone.

Even the big doors were off their hinges and leaned against one of the remaining walls. One of the doors was used to cover a large broken window in order to reduce the cold draft. There were some homeless people trying to sleep in the drafty waiting room. Most of them lost their homes to bombing attacks. The steel doors were very heavy it must have taken many strong men to move them. After a heavy bombing raid, my father had said to us, "Once the war is over, window glass will be at a premium.

We will be rich. We will start a glass factory. The raw material is cheap. It is mostly sand, and there will be no marketing costs. Almost every building will need new windows."

Now it had started to rain. We were prepared for anything; we wore our raincoats over our winter coats. By the time we got to our designated wagon after the long walk, carrying our heavy load, the perspiration was running down the back of our necks all the way to our underwear. The double socks we wore soaked up the perspiration from our legs. About one hundred and twenty of us settled in three wagons. By the time we were organized in the open wagons, the rain had stopped and a thin bright yellow stripe appeared on the horizon, indicating both the direction and the coming of the dawn.

It took the Germans five days to take us to the holding area about sixty kilometers away. The old, beat-up locomotive pulling our wagons often seemed to be required for some emergency, or it ran out of fuel or we had to stop for a bombing raid near the railroad tracks and stations. The Nazis would disconnect our locomotive and take it for hours and sometimes an entire day. We later learned that the many delays in returning our engine were also used as a method to slow down the deportation process by some of the courageous Hungarian railroad workers.

On the third day, we ran out of food. Fortunately, the weather improved, with only an occasional cold drizzle. It was November, and the nights were cold. The guards had their own food, but they would not or didn't have enough to share. There were about one hundred and twenty of us, and we were all hungry. It would have required a repeat performance of Jesus with the "loaves and fishes" to provide food for all of us. On the fourth day, the guards used the last of their food rations, which consisted of smoked bacon and thick jam made from mixed fruit that was known as "Hitler's bacon" and some stale bread. The guards were surprised and thankful when we shared the food we collected from nearby orchards while our train was stopped. We tried to be friendly with the guards, but they politely rejected us. We wanted to play games and often teased them. One time, we stole one of the rifles from a sleeping soldier who was taking a nap after lunch. To our surprise, he laughed and chased us until he got it back. Instead of beating us, he smiled and showed us the empty magazine in the rifle, no bullets.

We took everything in stride, as we were now veterans of long open wagon trips. Just a year earlier, we had escaped the Romanian invasion of eastern Hungary, Transylvania, in open wagons. During our ordeal, there were many difficulties, especially for the elderly, as we had no bathrooms on the train. Everyone had to use pails that were passed around during the night. During the day when we stopped, we lowered ourselves down from the wagon to dump the pails and to scavenge for food. For us children and teenagers, the most precious finds were small dried-up grapes left over after the harvest in the nearby vineyards. Most had some white to green mold on them this late in the season, but we just wiped it off. We ate them as fast as we found them. Perhaps some girl left them there on purpose.

According to our custom, the grape carriers, all young men, could collect a kiss for each bunch of grapes they found left behind by the girl harvesting that row. Of course, certain rows had a lot grapes left if the picker liked the young man. The grapes, which were chewy and sweet as honey, were an excellent substitute for candy. Even now, I prefer to give children raisins instead of candy–let them learn to enjoy the good natural food.

A few times, we really had to hustle to escape the guard dogs in the fenced area around the homes with small orchards. We learned earlier how to distract the guard dogs with worn-out corduroy pants or old heavy-duty leather belts. One would start hitting the fence at the farthest distance from the climbing point. We would continue to tease the dog, occasionally letting him bite the end of the pants or belt, and then we would have a tug of war. It proved to be the best and safest distraction for keeping my scavenging brothers and friends safe. If we were lucky, we would find some overripe plums, apples, or pears in abandoned orchards. The luckiest find was a big walnut tree full of nuts. We all ate walnuts for a few days. Our hands were jet black, as we could not clean or wash off the sticky stuff after husking the nuts. We had great fun knocking the nuts off the big tree with rocks and poles. We must have collected a ton of walnuts from the big tree during the few days of our stay. We used our rain and overcoats, tying the sleeves and neck, and stuffed them full of nuts before taking them back to the wagons. Surprisingly, one of the neighbors came to see what the commotion was. When he discovered who we were, he sent his wife back with some goat cheese. The fresh cheese was so delicious we ate it all before getting the next load back to the train.

When we finally arrived at the designated point, we had to walk another two to three kilometers to the holding camp. At the entry gate, two lines were formed, and at the beginning of each line stood a German and a Hungarian soldier. First, they checked our identification papers and fingerprints, then they rummaged through everyone's package and took what they wanted. We were not allowed to have knives, forks, belts, mirrors, flashlights, or other reflective materials, nor were we allowed to have anything that may be used as a weapon. They took most of the sugar, candy, soaps, and other useful items.

Everyone was anxious and wanted to go to the front of the line to see what was happening, so we got pushed back toward the end of the line. It was almost noon, about four hours since we left the wagons, by the time we got into the camp right after the fingerprinting. When the guards were searching our belongings, we pretty much knew what they were looking for. We had slipped our pocketknives into our boots between the two socks we were wearing. Soon we became very popular for having the only cutting tools around. The pocketknives proved to be an invaluable tool for our survival. They had many uses, from cutting up rags when our socks wore out to a surgical tool to open up boils. Our pocket knives also had a lot of use in cutting up sheets to make bandages for cuts and bruises. Since we didn't have pins and needles, it also served as the second best tool for removing splinters. However, the pocket knives had the most use in sharing food like bread and cutting strings for tying torn cloth and keeping loose pants or skirts on. My father had long ago taught us to handle knives safely. I believe every responsible person should have one just in case of an emergency.

The camp was surrounded by double wire fence about two meters high. The top of the fence was all barbed wire, and extra rolls were placed between the two fences, leaving just enough space for two guards to pass between them. We were given lukewarm farina soup for lunch and dinner.

The temporary tent to which we were assigned had some dirty clothes in it and a terrible odor. This and other smells bothered us for about a week, then they disappeared or we got used to them. After some cleaning up and settling in, we boys went to explore.

We estimated that there were close to a thousand people in the camp but very few men, and they were all old or crippled. The able-bodied men were either in prison or more likely in forced labor camps. The maximum capacity for our camp, we later found out, was about eight hundred.

Most families didn't know where their husbands or fathers were. Some sections of the compound looked shabbier, smelled worse, and were dirtier. We assumed they were the older arrivals—we were wrong. It was just that some people cared less about hygiene than others. The real way to tell how long people had been there was the length of their hair. No barber, no scissors.

The tents were set up for holding detainees only for a short time. The tops of the tents were slightly different shades from bleaching by the sun.

Within a day, we got a new military tent and we gladly moved from the terrible smell; it was the darkest green tent among them all. Each tent was dry inside, as there was a well-prepared ditch dug around the outside perimeter, and they all seemed to be watertight. On rainy or snowy days, the ground got wet just inside the entry flap from the muddy shoes. It didn't take long to find a stick that was strategically placed just inside the flap that we used to clean the soles of our shoes before stepping into the tent.

There were no assigned tents except for the civilian camp chief, a fellow prisoner. He lived alone on the highest point of the enclosed compound.

Our new tent came with three identical new metal buckets. One bucket was for drinking water, one for washing, and the third for night use. The latter had to be emptied every morning at one of the open pits. We boys supplied the drinking water. There were three wells inside the compound, but only one of them had good-tasting water, and it was the farthest away from us. I soon realized it was easier to carry two buckets of water rather than one, so I offered to help the neighbors by taking them good water every day. This is how I met my first love, Kati.

I first saw Kati when I brought back a bucket of water for her mother. She was leaning against the sunny side of the tent to get the warming rays of the early afternoon sun on her face and legs and soak up the warmth from the dark canvas. It was one of those early November days when the sun wanted to let us know that even though the winter was coming, she was still in control. Kati was wearing a pastel-green checked skirt with a white blouse that was partially covered by a light unbuttoned pink sweater. It was very colorful. The skirt fell below her knees, but it was enough to show that she had shapely legs. One knee was showing as she lifted her foot and held it against the heavy tarp. She was wearing white stockings, which were rolled down to the top of her shoes. Her long, thick hair was a rich bronze-auburn that took on a red hue from the sun shining on it. Her eyes were closed, and her thick lashes were the same color as her hair.

As I came closer, she opened her eyes. They were large and green with a hint of yellow, like glowing embers, giving them a bright, mysterious glitter.

Her eyes appeared larger because of her narrow nose and freckled face.

She had small but thick lips. She didn't blink; she just stared at me. I was mesmerized, and I could feel my knees shaking. She looked into my eyes, and it felt good, very good. I knew if I were made of chocolate, I would have melted on the spot. Neither one of us spoke. After a while, she smiled, and I felt warmth spreading throughout my body. I stood there close to her for a long time; my heart was racing, and I could not move.

The mood was interrupted by her mother sticking her head out of the entry flap, wanting to know if the full buckets of water were too heavy for me. I don't remember my response, but I picked up their bucket and put it inside the tent. My knees were still shaking. From that point on, I did everything to be close to Kati. I even complained to her mother that they were not using enough fresh water! I needed an excuse to come by at least twice a day. I did everything possible to see her often. I just wanted to be near her and to touch her hand. I did not even want to talk; I just wanted to look into her beautiful green eyes and to see and feel her smile.

I think my mother knew what was going on. She noticed I was smiling a lot more and that food was not as important. She mentioned to me that I had stopped complaining about always being hungry. The next day, I was delivering water for Kati's mother. I was stepping into the tent with a full bucket as Kati was coming out, and we bumped into each other. I think she had planned for it to happen that way. It was the most exhilarating touch and scent I had experienced. She touched my arm, and while holding it tight, she smiled, looked into my eyes, and said with the sweetest and softest voice, "Excuse me, please."

The next day, emboldened, I touched her hand. I remember telling her she was the most beautiful girl I have ever seen and I would do whatever she asked me. To my surprise, she asked for drawing paper and pencils.

It turned out she loved to draw and was good at it. Kati later showed me some of her drawings, mostly faces and portraits. Her collection included her mother, their neighbors, and some small children. The drawings were quite good. One could recognize each individual with a glance, but quality of the medium was bad. She even used torn-up bed sheets and light-colored blouses to draw on. Good quality or larger pieces of clean papers were impossible to obtain. I looked everywhere, but what little paper was around was hidden and guarded for toilet use. I noticed the lime used to treat the open pit toilets came in a double paper bag and they were stored behind an open shed close to the pits. Once it got dark, I went out and, with surgical precision, cut out the top parts of two bags lying on the top of the pile. Only the back side of the front sheet could be used; the rest had either printing on it or was saturated with the white powder.

The next day, I presented her with two pieces, almost letter-sized, light-brown drawing paper, slightly wrinkled. She must have had a photographic memory, as she drew some of the pictures without having the person model. It was amazing how she could draw her own portrait without using two mirrors.

A few years ago after my mother passed away, my sister gave me a flat box that had my name on it. She said, "Our mother left this for you." I peeked inside and saw some of my early compositions. I brought the box with me to America. A year later, I felt like composing some more music or orchestrating some of the old melodies, so I picked up the box again to review some of my scores. I started to go through the music when my eye caught one of the sheets of paper I had cut from a lime sack, which I collected and gave to Kati. This sheet had my portrait on it. I long ago forgot about the drawing, and I thought it was left at the tent city, but my mother must have rescued it.

KELE D. GABOR

Kati's Drawing of My Profile (1944)

When Kati finally let me kiss her, her lips were soft and warm, and she let me touch her breast. I almost fainted. She kept her lips locked on mine and would not let go. I remember breathing slowly through my nose first, and later we took each other's breaths. She took my breath away, and now I know what it means. The kiss lasted for several minutes; I was in heaven.

She explored my lips with her tongue, and I did the same to her. Her next attempt was to feel my tongue with hers, and I did the same. I closed my eyes and followed her lead, whatever she wanted. It is still so vivid in my mind, and I regret I didn't take a slower approach in developing our relationship.

I was deeply in love and had great respect for her. I didn't want to do anything that would hurt her.

Overcome by our emotions, we did not feel the cold evening breeze nor hear the baby crying in the nearby tent. If someone was watching us, we did not notice and we did not care.

This was my first intimate experience with the opposite sex. It was beautiful, incredible! If she meant to give me an unforgettable kiss and wonderful memories, she succeeded, as I have never forgotten them.

I waited until she gently lifted the tent door so as not to wake her mother, and she slipped inside, pulling her hand out of mine. I stayed around for a long time; I didn't want to let her go. Finally, a cold wind coming from the north made me shiver and realize it wasn't a dream. I turned around and went back to my tent.

I should have felt something wasn't quite right with her overly passionate kiss. Maybe it was not only an invitation to touch but to say goodbye— forever.

Three days later, she hung herself.

For days, I walked around in a daze with no awareness of what went on around me. I could not follow the family evening prayers or my sister's lovely singing. I could only think about Kati. Even today, I dream about that unforgettable kiss—long, sweet, warm, and passionate.

Her mother later told me she had welcomed our friendship, as Kati was too alone and always depressed. I often wondered if under different circumstances she would have kissed me as passionately. I also wondered if I could have done something differently; could I have prevented her from hurting herself. I endured the emotional roller coaster of denial, anger, blame, disillusionment, and acceptance over and over in fast succession. I blamed myself for a long time. Then I blamed her mother, her ex-boyfriend, the Nazis, the Russians, and it seemed the entire world. She was older and more experienced. I blamed my own inexperience, but I never blamed her.

Later, only the sweet memories remained.

Kele D. Gabor

Like birds of a feather, nationalities flocked together. Poles, Hungarians, Jews, and Ukrainian families formed little islands by taking tents close to their own kind. The man in charge inside the camp was originally from the Ukraine but lived in Munkács, Hungary (now Mukachevo in Ukraine). He had a shop there, but he made his money trading wine and spirits. He seemed to be discombobulated most of the time, and this might have been the reason he wasn't taken as an able body to a forced-labor camp. He was born to Jewish parents, and he spoke Ukrainian, German, Yiddish, and Hungarian. He reminded me of a Billy goat—tall, narrow shoulders, light skin, dark-brown eyes, long reddish black hair, and a goatee.

It was Mr. Billy Goat who told us initially that most of the Ukrainian population looked upon the Germans as liberators at the beginning of the war, including some of the Jews. The Germans had helped them a great deal by freeing them from Communist dictatorship; however, the Nazis started to kill indiscriminately and then began to deport the Jews. We later double-checked his story with other Ukrainians, as Mr. Billy Goat was the most mistrusted man in town. The Ukrainians confirmed his story and enlightened us as to why they welcomed the Germans. In the 1920s, Ukraine was comprised of all kinds of people, but the majorities were the German settlers, and less than twenty percent were Russian. Today, the demography is almost reversed. Stalin committed the greatest genocide in the twentieth century—far exceeding Hitler—as he eliminated over eight million Ukrainians, primarily by starving them to death.

A Ukrainian lady told other interesting stories about her husband working in an ammunition factory outside of Sopron (Hungary). He had organized a strike because of low pay and bad food. That explained why she and her children were here. She also told us about the Western newspaper reporters who had come to investigate atrocities committed by Stalin in the late 1920s. Neither the French nor the American reporters brought anyone who spoke the language, so the official Communist assigned translator told many stories but never the truth. In 1929, most Western newspapers reported that all reports coming from the Ukraine about human rights violations and starving were exaggerations.

Later, as an adult, I experienced similar situations with naïve, misinformed reporters. They did not have a historical perspective; they interpreted what they saw with their limited knowledge, experience, and often with a slanted view. If what they heard seemed unbelievable, they did not investigate it. They would form an opinion and report on that rather than search for facts and truth. One such encounter comes to mind.

Soon after my arrival in United States, I was invited to schools to talk about communism and socialism. After one of my presentations, three reporters approached me; they wanted to know more about the threat of communism and asked for a private interview as they were writing for the local newspapers. Two days later, I received copies of the reporters' articles, and none of them covered any factual information I had conveyed during the interview. Instead, they contained general ideas and their personal opinions on the subject of socialism and communism. During one particular phase of the interview, I predicted the fall of communism, as it was a very inefficient totalitarian system. I told them the timing of the collapse would depend on the amount of economical, social, and political pressures exerted on Russia by the US and the free world. According to my calculations, it should collapse within the next generation. They laughed and left. I wonder if they feel any guilt, as it did happen exactly thirty years later.

More than half of the camp population was Jewish, and they kept to themselves, like in the ghettoes they built in many cities. Some escaped from Poland, Croatia, or Romania, but most of them came from Slovakia, trying to find refuge in Hungary, where they had better chances to escape the Nazi concentration camps. Regardless of their origin, the Jews seemed to have more fights and arguments among themselves than any other group.

We were told about a sad story of Jews even killing each other. However, checking the story out, we found that a small gang of Jewish teenagers killed a newborn infant so they could suck out the nursing mother's milk.

This incident happened before we arrived at the camp. The gruesome story stayed with us for a long time. Some of the young Jewish boys justified it, saying the camp was no place for a child and the mother didn't want him. The constant crying of the colicky baby kept every neighbor up, and the nursing mother would get an extra portion of food, which they confiscated until the guards found out the infant was dead.

Kele D. Gabor

Supposedly, the guards never inquired about the infant's death. We did not believe the story for a long time until the only person we found that denied it was Billy Goat himself. Once we escaped from the camp, we wanted to forget everything that was bad or ugly.

The rest of the people were primarily dissidents from many different countries. We encountered very few Slovaks or Romanians, but there were many Hungarians, some Ukrainians and Serbians. A mother with nine children was the only Romanian. It was very difficult for her to manage on her own. I believe the numbers of each nationality represented at the camp were inversely proportional to how their government accepted or supported the Nazis. For example, there were very few Slovaks, Romanians, or Croatians because they were enthusiastic supporters of the Nazi regime and cause.

While we were there, we witnessed no new births, but we did see many deaths. The most common cause of death was suicide. It seemed that every week somebody died. While we were there, three teenage girls and a boy committed suicide. Each child came from families without siblings. These families were all well-to-do before arriving at the camp, and they could not endure the difficult situations and the harsh realities. They had been spoiled, had never known hardship, and did not understand discipline. The words "no" and "cannot have" were unfamiliar to them. They were aloof and alone and remained alone. They did not seem to know how to make friends, and if they did form a friendship, it was very short-lived. Their philosophy was to dominate, control, and to have everything their own way. They had a very hard time saying "Thank you," sharing, or showing any form of appreciation. They never apologized for anything. Even today, I am suspicious of people who cannot admit fault and never offer sincere apologies.

These teenagers sometimes threw tantrums or went off to cry alone and didn't seem to be able to find their places. They were always the first to break. They lived in their own world. They seemed obsessed with escaping the reality of their present situation. I found one of these teenage girls very attractive and spent as much time as I could with her, but she could not relate to me or discuss the current conditions and possibility of escape.

She communicated with touch and drawings, but only on her own limited terms. My words didn't matter. After she committed suicide, I made promises that I will never have only one child, even if we could not have any more— I would adopt the second.

Some of the single children became the "rats" of the compound, but they also ended up miserable, and many of them died prematurely. The common thread amongst these teenagers was that they were never disciplined (they were the best examples of the "Dr. Spock" rearing methods).

Regardless of how much the parent, usually the mother, tried to help, it made them worse and more dangerous, rejecting all the good intentions.

Some of the mothers could not be told to change their ways handling their children until it was too late. However, since I witnessed it, I believe the greatest pain a mother can endure is the death of her only child. I prayed often not to see that kind of suffering again.

I often wonder about the single-child syndrome and how it affects parents, neighbors, society, nations, and the world in the future. In China, where single-child culture has developed to curtail their population growth, resource depletion may lead to grave problems in the future unless there is a firmer rearing method adopted to compensate for overly permissive parents. I am concerned about the large number of spoiled children and their ability to lead or resolve conflicts. China might become a real problem in the future for the reasons mentioned.

The method of committing suicide was to use two long ladies silk stockings and a crossbar by the loading post at the back of the main kitchen.

I never understood why the camp commander never had it removed. It was seldom used for lifting heavy loads off the wagons or trucks. Two strong boys working together could have done the lifting of heavy sacks of potatoes without needing the loading posts with a pulley. After a mother's only daughter hanged herself, she went around for days with her index finger fully extended, shaking her hand, singing and yelling, "Single child is a curse. Two children is a blessing" (Egy gyerek átok, két gyerek áldás).

Families with two or more children seemed to have survived the demands and conditions of the camp. Families having two children or more could not only share the work and hardship better but were able to cope by supporting each other. When one child was feeling bad, the other sibling would typically go to great means to soothe the hurts and help. The hardship was a strong, unifying force for families. From my vantage point, families with multiple children were more supportive and sensitive to each other's needs than a single child. I remember when my sister didn't want to eat any more of the unsanitary food, the other sister would practically force-feed her until she regained her strength.

There was no stealing, even though everyone left their tent during the noon meal. There was frequent competition for the clothing of those who had died and for big-leaf plants, as the guards did not provide us with toilet paper. Typically, neighbors treated each other with respect. Peace was maintained for the most part, and one never wanted to upset anyone, especially neighbors. It was well known that unfair treatment of any tent dwellers could lead to the ultimate reprisal. We called it "switching the buckets." The three buckets we were provided in each tent were identical in size, shape, and color. Since there was no way to mark them, each bucket had its place in the tent. The position in the tent defined its use. It is more than amusing to imagine the consequences of switching the night or wash bucket with the drinking one, and I know for certain it did happen on at least one occasion.

It soon became evident there was a serious food shortage. Those who had been there the longest, such as the Jews, looked very undernourished.

We newcomers were better conditioned and prepared; we exercised and ate relatively well before the internment.

Just before coming to the tent city, after every rain shower, we would scout the neighboring hills of Zala for wild mushrooms. My mother would inspect them and discard the bad ones. She prepared them many different ways. Some were dried for later use. Mushrooms became our favorite food.

We later discovered some dried mushrooms contain more protein than any meat product. We probably would not have survived the war years without them. The potato peelings from the military kitchen did not compare to the delicious, earthy flavor of mushrooms. With the knives the soldiers assigned to kitchen duty, a lot of potato was left on the peeling to eat. We learned never to eat green or frozen peelings. The taste is horrible.

The guards and the German officer lived outside the encampment. Every morning and evening, they made the rounds, checked the numbers, and kept meticulous records on everything. Their military vehicle, an old, beat-up Opel, was permanently parked in front of the captain's office. It was seldom used, and we later learned that was due to the fuel (benzene) shortage.

Inside the compound, the man in charge was the nosey Billy Goat—an ex-merchant who constantly pestered us about finding more food for him.

In the beginning, we didn't understand his insatiable need for food, as he often ate with the guards and the officer. Later, we understood he used the extra food for sexual favors. From his appearance, it was obvious he had the best clothes, the most food, the only haircut, and, we guessed, the only sex inside the camp. He was given a chocolate bar every time he turned someone in for any reason; he was given two if he turned someone in who was planning an escape. Chocolate was very important to have; besides being a tasty treat, it helped to stop the frequent diarrhea we experienced from the inferior and unclean food we had to eat.

One day, a doctor came with a nurse to check on our physical condition.

The entire examination consisted of pinching our rear end after we dropped our pants. After the doctor pinched our "cheeks," he separated us in two groups. On the left where the nurse stood, people had to stay until she put an iodine mark on their wrists, leaving a yellow spot on the skin.

The spot was placed under the shirtsleeves so it would not show until one pulled it back or reached out with his hand. All those on the right side of the line could pull up and tie our pants and exit the large tent set up for the doctor and nurses. Jews mostly got the mark, as they were there longer, but they were lucky since they could get seconds at the chow line. When the food was palatable and tasted half-decent, we tried to paint the yellow mark on ourselves, but the cook knew the difference between clay and iodine marks and chased us away. The food did improve after the doctor's visit, but only for a few days.

The meals were terrible most of the time, although the flavor of it improved while my mother was assigned to kitchen duty. But we were hungry most of the time. I learned quickly that people who have experienced hunger will never waste food! It hurts me even today to see people serve themselves too much food and leave a lot of leftovers.

However, our bread in the camp was consistently good. Most of the time, it had different mixes of flour; whether it was corn, barley, potato, or rye, it was always tasty. Even the German guards were willing to trade their fibrous, sawdust bread for the camp bread. Sometimes there would be innocuous quarrels particularly among young boys attempting to get the largest piece of bread. The bread was good, even when it was stale; it was the only food we got that required chewing. The bread was delivered daily except Sundays, when we were served pasta or potatoes. One day, I was able to count the loaves. Horse-drawn wagons brought in two hundred and fifty loaves every weekday, just before noon.

During the first week, the boys' gang leader, a tall, skinny Jewish boy, came by to get my pocketknife. I refused to give it to him. He pinned me against the back of the kitchen wall, which was the only wooden structure inside the camp. One of his lieutenants proceeded to reach into my pocket for my knife. My quick temper took over. I was so mad that I kicked the gang leader in the groin so hard he collapsed. I then proceeded to work off my anger on his lieutenant. Word spread, and I immediately had the respect of the young boys among both old and newcomers. They all asked to be my friends. I must have been very angry. I beat up my foes so hard I made a lasting impression. I became a gang leader without wanting to be one.

I heard reports about things that I didn't want to know. On one occasion, the boys persuaded me to peek through a tent hole, and for the first time, I watched sexual intercourse take place between two human beings.

I then understood why Zoli, one of the boys, wanted to borrow my pocketknife.

The place I peeked in on the side of the tent had an L-shaped opening that had been cut with a pocketknife. One could pull up the cut flap only a few centimeters each side on the heavy tarp and get a good view with one eye through the triangular opening.

The couple engaged in the activity was Billy Goat and a much younger nursing mother. Mr. Billy Goat pointed to a small paper bag and told the young lady that the bag contained powdered milk. In exchange, he expected to get "the special." There were four military cots inside, twice as many as were needed for the baby and his mother. Two of the cots were stacked one on top of each other on the other side of the tent, and the baby was sleeping on the third. The doubled-up cots covered up the previously made L-shaped cuts to block the peek hole. The fourth cot was placed in the center of the tent.

During their sexual intercourse, I lost interest. It was worse than seeing animals mating. It reminded me of some pigs I had seen mating. I noticed the tears running down the side of her face, and I thought she must have been crying. I felt a lump in my throat as I realized that this was only for his pleasure. It seemed unnatural for two people to be having sexual intercourse without any kissing, touching, or show of affection.

Thoughts of Kati came flooding back, and I recalled the sweet and hot kisses we had shared and the way we had touched each other. I felt I had done something wrong, so I turned and left the rest of the boys to take their turns at the peeping hole. For the next few days, thoughts of what I had seen preoccupied my mind, and I had wonderful wet dreams. But after a while, the entire incident became insignificant, and it disgusted me.

I learned a few days later she needed the extra food in order to have milk for her baby. My mother explained about nursing; we boys began to find ways of getting extra food for the lady. One way was that people could borrow our pocketknives for half an hour for a half-slice of bread.

From this point on, we had to be very careful; we made Billy Goat very angry because the nursing mother would not provide services for him any longer. Her name was Olga, and she was in the camp because her family had tried to hide from the Nazis two American pilots whose plane had crashed. They parachuted out in time and survived. We boys all felt a little better about it, and we were proud of our effort to protect a lady. We even discussed why we had chosen to give up our bi-weekly entertainment, and we all agreed it was because of her crying and silent tears.

Within a few weeks, our conditions began to deteriorate fast, so very secretly we began to plan our escape. Our secret code for communication would be the use of colors. The color code was simple; the mention of any particular color would indicate its significance. For example, red meant danger, yellow meant warning, green meant "All is okay," purple meant sadness, and black was death. Later, our color language became more sophisticated as orange, brown, aqua, and others were added. It probably would have been fairly simple for someone else to decode if they had cared, but we felt very comfortable with it. We called it the "flower" language.

By the fourth week, we knew most of the "half" families, as we referred to them since their fathers weren't there. My mother assisted as a translator, and we children spied upon practically every tent, so we felt in control.

We noticed that on the second week, people began to disappear, but it was never a Jew. We knew why. They were afraid to be turned in by their own kind or by Billy Goat for a couple of sticks of chocolate.

On the evening of December the sixth, St. Nicolas Day, we left the camp. We hoped that the Hungarian guards would not care; all the German guards and the commanding officer had some serious wounds that would prevent them from running very fast, but they would still be capable of firing their weapons. The officer was missing an eye and half of the fingers on his left hand; the four German guards also had some problems, and in fact, one of them had lost half of one foot in Russia someplace. He was proud of his wound and fighting in Russia and often bragged about killing hundreds of soldiers with a machine gun before he stepped on an anti-personnel mine. He told us that the Russian soldiers came by the thousands, some without weapons. His partner often had to go outside the bunker to clear the dead and badly wounded soldiers from blocking the machine gun opening so he could continue shooting. The only regret he had about his military service on the front was he never had enough ammunition and often ran out of bullets before killing or wounding all his foes.

If we could run in the dark, we could make it. Our mother, in her weakened condition, could not run more than thirty meters. To be safe from being hit by a rifle bullet, she needed to be at least one hundred meters away. Our strategy was that once she stopped or firings began, we would all run a different direction and meet up at the old, abandoned kilns chimney. It was barely visible, even in the daytime, as it was about three kilometers away.

We waited until all the guards were preoccupied with some activities; their favorite seemed to be card-playing. It was very dark, in spite of a light cover of snow on the ground. We didn't have a watch; it had been confiscated or traded for food. We thought it must be close to ten o'clock when we gently opened the first gate. Once we all got through, we went to the second one that was slightly offset from the other. Opening the second gate was hard because it was heavier and unoiled. We were concerned the noise we made would call attention to our escape attempt. We worried that the squeaks from the metal latches and the hangers rubbing against one another in the quiet night would be magnified. We had already resigned ourselves to the fact we would not get breakfast the next morning. That was the usual punishment for the first escape attempt. We waited at least fifteen seconds, but no searchlight came on from the guard tower. We left without closing the noisy gate, leaving the obvious clue to the guards that someone had escaped.

We forged ahead as quietly as we could, although our steps made slight squishing noises, somewhat like stepping in mud. When we had gone more than ten meters from the fence, we all began to run. We had only run about another ten meters when a guard appeared in front of us using their military flashlight with red beam. It was difficult for us to stop because of the slippery mud under the snow. I think my mother must have bumped him a little, as he had to step aside to keep his balance. We were frightened and shaking, thinking we had been caught, but he waved us off.

Surprisingly, he spoke to us in a normal voice. "Please slow down, as the ground under the new snow is very wet and slippery. You can break a foot or, even worse, your neck. Also, be careful waving down motor vehicles, as most of them are German, and your smell will give you away." We did not realize that five weeks with an open pit toilet and no showering facilities, cold water, and no soap could make us smell unique and offensive among other normal people. When the guard saw we would not move, he said, "Go ahead, just be careful. No guard here will shoot you in the back." We told him we always heard shots after an escape and that we never saw those people again. I think he smiled, but we could not see his face, and he said, "We have no choice but to fire a few shots after someone escapes, or we get court-martialed. The German military is very strict. So far, we have hit no one intentionally." We left, walking slowly and carefully, trying to step in each other's footprints. In less than an hour, we arrived at the paved area of the old kiln. Then we heard five shots in quick succession.

We camped by the tower for that night. In the morning, I climbed up to try to get a sense of direction. The metal climbing steps on the side going straight up the brick tower was so cold I could barely hold on without my impromptu gloves made out of rags. The top of the high tower felt and looked like it was moving in small circles.

The trip home was very difficult, worse than we had expected. We were relieved that our bags were much lighter than what we had come to camp with. The second day into our escape, we approached a farm. An old man named Sándor lived there. He took pity on us and gave us hot water and food. When we looked in the mirror, we were shocked; we did not recognize ourselves. We had grown used to how one another's face changed, but to see ourselves as we looked thin and dirty was scary. We all washed in the kitchen area. Mother was last. She ran out of soap, so she called me to find some and pass it to her. Not thinking, I just swung the door open to give her the soap. It was the shock of my life! I didn't see my mother. I saw an old woman, disheveled, stringy, dirty hair, a gaunt, thin face with eyes almost completely sunken in, thin arms, and a body that was not more than skin and bones. If she had not spoken, I would have turned around and run away. It was like having a scary encounter with a living ghost. Her breasts had shrunk and looked like small, empty white paper sacks. What had been beautiful, plump, firm round curves were gone. It came to me in a flash that all the "extra" food she had given us and claimed to get from helping in the kitchen must have been her own portions. From that point on, I never accepted any offering of food from her hands; regardless of how sweet her smiles were, until I saw her eat her own portion first.

We had to stay at the farm for two days for my mother's feet to heal, but she never complained. She and my sisters had big boils on their feet. My mother had given her second pair of socks to Olga, the nursing mother.

The girls washed their socks and hung them up to dry. In the cold air, they froze, and when they wanted to put them on in the morning, they broke apart. We didn't want to take the time to wash our clothes, so we slept in the woodshed, the warmest place next to the kitchen. We still had about fifty kilometers to go. After the second day, when my mother's feet got better and she received a second pair of socks from the farmer, we started up again. We were clean and fed, but our clothes still looked shabby, well worn, and were too smelly. It would have been too risky to wave down any motor vehicle. We also stayed away from the main highways and followed dirt roads whenever possible. Without a map, we often meandered. People were very good to us, so we managed to get some food and water every day.

On occasion, we got rides on a horse- or oxen-drawn carriage, but just for a few kilometers and always in the back of the wagon so as not to offend the driver with our camp odor.

It took us more than a week to get close to home. Here, we split up. My mother, sisters, and my youngest brother stayed at an old and empty, badly damaged building on the outskirts of Zala. My other brother and I went ahead to find a friend. We first tried the church, where we thought Father Tibor would be. We waited until dark before we got the courage to knock on the door. The porter would not open the door but asked who we were and why we were there. After hearing our young voices and looking through a small window on the door to make sure we were not the Gestapo, he opened the heavy door and invited us in. We were asked to sit on the bench in the waiting area of the hall; the stone bench was ice cold and very uncomfortable. The seat of my trousers was worn so thin, it was all but gone. It seemed like we waited a long time, as I was half-asleep when a candle was pushed close to my face. Behind the flame, I could make out Father Tibor's features, but it took him a while to recognize us.

He knew exactly what to do and sent the porter on a one-horse sleigh to get the rest of the family. In the meantime, he asked another priest to find our father and tell him the good news. As far as we knew, he was still in prison. We had no idea of the ordeal he had to endure and of his subsequent rescue by the people who loved him and respected him.

I was barely awake that night when I felt my mother's hand touching the top of my head. Her stroke was soothing and comforting, like a gentle sedative. It was all I needed. That touch that evening has since remained with me, and it will for the rest of my life.

I wasn't awake when my father arrived, but his smiling face greeted me in the morning. He hugged me, ignoring the stench and the dirt, and I just cried and cried for a long time. It was the longest and sweetest cry I ever had.

Kele D. Gabor

Homeless

I have been a political prisoner, brainwashed, tortured, drugged, interrogated, sentenced without a court, beaten, and lived under fear, but these things were easier to endure and survive than the constant pain of the rape of my country. Giving up your wealth or material things, regardless of how little you have, is easier than losing your homeland. Think of it this way: you live in Maine, New York, or Pennsylvania and one day you're told you belong to Canada and must adopt the French Canadian system and speak French. Or you lived in Alabama, Georgia, or South Carolina, then your schools will teach Spanish and you have to become a Cuban citizen. Please visualize this event, and you may be laughing at this impossibility. People living now in New Mexico, Arizona, and Texas might not be laughing if they would become part of and citizens of Mexico. But what if it should happen to you as it did to me? How would you feel losing your citizenship without due process of law and getting a new, different one that you don't want?

Losing one's homeland is akin to being raped. You may think I'm exaggerating, but these are some of the similarities. It is done by force and under duress, you don't want it to happen, it is very painful, it hurts deep inside, it makes you feel dirty, helpless, and you never forget. This comparison may only be really understood or appreciated by a woman. And if you want to fight back, they treat you like the "old court system." You are told, "You asked for it." I know my people and I didn't ask for it, and I know the rape victims didn't, either.

The politicians who drafted the Treaty of Trianon after WWI raped my country and at least fifteen million Hungarians, one of the largest minorities in Europe. The foreign politicians tearing up Hungary didn't even know they divided up a single watershed, a natural economic and agricultural unity that is the Carpathian Basin.

The treaty gave away over two-thirds of our land and over forty percent of the population. The displaced Hungarians became the sacrificial lambs of Europe. The new Romanians, Slovaks, and Yugoslavians, especially the Serbs, took advantage of the Hungarians living in the newly acquired land.

They deported Hungarians living close to the new borders and replaced them with their own people from the Balkans. Speaking our mother tongue became punishable and made it difficult to retain our culture, language, and heritage, along with closing many of our schools and universities.

There are several groups of minorities around Hungary, but the Slovaks got Csaló, which was ninety nine percent Hungarian. Many Serbs left Kosovo and migrated north to Hungary. However, the region of Vajda (Vojvodina) was over seventy five percent native Hungarian. Mura region has a lot of Slovenians and Croats, but they all asked to belong to Hungary, not to the new Southern Slavs (Yugoslavia). There was a constant influx of Walachians (Romanian) from the fifteenth century on from the south to Hungary, for a better place to earn a living and to escape from landlords like the bloodthirsty Dracula.

Even Dracula escaped from Walachia and lived in exile for a while in Transylvania, but only until he could safely return to his homeland. This region is now annexed and is part of the newly created Enlarged Romania.

The same scenario is going on between Mexico and bordering Southern states in the US. In spite of the large number of illegal immigrants, the states of California, New Mexico, Arizona, and Texas will remain, it is hoped, part of the USA.

Imagine, if you can, the pain and disruption of the life of the citizens of the Southern States when Mexico annexes them. The original thirteen Eastern states would become part of Cuba and Canada. The Western states would go to the Philippines, leaving one-fourth of the Great Plains as the dismembered United States. Imagine all these lands without mountains or large rivers as natural borders to ease the defense of your remaining people and the rest of your home land, with all their occupants suddenly gifted away to foreign governments. This is exactly what happened to Hungary!

It is nice to know there are better ways of handling border adjustments. In 1849, when California prepared to become a state, less than nought point one percent of the population was Anglo-Saxon or spoke English. After promising to the locals, mostly Spanish-speaking people, that their language will always be taught in the schools, the English-speaking minority had the added necessary vote to be the new state of the USA. This was done without using force and just gaining the majority of voters with promises that were kept. Spanish is still taught in

Californian schools, and now even the native Indian population can vote.

The Hungarians never had a chance. Nobody was asked where we wanted to belong. During the peace treaty and after the wars, every country was represented and heard from except the Hungarians! Why?

G. Ferrero, an Italian historian, wrote in 1871, "Hungary is a one thousand year- old state, with historical and geographical unity, welded together for centuries and held together by common desire which neither weapons, nor written words could break up from one day to the next." But they did, with terrible consequences.

Carpathian Basin— A complete natural geographical unity

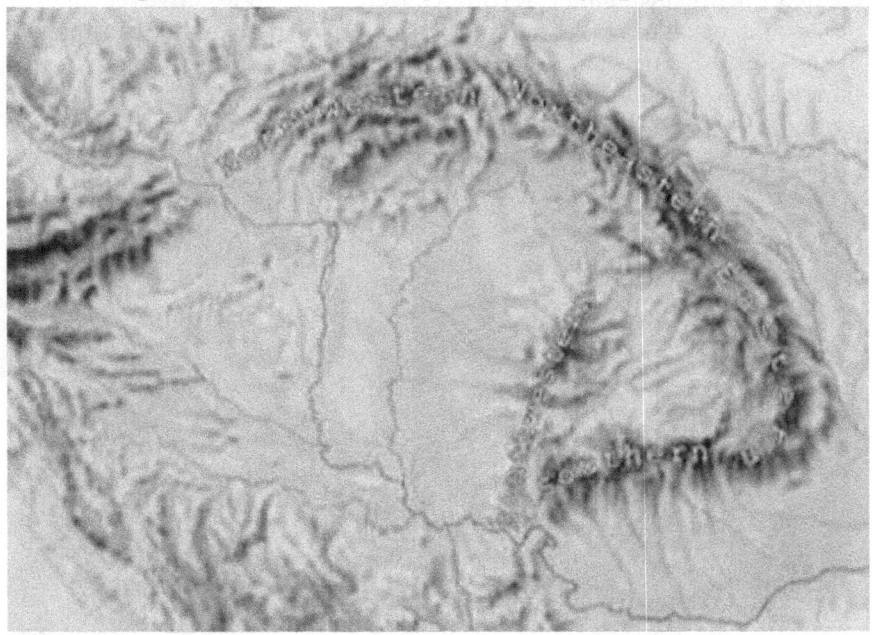

Before WWI, Elisee Reclus (1837–1916) wrote, "Hungary's great advantage is that it is a complete geographical unity. The Hungarian Kingdom is the most completely connected area of Europe. Regardless of what may happen in Central Europe, the Hungarians will play the most significant role in the arena of the Carpathians." Unfortunately, the treaty of Trianon destroyed this geographical unity and at the same time forced millions of Hungarians to live under intolerable conditions in newly created countries.

D'Annunzio, an Italian poet, wrote in 1926, "As long as Hungary is not given justice, the situation in the Danubian basin cannot be resolved. The war has truly mutilated Hungary."

The Hungarian Kingdom, over one thousand years old, was subdivided. The stabilizing force of Central Europe was left without defendable borders, access to the sea, and most of our natural resources were taken away.

They also totally disregarded the ethnic demographics, giving areas where the population was over ninety percent Hungarian to the newly created Enlarged Romania. Territories were attached to Slovakia, again a new country that never existed before, where the population was ninety eight percent Hungarians. The territorial provisions of the treaty liquidated the ancient state of Hungary.

Mutilation of Hungary

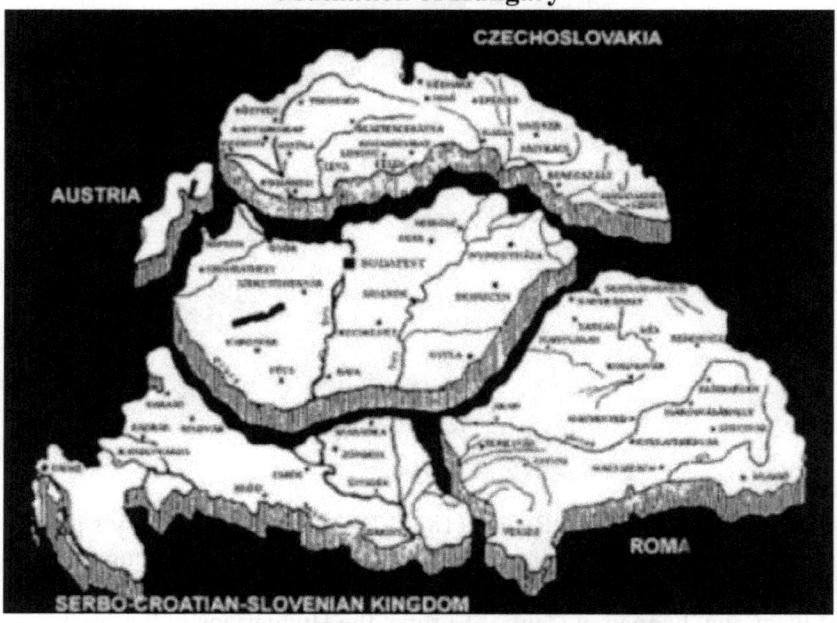

by the Treaty of Trianon (Versailles), June 1919

This map shows the broken off parts of the over one-thousand year old Hungarian kingdom without any logical justifications or explanations!

To emphasize this ignorance, here are some statistics quoted from the Encyclopedia Britannica on the Treaty of Trianon:

The census of 1910 had given the population of Hungary as twenty million eight hundred and eighty six thousand four hundred and eighty seven. Calculated from these figures, Hungary retained only seven million six hundred and fifteen thousand one hundred and seventeen under the treaty; while two hundred and ninety one thousand six hundred and eighteen went to [reward or penalize] Austria; twenty three thousand six hundred and sixty two to Poland; three million five hundred and seventeen thousand five hundred and sixty eight to Czech-Slovakia [a newly formed country]; five million two hundred and fifty seven thousand four hundred and sixty seven to Enlarged Romania [a new country]; forty nine thousand eight hundred and six to Italy; and three million six hundred and eighty one thousand two hundred and forty nine to Yugo-Slavia [again a newly created country of seven different ethnic groups].

The terms were bitterly resented in Hungary, and also by circles outside the country, as intolerably harsh and unjust. It was pointed out that the dismemberment of the old historic unit caused great economic hardship and dislocation, and even the ethnic principle invoked to justify this dismemberment.

The way the treaty was administered enhanced the emergence of the Nazi movement, the election of Hitler, and the beginning of WWII. The treaty also created a power vacuum in Central Europe, which led to much animosity and bloodshed in the newly created countries, and it will continue until the Carpathian Basin is unified to be a viable union or nation.

I remember the three good friends and their assessment of this situation forced upon us by the French radical Georges Clemenceau and their prediction of its dire consequences.

The Treaty of Trianon was unlawful for the following reasons:

- The treaty was based on false statistics exclusively provided by nationalistic, economic, and political lobbying by two Czech politicians, Tomas Masaryk and Edward Benes. Their intent was to break up the Austrian Empire and create a new

- independent Czech-Slovak republic.
- US President Woodrow Wilson published the fourteen-point requirements to ensure world peace. The tenth point dealt with ensuring the complete autonomy of all nationalities in the Austro- Hungarian monarchy. This point was totally ignored.
- Hungary was the only nation without representation and was never given the opportunity to provide a list of requests or have an appeal process. In fact, the Hungarian delegation was not allowed to take part in any discussions but, instead, was informed that any objections, regardless of their validity, would be ignored by the Western powers, which were the dictators of the treaty.
- Hungary lost over ninety percent of its forests and eighty percent of gold, silver, platinum, salt, and iron mines.
- Most natural borders disappeared, except a small part of the Danube and Drava rivers.
- The treaty destroyed the stabilizing power of Central Europe and was also a blow to the civilized world in money, prestige, and human lives for all affected parties.
- New countries were created with people who cannot mix, tolerate, or respect each other, which led to resentment and disillusionment. There is a better chance for a shotgun wedding to last a lifetime than for these newly created countries with a unique mix of ethnic groups forced together to live in peace and harmony (during one hundred and fifty years of Austrian domination, the Habsburgs did everything possible to create divisions among minorities based on the motto of "Divide and conquer."

After WWII, Stalin dictated the division of Central Europe, but the Allies went along and made the same mistake by recreating the new Yugoslavia, Czechoslovakia, Enlarged Romania and other countries, which would break up in the future).

Lord Sydenham, member of the English upper house, wrote in his book published in 1927, "I see with deepest sympathy the proud (Hungarian) people with glorious past who are now locked up and encircled by the fully armed new countries."

Father Tibor, a historian and archeologist, explained that possibly the most wasteful time spent in higher education is majoring in history without also learning how to make use of the information to help predict the future. If history would be taught based on unbiased evidence and its effect on current trends, we would not continue making the same mistakes. The best example of repeated mistakes is the division of Central Europe and the Middle East that could easily lead to WWIII. After WWII, the same grave errors were made by re-establishing borders similar to the Treaty of Trianon after WWI and without any help or support for Central Europe.

Only the western edge of Europe, primarily Germany and France, received financial aid to recover from the devastation of WWII—the Marshall Plan. Yet they committed more crimes during WWII than any of the central European countries. Hence, there is no justification in learning history unless the knowledge is used to help predict the future and avoid repeating similar disasters.

The totalitarian communist system did delay the eventual breakup and separation of these ethnic groups and forced unions, but I will never understand the still prevalent American foreign policy of not letting nature take its course in Central Europe, the Middle East, or in Russia. For example, the British forced the union of Kurds, Shiites, and Sunnis, naming the new country Iraq. We could avoid the internal civil war just by letting these diverse ethnic groups live in their independent states. If they want to unite later for economic reasons, let them do it by themselves.

The prediction of the three friends was absolutely correct, as most of these new countries have ceased to exist as a single or unified entity, but millions of people are still suffering.

The Serbs alone killed tens of thousands of ethnic minorities, and the mass graves of Croatians, Bosnians, and Hungarians are just beginning to be uncovered. The suffering was not only restricted to murdering thousands of Hungarian men, women, and children but also the closing of our universities, high schools, elementary schools, and destruction of our property, especially cemeteries and old churches, which would show to the world that this area is made up of Magyar, Avars, and Hun settlements dating back to the fifth century or more.

In 1944, the Romanian partisans massacred women, children, and men by the thousands, emptying nine villages to make room for Romanian families from Moldova. Finally, the killing was stopped by the Russian military, and the partisan leader Gavril Olteanut was arrested and given an eight year prison term, but he was released after four years. The Romanians then systematically moved the Magyar population away from the current common border to deep inside in Walachia, to the Danube delta, Dobrudja, or to Russian prison camps, never to return. The Hungarian Communist puppet government set up by Stalin and the Romanians even invented a plan to force the assimilation of the Hungarians by moving them from Transylvanian towns to Bucharest, deep inside the original Walachia. They set up Hungarian sections in the capital city, where the overwhelming population was Romanian.

The foreign diplomats and politicians responsible for the destruction of my country probably ignored the fact that Austria, and subsequently

Germany, started and lost the world wars. Nor did they seem to know why a country is formed.[2]

When the Hungarian kingdom was formed over a thousand years ago, the easily defendable Carpathian Mountains were chosen for protection.

There were only seven narrow passes, and it stayed that way for over a millennium. When I see political borders, I also want to see geographical and topographical maps of the same region. At a glance, one could discern which countries were formed in an artificial way or that the border was moved by force. Every time I see a current political map of Europe with the mutilated borders of Hungary, it gives me both physical and psychological pain.

Today, there are many forced unions of ethnic populations: in Central Europe, the Middle East, Asia, and Africa. For example, Kurdistan and Armenia ceased to exist. The Turks alone killed or relocated about one million Kurds and Armenians. Iraq did the same.

In any country, government responsibilities should be:

1. Defense of the people and country,

2. Internal security (police and justice system),

---

[2] The primary reason for forming a country is uniting against a common enemy. The original thirteen US colonies united against England , and the defendable border was the Atlantic Ocean.

KELE D. GABOR

3. Environment for growth, opportunities, prosperity, and the wellbeing of the people— (education, finance, and the necessary infrastructure to accomplish it).

Anything else is extra and never takes precedence over the three points
above.
Social programs are great if they don't destroy or discourage ambition,
independence, and the desire for self-improvement and a good work habit.
Everything beyond these activities by any government is another way to
make you dependent and, in some cases, enslave you. Ask yourself if you have a government by and for the people, as our founding fathers intended.
Paraphrasing what Thomas Jefferson wrote in his memoirs, "Our form of government will be the best and will be long lasting if we do not elect lawyers, as they're trained for years to question, interpret, reinterpret and delay things." I often wish we'd heeded Mr. Jefferson's advice.
All Americans should read our Constitution on a regular basis. After reading this great document, it will be obvious we have a representative republic and, fortunately, not a democracy. Voters and the news media often confuse the two forms of government and have no ideas about the qualifications for or differences between Leaders and Managers.
The following quote's origin is questioned, but the context and the logic behind it are definitely meaningful:

> A democracy is always temporary in nature; it simply cannot exist as a prominent form of government. A democracy will continue to exist up until the time the voters discover that they can vote themselves generous gifts from the public treasury (i.e., social programs, welfare, and the like). From that moment on, the majority always votes for the candidates who promise the most benefits from the public treasury, with the result that every democracy will finally collapse due to loose fiscal policy, which is always followed up with a dictatorship.

DECEPTION AND REALITY- LIVING THROUGH THE MISSING PAGES OF HISTORY

The average age of the world's greatest civilizations, from the beginning to the end of history, has been about two hundred years. During those two hundred years, these nations tend to progress through the following sequence:

From Bondage to spiritual faith;

From spiritual faith to great courage;

From courage to liberty;

From liberty to abundance;

From abundance to complacency;

From complacency to apathy;

From apathy to dependence;

From dependence back to bondage.

Where do you think we stand?

Yet if one understands our Constitution, it will be evident most of the power is in the hands of the Congress, not the president. Our president cannot even make peace or declare war without the approval of the Senate.

Therefore, if you want to preserve our great representative republic, please elect senators who are trustworthy and whose interest is centered on the future of our people and this enlarged country. There is a slow drift away from the original Constitution, mainly in the Congress and the judicial branches of the government, just like the old Catholic Church from the Bible.

The rape of a country or a woman, as sometimes happens, results in some new offspring. In the case of Central Europe, the new babies were the Enlarged Romania (even its name Romania was first coined close to the turn of the twentieth century and was known as Walachia), Yugoslavia (containing seven different nationalities who dislike one another), Czechs and Slovaks (they also mistrust each other), Greater Ukraine, and a larger Austria, all at the expense of Hungary and its people.

To add insult to injury, in the newly acquired territories occupied by Serbs, Romanians, Slovaks, and Russians tried to eliminate the native Hungarians by moving, arresting, or, on occasion, mass-murdering them.

The newly acquired areas also enriched the newly created country in natural resources, but in most cases, they didn't know how to take advantages of their situation. For example, Romanians didn't have good engineering schools for mining, so they had to sublease the gold, silver, iron, and salt mines to make profit from them, as they didn't want to use the local Hungarian experts and population. Ukrainians clear-cut all the beautiful forests, creating serious floods for the indigenous Hungarian population, polluting rivers, and killing fish at the same time. The Serbs mass-murdered all undesirables–Croatians, Bosnians, and Hungarians–and replaced them with Serbs from Kosovo. The void created by the departing Serbs in Kosovo was being filled with Albanians from the neighboring country.

I equate the plight of the American Indians and their tribes with the Hungarian people. The Indians also lost most of their homeland and territories and were put onto reservations. I often wonder what are worse, short term concentration camps or forced into living on Indian reservations through many generations.

Borders drawn around native Hungarians are now controlled by ultra nationalistic foreign governments. I sometimes wonder if those politicians who created the current unstable Central European governments feel guilty of mass murder and of creating an explosive situation or if they hide behind the cloak of some drummed-up justifications for their ignorance. It may be shocking to learn the displaced Hungarians far exceeded the total number of Jews taken to concentration camps from ten or more countries by the Nazis during WWII. Yet few historians make the comparison or report these facts.

The Indian population of North America was estimated to be eighteen to twenty million at the turn of the eighteenth century, according to American archeological history. This is based on the still undisturbed or known Indian sites, structures, and burial grounds. By the twentieth century, Indians numbered less than two million. That is about a ninety percent reduction in two hundred years. We learned that over thirty percent of the Indians may have died of white man's diseases because they had no resistance to them, but often the pathogens were purposely introduced to the Indians by the authorities. How about the other seventy percent? When it comes to killing Indians, a large part may have died of homesickness or starvation, as they lost their homeland and their main food source— the bison.

The Americans with compassion and understanding of the plight of the Indians could never drum up enough worldwide support to save them.

We now know the extermination of the large herds of bison was done on purpose to eliminate the food source for the Plains Indians. There is not a satisfactory answer for the fact that about ten percent of Indians who survived now have less than one percent of their home range. Victors do take the spoils, but this is more like the wholesale rape of all Indian nations.

As the story goes, the old Indian chief Two Eagles was told by a government official, "You have observed the white man for ninety years. You have seen his wars and his technological advances. You have seen his progress and the damage he has done." The chief nodded in agreement. The official continued, "Considering all these events, in your opinion, where did the white man go wrong?" The chief stared at the government official for over a minute, then calmly replied, "When white man find land, Indians running it, no taxes, no debt, plenty buffalo, plenty beaver, clean water. Women did all the work. Medicine man free. Indian men spend all day hunting and fishing, all night having sex." Then the chief smiled and added, "Only white man dumb enough to think he could improve a system like that."

No attacks are intended on the Spanish, English, French, German, Dutch, or other settlers in the USA. Some reparations are on their way, but we should show more appreciation for those who helped us survive and get rich. Even the significance of Thanksgiving has lost its sheen. This holiday should be dedicated to the Indians who helped our pioneers, the early settlers, survive. There is clear historical evidence about the Indians helping the pilgrims when they were starving. Without the Indians' assistance, most colonies would have failed and perished, as they had no knowledge of the American native plants, and they would have disappeared like the Vikings in Greenland. Don't forget, the original settlers only knew about the European staples—peas, cabbage, lentils, and the cereals wheat, rye, and barley. They didn't recognize the animals; they called the bison buffalo; the red deer or wapiti elk, the elk moose, the weasel fisher. Just think how limited the diet would be for the people around the world without knowing about turkey, corn, cranberries, sweet potatoes, squash, tomato, beans, chocolate, pepper, potato, avocado, and sunflower. The Indians gave the world a lot but got few things in return, and they do deserve our "thanksgivings."

Western Europe especially benefited and got rich on the hundreds of tons of precious metals, primarily gold and silver, they confiscated from the Indians.

The help of the Indians to the new settlers was an outstanding example on how to help others. These gestures from the Indians may be one of the reasons that the Americans became the most generous nation and provided the most help to mankind all over the world. In spite of the short history of the United States and its many blunders in foreign policy, it is the greatest country in the world. This form of government as a representative republic provides more freedom and opportunity than any other nation, thanks to the founding fathers and the great Constitution, even if some of the ideas were taken from the Iroquois Nation and the French Revolution. Let's keep it this way!

It was a sunny afternoon in Udvar, Transylvania, in the eastern part of Hungary. The smallest tank I'd ever seen was parked right across from our house. We youngsters went to investigate.

The German solider guarding the small tank let me take a peek inside. It had no cannon, except a turret for a large caliber machine gun that could be fired either from inside or mounted on the top outside. It had a lot of hand grenades inside, and they were also the miniaturized versions without handles. They called them the egg grenade, as they looked and felt like an egg, except they were all painted black, with a yellow and red narrow rings in the middle indicating the type and the amount of explosives in them. The tank had only two seats, but they could squeeze in a third person on the top. The soldiers would not tell who they were, but each of them carried a side arm instead of a rifle. We saw two of them, the driver and a major. We first were concerned about my father, as my mother got very nervous every time she saw German soldiers, especially the SS or the Gestapo. We boys guessed about why all the concerns, but we were never told. It was obvious there was something going on that our parents didn't want us to know.

When Father Tibor came to visit from Kolozs, the largest city of Transylvania, he and my father always retreated to our small library, which then was off-limits to us. They often talked all afternoon. Each time he came, he brought a large box of clothes and his charcoal gray umbrella.

The clothes looked like used religious garments— priests, seminarians, and nun's clothes. Even the headdresses were included. We knew nothing about who used them until one Friday afternoon, about a few weeks after Easter, a middle aged, well-dressed woman with a yellow Star of David[3] nicely displayed on her coat over her heart, showed up asking for her package. I let her in at the main gate, and I recognized her, as she always treated us nicely when we visited her little store across the school. She sold tobacco, writing utensils, sunglasses, pipes, cigarettes, candy, and my favorite, chewy licorice strings. A few months earlier, on Easter Monday, we went to visit her and her beautiful, very attractive daughter, Lara. Lara had large brown eyes, like a Persian lady, thick lips, and reddish-black wavy hair. We sprinkled them with fine perfume, as was the custom in those days.

According to old Hungarian customs, the boys went out on Easter Monday to girls' homes to spray cologne on them and, in return, got cookies and hand-painted eggs, chocolate rabbits, candy, or flowers. If you were lucky, you were given all of it and a kiss on the cheek if she

---

[3] The Star of David was a Sumerian symbol signifying connection between the Holy Trinity and Humans, and it was adopted by the Jews two thousand year later.

really liked you.

Lara played the cello, and I saw her a few times practicing in the afternoon across the gym where I was learning fencing. She attended the famous Lehar music school, named after the Hungarian composer. Unfortunately, she didn't kiss me. This last preferred gesture I always enjoyed from any girls I visited, and considered it an invitation for asking her out for a date.

That Easter, we went around with horse and carriage, as we wanted to visit about one hundred homes and at least that many young girls. Our trip was always eventful, fun, and exciting, as my father would enlighten us about how these customs came about.

I assume some of the readers may be familiar with most of the holiday customs, but a few of them need to be repeated, as I was often asked about what the chicken, egg, and rabbit have to do with Easter.

Like the Christmas tree, most Easter customs go back to pagan days. The Christmas tree was lighted and burned at the winter solstice. The chicken and egg were symbols of rebirth, renewal, and spring. The rabbit, also an old pagan symbol, as the goddess of birth, renewal, and fertility, was a beautiful young girl who turned into a white rabbit during the wintertime.

In the spring, the goddess renewed herself and changed back again from a rabbit, taking the beautiful young maiden form.

When I escorted the nice lady with the Star of David toward the house, my father came out, turned to our guest, and said, "Ida, I asked you never to come by the house, they are already watching us." Ida got red in the face and nervously turned around to leave. But in the end, she got a bag, which I knew contained a used nun's habit. After the lady left, my father didn't say anything, but put his index finger to his lip, indicating that what just now transpired was hush-hush.

The German major climbing out of the tank had double gold markings on his collar, indicating signal core. Soon I noticed the long antenna on the tank, and inside in the back it was full of radio equipment. They said they came in a hurry to talk with my father. They didn't know he was away on business. So they just waited there without saying a word. The date was August 2, 1944. About an hour after finishing our lunch, an army truck came and parked in the center of the town square, facing our house. At this time, the German officer asked to talk to my mother, and when the major went in, we were sent out. Later, my mother told me the major was instructed to get my father to safety and inform him on what had transpired on the Eastern front. The major was still talking to my mother when the announcement came from the military vehicle, starting at two p.m.

They announced the bad news: "You have six hours to vacate your premises and leave town. The Eastern front collapsed, Romania joined the Russians, and the Romanian soldiers may be here as early as tonight."

Soon after the announcement was made, the major came out of our house, and we went inside. While my mother was packing, she told us that the most trusted ally of the German army was Romania, who had changed sides and was now helping the Russians to take over Eastern Hungary. We were under the impression Hungary was able to come to a peace agreement with the Russians without the Nazis' knowledge. My mother must have read our mind, as she went on saying the peace treaty did not matter with the Russians because the Romanians are coming, "And you know what it means." We had heard enough stories about their officers wearing makeup, perfumes, and about their poor foot soldiers. Their army robbed us blind twenty-five years earlier, taking anything that was movable.

Breaking the peace agreement may have caused the Russians some headaches, as the Hungarians took this action as a breach of the treaty. We believed, erroneously, that the peace agreement was signed earlier, and we started to resist with the tiny remaining forces left behind. The approaching armies consisted mostly of Romanians, with only a few Russian units.

Later, the Russians had to take over, as the few and small Hungarian military units were able to stop the entire Romanian Army.

After Austria lost WWI, which Hungarian people only supported reluctantly, and our army disbanded or was in POW camps, the Romanians took advantage of the situation. They came in from Walachia, just south of our border, and occupied most of our country in order to burn and loot. Most of our fine furniture either ended up in the presidential suite or in theaters in Romania.

They had no idea of the value of our art collection, so most pieces were destroyed. They broke to pieces my grandfather's gun collection; some of the guns were from the sixteenth century. The Germans eventually packed up the remains of the art collection, but not having an available locomotive, it stayed behind for the Russians to take. We know much of our art collection is still in the basement of a museum in St. Petersburg in Russia, in spite of the international court ruling to return them to us.

We also know the Romanians stole wagonloads of beautiful furniture, sculptures, paintings, flatware, and silverware. So we started to pack some of the guns, rifles, and other favorite things while my mother concentrated on food and clothing. Beautiful and hand-carved furniture, pictures, silver and crystal glassware, pianos, statues, rare library books, and a lot more were just left behind.

We were lucky, as Colonel Álmos, knowing our situation ahead of time, sent us a military vehicle that could take us to a safer place, away from the Eastern front, about one hundred kilometers northwest. We had very limited space in the car, so we even had to leave behind some of the necessities, like extra food and clothing.

It turned out the Romanian army took much longer to reach Udvar, as boy scouts with hand-carved wooden rifles set up posts on the passes through the mountains. The Romanians had no idea that the guns were mock-ups with no ammunition and that they were just very young kids around age sixteen or less.

The military vehicle could only take us to Para, where we were able to get on a train with open wagons. When my mother found out about the boy scouts keeping the entire invading military units at bay, she hired a small truck to go back and get some additional supplies, some necessities, and some small valuables. She obtained a temporary permit to enter the city for four hours. When she returned, we were amazed at the amount of stuff nicely packed in big wooden crates, which were loaded into our open wagon. We asked her how she managed to bring so much on such short notice. She reminded us about what happened three months earlier in my brother's vision.

My brother Bende woke our parents up around three a.m. one morning in early May and told my father and mother he had the most interesting dream he thought was really a vision, as he was awake when he saw the pictures. So my parents, half-asleep, told him to tell them what he had dreamed. Soon they realized there was something special about his vision, so they both asked him to immediately sit down, get paper and pencil, and write everything down that he had seen in his vision.

We generally got up around six a.m. to get ready for school, and on the days when my mother baked bread, I got up at five a.m. to help her with kneading the fresh dough, as her hands often hurt. This particular morning, I felt the gentle tug on my shoulder and soon a kiss on my forehead from my mother. I knew it was bread-baking time and her hand was hurting. To my surprise, my brother was sitting in the library room by my father's desk, which usually was off-limits to us. The lamp on top of the desk was on, and the bright light bothered my still sleepy eyes as I was passing by the open door. I stopped for a moment and asked him what he was doing, and he didn't respond. This I found annoying and most unusual, as he was the kindest soul I ever knew not only in the family, but also in every place else I have ever been. He was smart, attentive, with an excellent memory, always looking into people's eyes, and very patient. In fact, I was always envious of his calm behavior, just the opposite of mine. This type of behavior probably helped him to become the best shot in the family. I had seen him hit five consecutive "bull's-eyes" on different targets right in the center, where the inner circle diameter was about the same size as the casing of the ammunition. During kneading the dough, I found out from my mother what he was writing. As my brother Bende finished and brought the paper over for my mother to read, she said, "My hand is full of flour, just read it to me." It was a story I should never forget.

This is not exact, but it is close to what he read from his paper:

> "Someone gently woke me up and talked to me. I didn't see him but saw the things he said. The vision started on a beautiful, sunny afternoon in front of our house. A military vehicle was parked, and the soldiers yelled, "Get out, the devils are coming." I smiled and asked him if he saw the devils too. He said, "Not exactly, I just saw strange soldiers in brown uniforms coming from the east, burning, destroying, and killing as they came and went."
>
> And he continued, "Big thunder clouds gathered by the town square, almost directly above our place, and a voice loudly

announced we should pack six weeks of food, clothes, and supplies for the children and go west to survive the onslaught. The clouds disappeared, and I saw more soldiers come with different uniforms, and they also burned, looted, and killed people. I saw churches, but mostly the old ones burning. Then I saw dark-faced men in brown long leather coats and big boots yelling orders everyone had to obey.

"I saw old cemeteries bulldozed and all the headstones removed and destroyed. I saw people starving in prison, in forced-labor camps, in iron, in handcuffs, in terrible pain and many villages burning. I saw big tanks coming through the passes, young boys were killed, and those who were still alive the tanks ran over. I saw dead people lying all over the place with heads missing and soldiers piling them up and burning them. I could smell the terrible stench as they were burning women; children and men still wrapped in barbed wire. Those who stayed alive had to march away in chains, with soldiers hitting them with rifle butts. I saw prisons in deep cellars, full of innocent people being tortured and killed with acid, torches, and electrical shocks.

"The men in the long brown leather coats with evil red eyes used other gadgets. I saw empty villages where new foreign people came from the south to live, and they were confused and looked lost. I saw the religious, the priests, and nuns yelling and praying while they were raped and burned to ashes. Nobody understood the strangers' tongue they spoke, and they had no features, just black faces and red lights coming out of their eyes. The red color emitting from their eyes started to cover everything, and dark, evil beings surrounded them.

I saw my next birthday was celebrated in an open wagon, on a train, far away from home, and people were hurt in the wagon, but our family was safe. We had to stay in the wagon for six weeks before we could leave. I saw us as grown-ups, my father killed, our land looted, and finally fleeing to a faraway place that was beautiful and peaceful. Then the heavens opened up, and I saw God in white cloths with a whip in his hand. He looked angry, and the people were shaking. The entire world was on fire, but our country stayed untouched by the flames."

Deception and Reality - Living Through the Missing Pages of History

When Bende finished reading it, I remember being scared and shaking, but I didn't want to show it. In fact, I forgot about it in the short run. I guess it is human nature to forget the bad and retain most of the pleasant memories.

Fortunately, my mother and father didn't dismiss the story and started to get ready for the "unexpected" evil invasion. My mother would start putting stuff away in big wooden boxes, which we might need in an emergency.

All these boxes were stored in a large storage room on the other side of the kitchen, where the steps led up to the attic but where we youngsters would rarely go. My father dug some holes in the back garden away from the house and put important papers and some valuable family antique items in them. He knew about and experienced the earlier Romanian invasion of our land after WWI. He spent time in their prison because he was Hungarian. He saw the Bolsheviks and the Red Guard at work and the secret police in long brown leather coats, as described in my brother's dream. My parents also knew my brother had never before heard or seen those things. Of course, we teenagers paid no attention to their activities of packing and getting ready for the eventual escape.

It took our wagon six weeks to travel six hundred kilometers to our destination, close to the capital. We did celebrate several family members' birthday, including Bende's, on the train in an open wagon. As Bende saw it, a lot of people were killed, arrested, charged with falsities, and kept in prison under deplorable conditions; thousands were marched to the Delta of the Danube by the Black Sea, where over fifty percent died.

The Romanians did burn villages; they did destroy cemeteries and old churches, as they were historical records and evidence of Hungarian origin. The Slovaks and the Serbs also followed the same course.

It was hard, very hard, to leave my homeland. It was extremely painful to leave behind my home, my mountains, and my trees, my friends, my ducks and dogs, the grazing bears in the thickets, the browsing deer on the hillside, the stags on the peaks, the beautiful views from the lookout, my creeks full of trout and crayfish, and all the wonderful wild berries and the delicious mushrooms. I was devastated and walked around with my head hanging low. My heart was heavy, and I often thought about not being able to enjoy again my favorite activity— going on hunting trips with my father or my oldest half-

KELE D. GABOR

brother, Ben.

Those of you who have had the good fortune and experience of tracking wild animals, not to kill but to see, will understand what I was missing.

Have you ever seen a capercaillie (a giant ruffed grouse) dance in the early morning sunlight, a mother bear nursing her cubs, or an otter catching fish? Ever tracked the wolf or seen a lynx catching a marmot? Did you ever have to run and climb a tree to escape a wild boar? Have you ever been caught in a big thunder or snow storm, get lost in a big forest, smelled and tasted the fresh water from a spring, stayed overnight without a tent and seen all the stars in the sky?

These hunting trips provided me with happiness and a lot of education about nature. There, I learned to respect and protect the environment, and I was being groomed, without knowing it, to take over the family owned forests, which were in our possession since the 1300s. It was amazing how my father and oldest brother got me totally involved in ecology without me realizing it. I learned about plate tectonics in 1944, even though it wasn't taught yet in schools or universities. I also understood the importance of recycling, water cycles, habitat protection, fauna, ecology, watershed, the interdependencies of all species, and the importance of varied vegetation, wild life, clean air, and water as the "liquid of life." It was interesting to learn that ignorant men sometimes could outdo the damages done by natural disasters.

The worst part of my loss was that nobody noticed, as we were all in shock. It was a week later when finally the hunger diverted my terrible mood, but just for a short period, and it started up again. It was not living, just existing. I never can or will forget where my homeland is, and it breaks my heart that it no longer belongs to the indigenous Hungarians.

My homesickness haunted me for the rest of my life. I only forgot about home for short periods when I was stressed or happy. When bombs were falling or bullets were flying, I was preoccupied with saving my life.

When I was happy, I really wanted to take advantage of those moments, allowing no bad memories to spoil the fun.

It is very hard to lose just about everything and only have hope left. However, in spite of my difficulties in losing my world, I have always been able to find good things to hang on to; I had my loving parents and siblings.

We prayed and sang every night. I feel sorry for those children who always had it good, never disciplined, never been exposed to classical music, art, have never really seen all the stars undimmed by city lights, tracked a wolf, drank from cold springs, or gotten temporarily lost in the wilderness.

We would only travel when the German military didn't need our locomotive. When we got it back, they moved us only short distances, and we were often left in the middle of nowhere. There were about thirty people per wagon, and it was unfamiliar and uncomfortable for everyone. We the young ones, however, made the best of things. We found some fun exploring the countryside near the train, as one never knew when we would get a locomotive to continue our journey to escape the Romanian and Russian Red Armies. A few times, we came very close to missing the train. We learned to put our ears on the track periodically to hear if the locomotive was on its way back. My mother would be worried sick.

Most of the time, we were looking for food to augment the canned fruits my mother brought, as we soon ran out of pork and ducks preserved in lard. We had to share our food with those in need, especially children. In some places, people would see all the hungry children and give us cheese, ham, bread, and some milk. When we stayed in no man's land, we had to climb down and forage in the nearby fields. Our favorite foraged food was fresh corn on the cob. Many times, we didn't have a chance to cook them, but it still tasted delicious. For days, we could only find potatoes. One other food we developed a taste for was sugar beet. They were delicious for breakfast, cutting them up in chewing-gum size pieces and sucking on them until all the sweetness came out. We never before ate as much uncooked raw food, as that was all we could find and fires were not permitted, especially after dark. We didn't like being parked close to cities, as bombing was a real problem.

The American and English planes were flying too high to tell that we were civilians, not military. One time, a bomb came so close that shrapnel killed one of the boys, Peter, the quickest climber, with large blue eyes and big ears that stood away from his short and straight hair. He was also a great singer, even though his voice just started to change. We didn't know him well; he attended the same school as I did, but he was a year ahead of me. The shrapnel cut off about a third of his head, and we had to scrape his brain off our shirts and blankets. It was the first time I had witnessed a compatriot's and a nice young boy's death. After the shrapnel hit, we only heard a quiet and slow moan. It was after the bombing stopped that we realized that he was badly hurt. He soon died thereafter. We really missed him, as he was fun to be with, always smiling and able to keep our spirits up with appropriate songs.

From this point on, we could not stay on top of the boxes in the open wagons to see the fireworks, as the bombs were falling. During bombing attacks, we had to stay close to the floor in the middle of the wagon or lay next to the side.

Peter's little sister was devastated, as she was very attached to her older brother. Their mother was a strong woman, but I caught her crying and shaking when her kids were not around. Peter's body was buried the next day nearby. The railroad guys helped to dig the grave and lower him down.

We, as friends, threw the earth back on him. No casket was provided. His body was just rolled in a white sheet, looking like an Egyptian mummy with a red head, as blood and body fluids were still coming out of the large, gaping head wound. The nearby police station provided a wooden cross, and my mother scratched his name on an old license plate Peter found earlier walking along the tracks and had brought the shiny object back to his little sister to play with. His grave is still there, close to Dés, near the tracks at the edge of a cornfield. We often talked about him in the evenings, and now I think he may have been the lucky one—no more hurt, starving, and suffering, as he was just resting peacefully in his native country. Peter was born and buried in Hungary, not Romania.

Soon after I had come to the United States, I fell in love with the country, both the land and the people, but my last wish is that my ashes will be returned to my favorite lookout, Szarka or Homorod, in my home, in Transylvania, not Romania.

The rest of our trip to the capital city was less eventful; we kept foraging for food. We played hide and seek around the places we stopped and slowly arrived at our destination, almost exactly six weeks after our departure time, just like in my brother's vision.

Arriving at our old home near Buda was the best thing that happened to us for a long time, as our father was waiting for all of us with open arms and heart. I remember soaking in the bathtub for an hour, not wanting to come out until my skin wrinkled, eating my best-tasting supper and falling asleep at the dinner table. The next day, we found out upon opening our boxes we had guarded and transported all the way to the Capital that they had mold in them. All the clothes, fine damask towels, table covers, pictures, Persian rugs were all damaged. The wedding gifts from Queen Zita for my parents, all the fine handiwork and pictures were soaked in one of the heavy downpours in the open wagon. It damaged most valuables to un-restorable condition. In spite of the damaged condition, I kept and still have the wedding gift from the queen.

As it is a custom in my homeland, Transylvania, the parents would plant their favorite tree for each child born. My father planted eleven silver-tip firs along the creek I used to fish in, in front of our cabin, to be visible from both the porch and the front windows. They planned to retire there and see us grow up with the trees, even after we were gone on our own. The first five trees were quite a bit taller, as they were planted for his children from his first marriage. After his first wife died, he married again, and with my mother, they had six more children. When they took photographs by the cabin, they would try to include the row of trees.

Every time I go to Europe, I make a special effort to visit our old place where I grew up. Sometimes it is very painful to cross over the border, as the Romanian government discourages visitors to Transylvania by holding them at the border for hours. When I took my three young boys to see their grandparents' birthplace and where I grew up, they made us wait four hours going and two hours coming back crossing the border.

My homeland is still a relatively beautiful place. Unfortunately, many of the forests are clear-cut, the rivers are polluted, and the roads are not maintained in order to discourage foreign tourism in the Hungarian portion of northern new Romania. Some of the natural springs have stopped flowing, including the one we used to give water to people who mistreated us, as it contained minerals that made them run to the bathroom within minutes after drinking it. When we felt justified, we provided the drinking water from there, and when the time came, we took our sweet time explaining how to get to the toilet.

Our land, home, and cabin now belong to the Romanian government, who used them as a playground for young Romanian girls from the south, and Hungarians were not allowed there. Even the young Romanian girls were told not to talk to the Hungarians, as they are bad and evil people.

Now it is no longer used, but they won't return it, nor can I buy it back. As an ex-native, I cannot own property, so I cannot have a piece of my home and country. It is very sad and hurts me a great deal.

During and after World War II, starting in 1945, some of the eleven fir trees my father planted were cut down one by one. The tallest and oldest tree was cut down when my oldest sibling was killed. Within a year after a tree was cut, the corresponding sibling died or was killed. Today, only four trees are standing, and the corresponding four of us are alive. I sincerely hope the last four trees and us will remain standing for a little bit longer.

I also planted three trees for my sons, and thank God both the trees and my sons are doing well.

Last time I was back visiting my homeland, I tried to put a green ribbon on each of our four remaining trees to protect them from poachers or the state-run timber industry, but I had to remove them or they would fine me for defacing state property.

Deception and Reality - Living Through the Missing Pages of History

Experiencing the Unbelievable

A few days after the great dinner with horse meat, Colonel Álmos called an emergency meeting for the three friends. It was already dark when I let the colonel in the main gate, and I didn't recognize him. It was the first time I saw him without his officer's uniform. While escorting him to our front door across the courtyard, I wanted to chat with him, but he asked impatiently if the other two had arrived. I said that my father has called and he was on his way and we could expect him any moment. The colonel asked again, before I finished my response, if we had heard from Father Tibor. My answer was negative. I could tell he liked the short military answers. He didn't have any more questions, and I was afraid to ask, considering his agitated mood. Secretly, I was hoping he had brought us some more horse meat, but he had no package.

From his demeanor, I could guess things had definitely turned for the worst. However, I could never imagine how bad it would be and what was really coming next. The evening air was cold, but he was not wearing a winter coat, only a long raincoat and a hat. When I opened the entry door for him, my mother was already standing in the doorway. She gave him a big hug and asked, "What's up?" His response was gentler now, and he just said, "We better wait for Vajk."

I helped taking his raincoat off and hung it and his hat in the hallway, then opened the door to the family room for my mother and the colonel, as it was the only room being heated and I considered him a close family friend. Colonel Álmos asked if instead they could meet in the formal guest room for privacy. My mother obliged and turned to her right, closely followed by Álmos. My mother continued, "I'll get your favorite apricot brandy [pálinka]. You go ahead and make yourself comfortable, and in the meantime, my son will entertain you." When my mother turned around and faced me, I could tell she was deep in thought, and I didn't like the expression on her face.

Before my mother could place the bottle and the three glasses on the table, the bell rang at the main gate. I knew it had to be Father Tibor, as my father had the keys. I left to go and open the gate for him, but as I was crossing the courtyard, I heard the big key turning in the lock of the main gate. The main gate was large enough to drive the largest tank through, but it also had a cut-in door on the side, which had to be opened first to be able to unhinge the big doors. It was my father who had arrived before I did, so he let Father Tibor come through. He bent down and unlatched the main gate. Sure enough, Vajk had his official car with him, but without his chauffeur, and he wanted to pull it in the courtyard away from the public view.

Father Tibor didn't proceed toward the house, but waited at one of the doors, propping it open with his gray umbrella while I went to hold the other side so the wind wouldn't slam it shut. Once the car was inside, we swung the doors closed, latched them in place, locked the main door, and followed them into the house. I took both my father and Father Tibor's hats and hung them right next to the colonel's while Father Tibor put his dark grey umbrella in the rack.

My mother came to greet my father and Father Tibor, but I could see on her face that what was said between her and the colonel must have been disturbing news.

The three friends were there a long time, and I was getting ready for bed when I saw them slowly emerging from the guest room. My father stopped me and told me to get the rest of the family together, as he had to tell us some very important things.

By the time I got my little brother up, the two friends were gone. My father was talking to my mother when we children single-filed into the family room. The light was on, and the door was open.

My father started to talk, watching the smallest expressions and reactions on our faces, and told us the Russian soldiers were coming and may be here as early as tomorrow night. My parents decided not to run anymore but face the enemy in our homeland, as my father's American contact assured us their Russian ally would do no harm to the Hungarians.

He added, "God Almighty, who watched out for us in these difficult times, please continue your vigilance over us and keep us alive and safe. Dear Holy Spirit, please help and guide us in our decision making so our entire family will stay safe in these trying times. Amen."

He added that my mother and father would need our help, as they also decided it would be safer to go to the ranch Colonel Álmos found for us to wait for the Russian soldiers. He also said he would take the car back to the office early tomorrow morning and return to walk us to the ranch, as it was only five km away. The good news was that Colonel Álmos would join us. Father Tibor had to stay with his flock.

The next morning, when I got up, my father was already gone, taking the official car back to the office garage. Mother was in the kitchen, fixing French toast for breakfast. She said, "I want to use up all the eggs. We only have two left for emergencies, along with stale bread. Eat as much as possible before packing up and leaving." She put in more flour than usual in the egg wash to give more substance to each piece of bread, then fried them in hot lard. She was around us, urging us to eat every bit, as we didn't know when we could eat again. I kept my word and said, "Mother, I won't eat until you do." So she took a piece, put some jam on it, and started eating it.

We boys didn't need much more encouragement. We even finished what the girls had left behind. The taste of that French toast with the thicker crust and cover is still in my memory, and I sure would like to try it again.

We were packed up with all the necessary items in our backpacks by eight o'clock in the morning. My mother got suspicious about our speedy packing, so we all had to show what we had put in our individual backpacks.

We all had a small towel rolled up, containing all necessary hygiene equipment like toothpaste, brush, soap, comb, disinfectant (iodine), gauze, and even a roll of strings with fishhooks. We also had our underwear, extra socks, sweaters, extra shirts, and another larger towel rolled up with the food my mother placed on top of our bed. She included a stick of smoked sausage (a pleasant surprise, as we didn't even know we had such a luxury food item), a small piece of smoked bacon, three pieces of bread, salt (in case we ran out of toothpaste), and a small bottle of honey. In addition, we all had our blankets neatly rolled up and tied to our backpack outside.

Spoon, fork, aluminum cup, and plate were put into the outside pockets, and a pocket knife in our trousers pocket. The girls had other things, but they didn't have to carry their blankets; instead, they had a much lighter waterproof tarp. My mother was very pleased and said, "It's a good thing you all went through some girl- or boy-scout training, and the escaping experience from Transylvania taught you well." Of course, we were also experienced in getting going quickly and fast, as we carried a similar load to the cellar every time we had an air raid.

Even after more than fifty years, the sound of sirens at night will bring nightmares for me, and I'm so glad the pitch and the melody has changed so I can get a restful sleep, even in New York City.

It was almost nine o'clock when my father got back after returning the car and taking care of some last-minute office business. Later, he told us he had to help select the entire secret correspondence and reports between the Allies. All these documents had to be burned, and it took longer than expected.

My mother was getting her and my father's stuff ready and laid them out on top of the bed. My father took a glance and said, "There is no way we can carry all that stuff. Let's just fill up my largest hunting backpack and go, as I can come back with one of my boys for a second load."

By ten o'clock, we were on our way to experience new things. We went to a nearby village, Szeg, and from there we cut over the hill to get to the designated ranch. We arrived early afternoon, just as the packs became very heavy for my sisters, and especially for my mother, who was still recovering from the tent city starving. She started to look really good, but her strength had not yet fully returned.

After finding the ranch, we were introduced to the owner, who was happy to see us, as his soldier son reported the Russians really liked children and usually behaved well when they were around. The owner was very polite and invited us to eat with them. Guess what? They had meat! A baked goose was waiting for us. The goose was big, but our appetites were even bigger as we finished it all. Of course, since the tent-city experience, we ate everything at the table, not just cleaning off our plates, even if it was too much. Even today, I'm afraid of hunger, and I know people who leave food on their plate have never experienced true hunger or starving, even if they tell you otherwise. We were already trained properly; our parents let us serve ourselves at an early age, so we learned to take a small amount of everything, as we had to taste all and could not leave the table until our plate was empty.

I have to say, the goose dinner was very delicious, looked great, and tasted just as good. Even the grown-ups took each bone by the hand, a real no-no for proper table etiquette, and sucked it, taking every drop of the flavor out.

Deception and Reality - Living Through the Missing Pages of History

Right after eating, my father and I headed back to get a second load. On the way out, the owner told us some shortcuts to the town, and it worked out well, plus not carrying any weight, just the empty back packs, we arrived there in about an hour. By mid-afternoon, we were heading back with a full load of stuff, but there remained many items, which were piled up earlier by my mother; like extra stockings, underwear, towels, jackets, gloves, extra shoes, some cooking pots, lamp and lamp oil, candles in case we lost electricity, the three older weapons with a lot of sentimental and antique value, and a beautifully decorated early eighteenth-century clock.

Going back to the ranch was harder, as we had to go uphill most of the way and we were overloaded. We had to stop and go around the shortcut, as a light rain made walking uphill very treacherous. When we got to the farmhouse, it was dark and still no sign of the colonel. Everybody was worried about him, especially after supper, except my father. He said, "I fought side by side with him during WWI, and there is no reason to worry until we hear the cannons."

The colonel did wake us up late evening. He showed up with his two favorite horses, one he rode and the other was loaded with stuff he wanted to bring. There were, of course, his two favorite violins, the chess set he used when he beat Aleksandr Aljehin, the chess world champion, in two consecutive games, all the medical tools and extra medication for the animals, and carving tools he wanted to keep for violin making.

To our surprise, the owner seemed the happiest to see him. The next day, I found out why. The owner raised Lipizzaner horses and had them moved west, out of harm's way. However, his favorite horse was left behind, as it was close to foaling, and there were some complications requiring top-notch veterinary help.

My father and I went for another load very early the next morning. This time, we took a wheelbarrow with us and packed it full and took turns pushing it after switching backpacks. In the early afternoon, we started back again, as we had one more load. We wanted to retrieve the last thing on our list, my father and grandfather's guns and rifles. We were less than a kilometer from the city when machine gunfire rang out on our left. We stopped immediately and took the prone position, exposing the minimum target for the shooters. Unfortunately, when I turned, I got two rounds grazing me— one shot off a button from my pants, the other not only burned but cut into my thigh, so it started to bleed. The wound burned, but the bleeding was so minor we didn't even bother to put a dressing on it.

The Russians must have had a lot of ammunition, as we lay there seemingly for hours before they stopped to reload. Bullets were flying all around us; the close ones had a distinct whistle from high to low pitch as they whizzed by our ears. Most of them fell short of the target right in front of us or on our sides. Each bullet made a little puff of dust as it hit the ground and sunk into the soft dirt. When the wheelbarrow was hit, it clanked. I began to feel scared, but my father's calmness and soothing words, "Just keep your head down," helped me to regain my composure. A few minutes into the shooting, six German soldiers came out of nowhere, just stepping over our bodies. My father asked where they came from, and they told us they were the last remaining six of a squad holding up the Russian Army from taking over the city and now they were leaving. The officer yelled back, "You should turn around and go back where you came from." When the machine gun stopped for reloading, we jumped up and started to run back to the ranch, leaving our last load of goods and the collectible guns and rifles behind in the city.

That late afternoon, the city of Zala was captured by the Russians several thousand strong, but we had to wait a couple of weeks before their first wave of soldiers came to check us out at the ranch.

When we got back and told our story, I went outside to assess our situation. My brother took me around the building, the horse stalls, and the corn and hay storage facilities. He showed me all the geese at the property and the hill in the backside full of wildflowers. Climbing up the hill, our shoes got real wet from the still cold and very damp ground. We went all the way up the hill to the crest, just to see the other side, which had rolling hills but were obviously used for growing hay. When we looked back, we saw the entire valley below. It reminded me of my favorite hiding place, Papkert, close to our home in Transylvania. It was beautiful and all green and the best place to roll in the grass or ski in the winter.

On the left side of the valley was our temporary home, but even from the top it looked like a very long building. On the right was the main gate, with a fence that kept the geese and the dog inside. You could clearly see the owner's wife tending her flock of geese. The geese also served along with the dog as sentinels and would make a lot of noise if a stranger came close to the ranch. The male goose often chased us, but he even attacked the horses if they came into his territory. It felt so good to stay up there and dream about my real home. This hilltop also served as an excellent lookout post.

My daydream was interrupted with clapping noise, my mother's way to call us home. I never heard her yell; she treated everyone well, her children and husband first, then friends and neighbors. She really appreciated my father's work; the pressures, responsibilities, and their respect for each other were mutual. I have never seen a better marriage or partnership. They really compensated for each other's weaknesses, and they could always depend on the other's strength.

I did take my time coming down the hill, checking out some of the magnificent oaks, wild lily of the valley, and violets sprinkled around the hillside. When I got down, my mother was waiting with a tray full of bread, with goose lard spread on them. I could have eaten all ten of them. They were so delicious.

Our room was the largest, taking about half of the entire structure. Next to the room were the two bathrooms, a hallway, then the kitchen and a large pantry that could have served as a separate room. Unfortunately, the big pantry had almost nothing in it. A small sack of flour, some dried beans, a larger sack of corn flour, a few bottles of preserves, sour cabbage jars (most of them empty), already dry red peppers hanging on a string, and a few eggs in a basket. Past the pantry was a separate living quarter, where the owner lived with his wife. Everything was painted white inside and out. On the other end of the building was our room, and it was sometimes used as a meeting place and projection room for the village folks, so it was quite comfortable and big. The measurements had to be at least ten by twenty meters. We all fit in one corner of the room comfortably. My mother and the rest of the kids made mattresses by filling big sacks with straw that they put down along the shorter wall.

They set up twelve beds, with blankets covering them; put a large table and two chairs in our end of the room. There were two doors giving access to the room. There were eleven of us, our family had eight, plus the colonel and two nuns from a nearby village church also joined us.

That evening when we all gathered for supper, we were formally introduced to the two nuns, and to our surprise we were later introduced to Uncle Álmos and were told the colonel had disappeared, but our new Uncle was an animal doctor. We got the message.

In our new home, my favorite meal was breakfast, as it reminded me of being back at home in Transylvania, having hot cornmeal mush with cold milk. Now milk was hard to come by, but one of the owner's daughters raised goats, which the Germans didn't want, and every morning we picked up a good-size can of milk from two farms down the road, where Juli lived.

Just before noon, my brother came running from the lookout yelling, "Soldiers are coming." We all went to the windows, looking down the road. Sure enough, about a squad of Russian soldiers in loose formation with weapons ready to shoot came along the dirt road, not in the middle, but on both sides. Uncle Álmos commented that they looked experienced.

They didn't stop by our building but marched on until the neighbor's house, where they stopped, took up a defensive position, and waited.

Uncle Álmos again said, "I told you they know what they are doing." Soon another new column of soldiers showed up, and they were dispersed. Four of them came in at the main gate. The geese made a lot of noise, but the soldiers ignored them and came up to our door first. Two soldiers kept their weapons trained on the door, while the other one kicked it in and slowly came inside. First, we only saw the barrel of the submachine guns; we called them guitars, as they carried them that way. Then with fingers on the trigger, they sneaked a look inside. They waved the muzzle of the guns, signaling to hold up our hands.

While standing there and looking at my family, I didn't recognize a single female. I only saw old, beat-up, dirty, filthy, wrinkle-faced grandmothers.

I finally could make out some features reminding me of my sister. Later I found out how and why they disguised themselves, and they were the lucky ones.

Once the soldiers checked our bedding to make sure there were no weapons hidden, they waved to let our hands down. Then they pointed with the machine guns to my father and uncle and asked them to raise their hands again. They asked for "nemetski" (German) and "Gitler" (Hitler), but we just shook our heads. While training their weapons on the two grown men, they asked them to empty their pockets.

They put the contents, consisting of a handkerchief, a box of matches, pocketknives, pipe cleaner, a small pouch of pipe tobacco, pocket watches, and large keys on the top of the table. My new uncle eased his way closer to the table, and when the soldiers were not watching, he reached out and grabbed his ring and later his pocket-watch and slipped them back into his pocket.

Then the soldiers proceeded removing the wedding rings from the ladies and any jewelry found on anyone. Once they finished, they looked on top of the table and started to take the valuable pieces and put them in their pockets, except the wristwatches. These seemed most valuable to them, and they put them on their arms. The one with higher rank had both his lower arms already full of wristwatches under the sleeves. Again, they asked for more watches: "Dovay chos." No response was given, but they checked our wrists also. They were very happy when they located an attractive wristwatch on my brother's hand. They pointed to my brother and said, "Boorzhooy," meaning "rich." We thought they were going to fight over it, but the higher rank soldier got the prize. They left, and we could tell the next stop was at the owners'. The owners also survived the first wave of the "liberators," just losing a pocket-watch and an alarm clock.

A little later, the neighbor asked for my mother's help to understand what the soldiers wanted. They were hungry and took the small basket of eggs and salt from the table. They cut the top off the raw eggs, put some salt in them, and drank them up one by one. They waved my little brother closer; one of them put him on his knees and started to rock him until he smiled. They offered him the last remaining egg, but he didn't want to take it.

The entire first introduction to the Russian soldiers took less than a couple of hours, and they left with the impression that they would not hurt us, just steal us blind, as our American contact had said. All day long, we laughed at how our new uncle fooled them and got back all the jewelry they took from him. We also came to the conclusion that it wasn't as bad as we were told. Our first encounter definitely left us with a false sense of security, but we weren't the only ones.

The next day, an entire company of soldiers came, and they wouldn't leave. They looked all over the place, asked for food, drinks, and "borishna" (girls). They took the girls' cologne and lamp oil and drank them as alcohol.

Kele D. Gabor

Not finding enough of what they were looking for, they lined up all the females and lifted their skirts up. Luckily, our family and the two nuns were better prepared, as they had done everything to discourage rape, including stockings soaked in tomato paste and placed in their panties, dirty clothes, and smelly legs. They even spread stinky cheese with garlic along the inside of their thighs, so when the bayonet or the rifle nuzzle lifted the front of the long skirts up, the look and the smell could save them.

The next morning, I went to get the goat's milk but was unable to find Juli. I looked at the goat stall, and I could see two of the goats were missing and the other three hadn't been milked, so I went around yelling her name. I saw their dog dead on the door jamb, with several bullet holes. I saw a mostly eaten goat on the kitchen table, along with an empty bottle of spirits (pálinka). I went to the bedroom but only saw a torn-up bed very dirty with mud, blood, and filth on the cover and pillows. I was just about to leave when I heard a faint moan, but I could not locate the noise.

I looked under the bed, under the kitchen table, in the pantry, but to no avail. Again, I heard the moan. I was just ready to leave and report the situation to my father when at the end of the hallway, the bathroom door slowly opened. Juli was sitting on the toilet, crying and obviously in great pain. The closer I got, the more scared I was. When I got about three meters from her, she looked up and waved me off. If she hadn't sent me away, I would have turned around and run anyway. I ran all the way home, over the hill under the bridge, across the field as fast as I could, leaving the milk bottle behind. I arrived out of breath, not able to say a word, but I didn't have to.

My mother and Juli's mother just got pale, turned around, and left running toward the place. We didn't see either one of them until my mother came home around dinnertime.

Juli was an average young wife whose husband had disappeared on the Russian front and might have been a POW somewhere in Siberia. She stayed alone on the small ranch in a small house away from her parents, and she liked it that way. During the first wave of "liberators," the parents were able to persuade her to be with them. I would guess she was about twenty-five years of age when I met her, and she let you know right away she liked to be the boss. Not the goats, not the chicken, not the cats, nor the dog, not even the single male goose could have his way with her. She was independent and strong-willed. I'm not saying that the crime committed against her was lessened by her comportment and behavior, but I never understood why she didn't take advice from the older and more experienced ladies, including her mother. She always knew best, talked harshly to most people, and usually would not listen but did what she wanted. I believe her harshness was a façade for her soft heart, as she would not take any money for the milk. She would just say, "Take it, the growing children need it."

It took about two to three weeks before she could walk normally again.

Both Juli's mother and mine would visit her every day, taking warm food to her. It was my mother who relayed the story, I think for the benefit of my rebelling sister, who didn't want to make herself look ugly anymore.

Juli heard the dog bark, so she immediately went up to the attic, pulled up the ladder behind her, and went behind a false wall to her hiding place, a separate hidden room at the end of the roof. She could look out between the shingles and see the approaching soldiers coming into her yard. She could hear all the noise as they walked around the seemingly empty house. She could even hear them laugh after shooting, and from the howling she could tell it was her dog, Pipi.

The platoon of soldiers stayed around for about ten minutes and left. When she was sure the area was safe, she came down very quietly. As soon as she turned from the ladder, she could hear quiet laughter coming from under the bed. Sure enough, two Russian soldiers climbed out. While holding her ankle, one went outside and shot into the air four times. Before the rest of the platoon came back, they cut the necks of two young goats and skinned them. Everything seemed manageable while she was baking the pieces and fed them. As soon as their stomach was full, they started teasing her. She ignored them but finally they grabbed her, threw her on the bed, tore off her clothes, and started the raping process. One by one, all fifteen of them had their way with her. Some of the soldiers came back for a second time, but she had passed out in the meantime.

When she came to, all were gone, but she was awash in semen and blood. She was able to crawl to the bathroom and sit on the seat, but she could not get up. When I came, she tried to stop her moaning due to the pain, as she thought the soldiers may have come back for the third time, but she heard my voice yelling her name. She claimed she didn't have the energy to talk to me, she could only moan.

We heard and knew of many similar rapes all around us and in the cities. Some of the young girls ended up missing or killing themselves, just like the single-child cases in the tent city.

>About five years later, a friend of mine introduced me to his neighbor to help me with the Russian language before an examination. He did help me, but in a unique and different way. He could tell I didn't want to have anything to do with the Russian language because I hated them, like the Germans, for occupying my homeland and giving most of it away. My Russian-language mentor shared the following story with me.
>
>He was twenty-eight years old, with an exceptionally beautiful wife, living on the next street to us. During the invasion, they retired to their vineyard a few kilometers away. Now and then, when they needed something extra, they would sneak back to the city and their home for the additional hidden supplies. They came and went during the curfew times at night so no one could see them. They found the house ransacked, with most of the clothes just thrown around, but undamaged.
>
>One night, they found a Russian officer using the house. Before the couple could get out, the posted guard woke up and, at gunpoint, led them back to the then awakened officer. The high-ranking officer called the HQ and, with the help of his guard, tied the man to a big, heavy double door hoisted up from the ground. Then right in front of him, they undressed his wife, and she was forced to have sex with the major. By the time he finished, there was a line of other officers who came down from nearby HQ and proceeded to continue raping her in front of her husband hanging on the door. According to the husband, he could only pray and count the number of officers having sex with her. There were nineteen officers who raped her, and he swore to repay everything for his wife's suffering and ordeal.
>
>After the officers finished, they untied him and let him go with his wife. His wife died within a year from the damages and diseases she received.
>
>The husband went to learn Russian, and when he was fluent

enough, he started his payback for his beautiful and beloved wife. He would hang out at any drinking places that were frequented by Russian officers. He bought them drinks until they were drunk enough to take them to his vineyard to kill and bury them. He even invented a drink mix that tasted good but greatly accelerated drunkenness so it would only take an hour to do one in. He was extremely careful and was able to do most of the payback. He claimed many people knew about or suspected his way of paying back, but so far nobody turned him in. He said he had to use his wife's old pictures sometimes to lure them to his place.

I got the message, and I studied hard to know more about my country's enemies. Now both Uncle Álmos and my newfound mentor have shown me that one must know his enemies to fight them effectively.

About five years later, I heard about my mentor's arrest; he was caught while burying his eighteenth Russian officer. I believe he got a life sentence but was freed during the Hungarian uprising and was able to complete his work getting the nineteenth.

My mentor might still be alive somewhere in Canada. The USA would not permit him to enter, as he admitted joining the Communist Party just to gain access to places frequented by Russian officers for what they had done to his wife. On the other hand, some of the corrupt Communists arriving in the US after the Hungarian Revolution were given the red-carpet treatment. There was no way for the Americans to tell who was who, and many times they didn't care. The real problem was that the FBI was not told by other agencies like the CIA that initially the Hungarian Revolution was successful and that most Communists, being afraid of reprisal, fled first to whatever border was the closest. The other problem was that the press underplayed the Hungarians' plea for help during our hopeless fight against the Red Army, but Radio Free Europe urged us on.

I know this and many other dichotomies in Western foreign policy resulted In losing many thousands of lives. But who cares? I often felt abandoned like the Kurds, who were persuaded and prompted by the CIA twice to rise up against

Saddam Hussein, then were left to fend for themselves without the promised weapons, food, support, and help.

When Juli halfway recovered, we started to feel safer, and my father went into the city with my brother. They left, and we prayed for their safe return. They did return, but they came close to a disaster. My father first went to the house, and to his surprise, our home, like the previous ones, had been taken over as headquarters of the local Russian Red Army.

My brother Bende relayed the story. "My father went up to the open main gate of the house and tried to go in-between the posted guards. They yelled 'Stoy!' meaning 'stop,' and pointed their machine guns to his chest.

Not speaking Russian, he pointed to the main house where we lived just a few weeks before, and with sign language, he tried to tell the guards he wanted to go in. One of the guards yelled, and an officer appeared in our entry doorframe without the door. My father must have locked it after the last supply run, and the Russians blew the heavy solid wood entry doors off to get into the house. Behind him stood a young officer who happened to know German, so my father could communicate with him. My father explained that we used to live there and would like to move back. He told us to stay standing where we were, then went into the house while yelling in Russian.

"We took the opportunity to look around the courtyard. To our surprise, our grand piano was moved almost to the middle of the courtyard, and the top and bottom were taken off. We didn't say a word, just looked at each other.

"A few moments later, the translator reappeared with a Russian colonel, the local commanding officer. The colonel had two shotguns, one in each hand, and he asked my father to whom did they belong. I immediately recognized my grandfather's guns, with beautiful gold inlays and carvings, which were given to my father for his birthday. My father responded that those guns and one more rifle were his and he would like to have them back. The colonel pointed one of the shotguns to father's head, but my father would never keep a loaded gun in the house, so he smiled. The colonel, impressed by his courage, moved the pointed gun toward the ground and pulled the trigger. The gun fired, and the pellets dispersed in every direction from the cement walkway, leaving only a small, shallow hole. Now we were both scared, but my father didn't show it.

"The colonel took each gun by the muzzle and proceeded to break them into pieces on the concrete steps in front of the entry door. Obviously, the Russian colonel had no idea of the value of those handmade double barrel shotguns, decorated with gold and made by the finest gunsmiths of Europe. One was a side by side, and the other an over/under combination.

They could easily be sold for more than the finest Parkers ever made. Once the guns were in small enough pieces, the colonel must have vented his anger as he invited us into "our" house.

"We didn't recognize the furniture. They were similarly broken up to pieces, the beautiful paintings, worth thousands of dollars from famous artists around the world, had bayonet cuts all over them, the clothes thrown around the floor. The pictures, especially ones depicting girls or ladies, were used for target practice by the soldiers.

"The translating officers asked to whom those children's clothes belonged. My father responded that he and my mother had six children and needed the clothes and a place to stay. The officer then invited us to the family room, where tables were pushed together, holding a side of horse already skinned and ready to be cut up. While we waited, the cook showed up with a short-handled ax and proceeded to divide the still-bleeding fresh meat in about ten-centimeter square pieces. With each chop, the fine tabletops with inlayed design were also cut up.

"They had no idea or appreciation of the handwork put into those fine furniture pieces. Once the horse was cut up, the cook put a few pieces at a time on a steel hook, stepped into the bathroom, and placed the meat in the toilet bowl. While holding the meat by the hook in one hand, he flushed with the other and smiled with his thin, wide Mongol lips and face."

My brother said, "We didn't believe our eyes." I also didn't believe him until my father confirmed it. Later, we found out the Russians had no idea of what a flush toilet was. They were using them as a wash basin, sometimes referring to them as "zobra," or "steeling" machine. It took them some time to figure out they had to hold on to the meat while flushing.

They thought even an outhouse was a luxury, and they preferred the open pits with two boards across to step on, just like we had in the tent city.

My brother continued, "After a while, the colonel showed up with the interpreter and took us across the courtyard to one of the smaller apartments, farthest away from the main gate. While going across the courtyard, we noticed they were building a fire under the piano with pieces of beautiful furniture. Later, we witnessed the use of our grand piano as a barbecue, using our expensive furniture to feed the fire."

My mother started to cry, but my brother and father continued with their account.

"The colonel smiled and said [through the translator], "You and your family can come and live here." My father entered the premises, as we had never seen them inside, and to his surprise, it had very little damage and a few useful furniture pieces, including a kitchen table and chairs. My father thanked them for the small place, and we turned around and left. To our surprise, the guards stopped us again, not letting us go until the interpreter reappeared with a handwritten note from the colonel with his signature, saying we had a pass and could occupy said premises, including the rest of our family."

The next day, we hired a man with an oxen-drawn wagon. We piled up everything, including Uncle Álmos's stuff, helped our mother up with our youngest brother, and the rest of us proceeded on foot back to the city, just as we had left it a month before.

Coming back to our new home, we had to go the long way, as we had to follow the road the wagon took. Uncle Álmos entertained us with songs and jokes, just like a real, loving relative. On the way, people asking for food and clothes or mothers looking for family members often stopped us. One mother was looking for her sixteen-year-old daughter who was taken away just last week, but no one had seen her since. Even though we didn't see any young girls, she insisted on showing her pictures to each one of us. It was a black-and-white photo of her, but she was obviously very well developed, blond, pretty and attractive. I remember my mother's comment after the crying woman left. "Her only way to survive is to befriend an officer and have him protect her from the rest of the men, as she looked attractive and desirable to any male."

We all carried a little backpack with a few items, just in case the family was separated. My new Uncle Álmos had a heavy pack. He left both of his horses and pistol hidden at the ranch but didn't want to leave anything else behind. On the way to the town, Uncle Álmos traded a bag of pipe tobacco for a delicious-looking large smoked ham. We were all happy and looked forward to a delicious dinner to celebrate our arrival at our new home.

When we arrived at the main gate, the Russian guards checked the document my father showed them and started to check our packages before we could proceed inside the courtyard. The wagon had to be parked outside, away from the main entrance, so we had to hand-carry all the stuff to our new apartment, back at the end of the courtyard. When Uncle Álmos wanted to come in, the guards would not let him, as the permit for occupancy was limited to two grown-ups and six young people. However, when my mother said, "Konyee doctor" (horse doctor), the Russian officer let him in and gave him a new and separate permit paper.

When we stepped inside the new small apartment, just beyond the entry doors, all our clothing that we left behind had been dumped on the hallway floor. Evidently, the Russian colonel decided to have the guards carry the clothes over instead of us bugging him again.

We were very hungry, so my mother started to prepare the dinner. While she peeled the potatoes for the ham, Uncle Álmos was happy as a lark and started to play his violin. Like bees coming to taste the honey, the Russian soldiers came to listen by the door and windows. When my uncle stopped, they started to applaud and dance, trying to persuade him to play more. They didn't care if it was Hungarian or Russian music as long as it had melody and rhythm. Álmos was an excellent player, so even the colonel invited him a few times to impress his commanding officers. Uncle Álmos was also in demand for helping with injured animals, and if the horse could not be saved, he was able to get a small piece of meat.

The potatoes were done, and we all sat down to say our prayer before eating. My father asked my uncle to slice up the ham, as it was his contribution to the family treat. Uncle Álmos was happy to do the honor and cut a big piece off for my mother first. As he picked up the piece to put it on her plate, small white maggots started to fall out. Upon closer examination, we found that the entire ham was infested. We all looked at the beautiful ham being eaten by little critters, and instead of turning our nose, we wanted to save the uneaten parts. My mother knew what to do. She cut the ham in smaller pieces, put them into a pot, filled it up with water, and started to cook it. Before the water boiled, the small white maggots started to float to the surface. It took her almost an hour to boil them out and pick them from the hot water with a small sieve.

We settled back to the table and cut the pieces into thin slices. We were able to save about half of the ham, and we were glad we didn't wait, as in a few days the entire ham would have been eaten by the maggots.

When one of my sisters was hesitating to eat, my uncle explained the maggots were not diseased, and he used them on occasion to clean up infected animal wounds. When they had done their job to his satisfaction, he would pour iodine into the wound to kill them. My sister asked for a little iodine, just to make sure, but we all laughed and ended up eating all the ham. Nobody got sick, and we went to bed with full stomachs. It ended up being our last good meal for a long, long time. It was more than a year later when we could fill our tummies again. Food, medicine, booze, and tobacco were scarce.

My father didn't start a new window or glass factory to get rich, as he had planned earlier. Instead, he was needed by the new government to help rebuild the country. Very few people survived who had the experience and knowledge to jump-start the reconstruction and manage the recovery process. Once we were settled in our miniature new home, my father sent me over to the church to let Father Tibor know we'd come back to the city and lived in the apartment in the same complex next to the old home.

Father Tibor sat me down and offered me some dry fruit, which I gobbled up as fast as I could chew them. He also asked me to tell him what had transpired since we saw him last. Not knowing any better, I started in chronological order on what exciting things had occurred lately. I started to tell him about the uncivilized soldiers, how they washed the meat in the toilet, how they barbequed the meat on our grand piano, knocking out the bottom and removing the top. He smiled, and I kept on going with more examples of uncivilized behavior.

He suddenly interrupted and said, "I think you mean 'primitive,' not 'uncivilized,' as there is a big difference. Like when three Russian soldiers came here with a large grandfather clock and asked to make many little wristwatches out of it— it was a primitive or ignorant request and has nothing to do with being uncivilized." I laughed and told him then that they were both primitive and uncivilized. He said, "There is a big difference between the two meanings, and I'd rather be with a primitive guy whom I could teach or learn from than a civilized man who thinks he knows it all. Let me tell you a story I heard during my last visit to India."

I kept quiet, as I knew it was always a pleasure to have him recite a story.

"On my last trip to India, I wanted to meet Mahatma Gandhi before returning home, so I asked to see him. I had to wait a long time, as many people were lined up ahead of me, as he was organizing the resistance to the British rule and needed to talk to as many supporters as possible. As you may know, he was a very frail man with a lot of wisdom.

"Each time someone finished talking with him, an assistant came out, counted the people in line, and every newcomer was asked to state his or her name, the purpose of the visit, and where they come from. There were about ten persons ahead of me when it was my turn to be asked. His assistant came to inquire about me in general. I told him I came from Hungary and just wanted to have the opportunity to speak with him.

After the next person left, the assistant came to me and told me, 'Mr. Gandhi is delighted to see someone from Hungary, but it will be an hour wait. However, he will send someone to make the time go faster.'

"In a few minutes, an elderly, thin, and tall gentleman with snow-white hair appeared at the door and headed directly toward me. He had to navigate and step over people and luggage lying on the floor, but he never took his eyes off me. When he got right in front of me, he introduced himself as Bill Bilawala, from the region of Bihar, speaking fluent English. Bill asked me the nature of my business and interests. I responded that I was a priest, history and archeology professor in Hungary interested in Mr. Gandhi as a human being, learning about Sanskrit, the Indian culture, and civilization as a whole.

"Bill said that Sanskrit is a very old language, older then Hindi, and claimed to have Sumerian origin. I agreed with him, as I found many common words, not only between the two languages, but also with Hungarian. Bill was surprised and asked if I would like to hear a true story about how civilization is viewed by his culture. My response was, 'Of course, I am delighted to learn.'"

Bill began by saying, "Right at the turn of the nineteenth century, a new viceroy was appointed by the queen of England to rule India. The relatively young viceroy was very ambitious and eager to enlarge the British Empire, to add another 'precious stone' in the royal crown. He was determined to acquire more territories to the kingdom, and without bloodshed.

"The new viceroy functionary gathered the best politicians, philosophers, statesmen, and diplomats he could find. He and his selected experts started to plan. They decided the most appropriate gift for Great Britain would be Nepal, with the highest mountains, the Himalaya [meaning "roof of the world"], and the highest peak, the Chomolangma ["mother of snow"], or Sagarmatha ["mother of earth"]. A few thousand years later, the British renamed it Mt. Everest, after an English surveyor.

"The Nepalese considered the English renaming of their secret places offensive. They claimed that they could go along calling it Ang Rita's Summit, as he was the first to climb the peak.

"The new viceroy and his respected team had to lay out a plan to acquire Nepal without bloodshed if they could enlist the help of the Dalai Lama. They thought with his blessings their success would be assured, as he commanded a lot of respect from all the people around, especially in the regions they were interested in. In short, their plan was to convince the Lama of their good intention in raising the living standard of the people through the introduction of modern civilization, and a better and higher form of government. After they carefully rehearsed all the steps, they hired a translator and asked for an audience with the Dalai Lama. It was many weeks before they got a response, and it was positive.

"The five smartest men of England against a primitive religious mind, they definitely had the advantage. So they thought. The five men traveled a long distance to Tibet to have an audience with the Dalai Lama. The English committee knew about the high elevation, so they all left in time to acclimatize to the thinner air. They were there about a week before the meeting time and were well prepared.

"The day came, and they all showed up at the temple and a Buddhist priest ushered them in at the designated time. They didn't have to wait, as the Dalai Lama was already sitting and waiting for them. The quiet, large, simple, and majestic reception hall where the meeting took place impressed them. Following the custom, they waited to start their presentation when the Lama gave the appropriate head signal with a nod.

"The English diplomat spoke first, as it had been prearranged earlier, and through their interpreter, he conveyed their mission of goodwill that would bring modernization to the region. They also explained that the British civilization offered would improve the lives of all the subjects of the land; they would lead a happier and richer life. Once they had presented the hook and bait without telling him their true intentions, they sat down and waited for the Lama's response.

"After a long silence, the Lama asked for more clarification and explanation of what modern civilization is all about, as it sounded very good.

"Encouraged by the positive response, through the translator, they explained they would bring in the railroad, build dams, roads, and improve the lives of all people without any cost to the Dalai Lama and they only wanted his support to convince the Nepalese to let them also do the same for them.

"After a long silence, the Lama spoke and told them, 'I'm a religious man believing in God, and my mission is peace for all, but everything else I measure. Tell me how you measure your modern civilization or weigh its benefit to the world?'

"The five smart English men looked at each other for answers, but nobody spoke up. Finally, the viceroy spoke and asked what His Eminence meant by 'measurement.' The Lama responded almost the same way as before that his beliefs are spiritual, but everything else is real and measurable.

"He also expressed some concerns that here is something new, a potential solution for problems of mankind and the world, but no way to measure the progress, results, benefits, successes, or failures.

"The Lama was ready to leave when one member of the dumbfounded delegation spoke up. 'Since we're not sure how or what standard method to use to measure or evaluate our civilization, please let us know what you think.'

"The Lama said, 'I'm a religious leader, but also concerned about the well-being of all living things, so ask your leader, as he must know, and come back tomorrow at the same time.'

"The Dalai Lama stood up, and so did the delegation, and they all did an about-face and departed. The delegation stayed up all night to come up with some ideas or examples of measurements, as they never considered this important part or the long-term effect of any implemented changes.

"When they thought they had the answers, they refreshed themselves and left for the second meeting with the Lama.

"Again, the meeting was very cordial, as they waited for the nod from the Lama before proceeding to tell him about how they would propose to measure modern civilization and its benefits for the world.

"The English diplomat spoke first, as they agreed earlier, and put forth a lot of measuring methods, like the number of trees they could harvest with new equipment, the speed and amount of wood that could be shipped by railroad, how many dams they could build to tame the rivers and improve the road system for easier approach to all communities, thereby improving health, education, communication, commerce, and living standards.

"Seeing that the Lama was obviously unimpressed by their dissertation, the speaker stopped and asked the Lama what he thought about how to measure the benefits of 'civilization'.

"The Lama said, 'I'm a religious leader interested in the welfare of all, but I must have a misunderstanding about civilizations, as you only talked about measuring progress without vision and goals, never mentioning the ultimate purpose or the expected benefits for all the world.'

"The delegation, realizing their mistake, turned toward the Lama and asked that based on his understanding, how would he measure the benefit of any civilizations?

"After a pause, the Dalai Lama said, 'If I understood you correctly at our previous meeting, I would define the purpose of 'civilization' and measure at least two things. One is how we treat all living things in the world, as it forms the basis of how we will treat each other. The second is measuring how well we prepare our youth for the future to manage and lead the next generation to benefit all people and the world.' The Dalai Lama smiled, nodded, and left the delegation without further ado. The members of the entire group stood up quietly, stood there for a moment, and left, deep in thought.

"The next day before they departed on the long way home, the viceroy made the following observations: 'The Dalai Lama was right. Our civilization, like the rest of them, will fizzle out like the Sumerian, Egyptian, Greek, Roman, and Inca without an all-encompassing purpose and proper measurement of the long-term beneficial aspect of our deeds.'

"The philosopher responded next and made the following observations: 'Mankind may be doing more harm than good in the name of civilization, we have not learned enough to tackle global issues or solve any complex problems, and we will fail like the rest of the men who tried.' Then he added, 'Not all is lost if we take the Dalai Lama's advice to have purpose, vision, and start measuring our progress.'

"During the return trip, they decided to meet again for serious discussions about civilization and set a new plan in motion and enlighten the world of their findings. The politician wanted to use the dictionary definition of civilization, but how do you measure a higher level of art, as it is subjective? Measuring civilization in light of architecture is also faulty, as we still could not build a pyramid. Does the highly civilized government employ fewer people but manage more or accomplish greater things with lower taxes? Regardless, politics should never be measured, as it has to serve the ruling classes and individuals. Therefore, politics has nothing to do with civilization and will take precedence over accountability and justice.

"After a lot of discussion, they decided that they should follow the Dalai Lama's suggestion of creating a vision and purpose for civilization to attain. Once they would come up with the charter, selecting the measurement methods will be much easier."

Father Tibor said, "Mr. Billawala concluded they never found out what the delegation did or accomplished after the meeting, as the hired interpreter who relayed the story was let go, but the "civilized" representatives definitely learned a lesson from the Lama they had considered primitive and uncivilized. The fact remained they tried to sell something they knew very little about and the governments don't really understand, either.

Luckily, at least four men out of the five delegates looked at 'civilization' in a different and more realistic light."

Our new apartment worked out to our advantage, as we were well-protected from surprise raids by drunken Russian soldiers in the HQ building complex. We only had to be careful while we were outside the well guarded HQ. However, we had to go outside to find food needed to feed the family. Schools were closed for most of the first half of the year after the war, so we had the time, among other activities, to forage for food.

Deception and Reality - Living Through the Missing Pages of History

Most of my siblings and I walked the countryside practically begging for food. We had very little to barter for an occasional egg, piece of cheese, milk, potato, or other vegetables. I had to trade my beloved pocketknife that survived the tent city for cooking oil, as there was no other way to get it. We didn't have any sugar or candies for three full years.

We soon found out the most sought-after items were tobacco, hard liquor, wine, disinfectants, and medicine. When the Bulgarian Army took over our school across the street, we started to bum one cigarette at a time from every soldier we could approach. The Bulgarian soldiers were more "civilized," less primitive, and better supplied than their Russian counterparts.

Even though the Bulgarian soldiers were in a supporting role of the Russian Red Army, they behaved better and would not rape any young girls, as far as we knew. On occasion, they even gave some food to my mother to feed our large family.

We often discussed the differences between the German and Russian Army occupation, and if we had had a choice, we would have picked the Bulgarians. When the three good friends got together, we asked their opinion about the selection of an occupying force, as they were more experienced, and experience is the basis of all knowledge. Their response was, of course, no occupation at all, but instead of giving the preferred ones, they elected to grade the armies that had occupied some region of Hungary in their lifetime. Based on their firsthand experiences, they all agreed on the following order, from worst to less bad occupational force: Serbian, Czechs, Slovaks, Romanian, Russian, French, German, and Bulgarian. They also thought American occupation may be the most acceptable, and we were very much hoping for it, as we would at least get some food and fair treatment.

The food situation was so bad that searching for it pretty soon took over our lives. My mother got thinner and thinner again, my sister whiter and whiter, only having energy to read or write. Later in life, she became a medical doctor, and reviewing her diary with our daily menu, she would say, "I still don't believe we could have survived with what little we had to eat."

One late evening after dark, someone knocked on our window facing the street. This was the room my uncle and we boys slept in. Uncle Álmos went to the window and could only make out a man's figure, due to the darkness and the partially covered windows. Window glass was hard to come by, and only small pieces of glass remained to peek through. The knock was gentle enough that the Russian guards didn't hear it at the main gate about fifty meters away. We felt safe inside, as we could always yell loud enough for the guards to hear us, but Uncle Álmos still grabbed his walking stick to protect us, just in case. He opened the double windows slowly, one by one, without making any noise. When he opened both windows, he bent forward to see who it was. He jumped back from the open window and whispered in my ear that it was the secret police, a young man with a long brown leather coat and hat with a red star on it. We were literally shaking in fear, as we had seen even the Russian Military HQ colonel shaking when a Red Guard political officer and commissar of much lower rank came to visit him.

After waiting and shaking on the floor for seemingly a long time, we heard the man whisper, "Colonel Álmos, don't you recognize me? I'm Alex, your violin partner." Uncle Álmos got up slowly, approaching the window.

I stayed on the floor waiting, as the only Alex I knew was the young Nazi officer who came to play duets with Uncle Álmos on a few occasions. He was an excellent violinist in spite of his political beliefs.

All lights were turned off inside, but I could make him out as Álmos bent to see outside from the open windows. They started to talk, but it was more of a whisper. After a while, Uncle turned back and asked me to join him at the open window that was wide enough for both of us. I took a peek outside as Alex lit a match and held the flame in front of his chin. From the small amount of light, we could clearly make out his familiar features, but with a mustache. I didn't want to believe my eyes—the ex-Nazi officer in a Communist secret police uniform. It took us awhile to come to terms with what we had just seen.

Alex finally spoke up. He said, "I joined the Communist Party, not to save my life, but because of my new convictions."

Uncle Álmos quietly remarked to me that he was always a lost soul, the only talent he had was music. Alex wanted to buy or borrow one of the violins from Uncle Álmos, with the promise to repay him in food. He gave a cube of butter, a kilogram of poppy seed, and sugar as a down payment.

Almos hesitated and said he had already promised the violin to

Bende, my brother, so he did not want him to take it. Alex upped the ante and gave the entire bag he was carrying to my uncle. It had tobacco, pálinka (fruit brandy), flour, and also bacon.

I remember standing there by the window and nobody moved or said a word. Finally I broke the silence, as the delicious smell of the smoked bacon made my saliva run. I told Uncle Álmos to let him borrow it for a while. Alex said, "I give you my word, I'll return it next week."

Alex became the local Communist Party leader, but we never saw our violin again. He systematically got rid of all people who had known him as a Nazi but left us alone. My father thought he might have felt safe from us. He knew we would not tell on him, as we kept his secret of being a half-Jew even during the German occupation. Uncle Álmos and Father Tibor had different opinions, and they asked my father never to trust him.

In hindsight, we should have had him shot by the Russian guard right there the night he appeared at our window right after he handed over the sack of goodies. In the dark, the Russian guards would have fired their machine guns if we yelled, "No-pomoch!" meaning "Help!" It happened once before, when a drunken soldier tried to climb in our open window on a warm summer night when my sisters were singing us lullabies. The poor soldier ended up with about ten bullets in him, but survived.

We boys volunteered to help the Russian Army demolition team in order to get at least one hot meal per day. The food wasn't very good, but it was warm, and a plateful of beans made a hungry boy feel good. The low-ranking officer in charge would typically send us to defuse damaged items, dig around unexploded bombs to expose the head and large ammunitions, or take apart handheld grenades. His commander, our mother, and father didn't know about it, as two of us did one shift of four hours a day. As time went by, we became proficient so the assignments were easier.

The standard procedures were to find the unexpended ammunition or other explosives, remove the mostly mechanical fuse to defuse them, and move them to a place where they could be disposed of with ease. The disposal was away from any structure, and usually an old bomb crater was used outside the city. The difficulties were with those items that we could not or didn't know how to defuse. Ammunition that did not fit the Russian firearm caliber or seemed to be old could be taken apart just with pliers and a vise. If we were lucky, we were spared from rim-fired and dum-dum ammunition, as these could explode easily in our hands and we'd never know what hit us. The black powder was collected in buckets and used to ignite the unexploded bombs and dynamite.

One occasion, after separating the casing, I found some dum-dum or explosive-filled heads. I wanted to find out how it worked on impact, as it didn't seem to have the spring or pressure release mechanism like other explosives. I slipped three heads in my handkerchief and took them home.

That afternoon, I decided to test them by throwing them against increasingly harder surfaces. I went to the farthest end of the courtyard from the Russian HQ, and when no one was around, I proceeded to throw one like a dart about three meters from the target. As soon as it hit the soft wooden plank, it exploded with a big bang without doing any harm to me. My ears were still ringing from the noise, and I could not hear when the guards came running, seeing me with two more rounds of the explosive bullets next to me. The Russian guards immediately arrested me, and the officer in charge promptly led me down to our old wine cellar, where we used to hide from bombings.

My mother was screaming to no avail while I was led away. I must have been in the cold cellar for a few hours in the pitch black when I heard commotion by the entrance. I could hear loud words in Hungarian and Russian, but I could not make out the meaning. The closer the sound was, the more it sounded like my father arguing with the guards. All of a sudden, there was a big bang on my door, the old lock broke, and the next kick of my father propped the door open. I was hiding in the back corner of the cell, where we used to keep the sweet wine for the ladies. My father came in, reached out, grabbed me, and started to pull me out. As we got past the broken door, I could see both guards keeping their "guitar" machine guns fixed on my father and yelling, "Stoy!" (stop). He just kept coming and pulling me out while the guards were following us back on the steps and out to the courtyard.

The colonel was already waiting for us at the exit. I expected the Russian command "Sterlat!" to shoot us, but instead he waved the guards off, smiled, and let us go. Later, he sent over his interpreter to say, "Don't play with fire, at least not at the HQ."

I was really concerned for several days that somehow this incident would give us away and my father might find out our work for the Russian demolition squad.

The hand grenades were also relatively easy to take apart, saving the light-brown small cup-size of TNT for blowing up the ammo collected in the dispensing area, but the land mines were trickier. We were crawling on all fours and poking the ground in front of us with long sticks to detect land mines. Once we hit a hard surface, we had to poke around to find the size and the shape of the mine before attempting to remove it gently. In fact, I did everything to avoid them after losing my newly found friend Solt to a land mine, as he tripped while carrying it to the demolition site. He was younger and less experienced but was an innocent boy trying to get hot soup to fill his stomach at least twice a week. His father died in the war, and his mother didn't know where her older boy was. The Russian captain just went over to Solt's mother and, through the translator, told her that her boy was in a deadly accident and "Here is his coat."

The mother was not allowed to see her son (I was glad, as his upper body was blown into pieces and a large part of his body was missing), but she was able to give him a Christian burial in a beat-up footlocker at the local cemetery. We were too scared to go to the funeral, in case his mother would recognize us and put two and two together.

A few days after Solt died, the captain eased off on us, and we didn't have to handle the really dangerous stuff; no more digging out antitank mines, of which the Russian soldiers were also deathly afraid.

We boys also had to be careful not to let our parents know, or we would not only lose our extra food source, we would have received harsh disciplinary action. Eventually my "uncle" found out about our extracurricular activities, and he put a stop to it without telling our parents. Now he had to provide somewhat safer work for us, but we had to wait a few more weeks until the maple, sycamore, chestnut, and linden leaves turned golden brown.

A new chapter started for us, and fortunately, I never found out what my parents would have done if they did get the word about either of our part-time jobs. Our new job was simple but dishonest. In spite of us trying to justify it, as we needed the extra food to survive, we never had true reconciliation.

Our work was easy; collect beautiful golden brown leaf specimens, dry them, and cut them up in thin equal-width pieces on a paper cutter.

Kele D. Gabor

Once they were the right consistency, our uncle Álmos would mix them with real tobacco and put the new mix into jars and seal them for two to three days. The real stuff came from or consisted of chewing, pipe, and cigarette tobacco. The ratio was varied to his taste and smell. Once he was satisfied with the "flavors," we put them in small pouches or he rolled up the finer stuff and placed them in old cigarette boxes.

Now the hard part began, as we had to sell them, rather trade them for food, but we knew the stuff wasn't genuine. If anybody would ask us about its quality, we probably would have told them the truth. Luckily, no one asked. Our customers were and had to be nonsmokers, as we could not take the chance to be discovered by someone sampling our inferior product on the spot. Luckily, everybody knew someone who smoked and wanted to get the hard-to-find and highly valued "currency."

We would go around smelling people without being noticed before we would approach the poor, unsuspecting potential customers, usually women, every place where they gathered— marketplace, bus, streetcar, or railroad stations. An old railroad worker in uniform once caught us and inquired about why we smelled other people. I could not say anything, but my smart brother Bende came to my rescue again and said, "We found out that people who smell good are more likely to have and share some food with us." The old railroad guy thought about the answer and said, "It makes sense, but don't bother anyone who cannot spare any food. Ask them only once, as you look clean, but miserable, and most mothers might give you food they need for themselves."

The mixed leaves with tobacco looked and smelled good, but it must have not tasted right when smoked, as in a few instances we did experience some very negative reactions after somebody close by was offered a sample. Fortunately, by this time we were far away and relatively safe from being caught. The only good feeling we had about the seemingly valuable stuff was that at any time, we could have traded it for services from beautiful ladies of our choice. Unfortunately, we were too scared, inexperienced, or too young to try, even though on a few occasions we did come close to succumbing to temptation. Anyway, I had beautiful, vivid, and full color dreams about having our way with pretty ladies.

We felt sorry for the girl we saw, not much older than us, with large blue eyes, almost every day at the railroad station. We decided to give her a pouch of pipe tobacco without any strings attached, as it was clear she didn't have much luck selling her obviously underage body, and she was getting thinner and paler with every passing day. She was delighted with our surprise gift and gave each one of us a hug and ran away happy. We felt really good about our good deed and decided to tell the truth to Uncle Álmos. To our surprise, he said, "I'm proud of you."

We soon realized how powerful habit-forming things can be, and its inflated value during hard times when availability was limited, yet life is fuller and better without them. This experience was a good lesson in Economics 101 about price dependency on availability and demand.

Therefore, price or wage control never made any sense to us! Price or wage control and wealth redistribution are senseless and only done by ignorant or dishonest politicians.

Sometimes, I wondered what my father's reaction would have been if he found out about our illegal activities. We didn't feel very guilty; we just wanted to stop doing it.

In spite of our success in fooling people to buy our inferior tobacco, we still starved on occasion and went to bed hungry many nights. The lack of food, vitamins, and being much undernourished started to show its ugly side by our getting all kinds of infections, boils, colds, runs, rashes, and coughs.

> Starving is an interesting feeling. It really hurts at the beginning, then it eases up and you get into a weakening stage. One can go on with very little to eat. It does turn painful when eating a "big" meal after not having food for several days.
>
> Based on a story of our relative returning from a Siberian prison camp with a missing hand, starving and freezing to death have a lot in common. He lost his hand while chopping wood, not from the sharp end, but the blunt end of an ax. He was weak, but he had to go to the forest to cut trees with a whole platoon of prisoners. When the ax got stuck in the bottom of the tree, he tried his best to free it, but the handle broke. He tried loosening the ax by hitting both sides with rocks. He got bloody hands and was so exhausted in the extreme cold that he grabbed on to the part of the ax that was sticking out from the tree trunks to soften his fall as he collapsed.
>
> He remembered the pain at the beginning when his bloody hand froze to the ax, but then the pain just eased off and he fell

into a beautiful, dreamlike state. When the rest of the POWs found him, he was ready to meet his Maker, but somehow they were able to revive him. As soon as he was warm enough, the pain returned, and he could not wait to have them chop off his extremely painful hand before gangrene would set in.

I thoroughly believe one cannot appreciate hardship unless one has experienced it to the same extent. People may feel for you and have some understanding of the pain and suffering, but it's not the same.

I think it was close to a miracle we survived. Working together and loving each other was a big help. Even during the harshest times, we cooperated and helped each other out. The hard times forged us together in one strong, impenetrable unit no one could take advantage of. Every night, we gathered together to pray and sing. Sometimes we just swapped stories and experiences of the day, which often led to laughter and more hope.

Without exception, we all wanted to go back home to Transylvania.

Our family continued to pray for better things every night, and God answered our prayers. In late November, my father's new assignment was in the middle of the country, where food was more readily available.

DECEPTION AND REALITY- LIVING THROUGH THE MISSING PAGES OF HISTORY

Road to Recovery from WWII

We arrived early evening at the new city, with new hopes. It was cold, damp, and foggy as we started to peel out from the jam-packed train— the only public transportation available soon after the war. Automobiles were hard to come by— there was no gasoline, and the Red Army took most of the horses.

By this time, we were hardened veterans of WWII, living through many difficult events and life-threatening situations, but we didn't know or anticipate the hardships we still would have to endure.

The cold drizzle woke us up from the long and relatively uneventful journey from the west to the central part of Hungary. Since the city was also a center of agriculture, we were looking forward to finding more and better food, eating right, and getting rid of the constant hunger. My father had to hire a porter, not for the luggage, as we had very little left to carry, but to transport some of us, as we were too weak from malnutrition. We could not wear shoes because of the many boils or infected wounds on our feet due to vitamin deficiencies, starving, and the wrong size shoes. The porter had a hand-pushed cart with two rubber tires, the only transport available, as bus service, taxi, and other intercity transportation were not yet available.

There were a few carriages, but no horses to pull them. Horses that the Germans didn't take were quickly butchered as red meat to feed the Russian Army.

We got temporary housing in a bombed-out storage house with an apartment on the top, but both floors were burned out and smelled terrible.

In the back, past the paved part of the courtyard, we found a small servants' quarter, still habitable. The front of the big building was totally black and smoky, the store windows were broken, and we could still smell the burned upholstery, even after six months of peace. Nobody bothered to come through the blown-off doors or broken windows to look for things or try to salvage anything from the burned out furniture store, as people were too busy finding important things like food, clothing, and medicine.

Our temporary apartment, without heating and lighting, was behind the store, roughly in the middle of the large courtyard. By the time we arrived, it was pitch black, but my father's flashlight helped us to clear the middle of the room for the makeshift beds on the cold stone floor. Our bedding consisted of blankets on the bottom and jackets and coats for cover. It was too cold and dark to find water, wash, or take our clothes off. We just all fell in our "bed" close to each other to keep warm, totally exhausted after the long journey.

The next day, we woke up to the smell of bacon and eggs. It was heaven.

I had to rub my eyes and sit up to make sure I wasn't dreaming. Looking around, I saw an old green beat-up door barely hanging on hinges; sunlight was coming through the cracks. Opposite the door was a small window about a meter and half above the floor. The old kitchen was small. A servant or gardener for the now demolished house and stores had probably used it. The back window facing away from the courtyard was unbroken. It must have been open during the blast, but the glass from the front door was missing, and now it was covered up with rough wooden planks. The blast must have come from the east side, where the burned out large store stood protecting the standalone bungalow.

My mother stood in front of the small cooking stove with her back to me, and all my siblings were still rolled up next to each other in the middle of the kitchen either sleeping or just resting, not wanting to get up. My father was gone, but his blanket and heavy winter coat were left behind on top of the children. As I was getting up, I must have kicked the legs of the only chair, making a terrible squeaking noise like the hard chalk on a blackboard. My mother turned around, putting her index finger on her lips, indicating to keep quiet, then whispered, "Please get me some water," pointing to an old, chipped white-enameled tin three-liter pitcher decorated with a thin blue stripe along the edges. It was a well-designed vessel, as it also had a handle just like a bucket.

As I got up, I found walking was still difficult with my infected wounds on the back of my heels. I slipped on the old shoes, which had been tailored for my injured heel by chopping off the back part of the shoe with an ax. I had to tiptoe for a long time, and my siblings teased me a lot about becoming a ballerina. I picked up the pitcher and looked around for the faucet, but when I stepped up to the wash basin, my mother grabbed my shoulder and quietly told me it didn't work and to go outside to find water.

I stepped out in the large courtyard but found no working faucet any place. The garden hose was neatly curled up on a stand and connected to an out side faucet in the unpaved part of the large courtyard that may have been used as a garden. However, the faucet was rusted, and I could not move the handle, even by applying extra torque with a broken shovel and a rock.

Concentrating on opening the rusted faucet handle and making all the noise, I didn't notice a young man, or rather an older boy, standing behind me until he spoke. "There is no water in the pipes. The water pumps have long been broken and never replaced." I asked if he could tell me where to get some water. He said, "Yes, but it will cost you." I looked at him very hard, like I used to do when I wanted something I deserved regardless of the opponent. This look helped me avoid fights, get my stolen pocketknife back, get extra food at the chow line, defuse anger, start a fight, or make some run away. It worked again. The young Jewish boy, Peter, led me to a working artesian well close by, where I filled up the pitcher by pumping on the long handle. I thanked him and hurried back to our place tiptoeing.

Peter, the young man I met in the courtyard, became a close friend, and I became his confidant.

My mother was waiting patiently, guarding my portion of the breakfast from the rest of the siblings. There were generous portions of at least three eggs, four strips of bacon for each one of us, and freshly baked flat bread (lángos), with hot tea sweetened with grape sugar. Since my siblings had already finished their meals, they stayed around watching me. It was a good, long-overdue hearty breakfast. We didn't ask where all the good food came from, in case it was just a dream from which none of us wanted to wake up.

After I finished our delicious breakfasts, my mother asked what would we like to do. We responded in one voice and almost in total unison, "We want to go home to Transylvania." She said, "Your father already applied for repatriation for our family so we can stay here as Hungarians."

We were at a loss to understand her reply, especially when it came to the meaning of repatriation, as it really didn't make sense. We asked for an explanation, and my mother, bless her soul, tried everything to justify his action. In summary, she passed on the following vindication: "It is almost at the end of 1946, but by 1947, the Allies under the influence of Stalin will decide the fate of Central Europe and most likely redraw the borders around us. Hungary may be considered part of the Axis powers and be penalized by Stalin and the Western politicians who may have the wrong impression or be ignorant of our situation; like Hungary had a choice to stay out of WWII. In that case, we may end up like after WWI, losing about seven million Hungarians and over seventy percent of our land to neighboring newly formed countries. If Stalin has his way, my birthplace will be in Russia, your father's in Slovakia, and yours in Romania. Therefore, those are the three countries we could choose to live in. In order to remain in this part of Hungary, we must go through the formalities of repatriation, and we hope we will be accepted.

"The reason we started the repatriation process early is to avoid the rush when a large portion of the seven million other Hungarians swallowed up by the newly created countries will seek political asylum in the remaining thirty percent of our original homeland. The maximum number our mutilated country could absorb is less than a million. After WWI, over one million Hungarians migrated just to America to avoid persecution by the newly formed countries. Our mutilated country had to absorb multitudes of Hungarians escaping from the newly created foreign states when the new borders were drawn around them. Many people had to leave, as they were perceived as a potential threat by the newly created insecure states. Among these were the well-to-do, highly educated people or ex-military officers. Your father was literally thrown over the new Romanian border in 1926 after being in prison for not being willing to take the oath to serve in their army.

"If we choose to go to any of the newly formed countries, your father will be tried, imprisoned, and sentenced to a long prison term. Over two hundred thousand Hungarians came just from Transylvania, our heartland, because the new nationalistic Romanian government labeled most Hungarians undesirables, and many young men who stayed were moved to the Danube Delta or to the Russian gulag and never to be seen again.

Over one hundred and twenty thousand escaped from the Czech-Slovak ethnic cleansing. Over eighty thousand came from Yugoslavia to escape the Serbian death march. These countries and their new governments were supercharged with nationalistic fervor. They were given even more land than expected or asked for at the completion of the treaty. The Western diplomats knew very little about Hungary and Central Europe. They were easily misled by the dishonest Benes, the advisor for the Trianon treaty, who falsified many records and even contradicted himself on occasions. An example of his dishonesty is the way he recommended drawing the border along seasonal creeks, which he called navigable rivers."

Some quotes from the newly made-up government representative: Benes in Kosice (Kassa in Hungarian) proclaimed, "There will be no minorities in Slovakia." In Slovakia, it is illegal to speak Hungarian even today! The Prime Minister of the new Enlarged Romania, Ionel Britannia's public announcement in Bucharest, "We cannot rest until the Hungarian people are destroyed economically and militarily."

My sister started to cry, and we didn't agree with my mother's logic, as sense. I spoke first after trying to comprehend what my mother's message was, but I could not find any logic in it.

My argument was that Stalin cannot dictate the peace alone. Americans stand for justice, freedom, and fairness for everyone. They must see through the Communists' lies; our family was Hungarian, at least for the past thousand years. Surely, no one in the world has the power to change our citizenship except us. Therefore, repatriation doesn't make any sense— it is a contradiction!

My mother tried again. "When it comes to politics, decisions will be made without proper understanding, knowledge, or perspective. You didn't see the division of Central Europe after WWI. These diplomats didn't only punish Hungary unjustly— they also subdivided and redrew the borders of Armenia, Kurdistan, and created new countries without blinking an eye.

They will just want to find scapegoats and end up punishing the innocent.

Those foreign diplomats have no idea about what we had to go through, how we resisted the Nazis or Communists, and how many lives it already took to try to stay independent. It would have been suicidal and impossible for a small and mutilated country like Hungary to resist with our ill-equipped small army. It took England, Russia, France, America, and the rest of the world combined to beat the Nazis."

- We tried again ...

There is already a Marshall Plan to avoid another world war. Foreign diplomats realized they were directly and indirectly responsible for putting Hitler in power and starting WWII. They won't make the same mistake again. There is no way the Western diplomats would bow to Stalin's dictates, punishing the innocent people, destroying Hungary again, and removing the stabilizing force in Central Europe. If they repeat the same mistakes, there will be terrible suffering for all the minorities, bloodshed, animosity, and general unrest, which can only be temporarily stabilized by force, fear, and genocide— it will be much worse than the Holocaust. We'd already lost more people and land than all the Jews in Central Europe.

My mother visibly agreed with our argument by nodding but decided to table the discussion and said, "Why don't we wait to talk when your father comes home, as he has a better grasp on what is going on currently and what is expected from the shortsighted or ignorant Western diplomats and politicians?"

We were so sure about being right we started to plan in earnest our return to our homeland in Transylvania. With full stomachs for a change and new adventures to look forward to, we were elated. For the entire morning, we discussed the first thing each one of us would do after arrival at our old home in Transylvania. We no longer wanted to explore our surroundings, as our curious minds were preoccupied with the changes we would see as a result of temporary Russian and Romanian occupation. I even remember the small interruption looking for the only comb, which was already missing most of its teeth, to quiet my sister who was in charge and responsible for this valuable tool, as we didn't want to use our forks.

We did eventually find it on the high windowsill, where most likely my father put it when he saw it on the floor.

My mother left to look around the premises, and we continued the packing process by throwing our limited stuff onto one of the open blankets laid out on the floor. When we had everything piled into one, we laid out two more blankets on each side and divided the contents to about four equal parts. We looked around for other things to pack, but only the greasy pan; plates and spoons were left. By the time my mother returned, we had all three blankets tied in the middle and ready for transport.

When my mother returned, she just looked at the four blankets tied in the middle containing all our earthly possessions but didn't say a word.

She stepped up to the stove and heated up some water to wash the dishes and asked me get more water, handing me the old pitcher. With the hearty breakfast, I was full of energy, grabbed the containers, and headed out to the artesian well. I almost forgot about the raw sores on my heels, but the pain reminded me to keep tiptoeing. By the time I retuned with the water, my youngest brother had cleaned up and looked real strange with his skinny legs in an oversized undershirt. I guess we got used to the dirt and grime on our face and clothing. One by one, we all had to get cleaned up, for a nice change, in warm water and soap. We put our only remaining clean underwear on; we just could not put the remaining filthy outer layer on.

My mother put half of the water on the stove, and the rest was poured out in a big wooden container like a small trough, and after shaking out all the clothes we had, she put them in the wooden trough to soak. When she rinsed them out to put them in hot water, the remaining water turned almost black. She said, "I need more water." Nobody volunteered to do the chore in his or her underwear. She ended up going to get the next load of fresh water.

We were all cleaned up with our clothes hung up to dry when my father appeared by the door. We all rushed to greet him with a big hug that he always returned twofold. He always came home for lunch with a smile, even if he was hungry. We children really appreciated his positive outlook on life, regardless of how desperate our situation was. My mother served him the same as we had for breakfast. We were all ready to eat again by that time, but we told him we were full. Of course, we didn't tell him it was over four hours ago. Once he finished, he said, "I have good news for us. We have a decent apartment right around the corner, and I already checked it out." He was ready to show us all, but we would not go without our clothes on. My mother was also eager to see it, so they left us alone. My sister said, "We didn't ask him about returning to our home in Transylvania." I said, "It is because we had to unpack for the wash and forgot to ask."

My mother came back smiling, with a small brown bag in her hands.

She opened it up and pulled out three thick envelopes with fancy writing on them. While she was heating up some more water, my sister read the printing on the colorful envelope aloud. On the top in big letters "Lipton" and with smaller letters soup were written. My mother took the envelopes from us, tore them open, and poured the yellowish green contents in the hot water. The aroma was delicious, and my mother wanted to taste it first to make sure they were okay.

We were no longer interested in packing and going back home. We just wanted to taste the delicious-smelling golden liquid. It was our first encounter with the American dried food. We all loved the soup and wanted to know where to get more. She said, "If you behave real nicely, we may get some more from the people who let us rent one of their apartments on the first floor in the back of their house."

We didn't need any more encouragement and started to pack again the four blankets. My mother finished washing the dishes, and we sneaked out one by one to get our half-dried clothes off the line. The girls' dresses dried much faster, but we boys had to put on the still damp clothes, especially in the crotches of the heavy pants. However, we all looked clean and smelled good. I remember us smelling each other as we all delighted in the fresh, clean smell. Ever since, I would rather smell the fresh scent of a clean person wearing outside air-dried clothes than any of the finest deodorants or perfumes in the world. It only took us fifteen minutes to get ready and get to our future place of residence in the early afternoon.

After we rang the bell, a middle-aged Jewish lady opened the large and heavy door that led to a small courtyard. She smiled and invited us in. She was well-dressed and looked elegant and spoke softly—ladylike. Once she closed the door behind her, she put on a real big smile and welcomed us one by one. As it was appropriate, we boys kissed her hand, and each of my sisters made an elegant curtsy. Our new landlady was visibly pleased and delighted with our behavior. She complimented us and asked us to follow her.

She led us past the entry to the stairs leading to her apartment on the second floor. Then she led us to the next living quarters on the first floor apartment in the back. The two stories and L-shaped building only had one living quarters in the back downstairs, one large apartment on top of the two shops in the front. The large apartment on the second floor above the shops was where the lady lived with her family, her husband and one son. She apologized for the small place for our large family and the musty smell, as this apartment was primarily used as storage for extra furniture, shoes, food, and odds and ends. It had a long glass-covered hallway as we entered and doors that led to a kitchen, dining room, and three bedrooms.

Each room had some old furniture pieces, but totally uncoordinated. There was an impressive wardrobe in the kitchen area, kitchen shelving in the bedroom, and a wooden bed frame in the hallway. Each room was oversized, the kitchen, pantry, and the bedrooms.

The owner let us settle in, and about an hour later, she returned with her son, Peter, whom I met earlier when he showed me the location of the artesian well, and now his arms were full with a load of goods and food.

She gave each child a small bar of chocolate with marzipan fillings. The fine clothing and the special treat we received mesmerized us. She said, "Some of the clothes are Peter's, but he has outgrown them."

My mother finally came to realize it wasn't a dream and started to cry. She thanked Ella, the landlady, for letting us rent this place untouched by bombs or fire and asked where she got the food, as she had nothing to feed us tomorrow. Ella said the Jewish Relief Fund would provide them almost anything they need or want, but she'd bring us more food today that should last until we go to the open market, where farmers bring in all kinds of fresh food. She said, "I talked to your husband earlier. We agreed on the price of rental, and he told me what he was doing and his assignment.

I'm sure that he will have enough money to buy you almost anything you need. The clothes are our leftover used ones, and you are most welcome to them. If you need anything else, just ask him," she said, pointing toward Peter, her son. She added her husband would be pleased she had rented the apartment to such a nice family. My mother thanked her again and said, "We're looking forward to meeting your husband." It turned out that the husband was very busy, constantly away on business trips, and we only saw him once or twice. As I recall, he only talked with my father and no one else in our family.

While my mother was arranging furniture, we went exploring, first inside. We looked in every cupboard, every nook and cranny. We even discovered a cache of ladies' shoes in a huge storage box. They were all new, different sizes and colors. We found out Ella and her family, among other things, owned a shoe company and brought home a lot of shoes before the Nazis took over the manufacturing facilities. They were able to sell all the men's and women's low-heeled shoes, but these high heels were left behind, and if we could sell one pair, we would get one pair free.

Kele D. Gabor

Fortunately, this family owned an honest and quality shoe factory, unlike the boot factory owned by other Jews, which made military footwear for the army. They substituted paper for leather soles, and our soldiers couldn't keep their feet dry in the snow or rain on the Russian front.

It was dark when my father came home, and we each got a large pear from him. His new secretary sent them to us. We had a very happy supper together, with lots of food—cheese, bacon, cold cuts, bread, onion, and a pear at the end for dessert. My father didn't want to believe the assortment of food my mother served, thanks to our new landlady. After the evening prayer, where we had thanked the Lord for all the good things we received that day, we all went to bed on the floor and slept better than any time during the past year.

My father awakened me early in the morning to go to the farmer's market with him. It was a pleasure to see him barter for items he wanted to buy. Besides the nutritious acorn squash, flour, and potatoes, we also purchased a live turkey. As soon as we got home, my father had to hurry back to his office without breakfast. I let the turkey loose in the courtyard until we finished breakfast. The dumb turkey made so much noise trying to escape by attempting to fly out of the two-story-high walled courtyard.

For the noise, Peter came down and watched me as I chased the turkey down, cut his head off, and let it bleed into a small dish. Peter was so impressed with my quickness and skill with the knife he would do anything I asked him, in spite of the fact that he was a year older and looked twice as strong and heavy as me.

It turned out they were some of the lucky Jewish people who hid away in the basement of the nearby Catholic church. They always had food and drink, so it really showed when we were together side by side. People called us David and Goliath, not for Peter's height, but for my skinny and pale looks. The big difference faded away in a few years. Peter was not much for sport except as a spectator, but he was clever when we tried to trick people, especially on April Fools' Day.

I remember the game we would play of leaving a paper-stuffed wallet on the pavement with a black thin line attached so we could move it from our hiding place in the cellar. We left a small crack in the basement window to the street, and when someone noticed the wallet he would look around, and if nobody saw him, he would stoop down to grab the unexpected find. Unfortunately for the person, the wallet would move just enough to be out of reach. The other trick was to climb out on the roof right above the second-story open window with a full pitcher of water.

When someone walked underneath the window, we would let him have a bit of water, just enough to confuse it with a bird dropping. We even got sophisticated and made small balls with water and flour. Invariably, they blamed a bird or the people on the second floor, where the window was open. We had so much laughter, sometimes our stomach muscles hurt. We kept changing the game, making it more challenging for each other.

Later we learned to play drunks pretty well, so Saturday night, preferably after midnight, we would go on the street and ring the bell of a house to wake the people. After we knocked, they would eventually come to the door or window, where they could see us as two drunks. When they asked what we wanted, we told them we were just looking for the other side of the street. When they would point to the other side, we would argue it could not be, as someone trustworthy just sent us here from there. I guess, after the war, hard living, and surviving the harsh conditions, we needed some outlet and made up for the lost time to be carefree and have a lot of laughter.

The first summer, I spent on a farm guarding a flock of turkeys, and on occasion, I played cowboy with the few cattle they had, but without the help of a horse. My salary was room and board, good food, exercise, and fresh air, which revitalized my body and soul.

This was also the high time of wanting to meet attractive girls, and we started to talk about sex a lot. When I told Peter my experiences in the camp (the tent city), he got all bent out of shape, as he missed that opportunity because his parents hid him underneath the church. There was no way I could convince him he was better off without experiencing the concentration camps and starvation. He eventually complained to his mother that he had to learn about sex from a younger guy like me. Since

Peter's father was always away, or for other reasons, the mother had to educate her son about sex.

To my surprise, Peter shared all his sexual encounters and education he had received soon after. I heard more and better descriptions about sex from Peter than all the rest of my friends. I believed for a long time that Peter pulled my leg with the stories he told. I found out later that he most likely had been telling the truth. Peter told me his mother invited three of her single girlfriends over for an afternoon tea with him present. That evening, his mother asked Peter, "Which of my friends do you find most likable or attractive?" After a lot of encouragement, he selected Fifi, as she was the youngest and smiled the most.

Peter spent two weeks for three consecutive months with Fifi that summer.

However, Peter and Fifi's adventures continued for a long time. You could see they both enjoyed the sex and each other's company. We almost broke up our friendship, as Peter would often cancel our prearranged meetings when Fifi showed up.

The most unbelievable part was that Peter's mother got periodic updates on his progress, and she even complimented him in front of me. Fifi and Peter's relationship lasted over a year until Fifi left the country and married a French military officer. Later, Peter's on-the-job training really paid off, as all his intimate girlfriends were all crazy about him. He knew how to satisfy a woman, and he also knew about the pleasures they could provide.

He was not successful in every case; he never learned when to lie low and stop, even with Jewish girls. He often became obnoxious, and the nicer girls avoided his company.

After college, Peter married one pretty Jewish lady, who would not give in until after the wedding. Peter even told me the Jewish girls also receive some similar but limited to verbal education, without performing any sex act before their wedding day.

My father was extremely busy helping to rebuild the country after the WWII devastation. My mother had her work cut out also. Before investing in fine furniture, which was hard to find, we decided it was time to visit our well-furnished home in Transylvania. My mother first wanted to go alone, but eventually she took me along for protection. Few people dared to go to an area that was already occupied by Romanian, Serb, or Slovak forces, in addition to the Russian Red Army. All my siblings envied me, even though they knew it was dangerous. My father's work required him to be close to the capital. Just before leaving, we found out about the Russians' planned killing of General Patton and imprisoning Wallenberg, the Swedish diplomat.

My mother was well-prepared when we boarded the train to our homeland, Transylvania. She had recovered most of her strength, but her attractive figure had to be camouflaged and hidden for protection from marauding Romanian or Russian soldiers, who still liked to take advantage of women. In fact, she looked like an old grandmother being escorted by her grandson. These special trains started up to accommodate the high demand of millions of people who wanted to return home after surviving WWII. Our train was so full that on occasion we had to climb up the top just to get some fresh air. On one of our nightly excursions to the top of the train, fine coal dust and smoke sprayed us so bad it took a few days to clean our faces. However, the black face came in handy, as it hid my mother's fine facial features, and the Romanians considered us gypsies.

The new borders of the newly Enlarged Romania were not cast in stone, but their border guards had already stopped trains and all vehicles that were heading home. The guards took everything that was valuable.

The Romanian guards claimed that since they now occupied these old Hungarian territories, it entitled them to have anything they wanted. I was furious when they wanted to take my new pocketknife, but my mother was able to control the situation by asking me to be a Christian and give it to them as a present and asked me to give it to the lowest-ranking guard. The guards were primarily looking for books written in Hungarian.

If they caught someone with a Hungarian Bible, he would be stopped, all possessions confiscated, and he would be escorted back to the border and never allowed to return. The Romanians made sure we felt unwelcome in our own homeland. It was interesting that all the Romanian guards spoke Hungarian well, but none of the returning natives spoke the Romanian language. After my pocketknife "present," they let us through without further search.

Each locomotive, coach, and wagon still had the original marking of "Royal Hungarian Rail" and the manufacturing place "Csepel," located close to Budapest.

That night, the train went very slowly and stopped at every little station, so we did not rest well. My mother used the time to tell me about the Romanians, as I have never seen one or heard their language before in my life. It was very strange and hurtful seeing them taking advantage of the Hungarians, and many times they treated us the same way as the Nazis treated the Jews, or worse.

Kele D. Gabor

We arrived in our home at Udvar on a cool morning, with very heavy fog surrounding us. Walking by the church, we could not see the steeple.

We practically felt our way home touching the sides of the houses on occasion just to make sure we were keeping on the pavement. It was quiet, no traffic or pedestrians around. No schoolchildren, no horse-drawn carriages— just dead silence. About a kilometer walk took us to our home. The main door was ajar, and no light was visible from any of the windows. We walked to the hallway door, which was closed. Pushing down the doorknob, I felt no resistance, and the door opened quietly.

The house was practically empty. All our fine furniture had been taken, and there were some odds and ends broken and scattered around the bedrooms.

There was nothing left worth taking back with us. The small treasures we buried in the garden were too risky to recover, as they would have been taken away by the Romanian border guards. Worse yet, most of the papers were too dangerous to take with us, i.e., the list of trustworthy individuals who could be involved in negotiating with the West. The lists of traitors who were now in power and control would also put our return in jeopardy.

We found some half-burned old photographs by the fireplace; somebody must have used them to start a fire. My mother started to cry. She started to blame herself for not taking these old photos and the paintings of her family members. I remember how proudly she used to show her father and family picture with the nice home or weekend house. I was more impressed with the grandfather's image with a huge brown bear in front of his boots.

With heavy hearts, we decided to leave the almost totally empty house and see one of our neighbors, Ilona, who had to stay because of the serious lung infection her husband contracted just before the Russians broke through the pass. She was home, but the husband was gone. Her little children were holding on to her skirt so tightly that she could barely move.

The children followed her every place, no smiles on their faces. It was very strange, as they used to run to my mother every time she showed up.

She would always bring those freshly baked cookies or pastry. My mother asked, "Where is George?" "They took my sick husband, and he died on the way to the Delta," she responded. We immediately knew it was the delta of the Danube River as it entered the Black Sea, the favorite place to exile the undesirables. Few, if any, returned from that place. Malaria, inferior food, infections, beating, torture, or other diseases annihilated the inmates of the forced-labor camp.

Ilona, with three children, was now without a husband or a wage earner.

Since they had a big orchard and were able to save most of the fruit in big barrels, she turned to making spirits. She said, "The Romanian police is so busy gathering young Hungarians for either deportation or turning them over to the Russians for work details, I can make the alcohol illegally and sell it on the black market. The only trouble is that so few have the money and there are very few men left around to drink my brandy."

She turned toward a big credenza, took out three small glasses, and started to pour out the gold colored liquid. I was at least two meters away but could smell the delicious fragrance of the plum fruit carried over by the evaporating alcohol. My mother raised her hand to reject the generous offer, but Ilona insisted we both needed the refreshing drinks. Also, in case we could stay a half-hour, she could summarize the way the Russians and Romanians took over the city. We ended up tasting and drinking the delicious booze, one for Ilona and two for us. She raised her glass and said, "God save the Magyars!" After taking a big sip, she started talking.

"The Romanians could not come through the passes because of the boy scouts, but the Russians did. Surprisingly, they seemed to be civilized and not like what we were told by the Nazis. The Russian soldiers, of course, collected all watches, took our remaining food, but did not bother families and liked the children. The Russians were soon followed by the Romanian Army that started to arrest all the young men and took them away on military trucks. When they returned, they loaded up again with the remaining group, but before they could roll out, a Russian vehicle pulled in front of them and stopped the convoy. Later, we found out they took the first load to a nearby mineshaft and machine-gunned them down. The Russians heard the firing, and they went to investigate. From that point on, the Romanians could arrest people in that city and region, but they had to turn them over to the Russians.

"From the first group of young men, only seven from the eighty-three survived the massacre, but they all were left there to die. The

Kele D. Gabor

Russians did let some of the younger people go who already had family and children, but they kept most of the single men, and we don't know where they took them." (About forty years later, we found out that some of the young men ended up in Kazakhstan and the gulag, much worse than the German concentration camps.)

She continued. "It seemed like the Russian soldiers did the fighting and the Romanians played the occupying force. After the Russians stopped the Romanians from killing Hungarians, they switched to the search-take-and-destroy mode. The soldiers would search out places and items that they regarded as old Hungarian relics. If they liked it, they took it. If it was too big, they destroyed it. Most Hungarian symbols were destroyed, such as famous paintings and the Hungarian flags and crests displayed on official buildings, roads, or cemeteries. Even headstones were broken to pieces if the Hungarian emblem was shown. It was scary, as nobody here speaks good Romanian, and none of the Romanian soldiers spoke Hungarian.

"After a week of search, they found a family close to the Békás Pass who spoke both languages. For our official city interpreter, they picked the oldest daughter, Malina. She was a sweet girl, about nineteen years old, and obviously preferred the Hungarians to the Romanians. However, she could not stop the looting and mistreatment of the indigenous population.

Malina told us a lot about events while she served as an interpreter until they found a new police chief who took charge of the city and knew enough of the Hungarian language to be very dangerous. The new police chief in charge of the region wanted to please the new government in Bucharest to excess.

"Malina and I became friends, and she told me a lot of stories, even after the Romanians fired her. She was unattractive to look at, with the exception of beautiful light-brown eyes, which she claimed to have gotten from her Hungarian father. Malina was the gentlest soul I ever met in my life. She had a sweet singing voice, a gentle demeanor, and a strong conviction about what is right and wrong. She ended up protecting a lot of people until the Communist chief completely took over. The commissar enjoyed absolute power and often took walks on the main street with his bodyguards and wearing his long leather coat and new boots. According to Malina, he was an evil man." (I remembered my brother Bende's dream and his description of evil. A momentary cold shaking came over me).

Ilona took another sip of the delicious strong liquid, so did we, and she continued. "I know from Malina that the new police chief was a midlevel military officer serving the Nazis at the time the Romanian government turned sides. In fact, during the infamous dinner when they invited the entire German Chief of Staff to celebrate the new joint offensive against the Russians, he was one of the many Romanian officers who pulled his side arm out right after the first toast and killed one of the German officers sitting next to him. The entire German high command stationed in Romania was executed at the same time and the same way in a matter of a few seconds. According to the police chief, it was a small price to pay to Stalin for the entire region of Transylvania, and in one fell swoop, the New Enlarged Romania was born again.

"The police chief also admitted to the fact that he had no idea there were no Romanians living here and only a handful of people spoke their language, but things will change. Sure enough, soon after the Romanian takeover, the official language became Romanian, and in schools that had a single Romanian student, the teaching must be in Romanian. Eventually, every community was assigned a Romanian police chief with children so every town, village, and city had to convert to teaching in Romanian. Since there were no teachers who could teach Romanian, they imported them from old Romania, south of the old border, called Walachia. There were many Hungarians who had nice homes, but they had disappeared, and the new Romanian teachers could just move right into their fully furnished houses."

We all finished our strong drink, and Ilona said, "You'd better have one more drink for the road." We respectfully declined, as it started to burn our empty stomachs, and we didn't want to ask for any food from the young widow with three children. My mother asked about our fine furnishings.

Ilona continued. "We saw the police chief personally supervising the packing and loading of all your furniture in trucks, and I asked Malina about it.

She found out, after she was fired as the official translator, the handcrafted furniture all went to Bucharest, the living room furniture went to the theatre, the bedroom furniture to different dignitaries."

"How about the family room furniture, since it was original Hungarian design with Transylvanian decorations?" my mother asked.

Kele D. Gabor

"They really liked the light-blue furniture painted with beautiful red tulips and colorful designs. I don't think they knew they were taking Hungarian folk art to Bucharest," Ilona explained.

My mother hugged Ilona and all three children, who warmed up to us during the conversation, and as we left Ilona said, "Please make sure that your sons and daughters remain Hungarians, as I don't know what the future holds for my children." We left quietly and didn't talk until we got on a train.

Leaving Transylvania was hard for me, but we had to go, as the Hungarian government failed to recover the recently lost territories. Even though they tried very hard, Stalin outsmarted the West.

Historians left out some important developments that occurred right after WWII. On April 9, 1946, all the Hungarian political parties, except the Communists, led by the Prime Minister Ferenc Nagy, asked for a fair peace treaty based on the request set forth by the French government on March 23, 1946. The United States also supported these peace talks. In fact, on February 28, Foreign Minister Mr. Byrens urged all participants to begin talks and asked for a fair and expeditious conclusion to the peace talks. He also made the army occupation restrictions public. For example, according to the proclamation, no foreign army may occupy sovereign states without their consent. Of course, the Russians ignored it. The peace talks among the Allied foreign ministers began on April 25.

The Hungarian government turned in their suggestions and requests for border adjustments by the end of April. These border adjustments were to reconnect the Hungarian population currently assigned to Romania, Yugoslavia and Czechoslovakia. The requests were made for territories where the original and native population was mostly Hungarian. For example, it would include twenty-two to twenty-three thousand square kilometers just from Transylvania. These claims for the territories were justified by demography, density of the native Hungarian population, by historical data, and backed up by legal rights and international law. Interestingly, the French government independently developed recommendations for Hungarian border adjustments, requesting twenty-two-thousand-square kilometer territory to be returned to Hungary from Romania, with slightly different borderlines.

Please note that as early as 1944, Stalin promised Romania the entire Hungarian Transylvania in lieu of taking half of Moldova and for turning against the Germans. This free giveaway was stopped by Churchill, and he demanded that the new borders drawn by the Soviets could not be accepted or finalized until the Allies' upcoming peace conference. With the French, English, and international laws backing the Hungarians, we felt confident of a more equitable and fair revision to the original peace treaty of Trianon.

The Hungarian issue didn't come up until May 7, 1946. This conference ended with a tragic result, not only for the Hungarians, but also for all the people of world who wanted peace, fairness, and human rights.

The Hungarians, with the help of America, England, and France, only succeeded in preventing Benes and Stalin from deporting two hundred thousand Hungarians from Slovakia.

My mother was right— Stalin's way prevailed!

Here are excerpts and some of the hidden facts from accounts of events leading up to this period and beyond, written after the collapse of Soviet type communism in the 1990s:

On October 15, 1944, the Nazis transferred power into the hands of the Arrow-Cross Party. Ferenc Szálasi's principal goal as a "National Leader" was to mobilize Hungary for war, since he was convinced that Hitler's promised "secret weapon" (atomic bomb?) would tilt the war in Germany's favor at the last minute.

The power of Szálasi's Arrowhead Party grew, following the introduction of the secret ballot, his social programs, his anti-Semitic demagoguery, and his radicalism. However, without German backing and support, he would never have been able to prevail.

Before the Russians closed in and blockaded Budapest around Christmas 1944, the Arrow-Cross authorities, as well as the "National Leader," moved across the Trans-Danubean region, and then to the western border, right into what they referred to as "border refuge," near Kôszeg. The Germans defended Budapest as a fortress, which gave the Soviet Army a six-week long and brutal fight before it succeeded in taking the city. The siege lasted from Christmas 1944 until February 13,

1945, resulting in great suffering and destruction.

All bridges in Budapest were reduced to ruin, public buildings were seriously damaged, and more than thirty thousand apartment buildings and homes were destroyed.

More than one million Hungarians fled from the Red Army to the West, and more than one hundred thousand never returned. In fact, fewer Hungarian Jews were missing after the short period in concentration camps in Germany than the number of Hungarians lost to the West. From the near half-million Jews taken from Hungary by the Germans, most of them returned except for about ninety one thousand.

The general mobilization ordered by the Arrow-Cross Party and the unmanageable terror of its activism increased the number of war victims by tens of thousands.

When the Hungarian Communist Party was re-organized in the wake of the Red Army, increasing the party membership became of paramount importance. As the Communist Party members got their hands on the internal and military political security agencies, they had access to the Arrow-Cross membership records as well. Consequently, the Communist Party was joined in great numbers by people who "to greater or lesser extent were infected by the poison of counterrevolution and fascism," admitted Mátyás Rákosi, the first secretary of the Communist Party.

The newly recruited "small Arrow-Crossers" (rank and file) had to declare when and how long they had been members of the Arrow-Cross party and state that their membership had been a mistake for which they were willing to make amends. Unfortunately, these declarations were excellent tools for intimidation and blackmail of those who signed them.

In Hungary, in the background of the Red Army, Soviet advisors began to appear almost immediately in 1944. The majority of these were political officers or military intelligence experts. Their responsibility was to establish a Hungarian administrative system, which would cooperate with the Soviet occupation authorities. No party or social organization could receive a permit to be organized or to function, to produce press materials, or to hold rallies without their permission. These advisors also determined the numbers of Hungarians and German minority needed to be forcefully sent to the Soviet Union. It is estimated that over five hundred thousand Hungarians were taken to the gulag from the Carpathian Basin, with the help of Romanians, Russians, Serbs, and Slovaks.

After the Nazis were driven out and the Soviets took power, the Allied Control Committee directed Hungarian political and economic life. First Marshal Vorosilov, and then Lieutenant General Sviridov led this body. When this committee was finally disbanded, the Soviet Ambassadors of the time became the "Hungarian governors" for the Kremlin. Ambassadors Pushkin, Thishkov, Kiseliov, and Andropov were all high-ranking members of the Soviet political police, too.

The Soviet advisors developed an extensive record system on all Communist leaders, opposition politicians, intellectuals, and prominent personalities in Hungarian public life. For these advisors, even Rákosi, Moscow's unconditional servant, was not reliable enough.

In important investigating and analytical work, Soviet advisors assisted or oversaw the political police, which later became known as the State Security Department (AVO) and the State Security Authority (AVH). These advisors also largely controlled the Political Military Department (KATPOL) and the Economic Police (GRO).

With the cooperation of the Soviet interior ministry experts, they carried out arrests and organized political trials, according to the Soviet model.

General Belkin, who led the political police in Central Europe from Baden bei Wien, Austria, frequently visited Budapest to personally observe that the advisors were working effectively.

The ministries and judicial organizations could rely on the work of the Soviet advisors, as well.

The Soviet advisors were important decision-makers in Hungarian economic life for a long time, directing uranium mining, air and river transport, as well as the defense and oil industries. They supervised foreign trade and all strategic branches of the economy and reshaped the Hungarian army to the Soviet model.

Soviet teachers, engineers, doctors, agricultural engineers, and miners arriving in Hungary not only shared their experiences about the "advanced" (truly outmoded and backward) Soviet industry and agriculture with their Hungarian colleagues, they also tried to make Hungarian people accept their foreign way of life and view of the world. The Soviet Embassy in Budapest and the Soviet political police also supervised the growing Soviet colony in Hungary. In the Hungarian countryside, the occupying Soviet troops became a part of everyday life, enmeshing the countryside with their garrisons.

In 1956, in collaboration with Ambassador Andropov, Soviet advisors prepared the way for the Soviet invasion to suppress Hungary's revolution. Soviet advisors Baikov and Kuptshenko were members of Kádár's (the new prime minister) close circle and never left Kádár unsupervised; even during the night, they slept in an adjoining room. In the fall of 1956, three high-ranking Soviet leaders, Malenkov, Suslov, and Aristov, came to supervise the first steps of the Kádár government and direct the retaliations from behind the scenes.

The Soviet siege of Buda was still underway when on 17 January 1945, the Communists set up the Soviet-style Political Security Department (PRO) in Pest. This PRO's official responsibility was to track down war criminals and bring them to trial. Before long, however, it became a notorious and dreaded force, made up of ultra left wing activists, criminals, and former Arrow-Cross hit men.

Following Communist Party orders, the PRO sought to prevent the establishment of constitutional order and pave the way for the Hungarian Communist Party's takeover.

The officers (of the PRO) were trained by the Soviet Political Police and at the Soviet-style Dzerzhinsky Academy in Budapest, where they were taught to acquire a merciless hatred of their class enemies. Following its Russian counterpart, the TCHEKA, the Hungarian political police, became the support and guarantor of the communist dictatorship.

In October 1946, security agencies in Budapest and all

around the country were united, and the PRO became the State Security Department (AVO). One of its tasks was to eliminate all democratic parties and to do all related intelligence tasks. AVO's undercover agents were planted in all parties. Chief among its mission was to infiltrate and annihilate émigré communities abroad and religious communities at home. The AVO monitored mail and phone conversations, and its moles and agents formed an invisible network in the whole country, right down to people's homes. Millions of people were declared political enemies and kept under constant surveillance.

Through the years, the communist terror organizations changed their official names several times, but not their mission. Citizens were reduced to subjects, and thousands feared the AVH (Alam Vedelmi Hatosag or Government Protection Agency), as much as its members feared one another. On command, its agents killed without hesitation, they committed burglaries, embezzlement, and torture to send their victims, based on false testimonies and confessions, to the gallows or to labor camps. A legion of informers, a shadow army, monitored and recorded the thinking of people at factory assembly lines, editorial offices, company offices, universities, churches, and theaters. No areas of life were shielded from them. They were the tool by which the communists seized power, implemented and sustained their system of terror that deported, crippled, or mistreated people in one third of the families.

According to BBC News reporter Nick Thorpe, "The deportation in 1944 of thousands of Hungary's civilians to the Soviet Union, although on a similar scale as the deportation of its Jewish people to the concentration camps, receives little official attention in Hungary."

An eyewitness of the deportation, Arpad Kovari has been trying to persuade the state to create a day of remembrance for the Hungarian Holocaust, not in competition with the Jewish Holocaust. Arpad took trips to the east in search of his father and the lost Hungarians. He had a picture of a group of men holding a cross on a hill in the city of Baltsi. "That hill," says Arpad, "is made of human bones."

Kele D. Gabor

> Many Hungarians ended up in forced labor camps in Siberia, where inhuman conditions far exceeded any Nazi concentration camps.[4]

On the way back from Transylvania to our new little subdivided Hungary, which was shrunk to less than one-third, we traveled through our historic and beautiful homeland where our family lived for over a thousand years, but again was unfairly given away to Romania, Russia, Czechoslovakia, or Yugoslavia. We both cried approaching the new border where the Romanian guards were happy to see some more Hungarians leaving the land rich in natural resources, reducing the Magyar population, culture, and heritage of Transylvania.

---

[4] To understand some of the extreme atrocities committed by Stalin, please read the book, "Martyrs of Magadan: Memories of the Gulag" by Michael Shields, ISBN 978-0-95533339-4-1. This book contains eyewitness accounts of a few survivors of the fifty million people sent to their mass graves in Siberia, in the Gulag.

Hungary

There are stories made up about subdividing the Hungarian kingdom after the World Wars to cover up the atrocities against the people of my land.

You can find the following story in American history books: Horthy, the regent of Hungary, recovered some of the land from neighboring countries by selling out to the Nazis and Hitler— this claim is totally false! The history books never mentioned that all the land recovered was always part of the Hungarian kingdom since before the tenth century, and the small parts that were returned still had the overwhelming Magyar majority, in spite of the systematic killing and deportation of the indigenous Hungarians. The historians also forgot to mention most that minorities now living within the Carpathian basin had come in for protection or economic reasons, and many came illegally, like the Mexicans to the US.

Hungary was the only country during the wars, and even under German occupation, that didn't allow the building of Nazi-type concentration camps.

Very few historians know or understand that the Huns, Avars, Magyars, Kuns, Pechenegs, and Scythians belong to the same family of people with common language and runic writing. They were also among the first in Europe to establish kingdoms. They also tend to forget the many good things we contributed to the so-called Western Civilization. Here are a few examples: better bows for hunting or fighting, the trousers— only wrap-around or togas were used, underwear was first used by Hungarians, hygiene— most plagues had diminished effect within the Carpathian basin because of our cleanliness, the first coach (named for the town of Kocs), military cavalry, the first telephone switchboard, the first metro in continental Europe, the electric Kando engine for trains, and electric shock treatment to revive the heart.

In America, many Hungarian officers served and helped win the Civil War, and Colonel Kovacs established the first cavalry branch of the US Army. You can find many Hungarian officers who fled to America and served in the Civil War after the failed 1849 revolution against the Austrians, and most of these men were buried in Arlington cemetery.

The Model T chief designer was Joseph A. Galamb; the technical advisor for Edison was Mr. Puskás, the jet-engine designer was Prof. Theodore Kármán; the father of the H-bomb was Dr. Edward Teller, just to mention a few. These men were all born, raised, and educated in Hungary. Very few, if any nations can trace back their ancestry for over five thousand years. Sumerians had similar language to the Huns, Avars, Magyars, Scythians, and Pechenges. There are about eight thousand words that are common between the Sumerian and the Hungarian languages. Many Hungarians could read and write thousands of years earlier than the Greeks and Romans. Our language is also unique in many ways.[5]

Jacob Grimm, the children story writer, was the first to establish a scientific base for the German grammar, and this is what he said about languages, "The Hungarian language is logical, and its structure surpasses every other language."

N. Erbersberg, an Austrian scientist, said, "The structure of the Hungarian Language is like it was created by a select group of linguists to make sure that it is orderly, compact, harmonious, and clear."

Ove Burglund, a Swedish doctor and translator, wrote, "Today I began to understand language structure, and in my opinion the Hungarian language is the peak achievement of human logic."

In the year 992, the Vikings ventured westward all the way to Newfoundland. In Yarmouth's Bay, there was a rock with runic writing on it, commemorating the Vikings' landing. It is the oldest written language found in North America. Tyrkir, a Hungarian, wrote the runic text in Hungarian and carved into the one hundred and eighty one kilogram stone. The Hungarian text is, "Erik jart e helyen is sok tarsaval". Translated to English, "Eriksson was here also with many of his companions." This

---

[5] Enjoy a better and more detailed description of Hungary and its people in the books, The Spirit of Hungary" by Stephen Sisa, ISBN:0-919545-02-5, and "Hungary and Hungarians" by S.J. Magyarody, ISBN:1-882785-23-1.

stone is on display at the Yarmouth County Museum.

We also have many runic writings dating back thousands of years, including cookbooks and many prayers.

The Scythians, Huns, Avars, and Magyars also shared a similar culture and had the same form of government, tribal democracy, where leaders were elected, and in case of war a warlord took over. Our culture predates the Bible, and our beliefs were centered on a single God. That might be the reason the Greeks and the Romans labeled us barbaric people when they encountered us in Central Europe. A prayer found written in runic alphabet around 410 AD on a Hun silver belt and displayed in the national museum of Kiev. (Kiev was originally founded by Ugyek, grandfather of Arpad who led the third wave of Hungarians into the Carpathian Basin in the ninth century.)

Our Father and God
You're within us.
We're led by your Holy Name,
Your wants are our laws.

You take our daily worries
And wear them for us.
Sins of our doings and others'
You forgive and eliminate.

Your hands guide us
Through temptations,
And you peal off our
Yoke of wickedness.

Yours is the Universe,
All powers and salvation.
From the beginning to the end,
And so be it forever.

Western Europe always labeled us as Eastern origin, equating us with Mongols. We had been the bridge between East and West for many centuries.

The first Hungarian writing using the Roman alphabet dates back to the eleventh century. Our unique language and writings dating back over many thousands of years are still comprehensible by today's Hungarians.

What other language could be understood just five hundred years later without a dictionary? We also had poets, writers, children's stories, songs, and cookbooks dating back at least two thousand years.

Ibn Ruszta, an Arabian Geographer, wrote about Hungary in the tenth century, "The Hungarians look like the Turks, and their leaders take twenty thousand horsemen to battle. Their country has many trees and plenty of water. They have lots of ploughland. The Hungarians are good looking, with strong body, well-to-do and exceptionally rich from commerce. Their clothing is made of silk, and their weapons are decorated with gold, silver, and pearls."

Byzantine emperor Wise Leo wrote in the ninth century, "The Hungarians can tolerate hard work, exhaustion, burning hot weather, freezing temperatures, and every kind of privation. They are freedom and finery loving people."

The ambassador of the Italian king Fruili Berengar (887–924) wrote about the Hungarians in 921, "Their wealth is great. They can assemble a huge military force! Military movements are guided by bugle signals.

They can ride for days by changing horses, and when the army is on the move, the land is shaking. Their fighting and courage are outstanding.

They are not afraid of death; they can die with a smile on their face! They are undefeatable."

Our universities were first established at Pécs in 1367 and at Buda in 1389. The Hungarian press was in full swing in the 1480s before the first English, Spanish, or Swedish book was ever printed. We had the second largest library in 1475, with five hundred books, after the Ferrari, which had five hundred and fifteen. The first mathematics book was written by George Mester in 1499, and Paul and John Bagellardus wrote medical books in 1472 and 1358 respectively.

Hungary was the first country to stop burning witches by the king's decree in 1096 and the first to declare freedom for all religions in 1557.

If I remember my history right, the West was burning witches up to the eighteenth century.

An expression of folk art shows up in paintings, carvings, music, and dance. Most of these art forms are registered and cataloged for the benefit of future generations. We have more children's stories than any other known country in the world. An example of culture is also shown with the high number of published folk songs. The top-three countries in the number of registered folk songs are Russia, Germany, and Hungary. The Russians have about five thousand, the Germans about six thousand, and the Hungarians over two hundred thousand.

Besides introducing new cooking methods in Europe, like dicing and boiling meat with seasoning, we also introduced eating with forks and spoons. The rest of Europe only knew roasting and eating most solid foods with a knife.

We also changed the European fashion, brought in the jacket (kazak), the long coat (kaftan), low boots with heels, underwear, and the use of buttons instead of strings to tie and hold clothing together. Even the cowboy boots are copies of the Hungarian military boots introduced by cavalry officers migrating to America after 1849. These boots were designed with pointed toes to easily slip into the stirrup and high heels to keep it there and were used by the Hungarian horsemen for centuries.

We introduced nine new breeds of dogs, three kinds of roosters and hens, even now a highly desired breed of steer and three different types of hogs (one of them is the highly priced and best liked pork, mangalica), goats, and numerous new species of pigeons.

In Holland, the tulip has been produced for four hundred years, but we have been growing it for three thousand years. The only genus of tulips that is from Europe is called Tulipa Hungarica, which originated from the Carpathian Basin. The tulip remained our national flower and our folk art's primary motif.

The very first constitution was written in Iceland in the eighth century, the second by St. Steven, king of Hungary, in the tenth century.

The style and form of the Renaissance art came from Hungary and was popularized by Austria and Germany.

The crop rotation in agriculture was first used in Hungary and later adopted in other European countries.

We successfully protected Western Europe from the Tartars and the Turks. Popes and Western statesmen referred to Hungary as the "Bastion of the West" and the "Shield of Christianity." In 1456, the pope mandated all Christian nations have to ring the church bells every day at high noon to honor the Hungarian heroes for stopping the Turkish invasion, thereby protecting the Holy Roman Empire and the rest of Western Europe.

Ottoman sultan Murad II (1404–1451) stated, "Whoever conquers Hungary will be the Lord of the world." (They almost succeeded and occupied over one-third of the country.)

Robert Johnson wrote in 1616 about Hungary, "This Kingdom had done more to reduce and hinder the ambitions of the Ottoman Empire than all the Christian nations combined."

Marzio Galeotto (1427–1497) and Antonio Bonfini, both Italian humanists, wrote about Hungary, "All European people are envious of the Hungarian Carpathian basin and its wealth; this is the reason hatred surrounds them. Hungary has the richest land, lots of fish, and huge amount of grains, and their wine is outstanding."

Not long ago, I was looking at the historical Smithsonian, where I found pictures of the emperors of Austria. The Latin and German subtitles plainly state Joseph II was the emperor of Austria and king of Hungary, but the title appeared in English as "emperor of Austria" only.

I even heard the story from a historian that Hungary, in the Western mind, reminds them of the country of Attila the Hun. Actually, Attila was well educated and spoke several languages.[6]

Historians see mostly the bad side of the Huns, and they cannot see some of the advancements and innovations they brought to the civilized world, such as their ingenuity in preserving dried meat as jerky stored under their saddles. When the Magyars joined the already settled Huns, Avars, and Pechenegs in the Carpathian Basin, they had no problem

---

[6] Read and learn about "Leadership Secrets of Attila the Hun", by Wess Roberts, PhD.

communicating among themselves.

Today, about fifteen million Hungarians live in the Carpathian Basin and the surrounding areas. There were eighteen Nobel Prizes awarded to Hungarians. There is no other nation on earth that could claim more than one Nobel Prize per million inhabitants. Similar favorable positions exist in the number of medals won by Hungarians in the Summer Olympics.

No country can match the number of medals won by Hungarians per number of inhabitants.

In addition to the Nobel Prize winners, Leo Szilard initiated and was instrumental in starting the nuclear program in the USA; Edward Teller gave us the H-bomb and later persuaded President Regan to start the Star Wars project that led to the demise of the Soviet type of communism and dictatorship.

Janos Neumann pioneered the modern electronic computers (1944) and invented the game theory. Michael Curtis (Kertesz) gave us the most loved romantic film, 'Casablanca', Alexander Korda 'The Third Man', labeled as one of the best films ever made.

In music, Béla Bartók, Ferenc Liszt, George Szell, Eugene Ormandy, George Solti, A. Rozsa, and Antal Dorati made the sound of harmony for the world's greatest orchestras.

The above people were all born, raised, and educated in Hungary, and there are many other great minds that are not well known in modern history.

It seems like the world has very little knowledge about Hungary and as a result have even less appreciation for the great and unique Hungarian history, language, culture, literature, inventions, music, and folk art.

The Hungarian nation deserves better treatment than it received after both World Wars!

Here are a few more examples of useful inventions by Hungarians:

- Janos Irinyi (1836), a Hungarian chemist, invented the safety matches.
- Donat Banki invented the carburetor.

- David Schwarz was the very first aerial navigator and designed the aluminum airship.
- George Jendrassik designed gas turbines.
- Ányos Jedlik (1861) built the first dynamo.
- Leo Szilard invented and designed the nuclear reactor.
- Sandor Just, Emeric Brody and Ferenc Hanaman invented the incandescent bulb, which are used in every household.
- Jozseff Petzval built and patented the first binoculars in 1840.
- Oszkar Asboth developed the first helicopter in 1928.
- Denes Mihaly invented the first film with sound and was instrumental in the development of television.
- First TV by Denes Mihaly (1919), and Peter K. Goldmark is credited with the first color TV (1948) and stereo broadcasting.
- Joseph L. Biro patented the most often used writing tool, the ballpoint pen (1931).
- Denes Gabor (1947) invented holography.
- Dr. Ignácz Semmelweis introduced the use of antiseptics in medicine.
- Otto Blathy built the first transformer.
- The first telephone switchboard was designed by Tivadar Puskas (1878).
- BASIC language by Janos Kemeny (1964), EXCEL by Karoly Simonyi (1974).
- 3D film with glasses, Daniel Ratai (2010).
- The first moon buggy was designed by Ferenc Pavlics (1960).
- Erno Rubik gave us the Rubik's cube (1976).
- The first automatic camera was invented by Jozsef Mihaly (1938).
- The contact lens by Jozsef Dallos (1928), and the first soft

lens contact by Istvan Gyorffy (1959).
- Diesel engine for the BMW was designed by Ferenc Ansits (1983).
- The automatic transmission for GM cars was invented by Laszlo Biro (1932).
- The unique design of the VW bug was by Bela Berenyi (1925).
- The Pulitzer prize is named after Jozsef Pulitzer (1917).
- The see-through "glass" concrete was invented by Aron Losonczi (2001).
- Gore-Tex and Fiberoptics were developed by Franz Salamon in 1970 and 1974, respectively (the most often used Hungarian invention might be underwear, as it is now adopted worldwide).

The United States of America became the first superpower with nuclear capabilities in 1945, thanks to Hungarian scientists, especially Leo Szilárd, who initiated the nuclear program. However, Communist agents soon gave away all the nuclear secrets to Russia.

The Italian-American physicist Enrico Fermi was once asked if he believed in extraterrestrials. "Sure I do," he said. "I know a lot of them personally. They are called Hungarians." Fermi's point was that Hungarians are too damn smart to be human.

For many a year, I searched for answers on why the West mistreated, made unfair treaties, and, in general, put Hungary in an unfavorable light. For example, I found no historians, diplomats, ambassadors, literatures, or any scientists who could explain or justify why the Trianon treaty primary penalized the Hungarian Kingdom and its people. We lost seventy two percent of our most valuable land, about forty percent of our population, ninety percent of our forests and mines. Yet we didn't start any wars!

Some might claim that we indirectly contributed to the cause of

Kele D. Gabor

WWI, as our justice system followed the Rule of Law. After the assassination of Franz Ferdinand and his wife in Sarajevo in 1914, the court and the judges would not give the assassin, Gavrilo Princip, the death sentence because he was not yet of legal age to be tried as an adult. Also, the fact that the Hungarian parliament would not approve a declaration of war truly infuriated the Hapsburgs and led them to feel justified in launching the war themselves.

Finally, I had a chance to read a plausible explanation by Mr. Robert Gyula Cel-Bert as to why Hungary is unfairly treated by the West most of the time. In essence, the reasons given were ignorance, prejudice, selfishness, and fear. But I will attempt to summarize Mr. Cel-Bert and a Swiss historian's points below.

Hungary, for centuries, served as a bastion of Western Europe from invading forces, especially the Turks, and for over a millennium, it contributed to the European culture in many ways: art, music, science, engineering, etc. The world should also be thankful for the 1956 freedom fighters who initiated the demise of European communism. Therefore, it is beyond logic why Hungary was so harshly penalized by the winners of WWI and after WWII. France, Great Britain, and the United States picked on a nation that had nothing to do with the start of these wars. Without any justification, they carved up our country and forced millions of Hungarians under our enemies' control. Here, they were subjugated and treated worse than slaves.

There was no justification for doing this, so the French made some up, like we mistreated the minorities and would not permit the use of their languages. This was not true, and we consider it the most hypocritical statement, as the accusation came from a nation where, in 1850, half of France didn't speak French but German, Alsace, Walloon, Dutch, Lorraine, Flemish, Breton, Catalan, Bask, Province, Italian. Fifty years later, almost ninety percent lost their mother language, as the French forbid the use of minority languages and French was forced on everyone.

The largest party leader in Slovakia, Andrej Hlinka, said on June 4, 1925, "Let the flames of the Hungarian Homeland burn bright in all our souls because we suffered less in one thousand years of Hungarian rule than the past three years under the Czech domination."

Great Britain dealt even more harshly with conquered nations like Ireland, Wales, and Scotland, and especially with people in the colonies.

The USA mostly eliminated the indigenous population, put some in reservations or resettled them, and replaced them with slaves.

The truth is that the primary countries engineering the Versailles treaty behaved as the real war criminals before WWI and continued in the same vein when the treaty was drawn up.

Vladimir Lenin commented on the Versailles (Trianon) peace treaty affecting Hungary, "This peace is forced on; this peace is extortion, peace of marauders and bandits...pillager's peace. This is not peace; these are conditions which are dictated by marauders with knife in hand for the unprotected victims."

Lord Viscount Rothermere, the publisher of the Daily News, wrote in his editorial, "Hungary's Place in the Sun," June 21, 1927, "I lost two sons in the war. They sacrificed their life for noble causes, but not for the unjust treaty for this noble nation [Hungary]. There will be no rest in Europe until the revision of this vile and dumb treaty of Trianon."

Hungary, on the other hand, was tolerant, never attacking neighboring countries, never taking part in the slave trade or subjugating people, did not massacre any minorities or killed any demonstrators.

The ill treatment of the Hungarians by Western Europe started early in history. In 907, the German bishop led the United Western European crusade against us with the slogan "Hunguros eliminandos esse!" (Eliminate all Hungarians!) Fortunately, Prince Arpad, with superior tactics but with much smaller force, was able to repel and beat the overwhelming and well equipped united army (Arpad's tactics on how to successfully fight such a superior force and win is still being taught in military academies).

In 1526, Ferenc I, the French king, as the ally of Sultan Suleiman, attacked Hungary at Mohacs. After the Turkish invasion and occupation came the Austrian colonization. All our attempts to free our land from the occupational forces were squelched by help from other European countries.

Why?

Even now, the European Union is very critical of the Hungarian government and its constitution. They falsely accuse and often penalize the nation and offer unfavorable contracts that would hurt the agriculture, import/export, and business. At the same time, they ignore the Benes doctrines, which are still in affect in Slovakia and contain many of the worst examples of human and minority rights violations. However, current attacks on Fidesz Party and the Hungarian Constitution could be attributed to the request by the Orban administration to provide accounting on who are the recipients of the huge amount of restitution paid to the Jewish community.

According to a European diplomat, the Hungarian people are still paying to over four hundred thousand restitution to Jews who were taken to the Nazi concentration camps toward the end of WWII. The audit showed that only about ninety-one thousand Jews who didn't return to Hungary, and the rest who returned got almost immediate compensation for their losses. Their total claims could not be satisfied as it exceeded the total wealth of the Hungarian nation. When the Orban administration asked for the accounting of the large amount of money sent to the US, the Jewish community refused; instead, they seemingly turned the entire world press against the Hungarian government.

According to the Swiss Historian, the general and misplaced distrust and animosity against the Hungarian people is because they were considered Eastern origin, which was feared all over in Europe, even though the Hungarians accepted the European culture, became a Christian nation, and contributed a great deal to the Western civilization for the past fifteen hundred years. However, this fear goes back fifteen hundred years, to when the Huns, Avars, and Magyars caused great difficulties for the entirety of Europe as they helped defeat the Eastern Roman (Bezant) and the Western Roman Empire. At the same time, they often deal harshly against the German, Goth, Gepid, Vandal, Frank, and Burgundy people and territories.

However, spreading hatred against the Hungarians is undeserved, but was publicized and preached by the leaders of the newly formed Holy Roman Empire. For example, the chief priest and historian of Rome, Marcellius Ammianus, started the campaign against the Huns. His propaganda was full of made up stories, lies, exaggerations, and long tails, but he has never seen, met, talked to, or known a single Hun. Unfortunately, his made-up stories and lies were readily accepted by most, including other historians. An example: Huns are the greatest enemy of Christianity, they are the friends of the devil, they live on killing and stealing, and all food is consumed raw, as they don't know about cooking, and the curing of meet is done under the saddle—they are all made up by Marcellius Ammianus.

The Huns had cookbooks two thousand years ago, which they customarily passed down in families, and they were far advanced in food preparations than the rest of Europeans. Children were taught to swim, shoot the bow, and read and write before other European children. A German commander conducting a prisoner exchange in the ninth century was shocked that all the soldiers could read and was dumbfounded when his counterpart would read off each prisoner's name from a list he wanted back.

The next waves of Hungarians in the sixth century were the even more cultured Avars and the ninth century Magyars, but they were all perceived as evil Huns.

The European fear, misconception, prejudice, and misguidance also extended to all Far Eastern people, like the Chinese, Japanese, Korean, Mongols, and Southeastern Asia also.

Therefore, the Swiss historian theory is most likely correct why many Europeans feel animosity against the Hungarians. However, we are proud of our Eastern origin and also feel no animosity against people of Europe or Asia. It is time for the rest of the world to accept us in good faith and fairness and appreciate our important function being the bridge between East and West!

KELE D. GABOR

Communist Takeover

By the spring of 1945, the Red Army drove the Nazis from Hungarian territory. The war came to an end, but the losses were staggering. Ten percent of the population had perished; the country was in ruins. People had to start a new life, and the country had to be reorganized.

In Hungarian political life, two opposing forces struggled to define the future of the country. One sought to protect the nation's independence and establish a civic democracy based on democratic traditions and Western European examples. Its supporters rallied around the Smallholders Party.

Opposing them was the "Left Block," led by the Communist Party, which presaged the Soviet-type system that would subordinate the country's autonomy to the Soviet Union.

The occupying Soviet army and the Soviet-led Allied Control Committee, which effectively had led the country until the peace treaty, backed a Soviet-type of transformation. But the great majority of Hungarians wanted to live in a form of democracy. In the 1945 parliamentary election, fifty seven percent of the voters were cast in support of the Smallholders Party, while the Communist Party received only seventeen percent. Despite the unequivocal electoral success of the Smallholders Party, the Allied Control Committee did not allow the formation of government without communist participation. In addition, they demanded that the interior ministry, and thereby the sole government-controlled armed forces— political police— be placed under communist authority. Through the political police, the leftists used any and all means, from political assassinations to terrorizing the population, to seize power. Once again, the people began to live in fear.

In 1947, when the international political situation seemed favorable, the Communist Party began to introduce an open and total dictatorship in Hungary. Torture and intimidation became part of everyday life. When the communists became concerned that their desired objectives were not being achieved quickly enough, the Soviets intervened. On February 25, 1947, the communists deported Bela Kovacs, General Secretary and MP of the Smallholders Party, to the gulag in broad daylight.

Shortly afterward, the communists organized a coup against the Prime Minister Ferenc Nagy, forcing him to resign, and then they dissolved the Parliament. In an election brought forward to 1947, the Communist Party, spearheaded by communist Minister of Interior Laszlo Rajk, ran a campaign of intimidation and, using all sorts of election fraud, received twenty two percent of the vote. This was the notorious "blue ballot" election, in which hundreds of thousands were deprived of their voting rights and two hundred thousand fake blue ballots were cast. Nevertheless, when the voters still managed to ensure the electoral victory of the civic parties, an additional seven hundred thousand votes were declared void so that the Left Block could form a government. Hungarian parliamentary democracy was thus suspended for over forty years to come.

The leaders of the opposition parties were either driven abroad or thrown in jail. With the fusion of the Communist Party and the Social-Democratic Party, new unified workers' party, the Hungarian Workers' Party was established (just like in Russia), which ultimately ended a long tradition of social democratic movement in Hungary.

A short time later, the formal leaders of the Social-Democrats were thrown in jail and party members persecuted.

The abolition of private property soon began. Industry, education, financial, and commercial services, as well as culture, were nationalized. A totalitarian state dictatorship was established. Again, we experienced the destructive nature of so-called "wealth redistribution."

Cardinal Mindszenty, Archbishop of Esztergom, head of the Hungarian Catholic Church, was arrested and, based on false charges, given a life sentence in a show trial. This trial demonstrated to the Hungarian people the Communists' lack of respect and consideration for others and that no one was safe from them. In the spring of 1949, for the first time in the one hundred and one year history of the Hungarian parliamentary democracy, voters no longer had the choice to cast their ballot for their preferred candidates. Instead, they could only vote for candidates designated by the party: members of the Hungarian Workers' Party or their comrades. Due to the increasing voter apathy, two hundred and twenty thousand "agitprop" workers tried to ensure the necessary votes.

They were aided by the State Security Authority (the Hungarian

KGB), the "first" of the party that every Hungarian came to fear by that time. In effect, the final election gave a ninety six percent win to the Communist candidates. The next free election in Hungary would take place only forty years later, in 1990.

Prior to the complete Communist takeover right after WWII, and before 1948, we were on the fast track to recovery. Most of the bombed-out buildings and roads had been repaired or cleaned up. Public transportation was in full swing; streetcars, buses, trains, and airlines were operating. Farmers, businessmen, and small stores flourished, and people started to smile again. The government gave a helping hand in tax reduction, providing ideas, goals, and incentives to recover. Leaders let people do what they were good at and put qualified men at the helm. New financial stability helped in the reconstruction. This was quite an accomplishment, as the entire country was looted and robbed, including the national treasures and the entire gold reserve was turned over to the USA for safekeeping.

The capital, where heavy fighting took place, was practically destroyed. Most of the recoveries were accomplished in three years after the war, without any financial help from the West.

The family's last hurdle of moving into our new home was accomplished in 1947, with unforeseen delays. The place was previously occupied by the Russian military but was returned when most of the occupying Soviet Red Army moved to the outskirts of the city. Our excitement and anticipation for the better and larger place turned to shock when the vacated premises of the Russian soldiers were shown to us.

We had never seen so much vandalism and damage to a beautiful building. We had seen barbaric and primitive behaviors, but the destruction of our beautiful living quarters made no sense, as they also had to live there. Even the kitchen was torn apart; oven, stove, and sink were removed.

All bathrooms and plumbing were destroyed; all tiles, plaster, washbasins, tubs, and toilet bowls were broken or removed. We could not figure out what they used for bathrooms until we went outside and found the primitive smelly holes dug and two pieces of lumber thrown over them. We couldn't figure out where and what the women used. One had to keep his balance while relieving himself. We wondered how many drunken soldiers had fallen in, as they all loved to over indulge when drinking alcoholic beverages. Even the ceilings were poked through. The only explanations we could come up with were that they must have been looking for small hidden treasures. I'm sure none was found.

By the time we finished the home inspection, we were itching and scratching ourselves all over; we must have collected every type of flea and bed bug. My mother had to wash all our clothes in hot, soapy water, and we took long baths to get rid of all the bed bugs. It took at least six months of difficult and accelerated renovation before we could move into our new place. The six months started with one week of cyanide-gas treatment under the tent for killing all the bed bugs. We had seen many buildings vacated by the soldiers of various nations, but nothing compared to the Red Army's vandalism. It was worse than a bombed-out building, as it remained clean; just the burned parts were removed and the broken walls rebuilt.

Once we got settled in our place, things started to look up. We bought new furniture, including a piano, and my mother and sisters started to play and sing again. My father was busy helping with the reconstruction.

After about a year from moving into our new home, my brother Bende had a new vision. Since I was sharing the bedroom with him, he woke me up at about two a.m. to tell me that someone visited him and asked him to leave this room and stay in our parents' bedroom till the morning. I was too sleepy to worry about his "dream," but he stayed with me until I woke up and reluctantly followed him to our parents' bedroom.

My mother woke up first and asked, "What's wrong?"

Bende said, "I had another encounter with the same person who woke me up at Udvar and showed me all the pictures in a vision. This time, there were no pictures, just a message: 'Please get up and go to your parents' bedroom and stay there until the morning.' So here I am and my brother, as I didn't want to leave him there alone." My father also woke up and asked if it could have just been a dream. My brother responded, "The person who woke me up did not say why, but let me know and feel it was very important to follow the instruction."

My father said, "Open up the fold-up bed and share it with your brother until the morning."

It was just about three a.m. when a terrible noise like an explosion woke us all up. We didn't know what happened. My brother just sat up and said, "Go and look in our bedroom." I quickly moved and was the first to arrive and opened the door to our bedroom. The rest of the family piled up right behind me and pushed me inside.

The scene was totally unexpected and unexplainable. Right over Bende's collapsed bed laid a five-centimeter-thick heavy gypsum board, covering his entire bed. We all knew if my brother had stayed in the bed, he would have been killed for sure. My mother hugged my brother and said, "Thank you, God." She added, "God wants you to live."

The broken-off ceiling piece was repaired, and the master doing the work did not want to believe that size and shape of the ceiling could just give away without someone tampering with the gypsum directly above his bed. He called it an unexplainable event and the room became an extra storage place, as none of us would ever sleep there.

We all made the grade and were accepted at the best schools in the area and started all kinds of new activities, including sports, in earnest. Music lessons, athletics, gymnastics, fencing, real football (soccer), and swimming filled up all of our limited free time, as academics were pushed hard, with lots of homework and special assignments. I remember we were lucky if we could afford the time to go to the movies two or three times a year.

The school demanded so much studying, homework, and extracurricular activities that most holidays, we had to catch up with book readings and writing reports.

Time for dating was not available. We, of course, developed good relationships with girls, mostly on a platonic level, as time and opportunity for close contact was next to impossible. However, during athletics events we could look at each other and on occasion congratulate the winners, but some who really liked each other would find ways to narrow the distance with a gentle touch. That ended up being the highlight of most relationships.

In retrospect, the occasional minimal contacts were wonderful and satisfying.

We were forced to concentrate on body language, especially the face, eyes, lips, and posture. Many of us substituted dancing lessons for a sport in the late fall time, where we could finally meet and touch girls. Since ballroom dancing was taught, where moving in tandem was essential, we had to use touch to signal the partner to change steps and turns.

The dance instructors and the girls' parents gave these dance lessons under close supervision. However, I was lucky, as mothers typically liked me enough to let me escort their sweet daughter home, either walking with or in front of us or, on occasion, following a few steps behind to keep an eye on us.

Our entire family, relatives, and friends returned to some normalcy, except for the many millions of Hungarians who had to live under Romanian, Ukrainian, Slovak, or Serbian occupation. Especially hard hit were the native Magyars, who fell into the newly expanded Serbia within Yugoslavia. The Serbian partisans wanted revenge for what the Germans did to them. They gathered people they considered undesirable and moved them out of their homes to make place for the newly arriving Serbs from Kosovo. Men were taken, never to be seen again, and the remaining family members— about forty thousand women, children, and old men— had to march in heavy snow carrying what they were allowed to take from their homes.

These were the infamous death marches in Europe, where over seventy five percent died. The partisans of Tito killed over forty thousand Hungarians.

Later, I met a young priest in a Communist prison who survived one of these marches. This type of genocide was practiced without the West knowing about it or wanting to know about it, and it was done with the full approval of Stalin. Stalin let the Hungarians know they had to shut up or suffer the consequences. Stalin said, "The Hungarian problem is a question of having enough wagons and trains to transport them out of Europe." Therefore, the final solution to the Hungarian problem, as Stalin perceived it, was to subjugate us to total Communist slavery. So began the Communist takeover.

After the war ended, the Russian occupation was in full force and the Communists tried everything to get the Hungarians to convert, without success, to socialism, a step away from communism. Unlike East Germany, we resisted the pressure to the best of our abilities, as we didn't believe in this "advanced" (truly backward) form of government, regardless of how hard the small number, but powerful Communists, worked on every level. In fact, according to statistics I could gather, we had a lower percentage of Communist Party members than in any other free country, yet we were considered a Communist state.

Many of the new Communist leaders came from Russia on direct orders from Stalin, but the most devoted followers of the new communist system were the East Germans and Jews who survived the concentration camps or came out of hiding. Unfortunately, Hungary became a magnet for the Jews from all the neighboring countries during the war years, as they were given better treatment and no internment in concentration camps.

The first commissar from Russia was Mr. Rosenfeld[7], who changed his name to Rákosi to sound non-Yiddish. He was originally a young, active Communist agitator in Hungary right after WWI and was promptly arrested after their brief bloody totalitarian reign collapsed. Mr. Rákosi was later exchanged for Hungarian flags captured by the Russian Army in 1849 when the Hungarians lost their freedom fight against the Austrian Empire because they received help from Russia. The Russian Army attacked Eastern Hungary with overwhelming force and took many Hungarian prisoners and flags. Around 1920 Rakosi was arrested for his crimes against the Hungarian people while working for the Communist Party. In the 1930s Stalin offered some of the captured loot to be returned in exchange for the Communist prisoners.

Stalin already had a plan to conquer Central Europe and had personally trained future puppets to control his satellite nations. One of the problems was that Mr. Rákosi, after spending ten years in Russia, forgot much of his Hungarian, supposedly his native tongue. He was frequently ridiculed by the Hungarians but seldom publicly for fear of dire consequences.

The Communist Party leaders, with the help of Stalin and the Red Army, wanted to convert Hungary to a socialist or pre-communist state, which soon led to a totalitarian system ruled by fear. This takeover method was not new and is still being practiced. After the election, as usual, the Communist Party had the least votes. However, behind closed doors, the winning party was forced to unite with the communists, and in a few days the entire country became the colony of Russia, led by

---

[7] Rosenfeld, meaning "Rosefield" in German, was changed from the original Yiddish name to Rakosi to sound Hungarian. In the late eighteen century, Joseph II, the emperor of Austria and king of Hungary, welcomed the Jewish immigrants as long as they changed their Hebrew names to German.

Stalin's designee, Rákosi. The leaders of the winning party conveniently disappeared.

We experienced the coming of Russian communism in stages; first, the press had to glorify Stalin and Rákosi, and then came the forced replacements of all the high leadership positions, cabinet, secret police, justices, finance. Without us knowing, our foreign representatives were also replaced, so most Hungarian ambassadors or country representatives didn't even speak Hungarian. When we called Mr. Peter, our UN representative in New York to help us during the 1956 uprising, the response to our requests in Hungarian was, "Nye ponyemoyou," in Russian meaning, "I don't understand."

The propaganda machine became unbearable. Everything that wasn't communist was evil, and blaming and finding scapegoats became the norm. The prewar Hungarian government was falsely excused of fascism, but it saved more Jews than the rest of the world combined. A new caste system was introduced— communists, workers, peasants, intellectuals, and the X-class. Practicing Christianity was a sin. Anybody caught attending religious services lost his job. Listening to Western radio stations became a crime. The clergy became the enemy of the people and were arrested, and most were sent to forced labor camps.[8]

The religious persecution reminds me of Irish and Hungarian connections.

In the church archives and record of the two countries are two martyrs because through the centuries, they suffered for their faith and fought for their independence. In spite of many persecutions, the Hungarians and the Irish have kept a love for the Mother of God. In Hungary, the Christian people venerate the Irish Madonna that is displayed in the cathedral of Gyôr. This painting—depicting a Nativity scene with the Madonna and the Child—was brought to Hungary in 1650 by an Irish bishop who had succeeded in escaping from Cromwell's persecution. On March 17, 1697, at the six a.m. mass, at the time when religious persecution had come to a head in Ireland, the Madonna cried tears of blood for three hours.

The eyewitnesses' accounts of this miracle are still kept in Gyôr and

---

[8] This type of religious persecution was not unique. The hatred of Christians started by the Jews and continued with the Romans. In the Middle Ages came the backlash in the form of the Inquisition, which was done by ignorant or evil leaders of the church. However, the Christians' persecution is still going on all around the world.

were signed by the bürgermeister (mayor), the military commander, the governor, Calvinist and Lutheran ministers, as well as the city's rabbi. Since this date, the devotion to the Irish Madonna has continued in Hungary, and large crowds come to venerate, especially on St. Patrick's Day and Ascension Day. (I also talked to many eyewitnesses of similar miracles of the crying Madonna in Transylvania after WWII, when the Romanians took control of the Hungarians living there.)

The communist government provided new incentives for snitches, who would turn anybody in with any accusation and were rewarded with half of the person's property, whether the charges were valid or not. These people became rich overnight, but most of them lost their ill-gained real estate to the state a few years later, unless they were Jewish or communist.

Soon after replacing the leadership with Communist Party members, things started to go from bad to worse. For some critical positions, the functionaries were given a choice to join the party and stay, or be gone.

After my father's repeated refusal to join the Communist Party, he also had to go. Some people gave in for the sake of family, but many of them were forced to prove themselves to be trustworthy communists by denying Christ, turning friends or relatives in, or making up false charges against undesirables. Pupils in schools could make up stories about teachers. Many good educators lost their jobs or ended up in prison. Only pictures or statues of Communist leaders, such as Stalin, Lenin, Marx, Engels, and Rakosi, could be displayed in public places.

The new court system required no judges, just a Communist Party membership. Anybody having a grudge and the "red book" (Communist membership) could have his payback just by becoming a judge in the new People's Court. There were unbelievable sentences given to good and honest people on drummed up charges. Ex-thieves, robbers, turncoats, and cheaters became the new judges and sought revenge on ex-judges, policemen, military officers, or just common people whom they didn't like.

From 1948 on, the entire country was turned upside down, and starting in 1949, the replacement of professional people with Communist Party members, regardless of their qualifications, started to show its ugly head.

Food shortages, large numbers of unemployed, and shortage of construction supplies were widespread. Even matches were hard to come by. The only construction projects were obelisks, statues for the living Communist leaders, memorials for the dead ones, or for building the Iron Curtain (fences with mine fields at the western borders).

Of course, the party blamed the former leadership for all ills, just like the liberals blamed others for everything that has gone wrong. Ex-businessmen, farmers, and leaders became the prime targets, and their homes were confiscated, with all their belongings, in the name of "wealth redistribution."

No private property was allowed except for the Communist Party members.

Atrocities continued with more fervor than before against Hungarian minorities in ultra nationalistic neighboring countries. The new puppet government of Hungary ignored all requests to object to the treatment or help native Hungarians who were caught on the wrong side of the newly drawn borders. Even the Slovaks fired all Hungarian workers and literally threw all Hungarian teachers over the new border to Hungary. The Slovak partisans killed and buried hundreds of young Hungarians, and their mass graves are just being discovered. Stalin's Hungarian communist puppet government remained silent.

New prisons had to be opened to accommodate the class of wrongdoers, consisting almost entirely of intellectual and X-classes. The political prisoners' numbers were increasing so much that a two-by-two-meter cell would contain up to four people. One of the most feared forced labor camps was built on the Soviet type of gulag at Recsk. There, thousands of innocent people suffered, hundreds died, starved, were hung, shot, and beaten to death, but their bodies were never recovered. These atrocities are still under a cloak of secrecy with the current Hungarian government.

When the few survivors complained to the international court in Strasbourg, it took them a long time to admit it was true, but no restitution was given to any of the survivors, even after some of the atrocities came to be proven. After the communist system broke down in 1989, no one was punished, no one was accused, no one was questioned, and no one was responsible for the evildoings. Why?

The real location of the Recsk concentration and labor camp was at Csákánykô for political prisoners, but no map ever showed its location.

The following information came to light after the collapse of

KELE D. GABOR

communism (1990):

The Second World War did not end collective persecution. Following a parliamentary decision, members of the German minority, the "Schwabs" were resettled— more than two hundred thousand of them. These times, again there were people who spoke up against another wave of collective discrimination, but to no avail. When the deportee lists were drawn up, the willingness to appropriate the lands and homes of the "traitor Schwabiens" played a crucial role, besides the hostile disposition toward them. During the almost two-year campaign, the humiliated, ostracized Hungarian citizens of German origin, completely deprived of all their belongings, were deported under inhumane conditions to Germany. Czechoslovakia belonged to the winning side and attempted to expel German and Hungarian speaking minorities the same way.

After the introduction of the totalitarian dictatorship, a program of persecution was launched against the Hungarian peasantry.

More than ten thousand people, referred to negatively as "kulaks," were coerced to leave their homes and land. The Ministry of Interior oversaw this campaign, keeping in mind the quotas established by the Party. The AVO (Allam Vedelmi— Government Protection Organization) was responsible for its implementation.

In the summer of 1951, and later in 1952, residents along the Yugoslav border were resettled as well. In many cases, the "unreliable elements" were taken away in the middle of the night, forced to leave all belongings behind. They were relocated by force to a different area of the country or locked up in labor camps. Those forcibly resettled lost all rights, were deprived of their retirement benefits, and could not leave their new location without permission. They were controlled day and night.

In the summer of 1951, mass resettlements began in Budapest and in the large cities around the country, such as Gyôr, Szombathely, and Székesfehérvár.

From May 21st to July 18th, in a well-prepared, large-scale

action, more than five thousand families or around fifteen thousand people were forced out from the capital. Each person was allowed to take two hundred and fifty kg of belongings with them. The communists inventoried the items left behind and made three copies. The more valuable items and furniture were appropriated to party members who moved into larger flats and villas. The rest became state property (this was called wealth redistribution).

Those of the resettled who had the most difficult fate ended up in agricultural forced labor camps called "social camps," which were surrounded by barbed wire and guarded by the AVH (Government Protection Agency) soldiers and police dogs. Prisoners were placed in sheep pens and barracks and were forced to work in horrible conditions.

Workdays were twelve hours long, and the laborers had to usually walk eight to ten kilometers back and forth to their work place camp. Due to the lack of food, the cruel conditions, strenuous work— as well as the lack of doctors and medicine— many died or suffered permanent damage to their health. From June 1950 to October 1953, around fifteen thousand people worked in forced labor camps, just around Hortobágy.

After the Soviet occupation, the new Hungarian government set up once again the conditions of internment, in secret. Internment, or "placement under police surveillance," was a type of technical means to isolate real or alleged enemies or to remove them from public life. Internment allowed authorities, primarily the political police, to place those citizens who were in the way, under police surveillance, without any restriction or preliminary investigation, on the basis of pure suspicion or political considerations. Internment was used when there was not enough proof to arrest someone. In these cases, the relevant special armed forces could take care of the situation without any preliminary investigation.

It was not only the members of right organizations, former military officers, members of the gendarmerie, those on the B list, those who were not allowed to work, the propagators of National Socialist propaganda, former political leaders, or civil servants who were interned, but anybody who was considered an enemy. Internment was a tool, which Communists with unrestricted power ambitions could use to get rid of their political enemies.

Between 1945 and 1948, in barely three years, the AVH interned forty thousand people across the country. By spring 1950, four central internment camps, much like concentration camps, were set up in Recsk, Kistarcsa, Tiszalök, and Kazinbarcika, where thousands of prisoners had to carry out forced labor. The victims worked in inhumane conditions based on techniques learned from the Soviets and Nazis, using primitive tools in the coal and ore mines and quarries, as well as in road construction and the timber industry. In comparison to the original maximum internment sentence of twenty-four months, which should have been reviewed monthly according to the law, the majority of victims served a much longer time, without their families ever receiving a sign that they were alive. The detainees, isolated from everyone and everything, were subject to the arbitrary whims of the guards, whose maxim was "The prisoners don't have to be accounted for."

In the Eastern part of the country, there were twelve so-called closed camps in operation, where people mainly from the southern and western borders were dragged off, beginning in 1948.

The decree dissolving the internment camps was issued in July 1953, after Stalin's death, and they were gradually closed down. However, investigations of certain prisoners were purposely delayed, many were transported to AVH prisons, and several hundred were only freed in 1956.

During the reprisal for the Revolution, the communists once again instituted internment and opened several former camps.

In the second half of 1961, the Kadar regime arranged for the centralization of ten thousand "unreliable individuals who were a threat to society" and their concentration in "appropriate camps" in a crisis situation.

The implementation of the plan was elaborated by the AVH's successor organization, the state security. The crisis plan for the establishment of these camps remained in effect until the fall of the communist system.

During the Communist dictatorship, those draft-aged young men who were considered "class enemies" eked out a meager living in inhumane conditions. Many noble and bourgeois scions, and also young peasants whose parents were accused of being kulaks, had to do labor service for the Hungarian People's Army. These "unreliable" people received no military training but, following a successful National Socialist model, "a special treatment." They lived in camps surrounded by barbed wire and worked in quarries, built roads, military facilities, and airports. The aim was not production, but rather the physical and moral humiliation of these youngsters.

In 1952, they counted ten thousand eight hundred and ninety nine people, which increased to twelve thousand five hundred and eleven in two years.

The Communist dictatorship, that was laid down in the footsteps of the Soviet invaders, from the very beginning considered churches as enemies and a target for destruction due to their moral and spiritual respect, and also to their financial power and internationally organized structure. The goal of the communists was to invent charges against church leaders and their institutions, which were considered reactionary and hindered development.

They humiliated the moral respect of the priests and pronounced their zeal to protect their beliefs and freedom of religion as a political crime. By forcing the churches to be financially dependent and restricting their role in religious practice, the communists tried to gradually cause them to wither away. The final goal was to eliminate the belief in God and religions and replace God with the State. The Church was considered to be a serious competition to communism that had to be eliminated. In an effort to totally subjugate the church, the communists removed those church leaders who were not ready to collaborate or who stood up against the party. I recall when priests and nuns were locked up in their church yards, but received no food or drinks for days. We could only provide limited amounts of water for them at night, stored in motorcycle inner tubes, which we could throw over the solid fence landing with minimal noise in order not to wake the guards up.

The Communist's interior minister, Rajk, issued a regulation that dissolved almost fifteen hundred civil associations. This seriously affected the Reformed church too. In 1947, certain members of this church were linked to the notorious Hungarian Community case and were accused of "plotting against the republic." The communist dictatorship began in spring 1948 to "settle" the relationship between the state and church, the so-called "separation of the state and church".

The Soviet occupiers introduced a new system that left no room for traditional values and morality— it was a Soviet world for Sovietized people.

It was alien and unacceptable for the vast majority of the Hungarian population. Religion was persecuted; the leaders of the party, Stalin and Rákosi, replaced God, and everyone had to worship them. Patriotism was forbidden; they expected Hungarian people to identify themselves with the goals and interests of the Soviet Union. Family members were turned against each other; people were under obligation to denounce their own relatives. Indeed, the Soviet child who requested the death penalty from the party for his own "saboteur" father was held up as a model. Finally, those who refused to accept all that were crushed by the terror machine, AVO, which spread its web everywhere, controlled everything, and harassed everyone. The system was operated by terror and fear.

The resistance against the Communist dictatorship spread to every level of society. Tens of thousands undertook the organization of armed resistance, or illegal printing and distribution of seditious leaflets, attempted to make connections with the West, or committed acts of sabotage. A number of people risked certain death when they collected and concealed weapons from the Second World War and were prepared to fight for freedom when the occasion would arise. Even when their death sentences were commuted, they could expect no less than life imprisonment. In ten years, between 1946 and 1956, in more than fifty cases, approximately fifteen hundred people went before the court for plotting against the state. They included fifteen- to sixteen-year-old kids who painted on the streets of Balatonfûzfô slogans such as "Hang Rákosi!" and "Death to the Communists!" as well as students who organized sabotage throughout the country and peasants who refused to deliver the food quotas to the regime. Resistance was organized throughout the country among people of all ages and social status.

As communists closed their schools, arrested their teachers, and intimidated their parents, students joined the resistance. There were military officers who could not accept that Hungary became a Soviet client state, workers who fought for their rights. Peasants persecuted as kulaks that were forced to meet delivery quotas and had to watch the AVO "sweep their lofts" also joined the resistance. Professors, teachers, and doctors who never accepted losing their political rights or who simply refused to live in fear and wanted a democratic Hungary also joined.

The Communists made everyone their enemy. It was enough to miss the People's Freedom (Nepszabadsag). There were many a newspaper including Nepszava/Voice of the People, Szabadnep/Free People, and Nepszabadsag/ People's Freedom all under government control. There was a half-hour meeting, where articles from the party's newspaper were read and discussed.

To tell a political joke, to show insufficient enthusiasm, to give money to families of the persecuted or even to publicly greet them was considered a crime, and the person becomes an enemy of the communist system.

The brave who stood up against the frightening terror were killed and buried in unmarked graves, since the Communists feared them even when dead. The Communists did everything they could to erase their memories.

Those who risked their lives for freedom of their country were called spies and traitors. We do not even know the names of many of them. Others are still smeared with Communist lies. But they are the real heroes of our time.

Unfortunately, these types of governments are still alive and well; a good example is North Korea.

In spite of the worsening conditions, my father's eternal positive outlook for the future was a tremendous help. My mother and we children didn't know about the frequent interrogations and some beatings my father had to endure in the secret police headquarters while in office and before they took his job away. He didn't give up after being replaced by a young, inexperienced communist Jewish girl and was ready to start a trucking company while farming our small ranch. Because of his unfavorable status by the Communist Party, we had to break ties with every relative and friend to keep them safe from the Communist secret police. I recently visited some relatives whom I hadn't seen for over fifty years.

Unfortunately, my father became very sick in early 1949 and died soon thereafter. He was hiding his pain and delayed going to doctors. I guess the beatings, prisons, and tortures, which started first in the 1920s by the Romanians, continued by the Nazis and later by the Communists, did wear him out, and we lost our safe harbor and rock. Our family was in shock, but so were the people who liked and respected him. During his funeral, more people showed up than the huge cemetery could hold. It was the first time I was an eyewitness to his extreme popularity. Later we found out that if he had not passed away then, the entire family would have been taken to one of the Communist concentration camps that same year.

Our father's untimely death had saved the family from the forced labor camps of no return, but living without income made our existence extremely difficult. We had to lie about our family even to get a part-time or seasonal job; the Communists would not let us attend universities or public schools.

Soon after the communist takeover, almost every prominent person was fired and replaced by card-carrying Communist Jews. We had nine ministers, and eight out of nine were Jewish. The party had to have a non-Jew in case foreign dignitaries arrived on a Sabbath. The prime minister, the head of secret service, and the head of the Communist Party were also Jewish. They continued to rob my nation of her history. New schoolbooks were printed, where only Communism, great Russia, Stalin, and his cohorts were praised. We often wondered if communism was made by or for the Jewish people, a sure and certain way to gain absolute power and control at a fast pace. The Rabbi Goldstein's stories, which will be written down in later chapters, have just become believable.

These were the times when I learned the hard way the dangers of evil leaders and evil governments who usurp power by blaming and purging the opposition, dividing people, and by fear.

Deception and Reality - Living Through the Missing Pages of History

Somewhere in Russia

Árpád, Colonel Álmos's son, finished his schooling at the prestigious military academy, Ludovika, similar to West Point. He graduated top of his class in 1938 and was invited to join the Joint Chiefs of Staff as a young officer. His only handicap was his good looks. Árpád was tall, handsome, with jet-black wavy hair, big light brown eyes, broad shoulders, and a well-toned body, soft and pleasant voice; one could go on.

Árpád was also talented in art and writing poetry (a poem to a girl's heart can be as sensuous as her lover's touch. It is hard for a man to judge another for appearance, as most men instead would prefer to look at girls).

When Árpád was wearing his officer uniform, women often turned around, looking at him as he walked by. His handsome appearance may have contributed to survival in the Siberian POW camp, but his honesty and honor led to his eventual demise and premature death in the Russian-controlled communist system. Because of his gift in art, he designed and fabricated the master emblem as a graduation present from the class to show appreciation to all the professors. Later, this experience working with metals was instrumental to buy his freedom and helped him survive and return from a Siberian prison camp.

His career had been on the right track; by 1940, he was promoted to captain, and he was also picked as one of the two representing our country in the long jump at the 1940 Olympics. Unfortunately, the 1940 Olympics were cancelled because of WWII. Most Olympians were very discouraged by the cancellation, but Árpád decided to keep training for the military pentathlon—horse riding, fencing, shooting, swimming, and cross country running.

I guess Árpád inherited his father's genes for constant working, learning, and improving one's self. I loved him like a brother, but I had no idea how much I would learn—just by associating with him—about historical facts and events, which might be contrary to what was taught or what was politically correct about WWII.

Árpád worked his way up and became a member of the pentathlon team representing Hungary, but to our surprise the Germans wouldn't accept their challenge. He did go to Italy and Spain, wherein friendly competition they always came out on top. In the 1948 Olympics, some of his younger teammates brought back the silver medal, and in 1952 the gold for Hungary.

Every member of our family was a big supporter of sports. I guess our enthusiasm for the participation came from three sources— the parents, friends, and schools. From the parents' side, my father was an avid gymnast and swimmer; from the friends' side, they were excellent fencers or sportsmen, and every school we attended had a three-pronged education: mental, spiritual, and physical training.

When the 1940 and the 1944 Olympics were cancelled, the three good friends reminisced about the 1936 Olympics, which all three attended.

They all came back happy from the experience, but were debating the pros and cons of the modern Olympics. Here are some of the historical facts, their arguments, and conclusions.

The Olympics started almost three thousand years ago. The first was held in 776 BC and was repeated every four years until a Roman emperor canceled them in ad 394. Very few, if any, events have lasted for eleven hundred and seventy years without interruption in human history. The three friends thought the secret of their success was directly related to the simplicity, honesty, fairness of competition without financial or political gain, and without gold, silver, and bronze medals as rewards.

Modern Olympics started in 1896, a little over a century ago, and there have already been three cancellations: 1916, 1940, 1944, and a couple of partial Olympics. One was in 1976 (the USA and some Western powers pulled back from the Moscow games as a result of President Carter's request), the other in 1980, when the Soviet bloc boycotted the Los Angeles games.

Modern Olympics have some advantages, as athletes don't have to compete in the nude. They're also open to women, and more new sports are added to the venue. However, media sensationalism, country nationalism, greed, and the political influence will eventually ruin these beautiful games.

The three friends believed if "medaling," or "metal-ing," became an obsession, athletes and countries would turn to advantage-seeking measures to gain unfair advantage over other competitors. They also agreed that in order to preserve the beauty, fairness, and honesty of these games, then fair judging and reporting of the modern Olympics had to turn back to the "laurel wreaths for the winners." If gold, silver, or bronze medals must be given, their significance must be diminished and just be a token of appreciation for the athletes' efforts. Also, they could make it a smaller medal and give a commemorative gold to all who participated and finished the events in an honorable way.

The three friends were right, as usual. Nowadays in the modern Olympics and other major sporting events, many athletes try to gain advantage over the other by new, undetectable doping, with drugs or blood modification.

In late 1941, Árpád was asked by his new commanding officer to submit his family background as a security measure and help promote him to major. To Árpád's surprise, he was not only denied promotion but was dismissed from the chiefs-of-staff duties in early 1942. He later found out that the reason for the dismissal was the total lack of German blood on either side of his family. This event took place about a year before the Nazis' takeover of the Hungarian government and the later invasion and occupation of Hungary.

The Nazis distrusted officers of non-German descent, so he was sent to the Russian front in 1942. He was lucky, as he was pulled back to serve behind enemy lines after one of the best shooters in the Hungarian army, Károly Takács, lost his right hand in a grenade accident, and therefore, all military members of the Olympic team were exempt to serve close to the front. Captain Takács had to learn again to shoot with his left hand and did become an Olympic champion in 1948 and 1952. Arpad, therefore, was assigned in the rear occupied territory to guard the German military supply trains from the partisans. After a year of service in the war zone and on the recommendation of a German colonel whose life he saved from a surprise partisan attack, Árpád did get his promotion to major. It was fascinating to read his handwritten memoirs about both assignments, on the front line and later behind it. For example, on the front the Hungarian units were always outnumbered by the Russians at least twenty to one. Their front line was so thin due to the long engagement line they could only assign one soldier for every twenty-five to fifty meters. After repelling the waves of Russian soldiers, they often found some of them shot in the back, and many of them had no weapons, indicating extreme cruelty by their officers. The Russian officers typically stayed behind the attacking waves, and all the soldiers captured, injured or dead, always smelled of alcohol. Most armies use alcohol before a frontal offensive leading to hand-to-hand combat, but only one or two shots per soldier.

Many Russian soldiers were actually drunk during an attack. The Germans and their allies could often tell of an impending offensive when the wind shifted toward the west and brought the smell of alcohol.

The Hungarian soldiers were so undersupplied they had to take warm clothing, boots, and some of the USA-made canned food from the fallen Russian soldiers to survive. Usually after the third wave of the failed frontal attack by the Russians, the few surviving soldiers surrendered and became forced laborers to strengthen the line of defense. Most Russian peasants and villagers preferred the Hungarian and Italian military occupation over the German, Slovak, Romanian, or even their own communist control.

The German military never gave the needed and promised heavy artillery support for the Hungarian army, as they had done for the rest of their allies. The Hungarian Army was completely void of heavy artillery due to the restrictions imposed by Treaty of Trianon after WWI. The Hungarian military attributed this less favored treatment by the Germans to the fact that our government refused to send the Jews to concentration camps. The preferred treatment of the other Axis members may be attributed to the total dependency on Romanian oil to conduct the war, and the Slovaks were the most avid supporters of the Nazi regime.

During Árpád's second tour of duty north of the Black Sea, in the region of the Ukraine, he went out in the late afternoon, just before dark, to check on one of his missing squads that was comprised of five guards.

Not finding any trace of them, he decided to stay and watch at least part of the railroad tracks until the scheduled supply train went by. Being very cautious, he worked until one of the newly arrived and inexperienced replacement guards came looking for him and started to yell his name out loud.

Before Árpád could warn him about his ignorance in a partisan country, a small caliber machine gun quieted him down forever. Árpád stayed for a while in his hiding place before heading back to HQ. He climbed out carefully and proceeded parallel along the north side of the tracks, but a good distance away. As he was slowly making his way back, he found three of his squad members, one seriously hurt and one with minor wounds. The guards told him they had followed three attractive young girls flirting with them down by the creek. They found out too late that it was a trap.

They were about a kilometer away from HQ, dragging one of the badly wounded men, when one of them heard some noise coming from the tracks. They stopped, and Árpád made his way closer to the tracks and saw the partisans setting explosives on the same side of the track. He froze and waited until the partisans left, then proceeded to dismantle the explosives. He had just finished defusing the dynamite when the approaching train, against regulations, put the high beam reflector light on fully, exposing him to anybody looking. Ten minutes later, all six were prisoners. The train went by without the expected explosion, so the partisans shot to death the badly injured Hungarian guard. Witnessing the brutal execution served its purposes— induces fear and shows extreme cruelty.

For a few weeks, he and his remaining soldiers were kept by the small band of partisans, all young people ranging in age from about fourteen to nineteen, many of them girls. The partisans seemed to be well supplied with weapons, ammunition, canned food, and clothing from the eastern side of the front, as the crossing back and forth was made relatively easy by the thinly manned front line of the German, Romanian, Hungarian, or Italian soldiers. The new prisoners carried the supplies, ammunition, food (mostly American canned meat), and extra clothes for the partisans.

One of Árpád's old guard was able to escape after a night crossing of a river, making it back to his unit, and that was how Árpád's father, Álmos, learned of his son's difficult situation in the partisan's hands.

One of the partisan's girls started flirting with Árpád. Her jealous boyfriend wanted to get rid of him, but the girl prevented his execution. Later, the boyfriend agreed to turn him over at the nearest Russian military post, just to eliminate the competition. The girl must have said something complimentary about him to the Russian post commander, as to Árpád's surprise, he ended up with the high-ranking officers holding area close to Lake Baikal in southern Siberia. He was extremely lucky, as they kept somewhat to the Geneva Conventions in treating prisoner-of-war officers.

There were a few exceptions; they had to work to earn their keep, and food and clothing replacements were less than skimpy. He and the rest of the officers, some Japanese, Italian, and a few Finns, were assigned to help build a sports stadium, hand-carrying bricks to the construction site. By the way, at that camp he never saw a German officer, and they all knew they were handled differently, all of them tortured and killed.

Árpád relayed some interesting stories about how the Japanese officers hated the work. They knew the Geneva Conventions and their rights as POWs. During the construction project, no wheelbarrows were provided, so they had to construct a two-man brick-carrying wooden platform. They used two-meter-long wooden posts and nailed one-meter-long wooden planks crosswise on the top. Two men, one man at each end, could carry a load of bricks to the construction site. They could easily stack twenty-five bricks on each, but it would have been too heavy to carry for a kilometer.

Most officers paired up only carried about twenty bricks per load. Two high-ranking Japanese officers only carried two bricks per load. One of the Russian guards got tired of seeing those two not carrying their fair share, and he sarcastically asked if two bricks were too much to carry. The answer from the officers was a definite yes, and they took one of the bricks off immediately. From then on, the two would only carry one brick at a time.

The Japanese officers gained the respect of the rest of the prisoners for their defiance. They established Mag-Ni-Fi (Magyar, Nippon, and Finn) camps command teams, and unlike the military hierarchy where the highest rank always leads, they democratically rotated officers and worked closely together to improve conditions, especially the quality of food and replacement clothing for the POWs, but with limited success. While Árpád represented the Hungarian side in the team, he became close to one of the Japanese officers who, to his surprise, knew a little Hungarian.

He picked it up from his father, who taught the Hungarian language at Tokyo University. It turned out they found more common words between Japanese and Hungarian than between Finnish and Hungarian.

When I asked Arpad to elaborate on his findings, he explained the Finno-Ugric family connection with the Hungarian language is mostly a political façade, as ours is a fully agglutinating (using many suffixes) language whose affixes are invariable and are juxtaposed instead of fused. It is a synthetic language without gender. The language is also phonetic, requiring no dictionary for spelling or pronunciation, and accents typically fall on the first syllable. These languages are Sumerian, Hungarian, Turkish, and Japanese. It was a big revelation for me, and later I found out that the Austrians and the Communists made concerted efforts to hide our culture, origin, language, heritage, and cultural superiority.

Vaitier, the French politician, wrote in the early 1900s, "The Hungarian nation's past shines, but its future should bring more glory. This nation, deserving a better destiny, was walled up by Austria to reduce access from the rest of Europe. This wall was built to give Austria a free hand to exploit, and also prevent the Hungarians' desire for independence to be heard."

Now with the help of linguistics, archaeology, toponymy (science of place names), and ancient history become more accurate, as before it was exposed to an even stronger political interference. A good example is Transylvania, which was unfortunately given to the Enlarged Romania, where all geographical places and locations are of exclusively Hungarian origin! I found a similar situation in Moldova, right east of the Carpathian Mountains.

However, history is not a required subject for reporters, as I overheard a respected news announcer to be dumbfounded over the actions of Saddam Hussein, who, in his mind, represented the center of the Babylonian and the Sumerian civilizations and cultures. It is a well-known historical fact that all of the Sumerians migrated north, west, and east at the beginning of a New Stone Age and were instrumental in spreading higher civilization all over Egypt, Greece, Rome, and Central Europe. The Persians and Arabs replaced the indigenous population of Sumerians, starting about five thousand years ago. Now that the Sumerian writings on clay tablets are readable, the linguistic relations to Hungarian are obvious. Even some of the old cities and place names in Mesopotamia (Babylon) and Hungary are duplicated, and as a result, the "historians" guided and led by the political machine had to change their tunes.

Árpád slowly learned enough Russian to become the amateur translator for the rest of the POW officers. He befriended the camp commander by providing engagement rings, the most important commodity to win sexual favors from young girls in the nearby towns. The camp commander, and later the guards, provided him the tools and the yellow copper wire to make the rings. I have seen these beautiful wedding bands made out of copper wire, and I was amazed how much they look and feel like the real gold ones. I asked Árpád how he kept it from oxidizing and changing color, especially the green copper oxide, and he just said, "It is my trade secret." He never revealed it to me, but he said he would pass it on to his children. Unfortunately, to the best of my knowledge this and many other secrets died with him.

On a few occasions, the POW camp commander took him along to nearby towns and villages, before his clothes got torn up and the heavy winter came. It seemed like the Russians were using Árpád as bait to attract good-looking women. Men were at a premium those days, especially the young, healthy, and the handsome. All able-bodied men were away fighting in the war. The rest were injured, captured, lost, or too old.

In many places, the women outnumbered the men two hundred to one. During the cold winters, the POWs could not wash. The water pails froze without heat, and the danger of freezing prevented them from cleaning up. The smell got to them, but when their clothes got worn out, no replacements were given, and they had to protect themselves from the extremely cold Siberian winter. After many of the prisoners suffered serious frostbite, they were given some seal fat from the guards, which they used to cover their entire body, especially the exposed skin. Once a week, when they could not take the smell of rancid grease and sweat, they started to scrape the old fat off to replace it with the less smelly one. The only good tool they had was a worn-out razor blade they got from the guards. Being there for the entire duration of two winters and having to shave their entire body every week resulted in profuse body hair. Those that made it out from the camp developed quite a bit of hair all over their body.

After his return from the POW camp, I remember Árpád as the hairy monkey man.

WWII officially ended for the Hungarians on April 4, 1945; however, at the Baikal POW camp, they didn't let the prisoners leave until all the many wagonloads of bricks were moved to the sport stadium site. Arpad and the few remaining Hungarian officers were released first. Since his fellow officers were all married, they hurried home using any means to travel, as no transportation was provided. So many of them worked their way back to Hungary within a year. Some were never seen again or rearrested right after homecoming. Árpád decided to take his time and take a scenic way home. With his linguistic curiosity and Russian language knowledge, he felt confident enough to track down and investigate the remaining Hungarian groups who had not migrated west but stayed by the Ural Mountains or just stayed east of the Carpathian Mountains.

I asked if it was the Japanese officer who talked him into this new adventure. Árpád said, "No. Back at college, when I read from Sir John Bowring's writings, the famous English linguist and statesman, I decided to do whatever I could to find the roots of our people, as historians just read and extrapolate." I told him I never heard of Sir John Bowring.

Árpád went on, "Sir John Bowring spoke several languages, among them Hungarian, and translated Hungarian poems to English. He also studied the origin of languages, and after long research, he wrote, 'The Hungarian language is unique, it stands by itself, it developed on its own, more logical than others and reaches way back in history, surpassing all the other languages of Europe today. Most other languages, including English, are a combination of many, and the rest of them are borrowed, imported or based on others.'"

Árpád further explained that according to Sir John Bowring, the Hungarian language stands by itself like a piece of basalt, which was not marred or weathered by time or history. It is independent, does not take from or give to others, but it is a living monument of mental superiority, independent and free, the oldest and most praiseworthy. There are many wonders in the world that cannot be explained or replicated by modern men, including the pyramids, the single piece of rock that serves as the roof on old Egyptian churches— where it came from, how it got there, how it was raised. The Hungarian language is even more mysterious, and whoever will discover its origin may have to reach way back and touch upon the biggest secrets of the world.

I told him I was impressed, and I wished him success in his ambitious endeavor. Árpád was not discouraged, just said, "I'll continue with my studies after my retirement and will be better equipped to find the origin of our language and culture." When I asked him what more he needed to learn, he responded, "In order to achieve my objectives, I have to learn and know more about archeology, as it is based on science and evidence, unlike history."

Kele D. Gabor

With Árpád's roundabout travels, it took him well over a year to get back home. He took his time, as he had no way of knowing his letters or the special messages he sent along with his fellow officer friends never made it back home. His father, sister, and the rest of the family and friends had just about given up on him when he finally showed up in June of 1947.

He was one of the lucky POWs, as many Hungarian soldiers and officers never made it back, or when they did, they were promptly rearrested, put on trains, and taken back as forced laborers to Russia again.

Árpád's reports on his Russian tour were fascinating. Right after they let him go, he put about twenty engagement rings, which also served as wedding bands, in his pockets. Then he started to backtrack to the town where his prison commander took him. He took a job to get enough money for clothes and clean up. It took him over a month to get the necessary money for used clothing that would fit him, a backpack, good boots, hat, coat, and his thick notebooks. He didn't need much help finding a bed. He ended up trading some rings for food and rail tickets. In the summer of 1945, the Lake Baikal and the southern Ural Mountains looked exceptionally beautiful. He raved about them so much I have made a special effort to watch every nature and expedition film about Southern Siberia.

Once he arrived at a station of a bigger town close to the Urals, he would continue on foot to close-by villages. He was particularly interested in villages where they spoke other languages besides Russian. He was amazed to find out that over one hundred and fifty languages are spoken in the Soviet Union.

He toured both the eastern and western side of the Ural Mountains and did find some villages speaking similar but definitely not the Hungarian language. His notebook was full of village and people's names, maps to homes, Hungarian-like words, and their meanings. He would seek out village elders to talk to and collected only about twenty words that matched the Hungarian word base (e.g., vad (wild), bika (bull), csecse (cute), marha (valuables), sziv (heart), viz (water), to mention a few).

He did eventually find an old lady who could sing some Hungarian ballads.

She came from Chechnya in the Caucasus, while her deceased

husband was from Moldova close to the Szeret River— and they could communicate with each other in their Hungarian-like mother tongue. This he found amazing, as he heard the Basks may be a remnant of the army of Attila the Hun but could not imagine Hungarians living close to, and as neighbors of, Armenia. He knew that Avars also settled in what is Southern Germany, and that is why they look, speak, dress, cook, carve, and live differently from the Northern Germans. Now Árpád thought he had to turn south to visit Chechnya for new discoveries. He never made it to the Caucasus, as he was rearrested in the Moscow Metro. They took all his remaining rings and locked him up, as he had lost his release papers somewhere.

He just about gave up on getting out when a young woman with two small children, where he spent a night before in the outskirts of the city, came to reclaim him. It turned out she hid his release papers to keep him, and when he left she actually followed him until he got to the Metro station. She may have initiated and definitely witnessed his arrest, but she was unable to obtain his immediate release from the military police.

Her persistence finally paid off; she was able to persuade the prison commander to release Árpád into her custody by showing his release papers from the POW camp.

This time, good luck was on his side. Only for two weeks did he have to play the new father and new husband routine in the family. One morning, the young lady rushed home from her work place, returned his papers, and told him to get out and leave. She also told him her long-lost husband had been found and was coming home today. Árpád didn't want to take any more chances, and he slowly worked his way back home, avoiding contacts, especially with the opposite sex.

Upon his arrival at home, the celebration was unbelievable; his father put on a welcoming party the likes of which the city had never seen. His father, Álmos, invited all the eligible young girls from all around town. The party lasted all day and night. Álmos wanted his son to settle down with a wife and hoped, a little later, to have some grandchildren. Even Father Tibor was invited and came for a short stay, still carrying his constant companion: the beaten up dark gray umbrella.

Árpád didn't find a suitable lady for himself at the homecoming parties but kept on looking. He did finally meet Éva, one of the attractive young ladies in town. She didn't come to the party, as she was already engaged to be married to someone else. She was a dark brunette, with large bluish green eyes, her wavy hair just long enough to cover the back of her lovely and feminine neckline; she walked like an angel and had an almost perfect body with a beautiful, symmetric face. As Árpád phrased it, "Just what the doctor ordered." They first saw each other at a public swimming pool about a week after his return.

I adopted Árpád as my big brother and often sought out his company.

I was spending one Sunday afternoon with him, doing our favorite activities, swimming, but mostly watching girls. While he was doing his turn to explore possibilities at the pool, I was reading his notebooks about his travels and discoveries in Russia. He had a lot of detailed notes, but they were hard to follow without a map. I was looking for stories about his encounters with the opposite sex, but unfortunately, all his notes were relating to places, tools used, eating utensils, carving, painting, decorations, folk dresses, folk songs, Hungarian words used by the Ural Altaic people, descriptions of their buildings and complexions with facial features, and a few songs where either melody or the words had a commonality in meaning, scale, or sound (the Hungarian melodies are in a unique scale of five instead of seven, just like the American Indian songs. Also, there are only five regions on Earth where this unique musical scale is found and used:

 (1) The entire Carpathian basin and around the Ural Mountains.
 (2) Far-East Western China and Japan.
 (3) A small part of central Africa.
 (4) American Indians. and
 (5) And a few in Scotland).

Here and there, I found a few verses of poetry intermingled with his research notes. I was just reading about a burial procession for a young mother and the unique head markers (kopja), the type used even today by the Transylvanian Hungarians, when Árpád reappeared. He had a huge grin on his face and said, "I just saw the girl I'll marry."

I immediately wanted to see her, and he obliged by taking me to the grassy hillside, away from the pools, where she was lying on her tummy reading a book placed between her propped up elbows and a boyfriend right next to her. While we observed, he was telling me about how she looked standing up and walking to get a drink. She was very shapely and her muscle well-toned, as we found out later that she was a physical education teacher in the local girl's high school.

Arpad said, "I looked into her eyes, and she turned her head." When I got to the drinking fountain, I sneaked another look while drinking and noticed she turned around and watched me taking a sip. The problem was that in those days, one needed a formal introduction to any lady before popping a request for a date. We went back, and he just sat there motionless, deep in thoughts, not even answering my many inquiries about his notes and about his travels in Russia. He explained, "I'm writing a poem in my head so when there is a chance, I can recite it to her."

When the boyfriend took a break, Árpád got up calmly, went and sat down next to her. From where I was, I could not hear a word, but I could tell she sat quietly while he was doing the talking. About a few minutes later, I could see her smile, and they shook hands, indicating that some kind of an introduction was taking place. Árpád was still there talking to the young lady when the young man returned. Árpád stood up, and after a few seconds, they shook hands while the young lady was talking. I was sure she introduced Árpád to her boyfriend.

When Árpád returned, he had that winning smile and look that now I call "the best of James Bond smile after a mission accomplished." I was terribly curious, wanting to know what happened and learn the technique about how to start conversations with ladies of my choice without violating the rules for gentlemanly behavior by not having been formally introduced.

He simply said, "As always, I find the attractive features of women and only tell them the truth."

I asked, "And what was that truth?"

He explained he just went and told her he had just got back from a Russian prison camp, had traveled a lot around Europe and Asia, and she was the most beautiful and most attractive lady he had ever seen and he had to see her again. I said, "You were talking much longer." He continued, "Yes, and I recited the poem I made up about her when I looked at her from the drinking fountain." It was a lovely short poem, but I couldn't recite it.

His pleasant voice, his handsome look, and the poem did it. Éva told me later it was a winning combination that was hard to resist. They met again that Sunday evening in a nearby bakery serving coffee, milk, and delicious pastries. They were married a month later on the same day she and her ex-fiancé would have exchanged the "I dos".

While Éva and Árpád were on honeymoon, he received the notice that the new Hungarian Army, entirely under Russian Red Army control, would be happy to take him back with his old rank, and the Army would be happy to get an experienced and professional officer back in service.

Because of Árpád's Russian language knowledge, he first served as an interpreter between the Russian high command and the newly created Hungarian Army. He told me that on a few occasions, he met some high-ranking Russian officers, among them Marshall Zhukov, who claimed to have Hungarian blood, as his mother was Hungarian. The general also claimed he was instrumental in stopping Stalin from shipping most of the Hungarian population to Russia.

The new army and command wanted him to join the Communist Party, but he kept delaying until they fired him, as the Nazis did before. The push and pressure to become a member of the Communist Party was horrendous at that time. The party was desperate to get at least eighteen percent of the voting public under its wings. Once a Communist Party member, he may only vote for the party's candidate. Once they achieved the seventeen percent, they forced a merger with the winning party with over fifty percent of the vote to take control.

It took them over four years after the war to get to the minimum threshold, and they accomplished it in Mafioso fashion. People were under extreme duress to keep their jobs, feed their families, or save family members from being arrested or unexpectedly disappearing. Beatings of grown men or imprisonment of innocent people were common, especially for the clergy. I know of a case where a young nursing mother was kept from her infant until the husband joined the party. They only went to extremes like this when they really needed a person's experience, knowledge, and was very popular.

During Árpád's stay in the military, he became a central depository for diaries, logs, and notes from deceased, imprisoned, or disappeared officers and ex-government employees. The big copper container by the door to his apartment served as a central receptacle for all these mostly handwritten historical documents, which were dropped off by the surviving family members, usually the wife or daughter. He never understood why he was entrusted with such important and historical documents. The Communists hated books or any written material, including photographs that contained an individual's observations during the war years and the period immediately following them.

These reports and documents contained all kinds of eyewitness reports, including experiences on the Russian front, the bombing attacks, the successful escape of Jewish people from Slovakia and Croatia to Hungary, the cruelties committed by the partisans, Serbs, Slovaks, Romanians, German, Czechs, and Russian military, including the Gestapo and KGB against Hungarians and German people during and after WWII. Possibly the most cruel were the Avengers, the Jewish paramilitary, to pay back for the treatment they received in the Concentration camps.

One short report even included a doctor experiencing the Allied bombing of Dresden. Possession of these kinds of writings of eyewitness reports in the Russian-controlled communist system constituted a grave crime and was punishable with long prison terms or death.

Since the very first notes Árpád received were the

observations of his highly respected commanding officer while serving on the Russian front, he read and hid the general's notebooks. However, when more and more other eyewitness reports showed up in his container, he had to find a way to hide them safely. He was not only worried about himself but his beautiful wife and infant son. One Sunday afternoon, he pulled me away from the dinner table and asked me to be his secret courier. I happily complied out of respect, wanting to protect him and his family, and it was another opportunity to save important historical documents that contradicted the official record. He already had over twenty documents when I carried out my first delivery.

Álmos, Árpád's father, now a semi retired veterinarian, dedicated his free time to building violins. In the corner of his small workshop stood a large wood-burning stove. It was round, about fifty centimeters in diameter, and about one and a half meters tall. The logs were fed in on the top of the stove and the lower half, where all the ashes fell. Uncle Almos made a metal round box to fit on the bottom of the stove that came only about three centimeters above the lower access door for the ash removal.

We opened the bottom door and turned the metal box until the two centimeter-high slot (like on a mailbox) appeared, where we deposited all the notebooks, letters, and photographs one by one. After dropping them in, we turned the round box so the slit didn't show. Right above this round box, one could easily reach in and take out the ashes.

Since Álmos lived about twenty kilometers from his son, I took these eyewitness reports, mixed them in with my schoolbooks, put them into a backpack, and bicycled them over to the woodworking shop. On the way, usually on Saturday or Sunday afternoon, I often stopped to cool off in the shadow of a big tree by the roadway. Invariably, I looked for notes from high-ranking military officers. Sometimes I had to scan all the notebooks to select reading material that interested me. I found one I kept until the next delivery, just to make sure I was reading the personal notes from a Hungarian general reporting to the German high command.

DECEPTION AND REALITY - LIVING THROUGH THE MISSING PAGES OF HISTORY

The notes were handwritten, often with pencil, and it was a real challenge to decipher some of the pages. However, I was able to make out a lot of interesting stories about the single-minded German tactics in conducting the war and handling the Russian front. It showed how the German high command only believed in forward thrust, no feint or tactical retreat.

According to his notes, the German general's staff would not listen to the Hungarian general's advice in shortening the front line and taking defensive postures when the attacks stalled for any reason. This blind faith in the German military superiority cost them many lives, equipment, and territory, in capturing Moscow— over two hundred thousand POWs in a single encirclement by the Russians, and ultimately the Eastern war. They just forged ahead, ignoring overstretched front and supply lines.

According to the notes, contrary to the Hungarian general's advice, the Germans pushed east all the way to the river Don. It may have been a clever defensive move by the Russians, just like against the French forces during the Napoleonic Wars, to let the enemy overreach its supply lines.

Once the German Army reached the river Don in 1941, their fate was sealed because of thinly manned front lines and the well-coordinated partisan attacks to cut most of the supply lines. The notes listed all the important missing supplies, from warm clothing to ammunition. Many soldiers went hungry and froze to death, but the German generals didn't know how to retreat and would not listen to better judgment or reasons. It was obvious from the eyewitness point of view that the Germans lost the war; the Russians didn't beat them until the American equipment and supplies propped up the Red Army.

Other interesting documents included the Hungarian government's resistance to the German occupation. It was the Hungarian agricultural press that printed the military furlough papers and letters of release for Hungarian soldiers from their German military duties. There were thousands of these papers printed with the necessary stamps and signatures, only the person's name and rank had to be added on the top line. The government press that was reserved for agricultural publication kept printing these furlough letters at night and used government employees as couriers to deliver them to trusted Hungarian military officers. According to the report, only about two thousand military men were saved from the Germans. Later, many of them were taken away by the Russians as forced laborers once the Red Army moved in. Some of the eyewitness reports gave explanations for the disappearance of the thousands of Hungarian men who were shipped to Uzbekistan, Kazakhstan, or other sparsely populated Russian states far from their homeland— or to the gulag in Magadan.

One of the saddest papers I read was written by a doctor who was one of the few who survived the Allied bombing attack on Dresden, which had been declared as a shelter city for women, children, and the injured.

The doctor was assigned as one of the hundreds of surgeons to help rehabilitate the badly injured civilian people from previous bombings of other cities. I had already seen a lot of horrible events by that time, but I could not finish his report. I stopped reading it after the doctor described the burning women, children, and patients that could not escape the attack as the English used firebombs with phosphorous. Besides photographs, he described the smell and the scraping of burned tissues, the facial expressions on the burned infants. He personally counted hundreds of women killed while trying to protect their babies. While searching for survivors, he took photographs for later identification purposes (evidently, many women with children would go to Dresden, the only city internationally declared to be a safe place). The doctor also lost his wife and their two sons during the attack.

The second half of his paper dealt with a camp where medical experimentation was conducted on Jewish girls who were twins. The team of doctors included many well-known Jewish physicians. The doctors wanted to find a way to help the German girls have multiple births. After a few weeks, this Hungarian doctor could not take the treatments of the unwilling participants, so he walked away and went to Dresden. When he inquired about these types of camps, he found no one in Germany knew about these hidden labs. Finally, a Nazi officer confided in him and told him about the existence of other similar camps. The Nazi officer invited him in order to show off his lamp collection, where all lampshades were made out of human skins, but only half of them were from Jewish people, as he explained that all enemies of the Third Reich are treated the same.

There was a cover letter with documents attached on "Statistics of the Concentration Camps" in German. The letter was an example of how the Germans were fanatic about accurate record-keeping. According to the attached report, the total number of deaths in all the concentration camps as of April 1945 was actually less than a million (much less than the six million claimed). This death toll included all inmates of all nationality from all causes including diseases or old age. The letter also stated that these reports were confiscated and they were not to be published.

However, further investigations at later dates also validated the letter. For example, in 1938, there were fifteen million six hundred and eighty eight thousand two hundred and fifty nine Jews in the world according to the World Almanac; and in 1948 there were eighteen million seven hundred thousand Jews in the world according to the New York Times. If the reported six million Jewish deaths is correct, in ten years the Jewish population had doubled. This would only be possible if every living Jew was cloned or every Jewish girl had at least five children (according to Raul Hilberg, there were five point one million Jewish victims; however, he might have counted twice in certain cases and included the non-Jewish people who lost their life during World War II.

I even found a short notebook by a disillusioned Communist Party member. His name was Stephan Black (translated), and he used to teach French in the foreign language school. He spent some time in France before WWII and as a young intellectual was quickly converted to communism. As he put it, "I was infected by a beautiful actress in Paris." According to him, it was a simple conversion, as many smart, intellectual, or socialist thinkers can get the virus of communism, as it is spread among people who think with their hearts and not with their brains.

The only reason I finished reading his notes was because I

was proud of the fact that no one could ever infect me with communism, socialism, or liberalism, and his handwriting was exceptionally nice and easy to read. In summary, he described his long fight with illusions and reality and how he went through a long stage of disillusionment in the Party, as he wanted to believe it so much until his young indoctrinated son turned against him.

According to Stephan, the most susceptible people to conversion to communism are the poor, uneducated people, the young ideologists, actors, actresses, artists, reporters, writers, professors living in the ivory towers far away from reality and people without strong convictions or religion. However, that is not the problem. The real problem, he claimed, were "the higher-ups using their job and position to spread this horrible socialist disease and willing to keep it going as long as humans will inhabit the Earth."

I hope he was wrong in assessing the situation, as I pray that through better education, and with a dose of reality, these lost souls will come to their senses. We should be more responsible for our own actions, as human weaknesses will prevent us from building a perfect society anyway, and communism/socialism, even in theory, is far from being a realistic approach to any form of government. However, I wish more schools and universities would teach how to think instead of what to think.

The next handwritten note started as a funny story because it was obviously written by someone who spoke Hungarian very poorly. Soon it became evident that it was possibly the saddest of all, as it was written about the Jews' payback on what Hitler did to them, written by a Polish lady. It talked about the concentration camps set up by the communists for German people on the territories that the Red Army liberated. One particular camp mentioned was located in Silesia, with a relatively dense German population. According to her, Stalin requested Jewish commanders for each camp to make sure all the German, innocent or not, women and children get a taste of what the Jewish people had to go through.

However, this was not an eye for an eye, but worse. It described German girls gang-raped starting at age thirteen and tying boys to posts and having their male organs chewed off by specially trained dogs. When blue-eyed and blond girls got pregnant, they doused their hair with gasoline and lit it. Few survived this treatment, but some survived with terrible head burns.

The author claimed that hundreds of thousands, if not millions, of German descendants were similarly mistreated, killed, and disposed of all over the Communist-conquered territories, especially Ukraine, Czechoslovakia, Poland, Moldova, Prussia, and Galicia. The descriptions were so horrible I had to stop reading it in spite of the beautiful feminine handwriting. Surprisingly, she didn't know about the Jewish Avengers, the paramilitary groups formed to kill German people indiscriminately to pay back for the Holocaust after the war was over.

My excitement grew when I encountered a German officer's gray map carrying pouch with a swastika on it, as I collected military maps during the war until the Russian officer found them and confiscated them all.

However, instead of military maps, I found the most shocking well-used notebook with a long list of people who could be trusted to cooperate with the Nazis. Each page was stamped with 'SECRET' (GEHEIM) and a swastika. I would say the list included about a thousand typed names with telephone numbers or some handwritten codes, and at the end I found organizations with a person's name attached. The most distasteful part was that at least ten percent of the names listed were Jewish (nowadays it's hard to tell, as most Jews changed their names to sound Hungarian). However, Mr. George Soros's name was left off, in spite of his known anti-Jewish activities (Maybe Eichmann didn't want his adopted son's name on the list). The paper also included organizations like "Committee to Protect the Jews," "Jewish Defense League," and "Save the Jewish League," and one of the group leaders was a Zionist called Herr Gruenboum ("Mr. Green-tree").

I concluded that this pouch must have belonged to a very high-ranking Gestapo officer and I could not understand why it wasn't encrypted.

However, I never came to terms with the fact that over four

hundred thousand Hungarian Jews were shipped to Germany by the Nazis, leaving another four hundred thousand behind, but not one of them shipped was ever chosen by the Zionist group or were found worthy to go to the Holy Land. The tragedy was that out of four hundred thousand plus shipped to concentration camps from Hungary, almost ninety-two thousand of them never returned, and many of them may have perished. It seems to me that the Zionist group agreement with Hitler and Eichmann to pick and choose who are qualified for the Holy Land left hundreds of thousands to die in concentration camps. The Zionist elite likely chose the rich and people of superior intellect with Zionist ideology and must have not cared enough about the other ninety eight percent. The group of only sixteen hundred and forty eight people who founded Yishuv (which became Israel in 1948) in Palestine never made the selection process or the list of names public. Trying to put myself in their place, I would have rescued as many of my people as I could!

All in all, I transported at least fifty reports in the forms of letters, notes, documents, and photographs. I now regret I didn't read them all. I even found a single letter in an enclosed envelope, detailing how Hungarian POW officers were assigned to a concentration camp liberated by the American army to build small cement structures right after the war ended. Before the cement dried, reporters and photographers were brought in to take pictures of the new buildings as Nazi torture or cremation chambers.

The letter was signed by a total of seven officers, with their oath that the text in the letter was factual and true. After reading similar eyewitness reports and hearing exaggerated Jewish claims, I often wondered how much of their plight and suffering was overstated.

As a young man, I was always in a hurry, combining these outings with girl watching and swimming instead of reading these very credible accounts of personal experiences and observations of important historical events.

When my uncle Álmos died, I went to retrieve these documents in spite of the danger involved in having any of them in my possession, but by the time I got to his small workshop, everything had been taken away, even the half-finished violins, all his woodworking tools, and the wood burning stove. I eventually tracked some of the woodstove parts down to a garbage dump, where I was told the iron parts were shipped to a foundry to make steel, as it had a huge crack due to mishandling. This was a better ending than all those incriminating records, eyewitness reports, and historical documents ending up in the wrong person's hands, such as in those of a communist sympathizer.

Árpád was out of work for a long time, as securing a job for an ex-military officer and non-party member had become a real task. Éva, his wife, was already expecting their second son when he finally landed a civilian job working as an architectural draftsman. When the Russians built their military airport, he was assigned there and worked both as a translator and as the technical leader. Again they asked him to join the Communist Party, which he declined, believing his technical and linguistic skills would be enough to keep his job. His idea worked till 1952, close to the end of the project, when he was charged with aiding in the stealing of construction material. He knew which communist chief did it, and he was able to prove it. However, they kept him in prison for not reporting it to the 'right' authorities. These kinds of drummed up charges were common and encouraged in those days.

During the Hungarian Revolution in 1956, Árpád was released from prison and was free for a while, but his wife with their older son were able to leave the country to go to Canada. The smaller child had to be left behind and was brought up by the grandparents, never knowing his birth mother was in Canada or how hard his father worked to find him. Árpád, in his search of his family, was arrested again and put back in prison. When the Russian puppet government finally released him, he was permanently marked as an undesirable and distrusted character by the Communist Party, just the opposite of what every other person thought of him— a very trustworthy individual, trusting him with historical and secret documents.

He attempted to reclaim his younger son, but the relatives discouraged him from even visiting him, as they were afraid of potential problems because of the father's political standing. His younger son didn't find out who his real father and mother were until after Árpád died under somewhat mysterious circumstances.

Kele D. Gabor

After his release from prison, not finding his wife, two sons, a place to stay, or a job, he accepted a young lady's offer of a temporary shelter.

In spite of the forced-labor camps and the harsh treatment by the Communist system as a criminal, he recovered fast, looking healthy and handsome even with his gray hair. He became a streetcar driver through the help of another lady acquaintance. He spent his free time carving and writing poetry. I saw some of his carvings, which rivaled the best of any sculptor, and read the lovely poetry about his lost wife, family, sons, homeland, and freedom. He kept most of his poetry and carvings private but did show some poems and carvings to some people close to him. I was one of the fortunate and lucky ones who had seen them all, as he proudly showed them to me in 1966.

It shocked me how sensitive of a soul he became, the pain and suffering resulting from the loss of his family and country. I was a man with a family of my own, but I could not keep my tears back while reading his poems. It was so unexpected of a strong military man with a battle and prison-hardened soul. He burned one of his wooden statues right in front of me, a beautiful carving of his wife, as he didn't want anybody else to see her nude figure. Before burning it in the fireplace, I tried to stop him, but he said, "She will remain with me in my memory, as I cannot forget her ever, but since you always appreciated her, you are the only one who could see her statue before I destroy it." This was the last time I saw Árpád alive.

His long-lost Éva returned from Canada, partly from being homesick, but primarily to reclaim her second son. Once Árpád found out the good news, he wanted to reunite his family. Soon after his jealous girlfriend found out about Éva's return, he died of food poisoning and the resulting intestinal complications. Éva had to go through double torture, as she did not only lose her husband and her second son but also her freedom. The Communist government imprisoned her for being either a traitor or a spy for the capitalists. The Communists could not fathom or understand that the love of her family, her left behind infant son, brought her back home.

It hurts me deep inside that his sons never knew their father or received any of the things he carved and wrote for them. I have seen the sealed envelopes with his sons' names on them, which also contained the secret for keeping copper rings from oxidation. To his sons, he must have been only an enigma. I wish they had been told the truth so they would appreciate and be proud of their father. Unfortunately, the girl he lived with forced open his large footlocker, passed these beautiful things to her relatives, sold them, or burned them. What a waste!

Unfortunately, many Hungarian families were broken up, forcefully separated, or deported, leaving many orphans after the communist takeover. Some of these orphans, educated in communist schools without God, morals, or religion, became the meanest freedom fighters against the Russians during the 1956 Hungarian Revolution.

KELE D. GABOR

Existence under Communist Control

It was the first Saturday of July 1950, early in the afternoon, when Father Tibor bicycled over to our home. He came to see how our family was coping with the loss of our father. It was exactly a year after our father died.

My mother was still devastated. She stayed in bed most of the time in the dark, not wanting to see anybody. Since my father passed away, my sisters stopped singing and my mother had not played a note on the piano. In fact, she traded it for a large can of butter (US military issue). The trade was made between my mother and the local Communist Party leader's wife. She needed the piano for her daughter, and we needed the food to survive. We made the trade knowing well the can of butter came from the American Red Cross for the flood victims along the Danube. Most charities didn't care to follow up where those goodies ended up. Like most of the Western foreign aid ends up in the wrong hands and does not go to the intended recipients.

Many of our family games stopped, and so did the sibling rivalries. One of the mean games we used to play with our sister was to take advantage of her power of concentration. She was an avid reader, and when she was involved in a story, no noise, yelling, or screaming could disrupt her concentration, except calling out her name. She became totally absorbed in her activities and also oblivious to events outside her domain. When we wanted to be mischievous while she was reading a book on the rug, we would put a chair over her then yell out her name. Being totally oblivious to our prior activities, she just jumped up and knocked herself against the bottom of the chair. We laughed, as we thought it was funny. Games of nine man's Morris, chess, football, tennis, ping-pong, ten-words, and all the other games stopped. With the piano gone, we boys also stopped playing. The entire house became a place of mourning. It was hard to lose almost everything that provided some financial security, our country, and our rock—the beloved and highly respected father.

In those few years, nothing was funny. Western powers traded one third of Hungary for one-third of Vienna. The Allies were supposed to occupy the western part of our country, but the Russian foreign politicians outsmarted the Western diplomats. Stalin, with the help of Molotov, the Russian foreign minister, very smartly offered to come out of the partially occupied Vienna and the most eastern part of Austria if he could have the whole of Hungary. Our homeland was now totally under the communist and totalitarian rules. Pieces of Hungary ended up under Ukrainian, Slovakian, Romanian, Serbian, Croatian, Slovenian, and Austrian rules. The carving up and mutilation of Hungary was complete. No one with power to stop the subdivision of my country had read Payot's warning, "Hungary is a wonderfully unified geological concord, where all areas are synthesized and dependent on each other and not separable without hurting its entirety."

The indigenous Hungarian population taken over by the new countries lost most of their freedom, except in Burgenland, which was given to Austria. Now I had relatives in every taken part of Hungary, so our family became truly international and members of one of the largest minorities in Central Europe. In the expropriated Hungarian territories, our schools were closed; we were discouraged from communicating in our mother tongue in public places. The occupying countries slowly converted the Hungarian geographical names to "sound alike" or just translated the names of cities, towns, villages, mountains, and rivers.

Each of these newly formed countries had its particular way to incorporate their undeserved Magyar land. The Romanians tried to destroy any monument, including churches, cemeteries, and headstones. This practice was also done by the Slovaks a few years later and still continues today. City halls and courthouses where the Hungarian emblems were permanently and proudly displayed were covered over, or if they could not reach it, photographing the emblem resulted in an automatic prison sentence.

The Serbs just conducted a search-and-destroy mission and mass murdered forty thousand Hungarians, mostly women and children, and confiscated their homes and lands. Then they proceeded to resettle Serbians from Kosovo into the vacated homes (this process is still going on in front of international observers in Vojvodina).

Possibly the harshest and most cruel official means of dealing with Hungarians was done by the Czechs and Slovaks via the Benes decrees (which is still in effect). The Benes decrees were the foundation of Czech and Slovak policies toward its Hungarian and German populations following WWII. Since the Slovak government would not offer a public apology for their atrocities against the Hungarian population (a million people) as of the year 2007, it deserves a few paragraphs below.

According to the Benes decrees, the Kosice (Kassa) Government Program aimed to eliminate all non-Slavic minorities in order to establish a "national state" of Czechs and Slovaks. The Sudeten Germans by the Czech border and the Hungarians who were trapped in Slovakia were not to be part of the re-established Czechoslovakia. Benes held these nationalities "collectively guilty" for the collapse of Czechoslovakia in 1938. Benes, on his way back from Kassa in 1945, stopped in Pozsony (Bratislava) and asserted, "After this war, there will be no minority rights... after punishing all the delinquents who committed crimes against the state, the overwhelming majority of the Germans and Hungarians in our fatherland."

Doesn't it sound like Hitler's speech against the Jews?

With the above objectives in mind, the Benes governments lobbied to have the Allies approve the ethnic cleansing of the Germans and the Hungarians. At the Potsdam conference, Stalin's aggressive support for the mass deportation of the Germans was obtained on July 25, 1945, with the reluctant acquiescence of Churchill (later Attlee) and Truman. However, the Western Allies did not approve the expulsion of the Hungarians. This reluctance may have been due to the awareness that Slovakia's Tiso regime was the most enthusiastic supporter of the Third Reich and the first to send the Jews to Nazi concentration camps. Even after the First Vienna Award, the Hungarians remaining in Slovakia were the most consistent opponents of Nazification. As early as 1942, the Slovak National Assembly voted to deport the Jews to Nazi death camps, with only one dissenting vote by Janos Esterhazy, the only Hungarian party representative.

In spite of the contrasting Slovak and Hungarian record, the Kosice program set the stage for the expulsion of the Hungarians as well. As a first step, it deprived the Hungarians of citizenship. This meant that "non-Slavic elements" were eliminated from public administration. All Hungarian landholdings were confiscated and all Hungarian schools were closed. The Hungarians were not allowed to participate in local self governing institutions, even if the inhabited areas were overwhelmingly Hungarian (such as Csaló, with over ninety eight percent Hungarians). A whole series of presidential decrees followed, which aimed to achieve this objective.

In the meantime, a ruthless press campaign of hate was unleashed against the German and Hungarian minorities (just like the Nazis against the Jews). Besides the hate campaign, the Hungarian population was targeted by intense persecution. The Communist-led "people's courts" were used to pin the label of "war criminal" on more and more Hungarians. In these trials, during 1946 to 1947, the accused were twenty eight point five two percent Slovaks, fifty nine point seven six percent Hungarians, while German, Ukraine, and other minorities constituted eleven point seven two percent.

After the expulsion of those found "guilty" of war crimes, the Benes decrees provided for the expulsion of all Hungarian schoolteachers and other undesirables. In quick succession, the Hungarian minority was decapitated. When the mass firing of the Hungarian civil servants took place pursuant to directive 44/1945 of the Slovak National Council, the overwhelming majority of Hungarians remained without earnings overnight.

Concurrently, all retirement payments to Hungarians were halted. The purge was not limited to government employees. Directive 69/1945 of the Slovak National Council ordered all "unreliable" Hungarians to be fired from private employment as well.

The negative legal repercussions of the eight Benes decrees

are still in effect today, even though in its July 1993 accession to the Council of Europe, Slovakia obligated itself to overcome these. Yet today, thousands of acres of land confiscated from ethnic and native Hungarians and given to Slovaks still remain in the latter's possession. Furthermore, of all the assets of Hungarian organizations that were confiscated between 1945 and 1948, only nine were returned to the rightful owners. The Reformed Church of Hungary similarly had the majority of its buildings and schools confiscated, but have no legal recourse today. And the western 'civilized' countries are still not speaking up for the Hungarians trapped in economical, ethnic, religious, and political slavery.

We were starved for freedom and food. Our family farm could not produce enough to pay the special taxes the Communist government levied against us. During the growing season, our weekends were spent working on the farm. We had to leave by four a.m. and walk ten kilometers to hoe, weed, or harvest, weather permitting. We had no money to hire people to work the land, and also as the "landowner" class, we were not allowed to hire, according to the new Communist puppet government. The grapes, corn, sweet peas, potato, tomato, peppers, beans, watermelons, and the fruit trees all needed our attention. The wheat and rye fields were given out to a young farming couple, as we had no means to cultivate grains. One was not allowed to sell any real estate, and the government would not take the land off our hand until the back taxes were so high that they didn't have to compensate us for taking our farm. We became very discouraged after all the exhausting work without any payback.

My father's pension had stopped a long time before, as he was considered an enemy of the people, and we all belong to the I class, the intellectuals, or X class, the undesirables. There were the factory workers, the peasants, with I and X classes on the bottom of the list. We belonged to the professional or educated group who, according to the Communists, were responsible for supporting the previous government that exploited the people. On top of it, we had no connections or help coming from the ruling Communist Party or government, as all our friends and relatives were also ousted by the new Jewish regime.

DECEPTION AND REALITY- LIVING THROUGH THE MISSING PAGES OF HISTORY

Relatives who were overlooked by the communist purge could not keep in touch, or they would lose their jobs just by virtue of association with us. It seems as though the Jewish people, wanting to avoid any more discrimination, took over the ruling caste, the Communist Party. The party ruled, dictated, and controlled everything.

At this time, it wasn't clear to me if the Jews just wanted to be in power and control everything or just craved the extra protection from the Russian Communist leader, Stalin himself.

Many of our cousins avoided us for fear of losing their jobs; some even changed their names not to show any links that may incriminate them by either bloodline or association. We discouraged our relatives and friends from keeping in touch so they would be able to keep working and feed their families. The Jews as Communist and secret police leaders took over everything— the press, the publishing, all the media, theater, military, finance, and everything that helped inform, control, or influence the people and the country. In short order, about eight percent of our population took complete control of our land, home, and country.

But they even wanted to have more. They tried to succeed, using many devious ways. We were forced to turn in all gold and gold jewelry, gold coins, guns, and ammunition, coin collections (as they may include coins from undesirable countries). We were told the gold was collected for Stalin's birthday, and it was used to form a miniature replica of the first suspension bridge across the Danube, tying the cities of Buda and Pest together, hence the current name of Budapest. Later we were told that through arrests of "enemies of people" and confiscating their valuables, enough gold was accumulated to also build a replica of the Budapest Metro and the telephone switchboard, the first to be built in continental Europe. We know whose pockets were filled with the confiscated gold, and the Communist leadership still had the gall to claim their lost riches during their persecution in the amount that exceeded the value of the entire country. According to their claim, the Jews owned the entire Hungary, plus some.

I guess the surviving Jews had to pay back somebody for what the Nazis did to them. It didn't matter if they were innocent people or even their saviors. The Jews did whatever they wanted, just as they do now in Palestine. In the meantime, they complained to make Hitler the most evil man in the world and successfully covered up Stalin's much greater and more numerous atrocities. They believed their grief and losses were greater than what the rest of the world suffered.

As President Harry S. Truman had described the Jewish comportment in his diary, dated July 21 1947:

> "The Jews have no sense of proportion, nor do they have any judgment on world affairs. The Jews, I find, are very, very selfish. They care not how many Estonians, Latvians, Finns, Poles, Slavs, or Greeks got murdered or mistreated as D (displaced) P (person) as long as Jews get special treatment. Yet when they have power, physical, financial, or political, neither Hitler nor Stalin has anything on them for cruelty or mistreatment to the underdog." (Truman Diary, parenthesis mine)

With the help of the most feared secret police, backed by the Russian Red Army, the Communist Jews took away our properties, homes, buildings, and businesses without blinking an eye. Furthermore, they approved and accepted the giveaway of hundreds of thousands of acres of our homeland to neighboring countries. In many cases, they drummed up false charges against innocent people just to get their property.

Most of the Jews we helped never bothered to thank us, with the exception of two families— one art dealer and one businessman's wife. Later, Lara, Rabbi Goldstein's granddaughter, did express a genuine apology for the Jewish crimes and injustices in the Communist era.

Since I was the only one home with my mother at the time Father Tibor arrived, we stayed in the hallway. The new communist government took our third room with the bathroom, flush toilet, kitchen, and pantry away, leaving no formal space for welcoming guests. Seven of us were forced to live in a two-bedroom apartment without kitchen, access to running water, or inside bathroom. Just as it was described and shown in the book and film 'Doctor Zhivago'.

Father Tibor said he had a few hours to spend before having to go back to say evening mass, so I offered him a big chair, a leftover piece from our guest room furniture we could not sell. It had been a year since my father died, and we were still under the spell of mourning. I was still mad about the whole incident of how my father's life came to an end. He was accused of the identical charges as the Nazis had brought, except that the chosen "enemies" were named differently. Instead of accusing him of loving and hiding the Jews, they called him a Nazi sympathizer. I did not experience big differences under Communist rules versus Nazi occupation.

The only changes were in the intensity of deportation to Russia (such as Kazakhstan), extreme fear and forced labor camps like under the Nazis, harsher penalties, and imprisonment for the I and X class, which included all Christians. Besides the undesirable classes, priests and nuns were also persecuted without due process of law. The communists established a caste system of five classes; there was the ruling class or the communists, the W class for factory workers, the P for peasants, I for intellectuals who had higher education, and the X class for the undesirables. One of the problems was that the Communist absolute-ruling class gave some privileges to the W and the P classes, provided they became party members. Many times, the children didn't know where they should belong, but all family members automatically inherited the class identification of our parents.

All these classes were ruled by the C class, members of the communist party. People started disappearing faster than under the Nazis. Just listening to a Western radio station or joking about the Jewish-controlled government could earn one five to ten years in prison, plus hard labor and confiscation of all his property. If they labeled one the "enemy of people or state," they had free rein on what, when, and how to hurt him.

When Father Tibor asked how he could help us, I blasted out, "How come you, my father, and all the clergy who helped the Jews survive are mistreated?

It was a terrible injustice what they had done to my father, mother, and the entire family. More Hungarian Jews survived the Holocaust and genocide than in any other country occupied by the Germans, thanks to people like you." He didn't say a word, just sat there looking at the credenza where the water pitcher stood.

I anticipated his wish and got up, took a clean glass from the top shelf, picked up the pitcher, started pouring, and asked my question again. "I know you people helped a lot of Jewish families, and some were later helped by Wallenberg until he found out the truth about the

Katyn massacre of Polish officers that had been erroneously blamed on the Germans, so the Russians arrested him. But why did the Germans hate the Jews, and why did your kind make sure that most Hungarian, some Slovakian, Romanian, or Croatian Jews will survive?" I kept on asking a lot of questions, trying to get answers to understand what was going on between the Communists and the Jews.

Father Tibor was looking down at my worn-out shoes and still ignoring my questions. I stopped asking and kept quiet. We just sat there with solemn faces, not even looking at each other, and the silence was heavy.

After the long pause, probably minutes, he looked up at me and asked, "Have you asked your mother?"

I didn't even respond to his question, not to pay back his silent treatment, but I had to think of my mother's mental health. She didn't speak to anybody for a long time, just gave hand signals. The shock of losing everything— husband, country, home, land, all valuables—was too much to bear.

Father Tibor finally started talking. "You know, if I were God and I had to choose a special group of people, I would choose the Hebrews, as they can be the most delightful, smart, well-educated company one can ever hope for. They are among the best comedians, the best lawyers, doctors, businessmen, spies, bankers, and whatever field they choose. However, God didn't have to pick a race, as God is not a racist. But you and I have learned that in spite of all their intelligence and good attributes, we would never pick one of them as a trusted friend."

I remembered at the tent city how untrustworthy they were, selling each other for a chocolate bar, not resisting the persecution or trying to escape, and also what they did to my country and each other.[9]

Now they run my country, and they are running it into the ground with the help of the great Communist Party, with Stalin at the helm.

Father Tibor continued. "However, if I were the devil, I would work very hard and make sure to get them on my side, as they can be the most racist, evil, vengeful, influential, arrogant, mean, and controlling people on Earth. There are many examples of this in the Torah, Talmud, Toledo

---

[9] Many crimes committed during the Holocaust were done by Jews. Examples: Adolf Eichmann and his adopted son, George Soros. While Eichmann sent hundreds of thousands of Jews to Concentration camps, Soros, as a teenager, took delight in confiscating fellow Jews' properties, gold, silver, jewelry, etc.

Jesus, and if they perceive you as a potential enemy, they will get rid of you, even if you're innocent. The best example is the crucifixion of Christ. The Jews specifically asked for the crucifixion because Jesus by that time had a large group of followers, well loved, became very influential, and represented the greatest threat to Judaism. This threat was real on all fronts, as Jesus even treated women and men equally, and that conflicted with their traditional and accepted ways. In those days, crucifixion was the only way to wipe out the memory of Jesus, as the Roman law prohibited even mentioning the names of those who were crucified. It was the way and the means to put famous people to oblivion and remove them from historical records. No way would Rome or Pilate want to execute Jesus, especially on the cross, without the Jewish lobby and pressure. Did you know it wasn't the Roman guards but the Jewish temple guards who arrested Jesus and turned him over to Pilate?"

I muttered, "Oops, you don't like them, either."

His answer was, "This is not a question of like or dislike, but we must treat every human being as an equal. If you hurt an innocent person, you are guilty and should be punished. Read and understand what Jesus said to the Jews in John 8:3-47."

I continued. "We have nine ministries in the government, eight are led by Jews. Also, our prime minister is a Jew, and so are all the top Communist Party leaders."

Father Tibor said, "You left out the head of the secret police, Stalin, Lenin, Marx, and Engels, but let me answer your original questions. I helped hide Rabbi Goldstein in one of the old but never used crypts in the Greek Orthodox cemetery, along with his daughter and granddaughter, Lara. We took them food and clothing for almost a year. Even your mother helped with occasional meals when she had enough to feed you all. Before the rabbi died, he told me the following story in which I'm now beginning to believe."

I cut in and asked why the change of heart about believing stories without archeological or other supporting evidence.

He ignored my interruption and continued. "There is also no archeological evidence the Jews were enslaved by the Egyptians. In fact, the uncovered housing for the Jews was the type built for the high middle class.

"When men touch perfect things, they make it imperfect— like meddling with nature or rewrite, augment, select or translate the holy scriptures, the Bible. There are more versions of the Bible than any other books. For example, reading some of the Sumerian and Hebrew text, then Aramaic, Coptic, followed by the Greek and Latin translations, one wonders how much has been added, deleted, changed, or lost in the rest of the texts and what was the motivation behind it. Don't forget some of the scriptures for the New Testament were written in Aramaic, Jesus' tongue, but were destroyed by the Jews as they converted Christian teaching to Judeo-Christian. Rabbi Goldstein used to tell me, 'There are no Christians anymore, but only Judeo-Christians— we made sure of that.'

"In the new Gnostic scripts found in Nag Hammadi, some of which were written by eyewitnesses to the crucifixion of Christ, like Mary of Magdala. Mary of Magdala, Thomas, and Phillip seem to shed a better light on Jesus' life. Also, there is a lot of important material in the Gnostic scripts that should be either included or used as references in the New Testament. As Rabbi Goldstein told me, they pushed the hardest to canonize the Bible so no potentially damaging new evidence or Gnostic scripture would find its way into the book.

"Other important observations: there is a real conflict between the God described in the Old and New Testaments. Many stories, like the Genesis, the Ten Commandments, and the great flood, can be traced back to Sumerian writings predating the Bible by a few thousand years. The Old Testament talks about a vengeful God and the New Testament of a loving God. The Jews identify more with the vengeful God and prefer the 'eye for an eye' policy, which makes them a potential danger to society when in positions of power. In fact, if they had the military power of Germany, they could have been more destructive than the Nazis, just as Stalin was."

"Could you give me some examples?" I asked.

"Of the translation errors, the one that stands out the most is, 'Elio, Elio! La-Ma Sa-Bag Ta-Nim!' which Jesus spoke from the cross and said in Aramaic language, not in Hebrew, 'O God, O God! Lift the injured into heaven,' instead of 'O my God, O my God, why have you forsaken me?' That makes no sense. Luke's version of the last words of Christ uttered on the cross in Luke 23-45, 'Father, into your home I commend my soul,' is closer to the truth."

"That might have been an honest mistake by the Jewish eyewitnesses who only spoke Greek, some Latin, and practically no Aramaic or

Hebrew," I argued.

"My son," he responded, "there are thousands of changes, like the original Lord's Prayer begins also in Aramaic and was recited that way for centuries.

'Our Father and Mother, who are above and in us, blessed be Thy name.' The rest is a fair translation with the only exception of "Don't lead us into temptation" instead of "protect us from temptation," but somebody left off and changed the beginning on purpose, leaving the Holy Ghost out. In fact, the Huns had a better translation of the Lord's Prayer from Aramaic in the fourth century than our current version of the Our Father.

"Going back to the 'enslaved' Jews, evidence suggests, based on their housing facilities discovered in Egypt, that they worked there because they were needed in the crafting and/or the trade side, not as slaves. In fact, as usual, they end up in the high classes wherever they settle. As soon as the Jews gain power, they become arrogant and lose their popularity. The Negroes and enslaved Arabs were stronger, more efficient, and required less trouble to control and make them work for less. Just read the Bible, i.e. John 8:33, the Jews claim 'Never have been slaves to anyone.' The departure of the Jews from Egypt might have been arranged by the pharaohs or mutually agreed upon, just as shipping out all the Jews from England in the fourteenth century. If they had been really slaves, the Egyptians would not let them have or take so much gold so they could erect the false god in the form of the solid gold bull.

"Historians and reporters should also tell more of these historical events, but they are very quiet about some facts, like the genocide in the Ukraine and the massacre of Polish officers in Katyn by Stalin. The English getting rid of the Jews and shipping them to Europe is an interesting historical fact, as they were ordered on one set of ships and all their belongings on other ships. The ships with the Jews on sailed, but all their wealth stayed behind. This time also coincided with the sudden richness of the English royal family. The expulsions of the Jews are too numerous to list, but here are a few more examples: 1394 from France, 1492–1497 from Portugal, 1650 from Belgium, and 1100–1400 from Germanic lands.

"The Sumerians had seven commandments, the predecessor of the Ten Commandments and it predates the Biblical version by thousands of years. The story of Eden, Cain and Abel, the Tree of Life, Adam and

Kele D. Gabor

Eve, the great flood were all written in Sumerian thousands of years before the Bible. As a side note, there are many Sumerian and Aramaic words, other than geographical names in these stories, which match Hungarian both in meaning and pronunciations."

"Before you get too far ahead of me or change the subject, please provide some examples of just what you said," I asked.

He responded, "It may be a curse to know and read many ancient texts, as I can see a lot of stories, events, and words that are common in Sumerian, Sanskrit, Aramaic, Egyptian, and some Hungarian. I should start with Sumerian words like Ar-Am and Ar-Ab, where 'Ar' means many or people, and 'Am' and 'Ab' means mother and father, respectively. Therefore, the 'Aram' and 'Arab' languages mean 'people of mother and father,' respectively.

Even today, the meaning, spelling, and pronunciation of' 'ar' are the same in both Sumerian and Hungarian languages.

"Another example, Hun-ar is the basis of today's Hungar people of Huns or Hons— meaning 'people with homes.' Mat-ar is the basis of Magy-ar, meaning 'people of Mats,' or Mat-ar-i in Egyptian. The word Eden means in Sumerian a flat land surrounded by mountains. In Hungarian, we referred to all flat-bottomed objects as eden (or edény), resembling the flat valley.

"Another example is Arat, and in Hungarian aran, meaning gold, or Arata, which means 'place of gold.' Arat is also used in Hungarian, meaning 'golden harvest.' The city of Ar-ad also has identical meaning, spelling, and pronunciation in both languages, and translated to English, it means 'adding many' and implies flood. I ran across hundreds of words like that while interpreting ancient texts. Probably the most commonly used words in Sumerian and Hungarian are ur–meaning lord; Isten (or Istar)– meaning God; nap or nip-ur, meaning son-god. I could go on, as I found many geographical names which are almost identical in spelling and meaning between Sumerian and Hungarian."

"How about an example of common words in Sumerian, Aramaic, and Hungarian?" I asked.

He responded, "A good example is the word sub, meaning cut in all three languages. Even the Hungarian words szabo (tailor) and szabja (sword) have the same origin as the sound 's' is written as 'sz' in our language."

I didn't interrupt this time, so he continued with the rabbi story.

"Rabbi Goldstein was already in his mid seventies when I first met him in 1936 but still sharp and could keep up with most middle-aged men. By the way, you have to meet Lara, his granddaughter."

"I want to meet no Jewish girls," I responded. He winked and continued. "The rabbi told me on his deathbed, just after the German invasion and occupation of Hungary in the late spring of 1944, his father and two other rabbis approached Friedrich Engels, the famous philosopher and textile manufacturer in the 1840s. They asked for his help for the Jewish cause in Europe because of the discrimination and difficulties in gaining power and control. They believed it was not a racial, but a religious issue, and plain persecution.

"These three rabbis met earlier on a regular basis for years in Germany before coming up with a viable solution to their predicament. When they were convinced a new religion could truly combine Christian and Jewish values, which would also appeal to the masses, could ensure more tolerance toward and acceptance of the Jewish community, they went to see Engels.

He wasn't receptive to the idea, as he was concerned about introducing a new sect on a very competitive field where religious leaders already took advantages of poor, undereducated, and gullible people. In addition, Engels feared it would be immediately recognized by others as a means of usurping power and control over people.

"After trying a few more times without much success, they went to see Karl Marx in Brussels. Marx was very quiet and listened carefully to their ideas, and after the third meeting, he said, 'We must make it a new sociopolitical movement, as there is less competition and everybody is ready for a change and a new form of government. In fact, we don't want people to convert the current Christian religions. If they do, they will not only be competition but also our greatest enemy, like Christ was to Judaism.'

"In 1849, the rabbis' persistence paid off, and the new Communist Manifesto was born and published. The Manifesto had all the elements of Christian and Jewish values, except for God. However, one had to believe in and live by it, just like a religion, and was camouflaged under the name of manifesto, a political angle."

I told him the story was fascinating but unbelievable because it is a new political view of trying to make everybody equal, and we are not. We all are different, and the equality should only apply to giving opportunities, in law, justice, religion.

His response was, "Read the Communist Manifesto, and you will see the Christian and Jewish values, creating a heaven on earth but leaving Christ and God out of it. In principle, it should appeal to all the people, especially the poor and the persecuted without strong conviction or faith. As it was conceived then, their greatest enemy is the Christian church, wherever the communists or the Marxists take over, they will do everything to discredit or even exterminate the Christians."

Sure enough, all the religious leaders have been arrested and put in forced labor camps or prisons, including the Hungarian Cardinal Mindszenty.

After living under Communism for six more years, every year that passed, the story became more and more believable, as communism has all the attributes of a religion, even in taking advantage of the people, the hierarchical organization of the communist leadership had to accept a lot of things based on faith alone. Philosophically, it was a great sounding new form for society, like heaven on Earth, but in practice it was just the opposite, controlling the people and hell on Earth.

Father Tibor took another glass of water and continued. "You should have also asked why it was easy for Hitler to sell the German people the idea of putting the Jews in concentration or labor camps. There are many reasons, but here are a few. The Hebrews typically stand out by their language, including Yiddish, their mannerisms, clothing, hat, facial hair and style, body odor, and they keep to themselves—making them an easy target as a nonconforming group. They're also very shrewd businessmen, which make them hard to compete with, especially in the marketplace.

Also, most animal activists dislike them for the way they slaughter to make the meat kosher, i.e., they have to let the animal bleed to death, and the easiest way is to break their legs first so they won't run away and then cutting the main arteries in the throat. These poor animals sometimes may take a whole day or many hours to die, and it is hard to watch as they try to run away on broken legs.

"In Amsterdam, at the Jewish world conference in July of 1933, they requested the release of all Jews from German prisons, guilty or not. The delegation leader, Samuel Untermyer, gave a radio address where he declared holy war against Germany and promised the total boycott and destruction of Germany. The message was not well received by the Germans.

"They also don't believe in the New Testament, and that makes them good candidates and often used as false witnesses for the right amount of money, where swearing on the Bible is required."

Now I understood why all those young Jewish men stood in front of the courtrooms, offering to be witness for a fee, when I went by to deliver to my grandfather, the local judge, his hot coffee and doughnuts my grandmother sent.

"The word holocaust came from the Hebrew 'holocaustum,' meaning human sacrifice by burning. This had been practiced by certain Jews for many hundreds of years just before Passover to taste the innocent's blood.

There are some historical and judicial records dating back to the fourth and as recent as the twentieth century of bloodletting by some Orthodox Jews, but Rabbi Goldstein assured me these killing of young children were all done by mentally sick people, not only by Jews." Later I found out that certain evil cults still sacrifice children.

I asked what he meant by the mannerisms of the Jews. He responded, "Do you remember when you told us about the spoiled single-child syndrome in the camp? They are very similar in behavior. They are human beings, and they do make mistakes but cannot apologize, only accuse."

Father Tibor continued. "They typically learn many languages, know how to enter illegally into any country, and they are also excellent spies.

They're also known as the world's best smugglers."

I said, "This is not enough to punish a group of people. Just look at the Gypsies, the same applies to them."

He went on. "After World War I, a bitter, lonely, and radical French statesman dictated the terms of the peace treaty at Trianon. The winning side wanted to penalize all the countries that helped Germans fight the war. Even though Austria started the war without the full support of the Hungarians, they rewarded it with a piece of Hungary. In other words, he and his cohorts made a lot of serious and grave errors that eventually led to WWII.

"Some of these terrible errors included the breakup of Central Europe [no more central power] without regard to borders and resulting in the neighboring states' enslaving at least seven million Hungarians. But what the treaty also did is limit the industrial growth in each country. For example, the French bankers who were mostly Jews controlled the financing. If a German asked for a loan to get a company or business going, he first had to be a Jew or had to have one-fourth Jewish blood or more. Hence, the Nazi rule of accepting people with one-fourth or less part of Jewish blood, just as Hitler was. A letter of recommendation that had to come from the local Rabbi enforced this secret agreement.

"As a result, only Jewish companies and businesses flourished. It got so bad that during the Depression, only the Jewish people were prospering and well-off; everybody else suffered or starved. The Germans and the government had no money, so Hitler had to turn to the rich Jewish community and used their immense wealth to start and conduct the costly war. War takes money, money, and more money. Germany could not build up and finance a large army without money. By the time the Depression loosened its grip in Europe, some of the Germans built up quite a bit of resentment against an already disliked and distrusted race. The Jewish people also have a tendency to exaggerate and claim the six million lost in concentration camps is absurd. However, none of them deserved to be killed."

Father Tibor stood up, and so did I, as I knew he had to leave to celebrate the evening mass and he was already running late. As I walked him to the outside gate, he was holding on to his bike, he stopped and looked at me. He smiled and said, "Don't be angry. Keep your cool, and next time, I'll cheer you up and bring Lara along."

I didn't say a word, as I had already expressed my opinion

earlier about not wanting to meet her. I should have at least thanked him for his dissertation in trying to answer my questions with a new and fresh look at the adversarial position I took against the Jews.

The next day, I really felt guilty and awful, as Father Tibor was arrested that night after the evening mass and nobody knew where the secret police took him.

Almost exactly a year after Father Tibor was arrested, somebody knocked on the outside big door leading to the courtyard. By coincidence, I happened to be at home from school to look for a temporary summer job.

Getting any kind of jobs those days was difficult for young men classified as I or X class by the Communist system. Of course, I had to lie about my family and my father to be able to land a job. Instead of listing his former occupation, education, company he worked at, I added the word deceased in every column and question on the application list. I knew that whoever knocked on this beautiful Sunday early afternoon was a stranger, as he didn't use the proper code.

Since my father's death and the total Communist takeover, we had to play it safe, keeping all doors locked. We installed a special hidden electrical buzzer under the outside window for family members' use. Other friends used the coded knocks, which were different for the outside windows and the large entry gate to the courtyard. These precautions were necessary to protect the six families living in the three family complexes, as rogue or drunken secret policemen or Communist Party members could go in any house without warning or warrants and conduct house searches.

In a few cases, contraband was smuggled into a neighbor's house immediately before or during the unscheduled search, and the stuff was, of course found without delay a short time later. Most of the contraband used was DOD ammunition, as it was easy to carry in the pocket and even easier to put to an unsuspected "hiding" place during an impromptu visit.

Our poor neighbor was dumbfounded when an unexpected visit by the secret police produced not one but two .50-caliber bullets, and he got five years in prison and lost all his property and belongings. The only way to protect ourselves was to stay low and lock up everything and hope for the best. Breaking in was usually done when they had the necessary papers, but on most occasions, the Communist police didn't have to prove or show them. These types of activities by the already feared secret police put a lot of extra stress on anyone who was not a member of the Communist Party.

When the second series of knocking came, and it seemed to follow a pattern, I was really scared, as it was the typical method the secret police used to gain entry to an unsuspecting family. How I wished then and many other times to have a weapon to protect our family.

I often think about the idealists who don't believe the American Second Amendment— the right to bear arms. As I experienced, each time my country was taken over by a totalitarian or foreign government, taking the power away from people, the very first thing they did was to collect all the firearms, leaving us totally defenseless. That was what happened with the Hungarians when the Russians, Communists, Romanians, Germans, Slovaks, French, or Serbs took control. I know I will never trust a government who denies your right to protect your family with the appropriate means. The most ridiculous excuse not to give you a permit is the accidental death caused by a firearm, which is miniscule compared to almost any other type of accident. People with felony or criminal records should be automatically denied buying or using any firearms. However, I do believe and strongly support good training with the weapon of your choice before putting it to use.

I was just about to ignore the person or persons by the main gate when a soft, almost crying, female voice came through, "Please, let me in."

I carefully approached the main gate, and when I got close, I tried to peek through a crack close to the doorjambs. The only thing I could make out was a lady in high heels wearing something light gray. I made a command decision and with my deepest voice asked, "Who is it?"

A gentle voice responded, "I'm Lara, and I have to speak with Anna."

I reached in with my right hand to get the huge spare door key hidden inside the brick wall and next to the main entry. I put the key in, and with some difficulty, the purposely un-oiled lock mechanism moved with an ear piercing squeaking noise that could wake the dead. I opened the heavy door just to stick my head out, but the lady on the outside was pushing the door inward and with a sweet voice claiming, "You better let me in, they may be watching." Since I knew what that meant, I immediately opened it just wide enough to let the lady slip into the courtyard.

As soon as I looked at her face, I knew she was the Lara Father Tibor wanted me to meet. After closing and locking the main door, I turned toward her for a better look. She was exceptionally elegantly dressed, with a light-gray custom suit and a white blouse that barely showed with the formal top on. Her eyes were big and dark, with large pupils in spite of the bright sunshine, long eyelashes, and a pronounced set of dark eyebrows. She wore her hair up in a bun, obviously to look older or mature. She had a faint smile, just enough to see her white teeth. She was definitely a year or two younger than me, but carried herself as a grown up and mature lady.

Her chin, lips, and nose were a dead giveaway of her Jewish origin, but her neck was unusually long and feminine. Looking into her eyes, I was mesmerized and almost missed her extended right hand as a sign of greeting. She seemed familiar, as if I should have known her. When our hands touched, I remembered Kati, my first and so far only love. The identical feeling came over me, but no knee-shaking and no confusion. After the handshake, I knew I had met the most attractive Jewish girl I had ever seen. The only problem was I felt so attracted to her the first moment I laid eyes on her that I got scared, and it took awhile to make peace with my strong and strange feelings toward her. Call it chemistry or magnetism, but whatever it was, the attraction was very strong. During the long and firm handshake, like friends typically use, I felt her small hand with long fingers, which at the tips had some roughness or calluses. It made me wonder what she did for a living.

While I was escorting her toward our entry door, she turned around and, with a lovely smile, said, "You must be Kele, and you look as Father Tibor described you."

Obviously, I either had forgotten to introduce myself or didn't want to take the time during the handshake. Maybe she was holding on to my hand so long to give me time to say my name. That thought made me uneasy, as it may have meant that the attraction was not mutual.

We had to turn left and go up on a few steps to get to our entry door. When we got to the door, I asked her to wait and let me check on my mother's condition, just to make sure she was presentable. Lara immediately apologized as she explained, "I didn't want to announce my arrival ahead, as Father Tibor instructed me to do."

"You mean that you talked with Father Tibor?" I asked.

She responded, "Not lately, but he is the reason I'm here, and I'm determined to find and free him."

I let Lara into our hallway and offered the same old big chair Father Tibor used the last time he visited. Once she sat down, I walked into our all-purpose room— bedroom, kitchen, workroom, and library. My mother was already coming in from the back bedroom and said, "I hope you didn't let the stranger in." I explained that Lara was here to talk to her, as she had a message from Father Tibor. My mother was suspicious, for all the right reasons, and said, "How do you know it's not a trick"? I told her she asked for her by her first name, not like others who referred to her always as "Mrs."

My mother was already putting on her more formal but worn-out black silk robe but kept her comfortable slippers on, pushed me aside, checked her hair, and which was similarly arranged as Lara's, in the small mirror by the door. She reached over and opened the door to the hallway. With a very cold voice, she asked, "Who is it, and what does she want?" Back came the answer, as sweet as can be, explaining her mission while she was getting up from the big chair. Lara introduced herself and bent down to kiss my mother's hand. My mother pulled it back, rejecting her attempt of showing her deep respect and admiration.

I was just about ready to leave the two of them alone for a private chat, but my mother directed me to bring another chair for myself. Lara would not sit back in the big, comfortable chair. She insisted my mother use it.

I got two other semi-comfortable chairs, one for Lara and one for myself, and I asked if I could bring her anything. She politely responded a glass of water would be perfect, as the walk from the bus station was long and hot.

My mother still had her serious and mistrusting stiff look when Lara, trying to break the ice, said, "If I may call you Anna, first I want to thank you for what you and your husband did for us saving our family from the Nazis, and second, I have some sad but promising news about Father Tibor. It took me almost six months of searching after his arrest, turning over every rock to find him. As you may know, he became my mother and father after losing my parents, and I have great respect and admiration for him and also for your husband. I used all my contacts, both political and the underground, to find him. Father Tibor is in a forced-labor camp up north in one of the rock quarries, probably by Recsk. I already contacted some official to try to help him."

Lara reached into her small purse and took out a small, slender box and said while putting it on the table in front of my mother, "This is a very small token of appreciation for all you have done for us in the war years, and I know you also write poetry, some of which I have read and love. Please use this tool for your future verses."

My mother interrupted, "Why are you telling me all this? I don't know who you are talking about. And why did you take the bus?"

She responded, "You are just like my mother was when your husband and Father Tibor tried to help us. The bus I had to take and sit in the last row to make sure no one followed me. I know the railroad station is closer to your place, but it is hard to spot a secret police on the train, and I didn't want to be followed."

Without going into too much detail, it took Lara close to fifteen minutes to convince my mother she could be trusted, she was genuine, and she meant well. I was embarrassed about my mother's way of handling Lara.

Later, I asked my mother why it took so long for her to know if Lara was trustworthy, as she can usually tell from the first look and touch if some one can be trusted or not. Her response was a big surprise. She said, "I could tell she could be trusted the minute I met her. I even recognized her from Udvar and knew her parents. We asked her father to help us smuggle back some of our family-owned art pieces from Pozsony [Bratislava], Slovakia when he was arrested. I could also see the great attraction between you two, so I had to teach you a lesson about how to handle people if you are not sure, as love is blind."

I had great respect for my mother; she had many talents, painting, writing, music, poetry, and, most of all, the ability to identify people's character at the first meeting. I now believe I inherited a little bit of her talent of reading people, as I have hired at least three hundred professional people without misjudgment. Every time a company president hired someone with my disapproval, it always ended up in some kind of trouble and, in some cases, disaster.

Kele D. Gabor

My seventh sense[10] of recognizing honest people is a curse when it comes to politics, as I have a hard time understanding why the voters get so easily fooled, not recognizing lies, half-truths, staging, acting, ideologues, and posturing.

From that Sunday on, I could not get Lara out of my mind, and I tried everything— sports, extra labor, games, friends, other girls' company, camping, walking, swimming, running, ping-pong— but nothing helped. I had a similar feeling to what I had with Kati, but still quite different. I give up, I cannot describe or explain— I'm not a poet or writer, who could possibly do justice in describing my feelings; I would only spoil it. It should suffice to say I had an empty feeling every time we parted company or she was not near me.

It didn't take me a long time to share my disappointments about the Jewish people with Lara, but it turned out she knew. She helped me a great deal overcoming some of my misgivings, as Lara told me numerous times based on our experiences we had all the rights to feel the way we did and that there are good and bad people in every group. She went so far as equating the Holocaust with the plight of the Hungarian people. To prove her point, she showed me a copy of a German document where all deaths were listed from each of the nineteen concentration camps from 1939 to 1944, and the total was less than four hundred thousand. When I finished looking at it, she said, "This is closer to the truth than anything else you see or hear."

She said, "When I went back to Udvar in Transylvania to reclaim some of our belongings, I got the same treatment from the Romanians as you did. I have seen Russian soldiers stopping the mass execution of young Hungarian men by the Romanian military. I have seen thousands of innocent people being deported and shipped away, just like the Jews were by the Nazis. I have seen Hungary being carved up. Most Hungarians, the indigenous people of the area, who found themselves in newly created countries received the same treatment as slaves or second-class citizens.

Their homes were ransacked and their property taken away. I even went to Slovakia to retrace the steps of my parents, and they were even worse in the way they treated Hungarians. I didn't see what the Serbs did to the native Hungarian population, but I did hear about the mass

---

[10] Most schools do not teach about the sixth sense, BALANCE, without it we could not stand or walk. It is located in the inner ear, but it is independent of hearing.

executions, slavery, internments, and the deadly marches.

"I often wondered about which one is worse, being taken by the Nazis or the communists to concentration and death camps, or totally losing your homeland, identity, citizenship, freedom, and being treated like the Jews throughout history. The number of Hungarians ending up in other and usually more primitive countries was likely to be much more than the number of Jews taken by the Germans. We are free now, but the millions of Hungarians are still enslaved or are treated as second-class citizens."

I appreciated her comments, as I also had to live through and experience similar events and mistreatments.

After feeling and seeing some of the small calluses on her fingertips, I was sure she was a violin player. As often happened, I was wrong again— she was a cellist. I should have remembered Lara, the young pretty girl I went to sprinkle with perfume on Easter Monday in 1943 but received no encouraging kiss as I did eight years before. Now she performed with a small chamber orchestra and only played classical pieces.

I had to go back to school in the fall and finally saw her again, and our first "date" was a disaster. I was planning to tell her how much I was attracted to her and take her to a dance, but she could only talk about rescuing Father Tibor. She had laid out some plans to free him that she wanted me to review and approve, but I got so jealous of Father Tibor that I paid no attention to her efforts. The "date" ended with hurt feelings on both sides, and it took me a long time to get together with her again. A few days later, I realized it was my fault and we should really concentrate on freeing Father Tibor.

I went to the concert given by her quartet at the university theater and literally grabbed her coming down the back steps from the stage. The backstage was poorly lit, so unintentionally I really scared her. I apologized and started out by saying that after reviewing her plans, one looked more viable than the others did. I also had a few suggestions, like not writing anything down, instead memorizing it. Nobody should know more than absolutely necessary, especially names and places. She assured me that as a Jewish girl, she never has to worry about a house search, as she was now in the privileged class and totally trusted by the current government.

My new approach worked, and we both became involved, I on the sideline and she did all the legwork. There was no other option, as I had no way of selling myself either as a Jew or a Communist Party member. We both learned a lot about covert operations, and later in life, we both benefited from the experience. In fact, some of the finer points of executing the plans and some failures enabled me to help identify some Western double agents at a later time. For the eventual success of freeing Father Tibor, Lara deserves all the credit, as I was more of a sounding board for her than anything else.

By the way, I sincerely hope that one day she will also write her memoirs, as it will be better written and should be more interesting than mine.

Every time we met, I had a great urge to kiss her, and she knew it but would not give in. She led me on by saying, "You get your kiss when Father Tibor is free." I could hold her hand, hug her, and kiss her on the cheek but never on the lips. How I longed for those beautiful thick lips, but I tried to be a gentleman as much as possible. I did try a few times, but at the crucial moment, she turned her head away. We were so close sometimes, but still far apart. I finally collected her promised kiss, and I'm happy I waited. I received another unforgettable kiss, passionate and sweet. After that kiss, I was set on persuading her to be my wife, and I figured she would have a more difficult time to sell me to her relatives, which she denied, than I would.

I will not detail the plans we came up with to free Father Tibor from the forced-labor camp or how she finally succeeded, as we still need to play it safe. Here are a few highlights.

She had to join the Communist Party; she invited and entertained many Jewish people in power, using the rabbi's help to do things for her, promising everything to a Jewish doctor for hospitalizing Father Tibor, where his actual escape was planned. It turned out she didn't have to pay the heavy price, as it was easier to get a special medical release for him than have him be an escapee and fugitive for the rest of his life. Lara's rabbi grandfather must have had a lot of clout and respect, even after death, to open many doors for her.

Father Tibor was released from the labor camp and prison about a year later for health reasons. As far as we knew, Father Tibor was the first and last who was ever released from the hated prison of Recsk. Since he was already in very bad physical shape, Lara dedicated herself to nursing him back to life. In fact, he and Otto, my ex-scout leader, were the only persons I knew who got released from the prison camps for medical reasons and survived. My classmate, colleagues, friends, and relatives, including my father, didn't have a chance. Usually the beatings, interrogations, and experimental poisons and drugs had done so much damage that after the release, they only had weeks to live.

Most of the time, these released prisoners were so incoherent we could never really find out what the KGB agents and prison guards had done to them. The other exception was Otto, who was able to talk about the "highlight" system, where they stood him up in a single-body-size cell, with iron gadgets locking him and his head in so he could not turn either the body or the head. As soon as they closed the door on him, two high-powered light bulbs automatically turned on in front of his eyes, and regardless of how tightly he closed his eyelids, the strong lights kept him awake and burned his eyes to the point where blindness set in. Otto was lucky, as one of the light bulb burned out soon after the first use of the cell and the interrogators had not noticed. Still, temporary blindness lasted for many months, but after a half a year, he could get around with wearing very dark glasses. Otto was charged with interrupting the public speech of a Jewish Communist Party leader and prime minister by ringing the church bells during his speech.

Peti, our high school best long-distance runner, wasn't that lucky; he only survived five days after release, and his mother was shocked by what they had done to her son, as the marks of the heavy beatings were quite visible all over his body, even after death. Peti was charged with making fun of the Hungarian Communist Party leader and our Jewish prime minister, as they spoke better Russian than Hungarian. This reminds me that during the Hungarian Revolution, when the Russians attacked us on November 4, 1956, we called upon our United Nations representative to speak up on our behalf in New York, but he could not speak a single Hungarian word, only Russian and French. How would you like to have your country represented by a Red Chinese colonel who doesn't even speak your language?

After Father Tibor's release, Lara and I slowly and steadily pulled away from each other, but I still have warm feelings for her. Lara and I met again a few years later at an archeological site, a few months later in Austria, and about ten years later in America. Each of these meetings was very memorable, as she explicitly trusted me, and then I found out she also loved me but couldn't afford to reciprocate my feelings to ensure the success of her mission in life. She became a special and very valuable friend for the rest of my life.

At this time, I came to the conclusion that our families had suffered enough and could not be worse. After seeing, learning, and experiencing so much suffering and horrors on my own, I felt empowered, well-prepared, and ready for the future, regardless of the difficulties ahead.

While Lara's situation improved, as she became a very powerful person in Communist Hungary, my situation stayed this way just a few months, and then— if I knew what was coming, I'd have tried everything possible to escape the future.

My Picture (1956)

Amateur Detectives

Before finishing my training in surveying, I worked at a canning factory for two summers by the grace of a friend who knew the Communist political officer at the plant. By not telling them who my father was except that he died, they hired me as a laborer, delivering onions for drying. Those summers, while working there, people I knew would go on the other side of the street if they saw me coming. The stench of the heavy onion smell drove everyone away. I figured if I had survived the open-pit toilets and the terrible stench in the tent city, I'd be able to adjust to the strong smell of onions. I was right, and ever since I had my sinuses cleansed by the strong onion odor, I've never had a bad flu, allergy, or cold. The onion treatment might be a better and cheaper method to cleanse your sinuses than other vaporizers, inhalers, pills, or allergy shots.

The freshly picked onions came in big wooden boxes, about thirty kilograms per container. I picked them up at the railroad docks and loaded them on a hand-pulled cart. Only twelve boxes fitted on the top of the hand-drawn wagon with rubber wheels and, once loaded, I pulled them over to the cleaning facility next to the dryers. From the railroad to the loading dock, the road was flat and paved, and it took little energy to pull the cart about two hundred meters each trip. On arrival, I unloaded the boxes and put the contents on a conveyor belt that took them to the cleaners and washers. I was amazed at how efficiently and fast the women worked and cleaned off the outer shell of each onion. During my break, I sometimes stood behind the working ladies, watching their hands and fingers move so fast that I got mesmerized and found it fascinating and entertaining. The speed of their hands and their nimble fingers worked just as fast as any concert pianist's during a performance.

Then the onions were washed and dumped into huge cutters, each about three meters in diameter, which looked like giant food processors.

Kele D. Gabor

The sliced onions dropped down underneath to another conveyor belt, which could be guided by hand from one dryer surface to another. We had at least twenty-four dryers, each made of stainless steel, with a size about three by six meters. Workers with long-handled rakes constantly moved the contents around to dry the produce evenly. Hot dry air, fanned in from underneath, dehydrated the onions or other vegetables in a few hours. Only one row of four dryers was used for the onions; the rest were reserved for other produce and fruits. While transporting, cleaning, slicing, and drying the onions, the 'fragrance' increased at each station, and my skin, body, clothes, and soul became totally penetrated by the onion smell.

The second week I was there, they let me drive the battery-operated cart to carry the full boxes of onions. What had happened was that Russian KGB agents in brown leather coats, in many ways resembling the Gestapo, whisked the previous driver of this vehicle, Laci Makk, my immediate supervisor, away from the factory floor in front of my eyes. They didn't have blue epaulets like the Hungarian uniformed secret police (AVH). I would have never guessed that witnessing this terrible and scary event, and remembering the faces of the arresting officers, would play such a significant role in helping me to identify Western double agents. I could only load eight boxes on the smaller battery-operated vehicle, so I had to make more runs to keep up and supply the cleaning ladies and the machines. I didn't have to pull the heavy load and was happy about the sudden promotion but wished it had not come with such a heavy price of losing another young Hungarian to the KGB.

A short time after his arrest, someone grabbed my arm from behind. I turned and saw a middle-aged lady with fine features staring into my face.

I immediately smiled, as I knew it wasn't the KGB. She looked at me hard and asked, "Aren't you the son of 'so and so'?"

I knew if I didn't lie, my working for that summer was over at the factory, and we needed the money very badly. At that time, I was the only one working for money in my entire family of seven. We had no other income, we had run out of things to sell, and they took our land, house, and all the valuables without any compensation. For some reason, I wanted to say, "No", but it came out as a shaky "Yes'.

She said, "Don't worry. I'm Perl, the daughter of the ex-owner of this factory, but nobody has turned me in yet, and they just think I'm a very knowledgeable person about the canning technology." For Perl, using her married name was enough to hide her identity for the time being, and the Communist political officer didn't connect her to the previous factory owner. She told me she worked in the new president's office. They wanted her to join the Communist Party, promising her great rewards, and since they followed her advice, things started to go well at the factory and now she had a lot of authority. This factory actually made money, but most state-controlled companies didn't. In countries where the government runs them, businesses are typically inefficient!

The next summer, they hired me again as a lab assistant, thanks to Perl's help. I measured the water content of all dried produce shipped primarily to Russia. Unfortunately, after they found out about Perl, she was to be arrested and tried for treason. Luckily, someone warned her in time, and she was able to slip away out of the country and join her mother in Austria.

She was very lucky not to be caught, as by this time all of our borders to the west had the Iron Curtain in place, properly peppered with land mines.

I remember well when the Russian officer rechecking my calculation for the dried corn gave me a bottle of vodka, as he was very satisfied and happy with the shipment. He even invited me for a glass of beer in the nearby pub, and when I asked him why the great communist Russia needs the Hungarian produce, he responded, "You are better producers of goods than we, and we need to take as much food from you as possible because people with hungry stomachs do not have time for politics."

Three years later the factory, without Perl's help, had to close its doors because of gross mismanagement and even greater losses. Many a factory and company ended up this way. The Communist-run Socialist government turned out to be more inefficient than any other type of government— and that was a fact. The liberal democrats, Socialists, and Communist sympathizers worldwide contributed a great deal to the prolonging of the totalitarian Russian government. Industrial espionage during the Cold War aided the communist regime to continue the genocide, prison camps, political concentration camps (gulag), slavery, and atrocities against mankind, creating an evil environment far exceeding that of the Nazis.

After my engineering training, my first assignment was a real eye-opener in more ways than one. With my new colleagues, we had to experience firsthand how bad the communists were under the protection of the occupying Russian Red Army. The oppressive and totalitarian puppet government required us to do things we despised from the bottom of our hearts.

This government served the Soviet and Stalin's appointed elite. They also worked to rule the world by fear, but definitely not helping the people of Hungary. We felt, saw, experienced, and, unfortunately in some cases, had to help indirectly the evil Communist system when we had to execute unjust and cruel orders given by the "devils" themselves.

After the devastation of the Second World War, the Hungarian peasantry began to rebuild the country in hopes of a better life. Through the expropriation of large estates in 1945, hundreds of thousands of Hungarian peasants came into the possession of land. The old and the new landowners hoped that their land would ensure them a dependable livelihood.

However, wartime regulations did not end with the end of the war. Farmers still had to first meet their delivery quota obligations, and only then could they sell their products freely. Hungarian peasantry not only had to provide food for the population and the occupying Soviet army, but for war reparations as well. The delivery quotas were categorized: first came the per-person ration; next the sowing seed, some of which remained with the farmer; and thirdly, a general agricultural levy.

With the communists aiming at a total grasp of power, they sought to dominate Hungarian peasantry as well. Between 1948 and 1953, the tax burden of farmers increased threefold, and in 1952 they changed the order of taxation: first came the general levy, second the sowing seed, and lastly the per-person ration. Most of the time, nothing was left over after meeting the quotas. Often, collectors showed up in the company of secret security men for 'loft sweeping', i.e. looking for hidden produce.

The communist party tried everything in its power to destroy the traditional peasant way of life and force peasants to leave their land. This had two objectives: first, the Soviet Union was preparing, with the satellite countries, including Hungary, for World War III, with significant investments in weapons production and heavy industry. These huge investments were founded in part by the plundering of the agricultural sector. In addition, they needed manpower in the heavy industry. The communist system would not tolerate in any way the existence of an economically independent community with its own value system. The liquidation of land owning Hungarian peasantry, with its common lifestyle, its tradition and customs, was essential to the consolidation of the party's total control over its citizens.

Following the Soviet model, the "kulaks," or wealthy peasants, were caught in a cross fire. There is no equivalent in Hungarian for the word "kulak," and the Communists did not bother to translate it. Anyone was easy prey to be designated a "kulak," that is to say, a public enemy. The 'kulak' lists that were drawn up always included the most important and productive farmers in the villages. In principle, a "kulak" was supposed to own over twenty five acres of land; in practice, however, local party bosses were free to label just about anyone a "kulak." The "kulaks" were hit by surtaxes and increased quotas, as well as with psychological and physical terror. Bands of "kulak beaters" regularly made the round of villages and committed open acts of brutality and threats to keep the population in a state of fear. They wanted to wear down the peasants with forced labor and resettlement, as well as property seizures; trials based on fabricated charges, and severe prison sentences and executions. For the crime of non-compliance to meet quotas, four hundred thousand peasants were convicted. The resistance was so great that in certain villages, scores of people were thrown into jail for "plotting against society," and many lost their lives.

It is no wonder that some three hundred thousand peasants abandoned their land. Ten percent of previously cultivated land was left fallow. The farmers who stayed behind quickly lost any incentive to produce, leading to an enormous shortage of food and the introduction once again of rationing.

Since every failure of the socialist system was blamed on the "people's enemy," the communist bosses would seek out the "saboteurs." Scapegoats had to be found. A series of peasant trials ensued, leading to heavy prison sentences. The communists would claim that the meat shortage was the fault of the managers of the state Meat Distribution Company and they were executed. "Trashing sabotage" was punishable by death; secret slaughtering drew long prison terms.

"Modern Soviet agricultural methods" (unproductive) were forced upon the farmers in the Hungarian countryside, a model that resulted in severe grain shortages in the Soviet Union itself.

Following these "advanced" methods, they centrally planned and controlled what could be produced, when, and where. Some of the most "memorable" experiments included forced production of cotton and rice, originally not indigenous to Hungary. Eventually, the resistance of the peasantry was broken, and private farms were liquidated by forced collectivization.

I received my order to report for work in the state surveying office, located in the center of Hungary. The director invited me into his office and confidentially told me he knew my father; he respected everything he stood for, and he was happy and lucky to have me. He continued that in his and most other cartographic subdivisions, there were very few Socialists, Communists, or Communist sympathizers, but one never knew, so he cautioned me to be careful. I assured him I would be careful and confide only in a few close friends, and that was the reason I survived. I thanked him for the warning.

I had a delightful experience and wonderful working conditions in the office compared to other previous work I had done at other state-run organizations. By this time, all private enterprises had been wiped out. The "people's courts" found all company owners to be the "enemy of the state or people," and they were given prison terms or only their property and company were confiscated, if they were lucky.

The work in my new engineering office was heaven compared to any one of my previous jobs, including the one in the canning factory. In the first few weeks, I just learned about the new theodolites received from Switzerland (similar to Transit but more accurate, with more options).

Deception and Reality - Living Through the Missing Pages of History

I had to assemble and mount them on tripods, check the optics and all the features, and field-test them. After gaining some familiarity with the new tools, I was sent out by the Tisza River to readjust the map, put in new triangulation points close to the bridge to ease preparation for building the new and wider bridge that was on the drawing board, but never built.

The new senior engineer heading up the crew treated me like a true professional. He called me his personal helper and told me about many interesting events associated with his recent works. Our senior engineer, Ben, was earlier assigned to the team to re-measure all the new borders around our miniaturized and cannibalized Hungary. Since we just lost most of our land and about half of our population, the Russians approved the expenditures to redo the temporary and, many times, erroneously marked new borders. It was a good thing, as all the newly created governments and nations around us tried to grab as much land as possible and frequently usurped more than was already gifted to them by the radical French Clemenceau and Stalin and approved by the ignorant or misinformed Western leaders.

As Ben described his assignment, it was both good and bad. The good part was that in all cases, we were able to correct the mistakes made by the Romanians, Russians, Slovaks, and Serbs, which, for some reason, always ended up in their favor, getting even more territory from Hungary than they had already stolen. Most of these errors (the politically correct expression was 'inadvertent mistakes') were blatant. The sad part was the many Hungarians got stuck on the other side of the border. Some of Ben's stories almost made me cry about how some old folks would offer their only valuable possessions, even their last sack of potatoes, to move the border only one or two meters over so the family could stay and be buried in Hungary.

The new borders were drawn without regard to the Hungarian majority, and they were cut off from their homeland. The borders were often marked with just about a straight line between larger communities, also cutting off roads, bridges, cemeteries, natural borders, rivers, railroad lines, and paved roads. Even the natural contour of the land was ignored.

All his stories really hit home, as I was one of those who had to escape from my own homeland just because of my ethnicity. God was with us, as only about half of my family was divided this way, and at least my mother and half of my siblings were able to flee the Romanian, Serbian, Slovakian, or Russian ethnic oppressions. Some villages with populations of less than a thousand, like Lud, were divided in half. A mother's house stayed in Hungary, but her neighbor, who happened to be her daughter, was across in Romania. The actual distance between the two dwellings was less than twenty meters.

This type of insanity to satisfy the greed of a neighboring country was unbelievable and would not compute in the mind of the indigenous

Hungarian population. Hungarians typically blamed these crazy border changes on the ignorance of the Western diplomats who approved the treaty. Instead of following natural geographical and ethnic lines, they just drew the borders by connecting cities, towns, villages, or other settlements.

One of our good friend's families was affected at Szolos, where the cemetery was divided into three countries; his aunt, uncle, and their families were all buried close to each other in the same cemetery. When the borders were redrawn, the cross on his aunt's parents went to Russia, his uncle's family to Romania, and his parents stayed in the new, mutilated Hungary. I even saw a farmhouse where the only source of water in the nearby well fell on the other side of the border. Poor guy eventually had to abandon his farm, as he was not allowed to even get drinking water from his own well five meters from his house.

Lord Rothermere wrote in June of 1927, in response to the newly created countries and border adjustments in Europe: "The unjustly drawn new European borders will put the peace of entire Europe in constant danger."

Sure enough, the new countries formed at the expense of Hungary have now fallen apart or are in danger of splitting up, except for the Enlarged Romania. The Transylvanian Hungarians are still under the Romanian control but should be freed and be independent. The European Union needs to make this process a top priority, and ASAP!

After the breakup of the Communist bloc countries, the only place where border adjustments have not been made is Hungary.

After finishing my training with useful work and getting familiar with the new equipment, I headed back to the office. I worked on different assignments, checking field measurements against the current maps, drawing and printing the necessary information on the new maps. I was also frequently sent to the main cartographic office, where close to a hundred draftsmen were working.

Engineers, especially in the main office, were often courted by Western agents to gather intelligence; in other words, spy for them. They knew Russia was ahead in jet and rocket engine design, and both were scheduled to arrive in Hungary. The Russians got a jump start in rocket technology by capturing and receiving most of the German engineers and letting them experiment in their own field of expertise.[11]

Our regional office did all the surveying for the new military airport to accommodate the new MIG jet fighter planes. Next, the new rockets arrived and we did some of the surveying and maps for the silos.

A young cartographer, Sándor, his gorgeous sister, and I developed a close friendship and spent both professional and leisure time together while working in the main office in the capital. My new friend Sándor had exceptionally nice hand-printing on all his maps. His letters and numbers were as good as printed information, and often his work was mistaken for printed material. He worked strictly as a draftsman in the main cartography office. In the summer and early fall, he, his sister Piri, and I often went swimming together on the weekends. In the winter and early spring, when weather didn't permit outside activities, we played ping-pong doubles.

Sándor was left-handed, and I was right-handed. We successfully reached many finals and did very well in the industrial league.

After losing one of the finals, Sándor told me about a plan to save the small vineyard his mother wanted to keep. They lived just outside Eger, in a small house in the middle of a five-acre vineyard. I spent only one weekend with his family and also met his younger brother, Zoli. Piri, Sandor's sister was exceptionally attractive, with a lovely and pleasant voice. Her beautiful, clear blue eyes were captivating. When I looked in her eyes, I felt warm and comfortable. I liked and respected her too much to start a serious relationship, so I didn't want to ask her for a date. However, I really enjoyed her company, and I was happy when she accompanied me and her brother often. They lost their father,

---

[11] The USA let many of the German and Hungarian scientists be taken by England and Russia. Therefore, America fell behind in rocket technologies. The English put the scientists to a place where they could be observed and listened to, but unlike Russia, they did not give them assignments. What a waste!

just as I did, but their mother was able to cope with the difficulties better than my mother. Because of the drought, their mother could not make the increased tax payments and wine deliveries, and now the family vineyard would be taken away by the state.

Sándor's plan was to turn over some maps to some Western agents, who paid well for any such information. I remember telling him he should not have told me his plans, as everyone knew we were friends and the secret police with the new drugs could come after me; and without wanting to, I might implicate him or be an unwanted witness in his case. He told me not to worry, as he was working with the same agent, Mr. White, whom Laci had been doing business with for many years in our main office. I argued, "Don't you remember every time someone new tried to pass on information to the West, the individual was arrested within days, only Laci seems to avoid detection?" He went through the procedures he was going to follow, just like Laci. Like Laci, Sándor would select both the place and time for the drop, giving less than an hour for the agent to make the rendezvous for the pick up. Sándor believed that most people who were caught by the secret police let the Western agent specify the pick up time and place.

Two days later, I saw Piri come to pick up the cash for her mother. Everyone was happy, and we celebrated by going to the finest pastry shop and filling up on goodies, which we could not afford, as we both provided the badly needed financial support for our families. I remember eating several bowls of fresh strawberries. I loved them but could not afford them from the small amount of money I kept for myself.

I know the entire family was hoping Piri and I would fall in love and get married. Piri was smart, attractive, with a good figure and bright, big blue eyes. She was intelligent, sang beautifully, and was a delightful person, but I still had feelings for Lara and was not ready to give her up.

The next day, I witnessed Sándor's arrest by the KGB around ten a.m. in the office. They looked and acted the same way as I witnessed before at the arrest of Laci Makk in the canning factory. It was easy to remember, as one of the agents was missing almost half of his right eyebrow, close to his nose. At that time, I wondered if the Russians had only three KGB agents who did all the arrests. I was very nervous, but I tried not to show it and followed my routine for the entire week, but without the company of Sándor or Piri. I missed him, and that weekend, I decided to do something about it. I still had the phone number of his contact at the embassy on the backside of the rubber pad on his ping-pong paddle. His paddle was in my sports bag.

I wished I could contact Lara and have her be my sounding board for when I came up with a plan to catch the person or persons responsible for turning my friend Sándor and others over to the KGB. After long deliberation, I decided everyone around me was a potential suspect for turning in people who wanted to help the West. However, I really suspected Mr. White, as he organized the entire operation from the embassy side, and I could not come up with another strong suspect in our office, except for Laci, who was actively providing useful secret information but never had been arrested.

That weekend, Piri showed up with her brother Zoli at the ping-pong club where Sándor and I hung out on rainy or cold days. She was crying her heart out, and I could feel her hurt. She said, "Sándor should have come home this weekend, but there was no trace of him anyplace." I just realized I made a mistake of not notifying the family immediately after Sándor's arrest. It turned out for the best, as their house and Sándor's small one-room apartment were already under surveillance by the AVH (the Hungarian secret police). Piri kept on crying, and I had to quiet her down before telling her what happened. I sat her down and asked her to tell me exactly what had transpired since he didn't show up.

She said, "We went to his place, but my brother Zoli would not let me go up to his room and made me stay on the other side of the street. We were waiting there until Sándor's neighbor, whom we had met several times before, came out of the apartment building. Zoli ran across the street as he was just coming out from the main gate of the apartment building.

The neighbor who had not seen Sándor for the entire week went and asked the apartment manager to check, and they both went up to Sándor's room. They unlocked the door, found nothing except a big mess and an unused bus ticket to Eger, their home. According to the neighbor, the room was turned inside out, including the bed. It was obvious someone went to search Sándor's room, leaving nothing untouched.

"The apartment manager said, 'The secret police were already there earlier in the week, borrowed the master key, and asked about people visiting Sándor. Then after a few hours, they left.' When Sándor's neighbor asked what the manager said to the police, his response was, 'I told them I never saw anybody and that he was away most of the daylight hours, just came home to sleep in his small room. I also told them he is a handsome boy, so he'll turn up in a few days.' Sándor's neighbor thanked the manager's efforts and left to pass on the message to Zoli, who was by then waiting across the street with me a few meters away."

In retrospect, we did all the right moves, thanks to Zoli's suspicious mind. We went totally undetected, even while Sándor's place was under surveillance. Zoli became an invaluable help, and he deserves most of the credit for our eventual success of locating the guilty parties. Zoli was two years younger than his brother, but as Sándor used to say, "He was the brains of the family." He was much darker than Sándor, and instead of brown eyes, he inherited his mother's dark blue. He was taller than Sándor and very thin, so he always looked even taller than the few centimeters between us. I only saw Zoli in his dark-brown worn leather jacket, and he probably never had the money to buy himself another one.

We went to the zoo to be in a crowded place to avoid detection, in case someone was following us. Again, Zoli's ideas paid off many times over during our amateur detective work. Once it was dark, Zoli and I went aside to talk. When I told him I wanted to find the rat that turned Sándor in, Zoli responded, "We have to do it, not only for my brother, but all the other young Hungarian men needing to be saved in the future from the KGB and the AVH." At this point, Zoli took over most of the planning and the legwork part of our detective work. We agreed to meet again in public places and find safe spots to discuss our plan of action. Before departing, Zoli asked that we refer to each other with new names, no written communication, but if we have to leave a note, it would be coded.

The next week, we met under the Margit Bridge and greeted each other with the previously discussed method of changing the state of the top button on our shirt collar, either opening or closing the top as a sign of all clear to meet and talk. From this point on, I had to make sure all my shirts had a button on the top. On a few occasions, Zoli or I passed each other without the signal, as one of us suspected the coast was not clear. In this situation, we just ignored and walked by each other, and we would walk up to the center of the bridge separately and take the bus or streetcar and go to the railroad station, the secondary meeting place. Usually the coast was clear, and we just walked up separately to the middle of the bridge, where the connecting second bridge led to the island of Margit. It was close to a pickup point, bus, and streetcar stops, and at the same time an easy lookout to detect if someone was following us.

When each of us presented the plan, we found a lot of common ground and both agreed our prime candidates for betrayal were Mr. White and Laci. We decided to tackle both at the same time. I would call Mr. White to meet me using my code name and have Zoli just as a lookout to observe the situation.

While Mr. White was away hoping to meet me, I called again the same number to get another contact at the embassy. I asked to talk to someone urgently, as we had an important thing for Mr. White, knowing that he was already on his way to meet the new informer. Since I didn't speak English, it was very hard to find someone else to help me, but finally a person named Al came on the line, and with broken Hungarian, he was able to communicate. I introduced myself with the "opera" name and told him on the phone Mr. White was a double agent, as everyone who contacted him was caught in a matter of days after a drop. He responded with disbelief and persuaded me to meet him ASAP. I told him he had fifteen minutes to meet me at a park close by on the corner, but he must wear something green for recognition, as I did.

In sixteen minutes, a young guy showed up by the designated bus stop on the corner, with a small box under his arm wrapped in green colored paper. I just stepped up to him and said, "Te vagy Al?" (Are you Al?) He explained with his broken Hungarian that he had a hard time finding some green-colored item he could wear. That was the reason he was late.

He was just a year or two older than I was, and he originally came from Michigan. His mother was Hungarian, who taught him what he knew.

I explained the situation and why I suspected Mr. White. He pretty much convinced me Mr. White could not work for the KGB, as he was a great admirer of General Patton and he didn't care for the Russian communists, as he was convinced the KGB killed the general. Al also told me they have known about the leak or problem for some years, and after an exhaustive investigation, they believed the KGB agent must be working at the cartographic office. He also told me much later the reason he had to meet me was to identify me, in case I was the rat.

KELE D. GABOR

Later, I also found out that for a long time I was their main suspect, as I didn't provide the telephone code word after my first call. This situation really worked to our advantage, as they were almost always ready to meet me, and they often followed me to either set me up or catch me red-handed. For example, they gave me false names of people helping them obtain secret information. They also gave me the name of one of the Communist Party leader's son, Peter O., a red-headed, smart Jewish boy who worked at the office but in a management position with his own separate office.

By this time, most of my prejudice was gone toward most of the Jews, thanks to Lara. She totally convinced me to forget about classifying people under one umbrella but, instead, always to look at the individual. She did admit the Jewish people in general are the most racist group, they almost exclusively help each other, they have a tendency to look down on others, and they're likely to be paranoid. They trust no one, including their own kind. The majority of them are even afraid of healthy patriotic feelings expressed by others, and it is hard for them to closely identify themselves with a nation or nationality other than their own. Sure enough, I did find a few very decent and honest individuals amongst the Jewish people during my professional career.

It took Al over a month of investigation to conclude I was legitimate. I never told Al about Zoli's help but kept Zoli informed of any new developments.

When I was on assignment, Zoli and I kept in touch by coded messages. He came up with the idea of writing notes no one could interpret.

When I returned to Zoli his brother's ping-pong paddle, he looked it over and said, "You both have the same paddle make, with identical handles and a spiral leather grip. The only thing we need to do is cut up strips of paper matching the rolled up leather handle, put the strip of paper over the wrap matching its line, and put the message vertically on the paper.

After unwrapping it, fill in the blanks with meaningless information." We only had to use this communication a few critical times when we could not meet as previously scheduled or when passing on secret messages. Zoli's idea worked like a charm. The paper could be placed in a letter, put in the pocket, or passed by hand, but only readable by those people who had the same make and model paddle and knew how to match the paper to the handle.

At that time, I was still convinced Mr. White was the double agent working for the KGB, so I made Al promise that Mr. White would be out of the loop, and he kept his word. Zoli still believed it was most likely a person at the embassy and less likely Laci. It was one of the coded messages that got Zoli's attention. I remember writing Zoli a note saying I found out our suspect's name, "Laci," was his middle name and officially he was called "Vitéz." He immediately responded back that he was convinced Laci could not be our suspect anymore.

It was a few days later when we met and Zoli clarified his conclusion.

Zoli said, "As I recall, you told me about the same KGB agents arresting both my brother and your ex-boss a few years ago." He didn't have to say anymore, but we both said it at the same time. "They both had the same name, and the arrest came a few days after Vitéz Laci Makk started to provide information for the Western Embassy, not using his full legal, but only his middle name instead." This time, the only thing we had to do was contact Al and let him know our new discovery. We were proud of our detective work and were eager to share it with Al.

That meeting was on a "brown" day, as we both wore brown hats. I started to explain to Al it could not be Laci, that it must be someone else at the embassy, as the KGB did arrest a "Laci" with the same last name and about the same age at about the time he started to pass on information to Mr. White. A KGB informer must only pass on the name and possibly the age and not the identity of the individuals involved in espionage. The KGB still does not know they arrested the wrong person. Therefore, somebody is giving out the names only and possibly ages, and most likely, the rat does not know what the accused looks like.

Al's reaction puzzled me, as his response was, "We have others helping us, like Hodos, who has never been caught, and we need proof of your theory. I knew Hodos. He is the son of a well-respected military officer who was kicked out from the chiefs of staff office for the same reason as Árpád was— no German blood." I went back heartbroken with the new suspect's name, as I trusted Hodos with my life. Zoli, who never wanted to be seen by any Western agents, was waiting for me at the rendezvous point.

Zoli could tell something was wrong but just waited for my report. He was usually very quick with ideas, but this time, he didn't say a word. I could see he was thinking. After a while, he asked me to describe Vitéz and Laci, concentrating on similarities, not the differences. I just stood there and smiled without saying a word. I could see Zoli started to get mad, but I kept on smiling. When Zoli could take it no longer, he asked me to share my thoughts. I just told him this might be proving our point to Al, as they are both young males, but there are no other similarities. If Hodos was involved; he could also provide a short personal description besides the names.

Back to the drawing board, Zoli said, "The only good thing we got out of all this secrecy and hard work is that our code names will work, and so will our coded messages. It is time to relax a bit." Only those people who lived under the fear of communism could understand our extremely stressful situation, as we pretty well knew what price we would have to pay if caught. The real fear was, however, for our family and close friends, who are typically tortured by the secret police after an arrest.

I went home and changed, put my sweats on, and headed down to the club to play some ping-pong. Hard exercise and sporting activities usually got rid of some stress, and afterward, I dreamed about some of the solutions to difficult problems.

By the time I arrived at the club, a letter was waiting for me, and in it was the coded message from Zoli. I went to the restroom, closed the door, and wrapped the paper strip on the handle of my paddle. He wrote, "Level with Hodos and find out what he does differently from Laci." He also indicated he wanted to talk to me tomorrow at the usual place and time.

I could only find a much older guy to play with, but he played very good defense and gave me a good workout. (Ping-pong is a fast, furious, and exhausting game, especially on a professional level. For at least a month before competition, we used to run every morning about five kilometers and play every evening, except the day before the tournament.)

The next day, I was refreshed, went to work early, and left a note on Hodos's desk, saying I must talk to him ASAP, but privately. Fifteen minutes later, he knocked on my office door. Hodos stuck his head in and, in front of my other colleagues, indicated something was wrong with my measurement on the map I gave him earlier and we must resolve the differences.

I responded, "I would like to go out for an espresso if he would be kind enough to join me to discuss the problem". He said he would if I picked up the tab. It made me think he must be a cheapskate, as he must have made some extra money for the information provided to the embassy. I told him since it was my error that slowed him down and brought him in, I felt obligated to pay for the coffee and possibly a sweet croissant too. He smiled and waited by the door while I put my raincoat on. We went to the closest coffee shop having an outside cover where we could find privacy and see if any undesirable person was around us or watching us.

I just looked into his eyes before taking my sip of espresso and told him I knew he was helping a Western embassy by providing information of the planned hiding places for the rockets. He took a sip of coffee and said, "So do others, except I don't get caught."

"You must do something differently than those who were caught," I responded.

"Not really, just don't talk to anyone about it."

"You are talking to me."

"You wouldn't squeal, even if drugged."

"How do you know that I didn't turn in Sándor?" I asked.

He simply stated people were picked up and arrested the same way much before I showed up in the office. Hodos also said, "I know that at least two more in the office are helping the West." I asked who they were, and he responded, "You must know if you knew about me, why should I tell you?" I thanked him, but I didn't tell him that I only knew about him and Laci.

I called Al to meet me at the park close to where we had met before and asked for the color code. He said he was wearing a blue necktie, so I had to look for something blue in the office before leaving for the day. The color match served as a code for the coast is clear. If one of us didn't wear the designated color, there was something wrong and the meeting must be postponed. Al told me later he had to go out and buy every color of necktie and keep them in the office, as I insisted on selecting the color code most of the time just before our meeting took place, even when he initiated the call. This day, I called and Al selected blue.

I could not find any blue on me or that I could borrow from someone else, so I ended up pouring blue ink over my white handkerchief to be placed in the top pocket of my jacket. The blue ink was hard to find in the supplies, as we primarily worked with Indian ink that was black. I made a mess with my newly colored blue hanky in the washbasin. The blue-indigo ink was so permanent, the stain stayed on the white sink for a long time, and everybody knew who the clumsy guy was, as I was walking around with blue hands for a few weeks.

I asked Al who the other guys were who provided information to the embassy, as I needed to know. He didn't want to give me a name and said bringing up the name of Hodos was a bad slip up on his part. I told him, "I don't have much time, as I have to meet someone else soon, and I'm at the breaking point, so if he doesn't want to help, he should just say so."

He said, "I really don't know the other guy's name, but I could find out."

I asked him to do so ASAP. He told me both Hodos and the other guy's name were very hard for him to get, as they were not on the list for reimbursements. I asked how much time he needed, and his response was three days, not including the weekend. I parted the first time without saying good-bye. Al knew I was very upset. I was late getting to the meeting place to see Zoli, but on the way, I already figured out where the traitor was.

Without expressing my conclusion, I talked to Zoli about Hodos describing our conversation, and before I finished he asked me to call and meet Al to find out who were the other guys. I told him he was a little late, as I already met Al and made the same request. When I finished my report on what had transpired between Al and me, he just blurted it out, "We were right the first time. The problem is at the embassy."

That night we stayed up, as we had to discuss and agree on the strategy of finding out the person or persons responsible for passing the names to the KGB. Al's response may have also cleared Mr. White, as people with false names or without payments were never caught. The exchange of money for information was the key. We were really fortunate that we used both methods for protection— no real name, no reimbursement, and hid our identities. I thanked Zoli for his original idea. We thought if the embassy was investigating this problem internally and everybody turned out squeaky clean, the people might be the in-house investigators or the financial office that provided the names to the KGB. We finally decided we would continue working with Al, not telling him our discoveries, but using him for our advantage.

We knew there was no way we could convince the proud and somewhat arrogant type of our theory; we needed more proof. This arrogance was easy to spot, as they got all upset about mispronouncing their names, but at the same time, they held a different standard for themselves.[12] They were typically oblivious to the fact that they mispronounced just about every foreign name, regardless of the stature of the person or place. They even changed geographical names. The first time I noticed this double standard was when I told the agents not to contact me, as I would initiate all calls.

The "Don't call me, I'll call you" request was hard to handle and swallow by Western agents, as they thought that they knew better.

Initially, our plan was that a guy with a fictitious name would put a call in to Mr. White and get the initial contact for some very hot information and demand immediate payment. Then two of us would observe what takes place outside the embassy, as we already knew the embassy phones were monitored occasionally and unlikely to be used for talking to the KGB. We also called Al and told him not to bother finding out the other guy's name helping with the intelligence gathering, as it could possibly tip off the double agent. Al didn't believe me but was happy not to get into trouble by asking for the other contact's name.

Our difficulties were more than we initially realized. We already knew Socialists, liberals, Communists, or Communist sympathizers infiltrated some Western embassies and governments. Zoli knew a lot; even today I cannot figure out where the information came from, but he either got it from somewhere or extrapolated it. At times, I was convinced Zoli had some training as a spy. When I confronted him, he smiled and said, "Since my brother was arrested, the only thing I read are spy stories, and I always wanted to be a detective." Of course, looking for double agents in a foreign embassy is much more difficult and dangerous than any detective work done openly. We had to hide our identity, change our looks, avoid detection, identify potential KGB or AVO individuals, live under constant fear, account and have an alibi for all our subversive activities, moves and travels, without financial or

---

[12] Commonly mispronounced names are Doppler, Kodaly, Karoly, and Budapest (should be 'Booda-pasht). Also, erroneously renaming names of cities and peaks, like Vienna for Wien and Mt. Everest for Chomolangma.

other support.

Our timing for the implementation of our plan was also critical, as we could only put an all-day watch on embassy employees on the weekend, and we could only follow two at a time. There was the added difficulty of getting the money for two good cameras to take pictures, as even film was too expensive for us.

We set our trap as a payback for all the young men who were picked up thanks to the hated Western double agents. We, of course, were ready to kill the double agent or agents responsible for the crimes. Now I wish we had killed them, as the discovery of the agents and consequential hell Zoli's family and I had to go through would have been avoided and also saved a few more innocent lives.

We found out there were new silos going in by the south side of the Kékes range, and the exact coordinates were only available at the highest levels of the communist political machines. That weekend we got Piri involved, Zoli's older sister, as we needed to get into the office of Peter O., the son of the Communist Party leader. We rehearsed every move, covered all options and our tracks. Zoli was a natural at planning for every detail, possible mishaps, and alternate solutions. Piri and I were more devil's advocates.

In short, our final plan was to enter Peter's office late on Thursday afternoon, just before quitting time, and use Piri's help to gain access to the office as a backup and steal an important paper, or at least get the coordinates associated with the new Russian military plans. Zoli would call using the name Peter O and demand to speak with Mr. White. He would offer the unique plan for a good sum of money on Friday night. That evening and the next two days, we would decide whom we should follow, and any time the person made contact with another via a public phone or at a potential drop zone, we would snap a picture.

Next Monday, I received a call from my office that I was reassigned to work on a long-term project of land redistribution in Southern Hungary. I was to report down there the following Monday. The remaining time was too short to take a chance on moving up the timetable on our plan. We decided to get Al involved without telling him our complete plan, just to slow down the recruitment or information solicitation, and forget about naming the other people helping the embassy from our office, at least until I returned. He was very receptive to our ideas and offered to help, either financially or with material supplies.

    We definitely didn't want any financial help, as it might jeopardize our plan, or worse, someone might discover our identities. I did call my boss to request a postponement, but he didn't want to, as he said, "I'm trying to save your life." We did put everything on hold but could not wait to conclude our investigation. My boss's comment bothered us a great deal. We were not sure what he meant by the "save my life" response.

KELE D. GABOR

First Arrest

I had to go to the office early that morning and talk to my director before leaving for my new assignment close to the taken away territory of southern Hungary, where the newly drawn Serbian border now stands (the northeastern part of current Yugoslavia, or in English, the Southern Slavs).

I just had to know what my big boss meant by his comment on the telephone about saving my life. Unfortunately, I had to wait until he showed up, and that particular day, he was late. I was nervous, like sitting on pins and needles, when the usually early riser came into the office late after ten in the morning due to family sickness.

When he saw me by his door, he smiled and asked if I was in love. I just said, "Sir, I need to see you at your earliest convenience." His response was that he had to make some phone calls and attend a short meeting before he could see me. I told him my bus would leave early afternoon and I had not packed. He responded, "Go home, pack up, and let's meet for lunch across from the bus station so you can talk to me before leaving. What is so urgent that cannot wait until you return or just phone me?" I told him simply we had better talk privately, as one never knows who may be listening.

When my boss wanted a meeting, it always started and ended on time, so when he didn't show by twelve-fifteen p.m., I really got concerned. Before each meeting, he would hand out the agenda in time to prepare for it. The agenda also included the allotted time, the person responsible for each subject, and general discussion topics. Meetings were limited to one a week unless there were special circumstances. However, he encouraged us to work in teams and paid special attention to balanced and mixed personality types, sexes, experience levels, and specialties. Only managers and people who needed to know the topic were invited to the staff meetings. His weekly status meetings always concluded in an hour for the six or seven managers.

I decided to stay in the back of the restaurant and observe things from a distance, just in case I detected any potential AVH (the Hungarian KGB) agents and had to take off by the seldom-used back door. At twelve twenty-one p.m., he finally showed up, and I kept on waiting in the back of the restaurant until I could be sure he was alone and not followed. He was just about to leave when I stepped forward and greeted him. He immediately apologized for not making the twelve o'clock meeting.

Since there was not much time to talk, I just looked into his eyes and asked, "What did you mean by your comment that you assigned me to this job to save my life?"

He said, "I didn't mean it literally, I just heard you were involved with a very attractive girl whose brother was recently arrested for espionage and aiding or associating with the 'enemy of the people,' and this is dangerous and may be life-threatening. I also understand why young professionals try to help the West shorten the grip of this totalitarian system. What I want to know is, are you in love?"

I was so relieved it took some time to answer his question, and I said, "Yes, I'm in love, but not with her."

He turned to me, and with a curious look he asked, "Are you in some trouble I should not know about?"

Without hesitation, I responded, "Yes and no."

He looked at me and said, "I hope she is not pregnant."

"Nothing like that."

With a real worried look, he shook my hand and left as soon as my bus arrived. To my surprise, he hung around at the exit doors until the bus left. I knew he suspected something awry with me, as he showed genuine concern.

I felt a tremendous pressure to execute our meticulously constructed plan ASAP to identify the guilty party at the embassy, trick him into a situation to obtain definite proof of his evil activity, and take a break away from all the pressure. The pressure started to wear on me, and I saw a potential KGB agent in every stranger. I was always on edge. One cannot fully appreciate the wear and tear of living in constant fear of your life unless it is experienced.

Leaving from or going to places, I had to be aware of my surroundings, and on many occasions I had to change directions, destinations, or the routes to avoid any possibility of being tracked. Even running into good friends required careful interaction in public places in case I was arrested later, as I didn't want to implicate them. Guilt by association was often used to handle the undesirables. Therefore, the unscheduled and unplanned meetings on streets or bus stations were also purposely shortened not to bring attention to or imply involvement in what I may have done against the communist regime.

Because I arrived late that evening in the city of Csaba, I could not get a connection to my designated destination, a small town. A hotel was near the bus station, and when I registered, I noticed some other familiar names on the guest list from my office. I got settled in my room and decided to go out for supper, but first I looked up one of my colleagues to see if he wanted to keep me company. Gábor was an experienced young engineer with light brown hair and blue eyes, and he was always helpful to me. He was in charge of the fine-precision equipment and often explained some of the intricacies of their efficient and effective use.

When I knocked on his door, to my surprise, a young lady's voice inquired who I was. Puzzled about the lady inside, I apologized and said the clerk at the desk gave me the wrong room number, as I was looking for my colleague. As I turned around, I heard the door open behind me.

An exceptionally pretty blond head with large blue eyes appeared in the narrow crack of the partially opened door. She said, "You are Kele. I saw you at the office once when I brought lunch for Gábor. He just went out to bring in some cold cuts and bread for supper, would you please join us?"

I politely refused, saying, "I really need to go out and have a hot cup of soup," which I considered as important as the main meal, especially during traveling.

She reached out, grabbed my arm, and pulled me in, saying, "We have hot tea in the thermos that should suffice." She offered me a chair by the window, and she started the conversation before I could sit down. "Gábor told me about you, and I have wanted to meet you. So tell me all about you, as Gábor should be here any minute and his only outside interest is music."

I asked, "Classical, folk, or modern?" She said since he got the new radio, he only listens to Western stations. I laughed and said, "That is illegal."

She also laughed and sat down on the other chair, turning it around to face me. She said, "We have good sound insulation, with one-meter thick walls between our neighbor and us, even though he wouldn't report us to the police."

"How about the window, as that is how most people get overheard and get reported?" She smiled again and responded that they took care of that by putting a stuffed bag between the double windows before turning the radio on in the back bedroom.

I started to feel uncomfortable, as she was very attractive and a pleasant lady. We were sitting alone in a hotel room with an inviting smile and bed in-between us. At that time, I would have never imagined that she and I would spend a whole night together at a place of confinement not too far in the future. I changed the subject and mentioned we had never been formally introduced while thinking it was too bad she was a blonde. For some reason, I was always more attracted to darker haired ladies, especially red heads, brunettes, and blacks with blue or green eyes.

She said, "I'm Viola. I have been married to Gábor for almost five years, but we don't have any children yet, so whenever possible, I join him on his official excursions to increase our chances for a baby."

Before I could ask my next question, the key in the door turned and Gábor appeared in the doorway with a bag of groceries. He first turned to his wife and gave her a big, noisy kiss on her lips and asked her where she picked up that mean-looking ugly guy, pointing toward me. Before I could respond, he shifted his bag to his left hand, and while smiling, he extended his right hand to greet me. He always had a firm handshake, so I also returned one.

Gábor said, "What a pleasant surprise. Please join us and have supper with us."

Viola added, "You're too late, I already invited him." She laid out all the food, two knives, and paper plates on a large towel on the top of the bed.

She stepped back to view the setup while putting her hand around Gábor's waist. As they were standing next to each other, inspecting the laid-out goodies, I noticed how attractive they looked together, in spite of the fact that she was slightly taller than he was.

I had a great supper and dinner combined. I totally forgot about my hot soup. Gábor bought some goodies I could never afford, and they urged me to try everything. When I thanked them for the superior, delicious, and plentiful food, they both smiled, and Viola said, "We know you give almost all your money to your mother, leaving very little for even an occasional splurge, and you always look starved." She went on to explain that they were well off because her mother was still working in Paris as a model, and she provided them with quite a bit extra each month; in fact, her Communist friend smuggled the new super-duper radio in for Gábor.

She was very cute while talking. I noticed she had almost identical lips to Lara's, but her complexion was much lighter. I guess every attractive lady had to have something in common with Lara, or it was natural to look for features that reminded me of her. However, she looked, talked, and moved more like Piri.

I became very tired after the unusually delicious big meal and all the running around, so I thanked them again, bid them 'Goodnight', and left.

The next morning, I saw them at the station as we boarded the train to our work destination. We checked into the same cabin and traveled together. The trip was delightful; she had a pleasant voice, so it was good to listen to her silly stories, as I had no interest in the subjects she covered, such as styles for women and men, tasteful use of makeup, and attraction by scent. Once we arrived, I was happy to learn they first wanted to see their assigned room. I needed to be alone to work out some plan to get back to Budapest expeditiously to finish our detective work. I headed to the local office to report to my new boss. The middle-aged but well-dressed office secretary, Rosa, sent me to a staging area, as the magnitude of our job required extra space and people. I was directed to a large old castle at the end of town, where the local communist headquarters was also situated. There they gave us the entire ballroom and connecting area, which was already set up with lots of tables of different heights, sizes, and colors. The chairs were also a mixed collection, obviously some of them coming from the leftover furniture from the castle. My new boss's office was right off the main entrance. He was away from his desk on a field trip.

The parquet floor was torn up in many places. Evidently, Russian soldiers had occupied it, as they typically picked the oak pieces up for firewood to keep the place warm during cold winters. The walls were badly scratched, and the little statues in the upper corners had their extremities missing, and some even had their heads blown off. This, of course, was typical of the Russian army personnel throwing their bayonets or shooting at art pieces just for fun, especially after drinking.

I went out to get an early lunch, as after the heavy evening meal I didn't feel like eating breakfast. There were no eateries nearby, so I went to the grocery store. It was a small store but well-stocked in preparation for the "land redistribution" project, which brought in at least twenty-five additional professional engineers and at least that many technicians in the very small town. There was a tall, shapely, but very pale young lady with a sweet smile by the cash register, an old man taking inventory, and one cleanly dressed middle-aged customer, a farmer. He must have been local, as he teased the pretty young girl while paying for his pipe tobacco. The man invited both the old inventory clerk and the young lady for a fresh and sweet watermelon. Both workers in the store declined, and the girl added, "We would not take any food from the eight beautiful children you have." The customer told them they had an excellent crop and plenty of extra watermelons to be shared with good people. I bought a small loaf of freshly baked bread roll (Buci), a canned liver pate, and a large, naturally fermented pickle fresh from a large oak barrel. With the small sack of goodies, I headed back to a partially maintained park area in front of the castle.

While consuming my early lunch on one of the old benches, I looked around, trying to find out about the family who once built and owned this place. The family name and crest had been long damaged and defaced to make it unreadable. Above the hammered-out family crest, which may have been done in plaster and painted with color, stood a large five-pointed wooden red star, the symbol of the Russian Communism, totalitarianism, slavery, injustice, and cruelty for all people, except the ruling elite. The thought came to mind that neither the Nazis nor those people who had that castle could have been as mean, evil, primitive, illiterate, and cruel as the ones represented by the red star.

A carriage drawn by two horses with five people in it pulled up to the main gate of the castle. From the way they were dressed, it was obvious they were some of my new colleagues. I stood up from the bench, and my pants got caught in a sliver, tearing a ten-centimeter section right behind my knee. I didn't pay much attention, as they were my traveling trousers. I just went inside to meet the gang.

My new boss was a big man with dark-brown hair, mustache, heavy eyebrows, and dark eyes. He was at least a head taller than anyone else around and built like an athlete. He was busy explaining something to another engineer at one of the tables with an opened map, so I stood back, waiting until he finished. His voice was pleasant but firm as he gave his final instruction to my colleague. He knew I was right behind him as he turned toward me and said, "Welcome to the dirty work."

At that time, I envisioned "the dirty work" referred to climbing through creeks, springs, riverbeds, and fences, where one usually picked up most of the dirt during surveying projects. But I was wrong. We had to do terrible injustices to decent farmers and their families, as the Communist Party demanded it. He invited me to his office, partially separated from the huge ballroom by bookshelves and old furniture pieces providing, minimum privacy. I suspected his current office must have been used as an open coatroom, providing the service for all guests and dignitaries who ever visited the castle in its prime.

My new boss's name was Sándor Nagy (big), and I commented on how appropriate of a last name he had. He smiled as he noticed I was aware of his imposing stature. He asked me about my experience level, and I told him what I had done in the field so far. He said, "Good, we can definitely use you in re-measuring some old roads, remapping the small river, as it had meandered a bit since the last survey was done in the 1930s."

Sándor, looking at the bag next to me, suggested I get the rest of my luggage and settle in the room assigned to me by the local commissar in a nearby kulak (prosperous) home. I told Mr. Big the bag was all I brought, as I was expecting to go back for mandatory military registration soon.

He said, "Don't worry about it. I can get you out of anything, as the party [Communist] wants to have this done before the winter sets in." I must have shown my displeasure, as he commented he also felt bad about doing this kind of a dirty job, but we had no choice. There was no way for my new boss to know how important the job I wanted to do was or why I wanted to go back to complete my mission, so I just thanked him.

I was ready to leave when he stopped me, looked into my eyes, and said, "If this type of work starts to get to your stomach, let me know, and I'll give you a break if we stay on schedule." I thanked him for his concern, not realizing the exact nature of our work. I wondered how I could get at least two weeks of a break in order to have a chance to identify the rats in the embassy that got my good friend arrested. Of course, I only found out later how dirty and terrible a job we had to do causing pain, suffering, and devastation for many of the farmers and their families.

The next morning, I had to report by seven o'clock and soon found out about the "job" we had to do. As it turned out, the local people didn't want to join any cooperative farming group as envisioned by the Russian-led Communist Party. The individual farmers had enough good soil to raise a family in spite of high taxes, without having to give up their land and share everything else with others. As an incentive to join the newly created farmers' association or cooperative where everything belongs to the state, the party took all the good land away from the individuals and made it the state farm. The lesser quality soil at the fringe of the collective farm area, about four thousand hectares of the association land, was redistributed to those who refused to join.

We had to pay particular attention to the redistributed parcel to make sure it could not be accessed by road. It had to be less productive land than what the owner had before, and most of all, as far away from his family home as possible. A person whose home fell into the association land and didn't join was always forced to move to a smaller, dirtier, and older house in the back country. The home-exchange program was run and supervised by the local Communist Party leader. I don't think anybody else there had such an evil heart or the stomach to do that work. The local party leader got the central-committee directive that the richer the family, the cheaper the new home must be, and these homes should not have working wells or good-quality water.

The economic pressure was so great on these independent farmers to join the Communist Party and the collective farm that many of them came to our office to protest. They were promptly arrested and threatened with confiscation of all their produce, including seed for next year's crop, without compensation. I had an intimate experience before with the "wealth redistribution" when my family had to give up our land and home, and I could see the similarity for the process to gain more and more government control where the end justifies the means.

I think it was the third farmer, whom I saw earlier in the store, being arrested when something came over me (I should have known better). I walked up to the commissar standing at the entry gate of the castle, yelling profanities, and I just calmly asked him to release the man, as he had eight children at home and they would be lost without a father.

The commissar looked me over like a meat inspector checking out a side of beef and asked who the hell I was. I looked in his eyes and said, "I'm the guy who is helping you create your dream."

Kele D. Gabor

He didn't return my look, avoiding eye contact, just watching his boots. I just noticed that for the first time, I was facing a non-Jewish local party chief. He was young, in his late thirties, with straight blond hair, a round face, gray eyes, and red cheeks. He bent toward me and quietly whispered, "We have to make an example out of the bad apples."

I responded, "How about making good examples of the good apples?" He asked what the difference was. I said it is just the opposite of what you do, but the good side is easier to sell. He asked for my name and asked me to join him for a drink at a nearby bar that night. I decided to thank him and even asked him to let the others go too. All of a sudden, I had clout among the people watching the incident. Later, I didn't know what to do with the trust they placed in me after this incident.

I sent my friend Gábor with strict instructions to meet the commissar at the bar at the designated time and to tell him I was reassigned by my boss to an urgent job, but I would look up the Communist Party chief later. It took quite a bit of convincing Mr. Big to give me some very important work on paper to cover my absence from the meeting with the commissar. It turned out it was a good move, as based on my important assignment, he started to respect and listen to me more. Maybe he thought I was one of the agents sent by the party to spy on him. He became very docile with me, and I was able to get the release of the other two farmers arrested earlier.

The young local Communist Party leader tried to get friendly with me and shared some of his personal problems with the opposite sex. Being afraid to advise him the wrong way, I just kept quiet, and he interpreted it as a sign of wanting to listen. He would use me as a listening post an told me about his escapades, which really turned me off. Not showing any sign of disgust with his affairs, he went on advising me on how to take advantage of women, as they are only good for sex, but the most important thing after sex is to urinate immediately after ejaculation, even if the urine goes over the lady and the bed. According to him, the immediate urination saves men from sexually transmitted diseases.

The passive listening didn't help; instead of solving a problem, I created the worst situation, as no farmers wanted to join the Russian Communist style collective farm anymore. I knew I was in deep trouble. In the meantime, I tried to find out as much about my potential adversary to give me some edge in future negotiations. I did find out about the commissar's past.

He used to be a leader in the Nazi Youth Group (Arrow-Cross) and served as the political officer during the German occupation, so I knew right away he was extremely dangerous. The Communist Party often used these turncoats, as they could always count on them, regardless of how terrible an act they had to perform. The Nazis did the same, using Eichmann, a Jewish officer, to commit the atrocities against his own people.

My difficulties really started the next day when I went for a haircut. The local barber called me 'Sir', which is an absolute no-no in a communist society, and asked if he could also give me a shave, as it came with a haircut. I hesitated, as the price of the haircut was already beyond what I should spend without feeling guilty, so I always waited as long as possible between haircuts.

My poor little brother, even as a teenager, couldn't afford a haircut and always had his hair unusually long. One time, I promised him he could go with me and have a decent haircut, but I could not deliver on my promise for a long time. When I finally took him, I just had enough for both of us, but without a tip. When his turn came, he just reached in his pocket and gave half of the money to my barber as a tip, turned around, and walked away. He had a heart of gold and never took advantage of other people, even when others took advantage of him.

This time, I figured on a larger tip and tried to forget about what happened two days ago. After the haircut came a scalp massage, and after the scalp massage came the shave and a facial massage. I never had such a nice treatment in a barbershop, and I was trying to count in my head how much change I had to give as a tip. It was not until much later when I went to Japan and had a haircut there that came close to the treatment I had.

I was so relaxed standing up after an hour-and-a-half-long beauty treatment, I almost lost my balance. I reached in both pockets, looking for all the change I could grab to pay the accommodating barber with all I had.

I put all my change in the left hand and reached in my back pocket for my wallet when the old barber spoke up and said, "This was on the house, and you can come anytime for a repeat performance." I was so surprised, I just thanked him, put all my change on the counter, and left. Afterward I kept thinking about the unique treatment, as I didn't then and still don't believe in a free lunch, but I figured it was a fluke, an early Christmas present.

That evening, I developed a scratchy throat on my way to my newly assigned place after work. I stopped at the local bar to have my favorite "mix" to relieve my sore throat, hoping the commissar would not be there.

I went straight to the bar and asked for a mix. The mix, as we called it, contained a shot of raspberry syrup and a shot of strong rum mixed together.

While waiting for the bartender to serve, I looked around and only saw about ten people, but they were all looking at me; even the small group playing cards stopped dealing in the back of the room. I knew something was wrong, as they all smiled, so I headed to the restroom to take off whatever my colleagues or the barber pinned on my back, but I knew it must have been very funny. The mirror in the men's room was small and dirty, so I had to clean it and take it off the wall so I could put it behind me.

I looked and looked, but nothing was on me, not even a loosely hanging thread or a tear sewn together; the tear at the back of my knee was almost invisible. I took my time going back, trying to justify in my head the weird behavior I just witnessed.

When I got back to the bar, two drinks were waiting for me, lined up side by side. So impatiently, I told the bartender I only ordered one. He smiled and said, "No extra charge." I returned his smile and relaxed a bit, thinking, Why not two for the price of one, and I'm assured of a good night's sleep in spite of my stupid involvement in the Communist politics with a man with a serious inferiority complex in a small town. As I lifted my shot glass, and before the rim touched my lips, almost as one voice, all the people, including the bartender, lifted their glasses and said, "God bless."

I automatically returned the usual toast, and then it dawned on me. I thought, this is trickery, as under communism, the name of God could not be used in public places or prayer in schools.[13] I got very nervous and looked around, but everyone was still smiling at me. I relaxed a bit, sipping down the sweet, strong, and thick alcoholic drink, holding it for a moment in my throat to get the full benefit of the syrupy, good-tasting medicine.

When I hesitated to get the second glass, the bartender assured me it was okay. This time, I lifted my second glass while turning around to face the audience and yelled back, "God bless all of you!" They returned my greetings the same way, and then I knew it wasn't a trick, as they would have responded differently the second time. When I tried to pay for the shots, the bartender refused and wouldn't even accept a tip. I figured that "the gods are smiling on me" and this was my lucky day.

The two shots of drinks did the trick. I fell asleep fast. I forgot about my troubles and woke up with a clear throat and refreshed. The family providing the room always had gloomy looks on their faces, I thought, in spite of the fact that they were paid extra cash for the big room I used.

(I later found out most of the money slated for our room and board was paid directly to the Communist party leader, but he 'forgot' to distribute it).

However, this morning they were all smiling, and the man of the house insisted I have breakfast with them. This was unusual, so I accepted their hospitality. It was a simple but nourishing breakfast, with scrambled eggs, a large piece of ham, and a hot cup of milk the way I liked it. At the table, everyone was polite and happy. When I made the usual cross with my hand to thank the Lord for the good food I was accustomed to, they all joined me with the same gesture.

I arrived happy, content, and well-rested in the office ahead of starting time, so I reviewed all the measurements we made the day before. About that time my colleagues started to arrive, and they looked at me funny.

When Gábor came in, he said, "Are you trying to start a revolution, or just WWIII?" I must have looked puzzled as he went on to say that what I did was not smart, intervening with the Communists. He continued, "Don't you know they are the meanest group of people, more so than the Nazis or the Gestapo? If you're trying to be a hero, don't

---

[13] I wonder about people who don't want to use the name of God, or even permit His name in schools or sport events. But the same people love the dollars where every bill has the inscription, "In God we trust."

forget, they all die young or they're already dead."

When Sándor, my boss, came in, he just gave me a dirty look and proceeded to his desk without saying a word. In fact, he ignored my "Good morning" completely. I got up from the chair to see him to clear the air, but he didn't want to see me. About an hour later, when all the surveying teams left on assignments, I got up and asked, "Where are you going to send me this morning?"

He looked around, and when he saw everybody else had left, he said, "I was instructed not to send you out and keep you in the office." I asked why.

He said, "Figure it out by yourself."

I was very upset when I left early to get lunch from the local grocery store. I asked for a can of pate and small round loaf of bread. The slender young girl behind the counter lifted off all the cans of liver pate, about six cans, grabbed a round loaf of freshly baked bread and placed it in front of me on the counter. I was upset and impatient, so I raised my voice and said, "I ordered one can."

She smiled and said, "There is no charge whatsoever. Just take your food to the nearby park, where you usually eat it in front of the castle."

My response was automatic and harsh. "You all confuse me with someone else, as nothing is free in this world. I'm not a confidant of the local or any Communist party, so how come everybody is treating me like that?

I also know the state-owned shops like this cannot give away anything."

She didn't say anything, but when I put the money on the counter, she grabbed my hand and asked me if she could hug me. I was so taken aback, I didn't know what to say or do. While she was holding and squeezing my hand, she bent over the counter and whispered, "I'm Elisabeth, the daughter of the family who used to own the castle you work in, but nobody knows except the people who gave me a place to hide. The rest of my family was tortured and killed by the Russians and the communists, even though my parents helped many Jews survive the holocaust." A familiar story.

She was still holding on to my hand when an older man came out of the supply room, turned toward me, and smiled. I just said, "I'm nobody important, and I don't understand why people don't let me buy anything in this town."

The old man smiled and said, "Since the Communist takeover in 1949, nobody had the courage to speak up against the ruthless people in control, and you are the first gentleman who did something for us poor peasants."

I was taken aback by his sincere words and didn't try to explain that it was a fluke, not courage, when I acted automatically against injustice without thinking of the potential dire consequences.

Elisabeth was still holding and squeezing my hand harder and harder.

The only way out was to look in her eyes, step closer, and bend over the counter to kiss her hand. After the kiss, she loosened her grip, but it took me a long time to gently pull my hand out without any resistance.

I thanked them and left with one small loaf of bread and a can of pate without paying.

While eating my lunch, I could tell I was being watched, but I kept on eating and visually replaying the recent incident. Elisabeth was slender, with large eyes and a high forehead. Her eyes were big and grayish blue, and her hair was medium brown, combed back in a bun, as Lara had it the first time we met. Elisabeth was an attractive young lady, with very light, almost white, skin that may have never seen sunshine. She had unusually long fingers and legs and small and narrow lips. I was thinking if she had voluptuous lips, I would definitely like to have a date with her and kiss her the first chance I had. I thought I was crazy thinking about kissing when I should be preoccupied with saving my skin and going back to Budapest to finish my most important "job." I wish I could have seen the future, as I later found out I should have been much nicer to her. She, however, remained to be the sweetest person I ever met and one of those ladies whom I will never forget.

After my unusually long lunch break, I headed back to the office.

Almost all the local people I saw, even across the street, tipped their hat as a sign of respect as they passed by. I was confused about the whole thing, and for the first time in my life, I had no idea what to do. The more I thought about it, the less came to my mind except to stay put, as things would turn out okay.

When I got back to the staging area in the castle, I went to Sándor, my boss, trying again to get a new assignment, as my project was completed and all the measurements had been checked out on the maps. He said, "I had to call your big boss, as we need to get you out of here immediately.

You create more problems than your director or I could solve, and I certainly don't want to see you again, even though I know what you did was done with good intention. Go ahead, sit by your table and look like you're working while we are waiting for your big boss's call."

I sat in my chair, looking around the temporary office room, trying to imagine what the castle and other rooms looked like before the Russian soldiers destroyed it. I thought of dancing a formal waltz with Elisabeth, Lara, Kati, and then Piri. I imagined them dressed in their formal gowns,

Elisabeth wearing a hot pink dress to give color to her skin, Lara in white to accentuate her big dark brown eyes, and Kati in green to show off her beautiful green eyes, tanned skin, and reddish-bronze hair. I imagined being invited as a special guest to Elisabeth's private quarters, a beautiful room richly decorated, with her playing the grand piano with her strong, long, and nimble fingers, and Kati was kissing me and Lara was holding my hand.

I was asked to select the next piece for Elisabeth to play, and I selected one of the Hungarian rhapsodies, as she had long-enough fingers, rhythm, and feelings to play Liszt. Before the piece ended, a beautiful lady came in a light-blue formal gown with a big smile. I didn't recognize her until she came closer and gave me a kiss on my forehead, sat on the empty seat on my left side, and said with her lovely voice, "Thanks for helping me."

Almost black hair, dark, big blue eyes, voluptuous lips, even the long gown could not hide her feminine shape or the gentle sway in her walk. She seemed to be floating on the parquets. I was mesmerized by Piri's beauty.

When the music ended, Lara joined Elisabeth to perform my next music request, Haydn's Cello Concerto with piano. I kept on turning toward Piri, sitting on the bench in her formal gown, as I never noticed before how beautiful she was.

I must have been daydreaming for a long time. I woke up to reality when my colleagues started to arrive from the field. As they came in, they looked at me oddly and were obviously surprised to see me there. Only Gábor stopped by, put his hand on my shoulder, and said, "Good, you're still with us." I knew what he meant, but I knew before they did that, I'd be arrested and taken away, but I wasn't sure where. Like in many difficult situations where one is not in control, I just prayed and hoped for the best.

I went back to my place late with an empty stomach, thinking I should have taken another can of pate from the grocery store at lunchtime for supper tonight. However, my hunger was not that bad, so I decided to skip supper.

When I arrived at my temporary place of residence, the lady of the house was waiting for me with a hot bowl of chicken soup. She said, "I found out this is one of your favorites, so I cooked this and you must eat it." Her genuine feelings came through as she spoke, and her affectionate voice almost made me cry. I figured I might as well enjoy life before they either take me away tomorrow or send me to a new assignment to delay my eventual arrest. I was really hoping and praying for a way out, as it got scarier and scarier to think about the possible consequences and the potential painful interrogations which usually follow.

While eating the delicious soup with a generous amount of chicken meat, which I know was hard to come by, I jumped up from the table, excused myself, and left the table. I turned back and told the lady of the house I would come back momentarily. I headed for my little suitcase and took out my ping-pong paddle, which I hadn't used since there was no time to play with anybody. I took one precut piece of paper, carefully rolled it around the handle following the leather, and started to write a short message for Zoli. I wrote, "Work with Hodos. I'm out." I took off the paper strip, filled out the empty space with meaningless letters and words, addressed the envelope to Zoli, sealed it, and went back to the kitchen.

The landlady said, "I thought there was something wrong with my cooking, and I was afraid you wouldn't come back." I told her she was a very sweet lady and I would never forget what she had done. She responded that they owed me more than they could ever pay me for getting the release of all those men. "Just look at all those children growing up without a father, or even if they let them go, after a while they'd be only half a man after all the torture. You see, most wives don't know how to restore the mental health of these tortured husbands."

I looked into her eyes and asked for a last favor. I took out the letter addressed to Zoli and said, "You must get the necessary postage and mail it from another town if I don't come back tomorrow, and don't even look at the name or address on the envelope." She understood, and without looking at the small envelope, she bent forward, untied the string on top of her blouse by her neck, and put the small envelope in her bra under her beautiful breast right in front of me. I tried to turn away out of respect, but I couldn't; I just stared at her beautiful breasts.

I went to bed and had a very restless sleep. I woke up around three thirty in the morning, hearing a gentle knock on the door. I asked who it was, but no answer was given, so I just got up, turned the night light on by my bed, and gently opened the door. Right in front of me stood the local sheriff, with a German shepherd dog sitting at his left side. My heart started to bounce and jump in my chest like a dancing ping- pong ball.

Even though it wasn't unexpected, I was visibly shaken.

The sheriff noticing my emotional state said in a very low voice, "Sorry about this, but I must take you in, by the order of the party of the people."

I turned around to get my clothes, and I was thinking about his statement about the "party of the people." I didn't know whether to laugh or to cry, as it was the most unfitting name for the Communist Party, as it had the lowest percentage of membership and the least liked but most feared, and lacked any kind of popularity.

The sheriff added, "I came alone, so please cooperate. I'll give you the time to get dressed and ready." He talked to me while I got dressed. He said, "I understand what you did, but I must follow orders. Please do not try to escape, as I brought my dog to help instead of another policeman.

He would shoot if you make the wrong move." He went on to say that he was in a Russian POW camp mining lead. So I looked up, and sure enough, I could see the signs of heavy lead poisoning. He was skinny, with gray skin, eyes in deep pockets, and most of his teeth missing. He explained he was the local policeman when he had been drafted and sent to the Russian front. He was captured, and after he came back in 1947, he was elected as the local sheriff. He knows he will be replaced soon, as he decided against joining the Communist Party.

I asked if he had a family, and he said he was sterile, but his wife adopted two orphaned children. I advised him to join the party so there remains at least one honest man on the police force and he would be able to feed the adopted children. His response was a surprise to me. He said in case he agreed to join them, there was an initiation process to prove his loyalty to the Communist Party; he would probably have to be a false witness, kill, or permanently disable an innocent man or woman to prove it.

I asked if I should take my small suitcase. He said, "It is better to leave it and have somebody take it to your family." He continued that he noticed it was easier for family members to deal with somebody taken away from them if there are some mementoes left. While he talked, I emptied my pockets into the small suitcase, except my personal ID book, and closed the lid.

I stood in front of him and stuck out my hand to have him put the cuffs on. He said it was unnecessary until we got to the station. I asked, "What are the charges against me?"

He laughed and said, "You must be joking, as it doesn't matter as long as it is not the enemy of the people. Anyway, I believe it is something like inciting riot and unlawful gathering, but believe me, it does not make much difference."

As we walked out, the lady of the house was standing in the kitchen door and visibly crying, but I went by her without saying a word. I wanted to show her that I was not afraid, but I felt guilty about it later, not thanking her for her kindness. It reminded me also of not thanking Father Tibor for his pleasant visit and talks the day of his arrest a few years earlier. I was very much hoping I'd see my landlady again.

We walked on the sidewalk, and it was still dark and hard to see, as there were no streetlights. I suggested walking on the street, but instead he walked ahead of me on the sidewalk, and his German shepherd followed me. At the next street corner, he made me sit in his sheriff car and then drove me to the nearest city. We stopped at the police station, and on the way, I was thinking it was better being arrested for something good I did for others and being arrested in a small town, not in the big city, where the newly created communist police force's brutality was already well known.

When we arrived, they were waiting for me, and I was ready to give information for the booking, but the officer in charge, with broken Russian, said, "Idyi sooda" [Come here]. I presumed he wanted to show off his Russian language knowledge, but I was not impressed. He continued in badly pronounced Hungarian that I didn't need to say anything; they already know everything about me. Then he turned toward the sheriff, saying, "You can go, and you did your good deed for today bringing here this stupid guy." I had been called everything but stupid, and I did certainly feel that way for acting before thinking.

The sheriff put the handcuffs on just before reaching the station, so the policeman escorted me down to the cellar, stood me by the door, and took off the cuffs, which were behind my back. I turned around, and the small square hallway was well lit, and I saw two doors with the marking above in Russian and Hungarian zheyenscki for women and muzhcoy for men.

This was the first time I saw a prison with clearly marked large cells with gender designations.

The policeman opened the door with a large key and pushed me inside. The only light was coming through a small window in the door, so it took awhile to get my eyes adjusted to see in the dark cell. There were two double bunk beds on each side of the small square room, with an open toilet between and behind the beds against the wall. On the right was a dark figure sleeping under a blanket, but I could not make out his face. Once I inspected the cold cell with the smell of feces, urine, and mold, I noticed a bucket by the open pit. I was thinking, Who would put our drinking water by the toilet? Then I noticed another bucket by the door, with four aluminum cups hanging on its side.

I estimated the cell to be at least one story below ground level. There were no windows or opening to the outside. Later, when breakfast arrived in the form of lukewarm black coffee made from roasted barley and two small pieces of bread, it reminded me of the "tent city" experiences, except that the bread was good there. I also noticed a small trapdoor about waist high in the door they could open with a latch from the outside to pass in the food.

I felt trapped and restless. At least in the tent city, we were not confined to a three-by-three-meter space. I went to the door to peek out and stayed there, contemplating my future. I figured if I admitted to all the charges they dream up, I could possibly avoid being beaten to a pulp or unconscious and suffering life with crippling internal damages to my body, like they had treated my father and other people. The best scenario I could think of was getting five to ten years of hard labor, as I was young and strong. I could be sent to a coal, bauxite, or uranium mine, or to a rock quarry like Father Tibor. I purposefully avoided thinking about the worst. When I thought of my friend Sándor, who was arrested for espionage, I stopped feeling sorry for myself.

I was still standing at the small door window, with six iron bars going up and down with about a three-centimeter gap between them, when the door to the steps leading up to the police station offices opened. To my big surprise, Gábor came in with a police escort. I was happy to see him but tried to tell him he should not have come to see me. He put his finger to his lips, saying nothing, just waiting until the police opened the women's cell door. Gábor went to follow the policeman inside, but he motioned firmly for him to stop. The policeman went inside, and I heard him talking and a woman's voice responding. There was no way I could hear the conversation, as it was at least ten meters away. They were exchanging a few words quietly, and the heavy buildup of mold on the walls soaked up most of the sound.

I could not imagine, and it was totally beyond my expectation what I saw next. Viola came out from the cell. She was mostly covered in a dirty prison blanket, but her beautiful long blond hair clearly showed. She obviously had a hard time seeing in the well-lit hall, but she recognized her husband's voice when he asked, "Are you okay?" She said, "Yes, honey, I'm sorry. How much did you have to pay?"

The commotion woke my cellmate up, and with a sleepy voice, he muttered something in a foreign tongue. It was obvious he slept through my arrival and was surprised to see another prisoner in his cell. With a heavy accent, he asked in Hungarian, "What is going on?" I told him they released the woman prisoner across the hall. He responded, "Wasn't she a beautiful dame? I sure would like to spend a night with her, but I'm not fond of whores, even if they are that sexy and good looking. That is what she gets for charging money for her services. If she would have taken a side of pork for her services, as she was worth it, no one could charge her."

He was right. The Communists claimed there was no prostitution in their system, but the Westerners didn't know they defined prostitution as happening if only money was exchanged between the consenting parties. Any other form of payment, like food, tobacco, or silk stockings, was okay. It was considered to be a business arrangement or trade.

I didn't respond to my cellmate, as I suspected he may have been planted to spy on me, and I had to watch what I said. He came close to the light, and all my concerns went away. He was a full-blooded gypsy, dark as some of the Hindu people and blacker than any Negro I had ever seen.

I soon found out he had stolen a colt from a farm but was caught later stealing hay from a communist party member for his newly acquired pet.

He asked me what I had stolen. I had to think about a response that he might or could understand. He couldn't wait and said, "You don't want to tell me because you still have it. It's valuable, and you're afraid I might take it after they let me go." A second later, it came to me, and I told him I had stolen the local commissar's pride. It didn't take him long to respond.

"You are in deep shit, and you will get a long sentence because 'pride' is much more valuable than any horse or hay." He added, "They will be rough on you, as commissars are insecure people who are afraid of your kind." I made the sign of the cross, as we usually do before for asking help from the Lord. He said, "God is the only way and hope for the Hungarians."

He got the urge to use the facilities, which was signified by smelly, loud farts. I asked him where the paper was, and he said, "I use my finger, as the rotten guards won't even give me the newspaper, and I know most of them don't read. I noticed they usually ask a prisoner to go up and read the important news from the Communist Party. Did you notice their accents? They are young Greek communists."

I thought the Gypsy man was making up a story, but I later found out quite a few of the Hungarian prison guards came from Greece after their failed attempt to take over the government in 1951. The young Greek Communist refugees were also welcomed into Slovakia, where they received property confiscated earlier from Hungarians. They lived like kings in expropriated Hungarian homes.

I looked around while he was squatting down, relieving himself. There were no sheets to tear off a piece, but I found some loose stuff on the underside of the mattress, so I tore off a few pieces. He watched me as I was working hard to tear the rough cloths, and he commented, "You will also be charged with defacing public property." His prediction came through about twenty-five years later when I tried to protect our "birth" trees with a green ribbon in Transylvania. By the time he was finished, I had inspected the walls and found Russian, German, Hungarian, and mostly dirty words scratched into the remaining mortar covering the brick walls.

Either because of nervousness, being scared, or the bad coffee, I also had to go real bad. He noticed my urgency and pain, so he hurried up.

Sure enough, he used his fingers and smelled his excrement by raising his fingers close to his nose and then rinsed his hand in the bucket nearby.

After he finished, I squatted down and emptied myself real fast. I used the small towels made from the pieces I tore off the underside of the bed and threw the used pieces into the hole. I picked up the bucket and splashed some water to wash off the cement to reduce the smell. I got my remaining lousy coffee and poured it on my fingers and washed my hand. My cellmate was watching me like I was performing a secret ritual, and he was amazed by my efforts. He commented I would die young, as there is not enough dirt on me to protect my body from sickness. I let it go without responding.

I continued my inspection looking for a hidden microphone, but I found none nor evidence of any wiring. My cellmate was again puzzled by my search and said, "No need to look for it. There is no gold here." We were still laughing when our door opened without any noise or dimming of the light that happens when they open the door leading to the police station upstairs.

A man stood in the door; we could not see his face, as the lighted hallway was behind him. He looked at the Gypsy and asked with a very soft voice how long he had been there. My cellmate responded, "I guess about a month."

The man said, "I have to figure out what to do with you later." He turned toward me, his features still shaded, and asked me to put my hands in front of me. He put on the cuffs so fast like it was the only thing he had done and practiced all his life. He said, "Come on, let's go," and I stepped outside the door, turning right toward the exit door to the steps leading up to the station. He shut the cell door behind us, turned the key to lock it, and said, "Follow me."

I still could not make out his face. He was so skillful hiding it that even after an hour of interrogation, and in spite of using all kinds of tricks and tactics, I could never put together a recognizable human face. In retrospect, I really believe he was an albino because during the interrogation, every time a tiny light fell on his eyes, a pinkish reflection came back. His hair under the military police cap was snow white, and behind his dark glasses, I could never see his eyebrow. I remembered my brother's vision in Transylvania about the black-faced men with red eyes doing terrible things to innocent people. I was scared, really scared.

Kele D. Gabor

To my surprise, he turned left and walked back toward the empty wall. I waited a second and followed him. When he reached the wall, he tapped on it, and a secret door opened up, with steps leading down opposite to where the police-station entry was and between the two cell doors. The stairs were narrow, so only one person could go at a time. I counted fifteen newly constructed steps before the next door appeared in front of me.

Inside was a large ten-by-ten-meter room with several tables on the side but one was located almost in the center of the room. The lighting was so dim I could barely make out anything else until I got used to the low light conditions. There was no visible sign of any windows to the outside, and I knew we were at least two levels below ground.

He pointed to a chair on the other side of the table and politely asked me to sit down. By the time I felt my way around the table without bumping into anything, he was sitting right in front of me on the other side. As soon as he sat down, he put on a narrow white light that only lit up my face. The light was not bothersome but made it harder to see.

He instructed me to put up my hand on the top of the table between two flat metal bars running in parallel with my forearm. The metal railings were toward the middle of the table, so I had to lean forward to reach them while putting my feet together for added support. I hadn't even touched the top of the table when he placed one flat bar with two curvatures on the top across my wrist, firmly locking me to the table with the handcuffs I was wearing. I didn't expect this, as all previously seen, heard, or imagined interrogations were conducted on a single chair strategically located under a bright light.

I became totally immobilized a few seconds later when my ankles got locked up a similar way. I could move my head, but it would not do any good. I was scared but amazed at the efficiency with which this guy operated in making me feel terribly insignificant, useless, and defenseless.

There is no way I could remember how long I was in there, as he kept me busy with questions. My best estimate for staying in the interrogation room is close to an hour, but at the time, it seemed like eternity.

If I hesitated for any amount of time, he would show different instruments he could use to get the truth out of me. The first time I hesitated, he showed me long, flat needles he could insert under my fingernails. He wasn't kidding. As I became more used to the general darkness, I began to see a lot of dark spots, like blood marks, on the table in front of my locked hands, on the floor, all around, even on the walls about head high.

I have forgotten, or probably don't want to remember, the exact sequence of questions or in what order the pain-causing instruments were shown to me. However, they included electric-shock treatment, acid, finger squeezer, razor blades, and a short-barrel shotgun that was fixed to the table and pointed exactly at my groin. I also remember him telling me that in his experience, the shotgun always worked the best because the pellets used in the ammunition were sterilized and especially made to make you survive for weeks in tremendous pain. They would keep me alive with intravenous feeding. He showed me the steel vises that could be used to squeeze my head or any part of my body, including my breasts or skull. I thought I had seen everything, but I was wrong.

His questions were focused on which Western foreign power hired me, who was my contact, who was financing me, and whom do I hate the most— Russians, Communists, or Jews? What was my purpose to shame the commissar, to what organizations I belonged, what was my next move supposed to be, who was marked for assassination by me or others? To whom did I report after my attempt to sabotage and who was my current contact or who was giving me the instructions?

The questions were so irrelevant to the incident I could answer with the necessary coolness not to make him suspicious. He was good at his job because he noticed any small inflection in my voice or my body language that could give me away when answering some of the questions. And sure enough, I was not certain in some of my answers, even though I tried to be honest, as I felt totally innocent. I just had to answer all his questions without hesitation— in full sentences if I could, unlike the lie detector machine that only allows yes or no answers.

I did argue one point he made when I stated what I had done was with good intention to save the children. He responded that the state and the party take care of orphans and one should not worry about them. I said, "I saw the Russian soldiers stopping the Romanians from killing young Hungarian fathers for their children's sake, were they wrong?" He didn't answer but went on with his questioning.

I was also amazed that such an efficient and professional interrogator was available in a small city. I learned later he came from a big city at night less than sixty kilometers away, just to interrogate me.

Kele D. Gabor

My luck was that none of the persuading tools were used. He, however, made random and loud noises right behind me by manipulating some electrical or mechanical machinery under the table. They were most disturbing, and even today I get very irritated and more nervous than others when unexpected or weird sounds are coming from behind.

Unfortunately, I had to experience the noise machine one more time. He told me not to tell anybody what had happened and what I had seen, as he would let me go. He thought it was a big misunderstanding, my stupidity and my fault.

It occurred to me that it was the second time I was called stupid by a communist. After being released from being locked to the table, I really felt a lot of discomfort from the rigid, motionless position I had to hold.

I could barely get up. My legs were shaking, my shoulders twitching, my wrist and elbow feeling stabbed by thousands of needles as a result of reduced blood circulation. I attempted to get the cramp out of my calf and the muscles above my knees but could not put weight on my feet to stretch, as my knees kept collapsing. It became obvious they just made sure that after the interrogation, no one would have the means to fight back.

The sunshine was bright after being in the dark room for a long time, in fact, too bright, when I stepped out from the police station. The cops took their sweet time to type up all the release papers and gather the necessary signatures. One of the policemen drove me back to the small town and dropped me off close to my workplace in front of the old castle. The only thing he said was, "You'll be back, I know." At that time, I could not guess why he said it and that his prediction might come true.

I don't know, and I still cannot explain why, but I turned around and headed toward the local surveying office instead of going inside the staging area. As I walked on the street, nobody noticed me or didn't want to show it because of fear for them or me. News must have traveled around the small town faster than the speed of light.

I was thanking the Lord for His help while walking in and breathing the fresh air. From this point on, my recurring thought was "freedom," and I made a promise to myself I would keep it this way, as it felt so good. I know from personal experience people don't fully appreciate what they have until they lose it.

DECEPTION AND REALITY- LIVING THROUGH THE MISSING PAGES OF HISTORY

Kele D. Gabor

New Experiences and Perspectives

After my release from the short but difficult stay in prison, the exhausting interrogation, topped by the mean attitude and the scary tactics of the Communist police, my instincts took over and guided me to the small regional office instead of my assigned temporary workplace in the old castle.

When I got to the office, it was close to quitting time, and the only person staying in there during the huge job was a lonely secretary, Rosa. Everybody else had moved to the staging area in the much larger castle to accommodate all the new people helping out with the inhumane and cruel land-division project.

As I stepped into the office, Rosa ran up to me and hugged me, yelling in my ear, "You're free, you're free, you're free!"

I had to pull back, as her screaming started to hurt my ears, and I wanted to call my big boss at my home office. I knew he was my only ticket out of this mess I created. My new intermediate boss on this project didn't know me well enough, and he may have been afraid of possible repercussions if he helped me. Also, with a lower title and position, he had less power and options.

Rosa, the secretary, wouldn't let me go but finally she asked, "Did they beat you, or did you have to squeal on someone?" Before I could answer no, she went on, "The big boss tried to reach Sándor, your new temporary boss, but the phones at the staging area stopped working." This was not unusual, as the secret police often blocked out phone lines while placing recording devices at desired locations.

Rosa said, "I was just getting ready to leave to visit you in prison and give you and your new boss, Sándor, the good news."

I said, "I'm here, just tell me."

She already had the note in her purse. She opened it and took out her paper written in shorthand. When I reached for it, she stepped back and started to read it herself.

The note said that in case I get free within a week and able to walk and work, I should be transferred close by to help an archeological project right by the Serbian border, less than fifty kilometers away. My job would be to map the area and mark or frame the site with the proper coordinates, as we must comply with the international laws so close to the Yugoslav border. Since the site was in the Communist-defined "border zone," I would need special permit papers to enter. Instead of mailing the new orders from the main office, I needed to type it up here and have Sándor sign for him and use the official stamp before handing it to me.

At this time, the thought occurred to me that with this assignment close to the border and with the permit to enter the twenty-kilometer zone, it may be a hint from my boss to give me the opportunity to escape the Russian-style communism. This time, my boss was asking for and counting on my full cooperation, so I had better not do any more meddling in political issues, even if they were done with good intentions. Within a week, he expected me to finish and report back to the home office.

The only good thing I expected coming out of my ordeal was a short assignment so I could return to my pressing issue of finishing our detective work. I had no idea about the complications I would run into during this short assignment. It looked like as if even if I didn't seek out problems, they just followed and found me.

Rosa said, "Sit down, you must be hungry. Eat the sandwich I made for you, covered under the napkin in the cooler. I wanted to bring it when visiting you in the prison today." I commented that those terrible communists even arrested Viola, Gábor's wife, but I didn't know why. Rosa responded, "It happened a day before they arrested you, and I reported the incident to the main office and was told not to worry. Then I called Gábor, and he said she went shopping without him, which she is not supposed to do. When I asked him why, Gábor told me, 'She has a problem, shoplifting, and Viola is a kleptomaniac.' You go ahead and eat.'"

What a pity, I thought.

It was a 'PICK' salami sandwich, my favorite. The slices were thin, plentiful, and the bread buttered. While I was eating, she called back my boss again to tell him the good news that I was free without visible marks of beatings and already safe in her office. When she finished, she handed me the phone.

I said, "Good afternoon, sir. I'm well and do appreciate your help to get me out of this hole I dug for myself."

He just asked if my internal and external body parts were in working order, and once I assured him I was okay, he said, "Your father also stood up for justice, and they got rid of him, so be careful." I was surprised that he would say such a thing over the phone, which might be bugged, but it felt very good to hear some understanding and compassionate words, especially from my big boss.

While Rosa finished typing my travel orders and permits to enter the border zone, I ate both sandwiches, went to the cooler, and picked up a raspberry soda. She yelled after me, "Never mind the payment, we're going to cover it." I told her I didn't have any money on me, but I insisted on paying for it as was the custom— as not paying for things had already got me into a lot of trouble.

By the time I finished the soda, she had both of my papers ready to go. Rosa told me I stunk like a skunk and I should use the bathroom here while she went to the staging area to make sure Sándor Big signed both papers and put a second official stamp on for the border zone permit. The surveying office had the authority to send me anywhere, so the border patrol or secret police stamps were not required, provided it came at least from a director's level.

I told her I didn't have any clean clothes and I could wait till I got back to my place. She said, "There is a full bathroom upstairs, as this office building was converted from a large home and we left the upstairs as it had been. You can hang out your clothes on the balcony and let them air out."

She put my freshly typed order and permits in a large envelope, grabbed her purse, and left me standing in the middle of the room.

I went upstairs and found the big bathroom fully equipped with shower and bathtub. I turned on the gas water heater and let the hot water run into the tub, undressed, hung out my clothes on the back balcony in the sun, and slowly eased myself into the tub.

A very good feeling came over me while soaking in the tub. I could not think about anything else but freedom and rest. Being interrogated is not only nerve-racking, but extremely exhausting. I never felt so tired in my entire life.

I was rudely awakened by a knock on the door, and Rosa's voice came through, asking if I was okay. I said, "I thought you'd gone to get the second official stamp on my permit and all the signatures. Why are you still here?"

She said, "That was more than an hour ago, and I have all your papers in my hand already— signed and stamped. Can I come in?" I stood up, grabbed the shower curtain, pulled it in tight, then said, "Okay." She opened the door carefully and said, "I went by your place and got clean clothes for you. I will put them on the basket by the washbasin. Your other shirt wasn't very clean, so your landlady sent one of her husband's. By the way, she is a young and very, very attractive lady."

I said, "Yes, and she has a good looking husband and two beautiful children to prove it."

She said, "Your landlady wanted to know everything about your condition after your release. She must be a very caring person." Then she left. I added some hot water, as my bath was almost cold, soaped up, washed myself all over again, and stood up. While the water was draining out, I dried myself thoroughly. My hair was standing up, as the soap really dried it out and I didn't have shampoo, comb, or hair cream. I put on the clean clothes and rolled up the stinky ones in a newspaper, making sure the dirtiest part of my underpants fitted over the report by The Party on the front page and headed down the stairs.

Rosa was urging me to hurry up. It was almost evening, and she had to lock up the office. I apologized, thanked her for her help, gave her a hug, picked up my papers, and walked outside. She followed me to the gate and I returned her a comb I had used to tame my unruly hair. I headed toward my place thanking God for how lucky I was and thinking that after I did my next short assignment, Zoli and I could finish our most important and urgent business— catching the mole or double agent working for the KGB at the Embassy.

It was after supper-time and dark by the time I got to my temporary place of stay. I knew the kids were already turned into bed, so I sneaked in very quietly. I went by the kitchen door, and to my surprise, no light was coming through the cracks. I paused then went past it and the other bedroom doors, as my door was the last one on the left. I gently opened my door, put on the night light by the bed, and looked around to assess my situation and make plans for tomorrow's early start. My small suitcase was propped halfway open. I reached in to find my wallet and put it in my pocket before I would forget. I had to stand up, as I didn't find my wallet just by feeling for it, and sure enough it wasn't where I had put it. It was opened up, so I checked if anything was missing. The money and my important papers were there, except my family and

Lara's pictures were interchanged. I left it as it was, folded it up, and slipped it into my pocket.

I was looking forward to tomorrow, except for having to stop in the police station, as they forgot to give me back my personal identification book (an internal passport and ID). Without it, I could be arrested and fined.

I wasn't sleepy, but I started to unbutton my shirt when someone came in. I could not see the person, as the night light was very dim. I was scared thinking of what happened the night before and that they might have changed their mind about releasing me. I asked who it was with a somewhat shaking voice.

A female voice whispered, "It is I. Just wanted to check on you and if you want to eat something before going to bed." She kept coming closer and stood right by my bed in front of me. I thanked her for the shirt, took it off, and wanted to return it when she put her arm around me and squeezed me gently. It felt good being pressed against her breasts, and she said, "You sure have a pretty girlfriend waiting for you."

I responded, "I love her more than she loves me." She asked me if I wanted the letter back I gave her the night before, as she could not mail it today. I said, "Of course, and I hope you didn't look at the name and address." She assured me that she didn't look and that I could have the letter back, but I would have to take it from her. I smiled and asked, "What do you mean?"

I was confused and said, "You're a beautiful woman and have a beautiful family. You're a mother, a good and caring person, and you are very attractive, but I cannot do such a thing."

"If you don't take the letter from me, I'll look at the name and address on it."

I pleaded that she could hurt herself, her family, and the person whose name appeared on the envelope. She thought for a moment, took her arms off my shoulders, sat down on the bed, and motioned for me to sit next to her. She said with a soft and sexy voice, "I know you went through an ordeal, even though they didn't beat you up, but you must have gone through at least a mental torture, and you need to release all the built-up stress and tension. I know how I brought back my husband after returning from the Russian prison camp and the ensuing interrogations. All the other families had serious problems, but I— with love, affection, a show of understanding, and letting him feel he was in control— had Feri [Frank] back on his feet, fully functional, in weeks after his return. Look at some of the others where the husbands still have not recovered from the war, shell shock, and prison-camp nightmares after many years."

Sure enough, I have seen many marriages fail after the husband returned from the war or Russia, and Frank didn't show any post-traumatic stress syndromes.

She continued, "Frank is away, helping his sister in preparation for the grape harvest, cleaning barrels, and both of our children are asleep. He told me to help you recover if you get back alive. I'm good in bed. I have saved myself from rape by befriending an older, high-ranking Russian officer, and it is okay for you to make love to me." I remembered what my mother said about how to save pretty girls from gang rape after talking to a mother looking for her lost, beautiful daughter.

Her explanation made good sense, but I could not get involved, as I told her I easily fall in love and I'm afraid of the consequences. She said, "I know it would be good for you, but if you cannot do it, I won't be hurt."

She said, "Go ahead, take the letter, and I'll be gone."

I did grab the edge of the corner of the letter closest to me and pulled my arm back quickly with the prize in my hand.

As promised, she left, and I felt alone, very alone. I smelled the letter; it had a sweet smell, just like her. I tossed and turned, wishing her husband, Frank, wouldn't be such a nice guy, her children wouldn't be so cute, that she wasn't married, and I wouldn't have had a strict moral upbringing with such a high respect for motherhood. We know well that the most challenging, difficult job deserving the most respect and most important for the future generation is motherhood.

Then I turned on myself. She must think I'm a homosexual, lost my marbles, not a real man, or I don't appreciate women. Then I prayed she would return during the night, as I was afraid to seek her out. I was still daydreaming about my hot dream when the children came in to tell me breakfast was ready. I looked at my watch. I had overslept. It was close to eight o'clock, and my train was leaving at eleven. I washed my face, my crotch area, and my hand. I put on my pants, undershirt, and went to the kitchen.

She had a big smile on her face when I walked in. She still had on the same sexy, light-lilac robe, but underneath, she also wore her white nightgown. The kids had already left for school, so just the two of us were at the kitchen table, sitting across from each other. I thanked her for most of everything she did for me while eating my breakfast.

She set there across from me, smiling, not saying a word. When I finished the fried bread, drank my hot tea, and she could have my full attention, she said, "You thanked me for everything except what I was willing to do for you last night. I had two older brothers, and I know how to help young guys. I admire you for your moral values, and in a way, I am glad nothing happened. However, I'm happy, as I can see my mission was accomplished. You look good, relaxed, and ready to start a new job without being nervous, tense, and frustrated. It looks like you had some pleasant dreams."

I looked at her nervously and embarrassed, but what she said was true and made good sense. I decided to thank her right then and give her a big hug. I expressed my sincere appreciation for her efforts, help, and willingness to give of herself just to make me forget about my ordeal, and it was over and beyond my wildest expectation. When I let her out of my arms, she said, "Don't forget, it takes a woman to teach a man how to love, as men are usually preoccupied with sex."

Later in life, I learned her statement was not only true, but contained a lot of wisdom. I started to observe married couples, and her statement stood up to the test of time. In every happy marriage, I noticed the leadership role the woman played in showing love through tenderness, understanding, affection, touch, and respect. These wives always knew how to defuse an explosive or difficult situation by smiling, listening, understanding, affection, and the right touch. The touch could be a gentle stroke on the partner's hand or a sweet kiss on the cheek or lips, but she always seemed to know how to express love and when. The key to their happiness was the expression of gratitude toward each other, respect, family members, and friends, and to other people as well. I recalled my father and mother always hugged and kissed, especially when they parted or met.

It happened at least twice a day. They often showed their affections for each other, all family members, and expressed some form of gratitude on a daily basis.

I really missed seeing that in the Western cultures. I also noticed men are awkward and uneasy in expressing similar feelings until the women take the lead. A feminist may argue that a lack of understanding and sensitivity from the male side is responsible for the marital problems. However, we must have evolved a different way, and women are better at keeping and making peace and harmony. Women are usually more effective at being the glue of the family. Which sex takes the initial move for conflict resolution or diffusion of dangerous situations is irrelevant, as long as the other partner is receptive, recognizes it, and responds to it positively.

After the Vietnam War, I also saw a lot of miserable GIs with distressed marriages usually ending up in separation or, worse yet, divorce. I remembered what my ex-landlady told me about rehabilitating men, and I wondered if the wives and girlfriends had any help or training to aid in the recovery process or the government tried to treat these people with the help of the feminine touch.

She made my day, and I made the train in time with my identification book in hand. Even today, I have pleasant memories of my landlady, and it might have been the dim lighting, but I have never seen a more beautiful, mature, live nude body than hers. If I could carve, I would pick her as a model. Traveling on the train, I was still thinking of how inviting she looked and the great opportunity I missed.

By eleven forty-five, my train arrived in the village, the closest settlement to a new archeological site. The border patrol checked my papers on the train, as this village was in the border zone, about ten kilometers from my destination. I stepped off the train and went outside to find some way to get to where the site was. I didn't feel like walking. My suitcase was small but heavy, and I carried a wooden box full of instruments I was given by Rosa from the office.

Two border patrols in military uniform stopped everybody, including me, and asked for the identification and border-zone permits. As customary, I reached in my pocket, handed my permit papers to the one with open hands, and waited quietly. They checked my photograph in my ID book, which looked almost like a passport, with all relevant information in it.

They pointed to my baggage and asked what was in them. I told them one was my suitcase and the box contained the tools of my trade.

Kele D. Gabor

The higher ranked soldier told the other one to pick up my bags and put them in the truck, as I was the guy they had come to pick up. The thought did cross my mind that they had come to arrest me again, but no handcuffs were shown, so I relaxed a bit. This type of checking had to be done in order to keep the Hungarian population within the border under the Communist rule— almost like a see-through Berlin wall, but with tall barbed-wire fences and a lot of hidden land mines.

The soldiers were not talkative, and the truck was noisy. It was an old American Dodge given to the Russians during WWII and later passed on to the Hungarian border patrol. The road we took was all dirt, and here and there we forded creeks without a bridge. I think they took me the long way. When we got inside the border patrol compound, I asked if there was anyplace to eat, as I was very hungry. They laughed and pointed to the mess hall and told me to wait there until we reported to the officer of the day.

The officer with the rank of a captain was a tall, skinny, but pleasant guy with huge hands and feet. He said, "First thing is to join me in the officer's mess for an after dinner drink, and then we get down to business." I told him I'd prefer to eat first, as I only had a light breakfast. He just pointed to my baggage and asked the soldiers who brought me to take them to my room by the first-aid station. Then he waved to me and started to go toward a camouflaged building across from his office. I had a hard time keeping up with him, with his giant strides. He grabbed the door handle, held open the single door, and motioned for me to enter first.

There were three long tables in the room, put together in a U shape. Behind the tables on the left, there was a small podium and a kitchen on the right. He headed to a small bar way back in the room and gestured again to follow him. He offered me a chair right at the bar, and he took the next one. He yelled out loudly, "I'm thirsty." Within a few seconds, the chef showed up behind the bar and asked what he might bring him and his guest. He turned to the chef and asked what was left over from dinner.

"Nothing, comrade, but we have fresh eggs and bacon. I could make some up for you." The captain pointed to me and asked if that was okay. My response was a definite yes. While the chef turned toward the kitchen, the officer asked for two beers, turning toward me with a questioning look. I nodded affirmatively.

Deception and Reality - Living Through the Missing Pages of History

The captain said, "This is a funny arrangement we have between the Southern Slavs [Yugoslavs] and Hungary. Since the diggings are just about on the border, they want to monitor our activities closely. This means Serbian and Hungarian border patrols will be assigned to the projects, with some additional observers from both sides." The captain went on, "I find this ridiculous and unacceptable, as I indicated in my memo to my superiors. We'd be better off with one man in charge, and I hope it is I."

I said, "That is fine with me, and I like your direct approach."

He smiled and said, "Let's hope they listen."

The beer came, followed by a generous portion of scrambled eggs and ham, with a large slice of bread. I took a sip of beer after raising my glass, and the captain returned the gesture without saying a word. I started eating, and he went on talking.

What was believed to be an old dam construction by the Tisza River turned out to be a series of family burial sites running northwest from southeast. The highest mounds were practically on the border, and the mounds tapered off in both directions, ending at the actual borderline.

In the sandy soil on the Hungarian side, we tried to put in an observation tower. During the digging for the cement footing, we encountered a human skeleton with very old weapons, like bow, sword, and lance. We were ready to pour in the concrete when the inspecting officer noticed our hesitation. He came and looked. After a few minutes, he said, "Stop the cementing. We need some experts to look at this, as it looks like a single row cemetery." The fort's commander called the HQ and reported the situation, and soon civilian professors started to arrive one by one. We received instruction to assist in setting up the site, making sure there were no land mines so the digging could start safely.

About two weeks earlier, an older professor was named to be in charge on the civilian and scientific sides of the project. However, I don't think he was an archeology professor, as he knew too much about military stuff and international relations. I said, "How would you know that?" The professor knew all about military issues governing international borders, rules of engagement, and the procedures on common finds across borders. He even reminded me about things that I should have known, as I was supposed to be the local expert in these matters. The professor was very friendly, knowledgeable, and I liked him.

Kele D. Gabor

I finished my late lunch, and I was ready to go and inspect the area.

I asked when he could show me the place where the excavations began. The captain got up and said, "Let's go," and started to walk out. He went to his office and asked to be replaced by an NCO, as his shift was almost done. He got into an old American made Jeep, also passed down from the Russians, parked on the side of his office, and waved to me to sit next to him. Before I sat down, the Jeep was moving.

The captain's style of driving was just opposite to his men who had picked me up earlier at the railway station. We were flying, and it only took ten minutes or less to arrive at the old burial site located between the border patrol compound and the Tisza River, or just east from where the border crossed the river. Behind the mound, on the Hungarian side, two large military tents were set up. I asked the captain what the tents were doing there. He responded the old archeologists wanted to stay close to where the digging would take place, and the other was set up for his assistant due to arrive soon.

We walked on to the top of the mound, and the captain, pointing to the south into Serbia, said, "All that land used to be Hungary. Some Hungarian people who survived the Serbian Holocaust are really angry about international injustice and unfair punishments. Any Hungarian who complained about the arrangements would be moved by the government far behind the border, their property confiscated, and Serbs would take their place in a much nicer home, just like the Romanians did it along their new border with Hungary. But there was nothing we could do about it, as nobody supports our cause or cares that millions of native Hungarians are in actual slavery." I kept my mouth shut, but I so much agreed with him, as I was from Transylvania, my homeland, from where I had to escape soon after the Stalin-dictated border adjustments.

The captain motioned it was time to start back, as he expected new people to arrive today and tomorrow. While returning, I asked the captain to let me use his office phone to call my regional office HQ, as I needed the location of nearby triangulation points and the border area maps, which were hard to come by. As soon as we got back, I called my office to inquire about who my assistant would be and to make sure I would get all the maps we needed. To my surprise, my boss decided to send a senior engineer, Ben, so my hope for the first independent lead position on a project was not to be.

I really didn't mind being second in command, as it always gave me more flexibility. Also, I respected and liked Ben. He was also very experienced in international border work, and there was mutual respect between us.

I went to check my room arrangement; it was a clean room with two military beds and a separate bathroom. I learned it was originally set up for nurses or doctors, but there was no need for them now.

The next morning, I hitched a ride with a border-patrol unit and took my theodolite with me. Not having the maps and the triangulation points yet, I set up the equipment as close to the border as possible at the highest point and decided to spy a little. After leveling the tripod, I started to look through the highly accurate optics to check every little thing around me. After finishing the southern area, where I noticed someone looking back at me, obviously the Yugoslav border guard with high-power field glasses, I turned around and swept our side, looking north, at our immediate area.

I was moving my instrument side to side when something familiar caught my eye. Right at the entry of the large military tent, which was occupied by the chief archeologist, stood a familiar object— the well-worn charcoal-gray umbrella. My heart jumped! Could it be Father Tibor? I looked again just to make sure, looked at the other tent, but there were no visible signs of occupancy.

I put the tripod on my shoulder and eased toward the tents, making sure I also passed by the half-open barrier spot. It looked much bigger than expected, about a three-by-five-meter area where the sandy soil had been removed to the lower side of the mound. Since I could not see any artifacts or a horse skeleton, I moved on to the tent with the umbrella at its entrance. The entrance flap was halfway open so I could peek in, and sitting across the opening behind a long table was Father Tibor, looking up at me. I could make out his unmistakable features, now with snow-white hair as the outside light fell on his face, but he could not see my face.

I politely greeted him, "Laudetur Jesus Christus" (a customary greeting among the religious, meaning, "Praise to Jesus Christ"). He looked more distinguished than ever, with snow-white hair, tanned skin, bright big blue eyes, bushy, still dark eyebrows, and when he stood up to greet me, he still had the spring in his walk. He came around the table and extended his hand, but I just stepped up and hugged him. He obviously didn't yet recognize me, as he hadn't seen me for over five years; there was no light on my face, so he whispered in my ear, "Whoever you may be, this form of religious greeting is frowned upon here and now."

I turned toward the light so he could see my face, and after a few seconds he smiled and said, "You look just like your father when he was young." Father Tibor hugged me again and asked what I was doing there.

I told him about my new assignment and later how I got there after my short stay in a prison cell. He just remarked, "There is no accident, it was meant to be that we meet again." I didn't say I didn't believe what he said, but he must have noticed, as he went on asking me when I saw Lara last.

I told him over a year ago, after my graduation. "Now if you still believe in accidents, let me tell you my assistant is due to arrive today or tomorrow, and you will be very happy to see her again."

It was the best news I had heard for a long time, but I must have shown some concern, as he asked what was wrong. It just came out. "It doesn't matter, as she doesn't love me."

Father Tibor offered me a bench by the table, and we sat down to talk. He said, "I know it is not so, but she has a mission in life preventing her from showing you her feelings or getting involved with anyone at this time."

I responded, "What's the difference?"

"There is a big difference," he continued, "as she made a secret commitment and promise to her dying grandfather, Rabbi G., but she may find out soon that those kinds of promises are too hard to keep and may not be binding. One never knows." I responded I'd like to have a family some day and I might not want to wait for her too much longer. Father Tibor asked me not to put that kind of a pressure on her now, just get together, seek each other's company, and see what develops.

Father Tibor showed me some of the early finds already laid out on the table, and it included a huge gold belt buckle with runic inscription, rusted arrow tips, picture of an almost totally decomposed bow, some slightly damaged pottery, metal dishes, and a cup, including a fancy gold plate with embossed design on it. He said he couldn't yet accurately date it, as it could be from the fifth to the seventh centuries, but once the digging starts in earnest, he will be able to pinpoint the date.

Then he showed me some sketches, as not all his photographs had been developed. The sketch showed a human skeleton with weapons surrounding him, pottery and vessels containing food fragments, and also a skeleton of a horse. I said, "This was left-handed, as his quiver and sword were on his right side."

Father Tibor corrected me by saying, "All individual weapons were placed in reverse side or a mirror image, as they believed their body and soul would reappear in the other world as they see their reflection in water or as a mirror image."

I was thinking about the possibility of taking a vacation and staying with him after my project was over. I was fascinated by archeology, and I just wanted to learn these interesting things from him. However, my "mission" of finding the double agent must take precedence over my personal interests or desires. All of a sudden, I realized I also had an important mission in my life that must take precedence over my other desires, such as Lara's situation.

I told Father Tibor I had to hurry back to Budapest after my project was done here, as I had some unfinished business needing my immediate attention. He responded, "In a couple of days, all the issues should be resolved soon after the political officer in charge [the Communist Party representative] will be appointed, as we already have plenty of military and local people volunteering to help to start the digging. However, for some reason, the party doesn't want to employ nor have college students involved from the archeological department. I find this very strange, as it would have been an excellent opportunity to have on-the-job training and truly learn about our own past." He invited me for a glass of wine and small talk when he found out I had two more hours to kill until the next shift of border patrols would arrive.

Father Tibor seemed to be relaxed and happy about his new assignment and also surprised he was selected to head up this project from the archeological side. He had a hard time finding a job after he recovered from the injuries suffered in the forced-labor camp. He knew that his fast recovery and finding this job was the result of Lara's dedicated work on his behalf. For the past four years, he worked as a janitor at a museum and a library. He had also done lots of tutoring, almost for nothing, and some pro bono work that was paid with an occasional meal, as he had to stay away from government facilities or universities, where food was available at a lower price. In spite of his many talents, he was a terrible cook, according to his own evaluation.

When he asked me about recent events in my life, I just gave him a short account of my mother's deteriorating health and of my siblings' progress in school, as they were all exceptionally good students. I had to brag about my sister, who finished high school in two years, completed her medical training, and received her MD. She finished with straight As all seven years and got awarded the highest honors anyone has received in the medical schools in the over two hundred-year-old history. She even received a special invitation from the Communist Party chief and the Communist prime minister to be their personal physician.

Father Tibor smiled and happily commented that he had predicted this and similar scholastic achievements for all of us, as he had known my parents and seen us grow in mind, body, and spirit. I stated I was far below his expectation. He assured me that I would succeed in whatever field I choose.

While refilling both wine glasses, he asked if I had any questions he could answer for me, preferably along his line of work, as I may know much more than he in the field of engineering. I told him I was wrestling with the evolution theory versus the creation and understanding God. He began answering my questions with a much lower voice.

"It is sad that the communists outlawed prayer, worship, and assembly of people for any purpose, especially for religious reasons. I'm also unhappy they not only despise but also forbid teaching about creation, as it is easier to comprehend because of its simplicity. However, I'm happy they try to teach more about evolution. While working on my degree in archeology, I spent some time digging for fossils. One summer, I found a mammoth-leg bone and decided to check out the differences from the elephants. There were quite a bit of correlations, and I expanded my private studies to the dinosaurs. In fact, I emerged into paleontology on my own and considered writing my doctorate thesis on the dinosaurs."

I must have looked surprised, as he went on to explain. "Dinosaurs living on land were much larger than animals today, so I theorized that seventy million years ago, the earth must have had a lower gravitational pull, and its mass was smaller to support those giant beasts. Based on bone structures I was able to view under the microscope and extrapolate their weight under current conditions, it became evident their bones could not support their massive bodies unless they stayed in water or didn't move fast. However, none of my professors would support or approve my investigation."

I interrupted and asked him how he could justify the increased mass of the Earth. He said, "The dinosaurs died out about seventy million years ago, and it must have coincided with the earth capturing a small moon or large meteorites, which increased the earth's mass considerably. Therefore, it made the animals less mobile, and it became more difficult to find enough food."

In retrospect, I wished Father Tibor's doctorate project would have been approved in the early 1920s, as it would have expedited the current theory of a meteor impact and subsequent climatic changes leading to the extinctions of dinosaurs in a relatively short period of time.

He continued. "Now back to evolution. You are a smart and educated man, so let's say you are God. After creating this constantly changing, beautiful universe with natural laws and all the forces interacting, the moving galaxies, solar systems, planets, and the laws of the universe, would you have created life that cannot adjust to change?"

I wasn't prepared for a blunt question like that, but the more I thought about it, the clearer it got— evolution is part of creation, and it had to be that way, or life could never have taken hold anyplace. God would not make the mistake of creating life without the ability to adjust and change to climatic or other external conditions that ruled the universe or the Earth. Evolution also proves that life began with a single cell and only once. Father Tibor added, "However, there is not enough evidence of evolutionary changes across species of animals or plants."

I told him he gave me a lot of ideas to think about and I appreciated his explanation about the theory of evolution, but what about God? Father Tibor smiled and asked me to imagine God. I looked at him funny and asked what he meant. His response was, "Just using your own imagination, try to figure out what He may or may not be like. A good place to start is making a list of His attributes, as we learned in religion."

I started listing the attributes: infinite, timeless, all powerful, invisible, perfect, limitless, omnipresent, unchanging, and then he stopped me by raising both hands and said, "Let's do it one at the time. Start with infinite."

I kept looking at him for help, but he just urged me to open up my mind and think about the meaning of infinite and finally asked what I knew to be infinite-like. I responded, "Numbers are infinite and we use the symbol for it, a horizontal number eight."

"Of course, mathematics is the basis for expressing the laws of the universe, as well as the basis for all science, but think of other things that are or may be infinite."

"Of course," I responded, "space in the universe."

"Okay," he said, "let's continue with the attributes. I think you mentioned 'timeless,' without beginning or end."

"Time is a function of change and measured by movements, so to be timeless, one has to constant and motionless. It also has to satisfy unchanging, invisible, omnipotent, and omnipresent."

Father Tibor smiled again and asked me to continue my thoughts, as I was on the right track. I wished he never said that, as I was more confused than ever. After a while, he interrupted my silence with the following question.

"What did I know or think that is infinite and motionless?" He made me feel like a little boy wanting to discover something I already knew. Finally, I said, "The only thing I know in the universe that does not move or is timeless is space."

Father Tibor raised again both hands, bending forward and saying, "Alleluia, alleluia!"

My brain started to race, and the more I thought about it, the more I liked the example of the vacuum in space to help me imagine God in human terms. For example, if God is space, it can immediately explain how God could be every place, as even the densest or heaviest atom has more space in it than matter. Also, space is powerful, as nothing else can exist without it— no universe, no galaxies, no solar system, no planet, no physical law or force, no birds and bees, not even black holes. Matter can be changed, destroyed, or converted to energy, but space must always be there, constant, without movement. Nothing can exist without space; matter and space complement each other like good and evil.

The big bang theory has been around since 1922 and was later confirmed by the background infrared radiation where subatomic particles blew up and eventually created the matter parts of the universe. However, there is no explanation given in the cause of the incidents, nor does the theory offer answers for the origin of space, laws of nature, or forces of the universe, like the dark matter that keeps the galaxies together. Was it always there? If it was, it's also infinite, motionless, and timeless.

I had to leave to make it to the meeting place for the military truck return, so I bid farewell to Father Tibor, thanked him for the lecture, and hurried to the designated spot for the pick up. While waiting for the ride, getting back to the base and the rest of the afternoon I could only think of my new discoveries, thanks to Father Tibor.

The next day, all hell broke loose. The new major arrived to head the military aspect of the operation, which angered the captain I had met the day before. According to him, the big brass picked someone who speaks both Hungarian and Serbian, and it made sense. My boss, Ben, arrived with all the maps and additional instruments and wanted his own private room, which I didn't mind. I had to help him offload all the extra stuff he brought, including two heavy concrete bases for the new triangulation points to be secured.

Then Lara arrived late in the evening, but I didn't even have a chance to greet her. She was in conference with the new heads of the project, and she didn't even know I was there. The following day, however, the digging started in earnest, and so did the surveying.

Ben told me he was selected, even though he was beyond retirement age, because we had to set up new triangulation points, as most of our close ones were now in Serbia, in the parts of our homeland that were taken away.

I liked working for Ben, as he was patient and he took the time to explain everything. However, he made me work extra hard and into the late evening, so I didn't have a chance to see Lara or Father Tibor for a while. It helped that Ben knew of my father and had great respect for him, so at least we could talk confidentially about our political situation or any sensitive topic when nobody else was around us. Some of Ben's favorite topics were the Communists' view of morality, their agenda of ruling the world, and trying to erase God from everyone's life and mind. Ben strongly believed religion and spirituality adds a new dimension to people's lives, gives strength, helps open their eyes, eases suffering, and makes us less selfish or egocentric. People without faith are not only handicapped in everyday living but also miss the boat to eternity. During the short breaks, we took one of the above topics or it would surface by itself, and for the most part I listened, as his views were new, very interesting, and logical.

Finally, early on Saturday afternoon, Ben asked me to take off and enjoy the weekend, as we all needed a break. I immediately went to the captain to get a ride to the field. I first took a warm shower, put on clean clothes, and headed to the site where the tents stood. There were now four tents and two wooden outhouses nearby, one for ladies and one for men. I knew Father Tibor hadn't said a word to Lara about me, as I had requested earlier; I just wanted to surprise her. I thought it would be easy to pick her tent, as it would be the closest one to her master. However, the tent next to Father Tibor's had a red flag on the top of the post, indicating the place for the political officer who is also the Communist Party representative and the "all powerful local substitute for god." I certainly didn't want to have anything to do with the party, as they only represented the evil, dirty, and ugly side of my world.

Father Tibor's tent had its entrance flap open, so I went there and looked inside. He was sitting at the table facing me and talking with a woman across from him. They were talking quietly, so I didn't want to disturb them until he noticed me standing by the opening. He just waved me in without saying a word, and I approached the table. When my shadow fell on the table, Lara turned to look at me. She hesitated a moment, jumped up, knocking the bench over and hugged and kissed me on my face. My heart started to hop and flutter in my chest like a Mexican jumping bean. I bent down to pick up the bench and took a good look at her.

Lara had become a beautiful, mature woman. Everything feminine was slightly bigger and better on her— legs, hips, breasts, curves, lips, eyes. She looked exceptionally sexy and voluptuous.

I asked for a second hug, took a step closer, opened my arms, and she returned the gesture. I gently squeezed her to leave a lasting impression, and she returned the squeeze. I felt like I was in heaven again pressing my body against her, and she was giving in like long-lost lovers meeting again.

Surprisingly, it was I who broke the embrace, as it was a very long hug, and I started to feel awkward and embarrassed doing it in front of Father Tibor. But she would not let me go. She just kept her cheek close to mine.

I said, "It is so good to see and hug you." She responded by squeezing me tighter and pressing her cheek even closer to mine.

When we finally got untangled, her clothes stuck to her body and her hair was also more tangled up. They must have had a hard day working up a sweat earlier, so her blouse stuck to her skin where our bodies touched. She had dark-brown shorts and a cream-colored blouse on that was slightly soiled and became slightly transparent where it was pressed to the wet part of her body. She said, "I have to get cleaned up, and you must stay with us."

She was ready to leave, but I insisted on a third hug. She

looked embarrassed about it, but she gave in and also gave me a small kiss on the lips. She turned around and left me with Father Tibor.

Lara stopped at the exit, turned around, and said, "So this was the special surprise for me. You're right. It is the best thing that's happened to me for a long time."

After Lara left, Father Tibor looked at me and asked, "You still believe she doesn't love you?" I didn't respond, but without being asked, I sat down right across from Father Tibor, looked in his eyes, and asked if I could talk confidentially. He said, "Yes, if you keep it down."

I said, "I want to take Lara with me, as I need her ASAP. I'm in the middle of a very sensitive investigation and identification of a probable double agent at a Western embassy, and I really could use her help." Father Tibor looked at me wide-eyed, the first time I had seen him surprised. I went on saying Lara and I worked very closely together before to gain his freedom and we made a good team, as we complimented each other well.

He just sat there for a long time, looking at his drawings on the table, then pointed to the corner of the desk where Lara was sitting earlier. On the corner of the table, there was a red armband.

I stopped cold, and a long silence followed. Then, "You mean Lara is the party's representative, the commissar?" I popped the question in amazement. He nodded affirmatively. I was shocked, totally surprised, and refused to believe it. After a while, I was convinced. I guess I needed to look elsewhere for help.

Father Tibor said, "I wish that was our only problem. Once I identified the burial sites as being from early seventh century and that they are Avars and show typical burial methods of the Scythians, Huns, and Magyars and spoke the same language, they took my camera, photographs, and all the artifacts from me. We unearthed several large gold buckles with runic inscription, which, judging from the size, weight, and damaged motifs on it, may have been also used as a protection or shield for the soft part of the body during battles. We opened up the middle hill closest to the international border and found a lot of gold artifacts, as we did in Bavaria when we opened up some old

Deception and Reality - Living Through the Missing Pages of History

Avars burial places there. As you may know, the Avars also settled there as craftsmen, hence the name Bavaria.

"I can only look, supervise the digging, identify, and date the artifacts found. I think the problem is that the new major in charge may be more than just a Serb sympathizer who doesn't want the world to know Hungarian people have been here much before the beginning of the fourth century and were the original settlers of all this area. According to Byzantine and Greek accounts, these areas were uninhabited before the Huns occupied it. This would be further proof Yugoslavia has no right to these territories. The officer in charge also brought along a squad of soldiers who don't speak Hungarian, only Serbian. One of his lieutenants has a crush on Lara, leaving very little time to discuss anything in private with her." Father Tibor raised his voice toward the end of his comments; he was obviously irritated about these recent developments when Lara stepped in, and she must have overheard a few of his last remarks.

Lara was shaking her head as she returned in disbelief and said, "You're smart guys, but brainwashed or gullible, like most people. Don't you know those guys are actually Russians, not Serbs? I can handle the Russian officer, Sasha's advances, and they just want to make sure there will be no international incidents resulting from the new finds."

Father Tibor retorted, "It is not enough to forbid picture-taking for us, but they are also taking all the skeletons, artifacts, and gold, loading them on their trucks, claiming to take it to our museum for display."

Lara started laughing quietly, making funny noises. "You guys really don't know what is going on. The Russians are claiming and transporting everything to Leningrad [St. Petersburg] to have the artifacts restored for their own display, just like the English and French did in Egypt, the Germans with Sumerian finds to hide the Hungarian connections, or the Spanish in South and Central America. In fact, some of the gold already has been pocketed, like the big belt buckle, and probably won't see the light of the day in any museum."

Father Tibor was visibly upset and demanded why he had not been told and said any further work should be halted immediately, as the nature of the work was an exercise in futility and should be considered grave robbing. She said, "This is the deal I made with the Communist Party and the Russians to save you from further political harassments or a lifetime prison sentence."

Father Tibor got even more agitated and said, "I won't sell out the Hungarian nation or the historical truth backed up with archeological finds for my bodily comfort. I would rather die."

I jumped in to support Father Tibor and said to Lara, "I thought you told me you are more of a Hungarian than a Jew? This behavior of selling anything for profit and changing sides when convenient and their abrasive attitudes are what made the Jews so disliked."

Lara got visibly furious, her face became red, and her eyes looked as though they could kill and she was ready to explode, but for the moment, she stayed quiet, like a volcano just before an eruption. In spite of my great disappointment in her, I hated to see Lara like that, but I didn't say a word. She started to take deep breaths, and one could see her normal color returning, but her squinting eyes sealed my lips shut like a welding torch fusing a wrought-iron crack. Even Father Tibor kept his mouth shut, not because of Lara's state of mind, but to be in control of his.

We must have been silent for an entire minute when the flap on the tent opened up and a young officer in Serbian military uniform stuck his face in and said in Russian, "Excuse me, I came to find Lara." One could easily see the big smile on his face when he noticed Lara standing at the end of the table, looking at us. The young officer, I presume Sasha, was practically salivating while looking at her. Now I saw and noticed what he had seen.

Lara looked stunning in white sandals, form-fitting dark-blue pants, and white, almost translucent, blouse showing the shape of her beautiful breasts, barely covered with a white thin bra. All of a sudden, I became terribly jealous of this intruder and it was my turn to get angry. It was infuriating when the officer walked toward Lara, referring to her as barishnia (young woman) and asking her out for Saturday night in the nearby town.

Fortunately, it was Lara who started to vent her anger at Sasha and told him to stay out of her way. She used Russian words, which I never heard or knew the meaning of, even after ten years of occupation and four years of forced learning. Once she spilled her anger, she pointed toward me and calmly said, "This gentleman is my fiancé."

Now it was the young Russian officer's time to get angry, and he did just that. However, his anger showed, but was not voiced. We could see the squinting eyes, the red and purple face, the down curved lips, the stiffening of the neck, the fisting hands, and the jerking motion of his body, but he did not speak; he just looked at me, and mostly Lara. His look was not of embarrassment for being told off in front of us but so mean that Father Tibor spoke up in Hungarian, saying both Lara and I had made a permanent enemy. The young and very angry officer nodded toward us like he understood what was said and left with a sneer.

Neither Lara nor I spoke, but Father Tibor repeated his warning that we had both better be careful as we had created an explosive situation and I had seen similar looks on primitive men before, which led to dire consequences.

" It may come to revenge", he added.

Lara spoke up next, as calm as she could be. She must have finished venting all her anger at Sasha, the young Russian officer, and started speaking like she was talking to herself. Her eyes seemed to focus on the middle of the table, not looking at us or anything else when she started her monologue.

"I was a teenage girl, happy as a lark, living a peaceful life in beautiful Transylvania with my music and many friends. All of a sudden, I was whisked away from everything I loved except my cello and my mother. She dressed up as a nun, and we headed west. Our cover story was that she was my teacher who had discovered my exceptional musical talent in the orphanage and now was accompanying me to gain acceptance to the famous Liszt music conservatory in Budapest. I later found out that this was arranged by Father Tibor and his friends to save us from the Nazis.

"When we arrived at the railroad station, our first trip took us to my grandfather, the rabbi, in a Greek Orthodox cemetery. I was not to be seen, talk, or do anything that may bring attention or suspicion of any sort. We had to hide ourselves and the only other thing I loved, my cello. I also had to stay quiet in one of the open places in the abandoned crypt we occupied.

The only outside person we saw was Father Tibor or his assistant bringing food and occasionally a change of clothing. I could only go outside after dark.

"Within a week of our stay in the cold, dark crypt, my mother put her nun uniform on again and said, 'I have to go to rescue your father.'

My father was an art dealer and was paid to save and rescue some of the old Hungarian valuable and historical art pieces from being destroyed or taken by the Slovakian government, like the Romanians did in Transylvania. He was in Pozsony [now Bratislava] to recover and smuggle back at least a fraction of the many art pieces temporarily hidden by the Esterhazy family. Unfortunately, one of my mother's close Jewish friends, in order to save himself, turned my parents over to the Slovakian government, and they put them into a concentration camp and both ended up in Auschwitz.

"I never saw my father and mother again. I could not go to school, but had two great teachers, my grandfather for a year and Father Tibor for almost eight years. I really learned a lot from both of them. I was there when my grandfather explained the birth of communism to Father Tibor, who still doubts the dying man's words, but I know that deep in my heart it was true. In fact, the rabbis financed Karl Marx in secret during his work on the Manifesto, and they stopped payment when he didn't want to change certain aspects of his work. That is how I know that both communism and the Jews have the same purpose— world domination.

"Every time my grandfather referred to Christianity, he laughed and said, 'There is no Christian anymore, only Judeo-Christians, and we made sure of that.' According to him, Jesus didn't sacrifice himself for our sins, but we murdered him like our enemies when we perceive them as a great threat to our ways of life, religion, laws, or our progress toward world domination.

Jesus was not only a threat to the rabbis but also to the way of family life, as he also introduced women's rights. I'm still researching when and how the sacrificial lamb story was invented and injected into the New Testament. There are many references in the Bible about Jesus not believing in sacrifices. In fact, the Jewish apostle Matthew included Jesus's words in chapter 9, verse 13, 'I want mercy, not sacrifice.'

"I had four great mentors— my mother, father, grandfather, and Father Tibor. I lost them all. The first three died on me, the fourth one doesn't understand the importance and the necessity of playing politics. Hungarians tend to seek justice and truth and look down on politics instead of embracing it and using it for their own advantage. Just like Kele's father, he could have joined the Communist Party, play the politics, but he would rather sacrifice himself, the future of his family, and his people. Old Hungarian culture puts honor, country, justice, equality, and personal responsibility ahead of the necessary evil, politics. Everything I did to save the last living icon in my mind has turned against me, and the only young man I really cared for and loved is leaving me forever."

I interrupted that our disagreement does not mean separation forever and instead she should vent the anger toward the Nazis. She responded, "I cannot waste my time on the past or on effects of the Holocaust. I must concentrate on the cause and how to prevent it in the future. You don't know half of the story, as you weren't there when I promised my grandfather to find out what turns people against us and what we did to deserve it. My grandfather told me a lot about his dedicated work along the same lines, and after checking out his findings, I had to agree with most of them, like why blue-eyed Jewish people were not taken to concentration camps.

According to genetics, people with blue eyes must have one-fourth or less Jewish blood, like Hitler, as the blue eyes are a product of recessive genes.

"I did uncover a lot of things that led to my people's persecution or dislike worldwide, and it will continue, as communism is not the final answer— we may have to change our ways. Now that Stalin, our protector, is dead, the honeymoon between the communism and Jews may be over, but only temporarily. In fact, in a few years, Jews might be expelled from Russia, as they were in 1910, and from England [1290], from France [1394], from Spain [1492], from Portugal [1497], and even the exodus from Egypt might have been an expulsion, but we'll prevail and return.

For example, my grandfather discovered that the Jews were not slaves but well-paid professionals in Egypt.

"Furthermore, there is no nation or race on this world that can overstay their welcome like us. Wherever we go and stay, the people eventually turn against us— not only Egyptians, Arabs, English, Germans, and Slovaks, but even the Americans. In the 1945 beauty pageant, Bess Myerson, a Russian Jewish immigrant's daughter, won the Miss America contest, but all her appearances were cancelled afterward because she was a Jew. None of the Western powers gave us visas when we needed to escape the Nazis.

"The discrimination against the Jews is worldwide, including our Semitic brothers, the Arabs, and I have to know exactly why. When Joseph II requested all Hebrew names to be changed to German at the end of the eighteenth century, many of my people applauded the idea to help us to integrate into the local communities, hence the beautiful German names for almost all the Ashkenazi's group, but it didn't seem to help. I have to know the cause for not being able to find a permanent home for our people.

"The solution may be to fit in, intermarry, identify with the people around us, and let their fight be ours too. Be patriotic in the country that gives us a home, opportunity, freedom, and chances of economic wellbeing, adopt their customs, names, and feel at home. Take up national causes, adapt to the people to help us conform. Forget about the internationalism, getting rich, controlling the world, and instead be patriotic about the people who give us a permanent home country to live in. Take less and give more."

We kept quiet, both out of respect for her and for wanting to know her perspective on the Jewish and non-Jewish conflicts on the global scale. She read our minds, as she kept on going and telling us what discoveries she had made in this area.

Lara continued. "We'll overcome, prevail, and succeed every place, even when we are not welcome. Communism is the easiest way for us to achieve our objectives, as the party rules and we rule the party. In capitalism, money rules and we rule the banking. Socialism is just a well-paved road to communism.

We'll always be on top, controlling all forms of governments. The road to power is controlling banking, trade, media, news, information flow, will eventually lead to world domination.

"However, we don't care about true democracy, as it doesn't exist or we make sure it only lasts a very short time and gets converted to socialism.

The easiest way to destroy a democracy is to inject it with a good and heavy dose of liberalism. Look at France and Italy. Every social program we introduce is really buying votes, using the working people's tax money and, at the same time, making the people depend on us forever. They don't yet recognize that making them dependent is degrading, and in some cases, it is like slavery.

"Probably the only form of government that can resist us is a benevolent dictatorship, unless we become the dictator. However, a representative republic is hard to dominate, as long as the representatives are real patriots caring about the future of the country and its people.

"We are not necessarily smarter than other people. However, we have a keen eye for identifying weaknesses and strengths of individuals, groups, governments, and leaders, which give us the edge in business and politics.

We are good at getting high grades, looking smarter, picking the right field of studies, matching people up, or just getting ahead of everybody else and getting closer to control of the world. I think many smart individuals and futurists recognize our potential and at the same time understand our weakness for power. These not only make people afraid of us but also make them look at us as a potential or real threat to world harmony and peace. Unfortunately, I believe, they are on the right track. Freud was wrong claiming that anti-Semitism comes from primitive minds against the superior intellects."

So as to get a better understanding of her remarks, I interrupted, "What are mine and Father Tibor's weaknesses?"

She first turned toward me and then toward Father Tibor while responding with the corresponding answers. "Kele, yours is emotional sensitivity, constantly fighting for fairness and justice, and Father Tibor's are regrets for not having a family of his own."

"So that is the reason you don't want to marry me," I retorted.

She smiled and said, "In marriage, sensitivity combined with commitment are the most sought-after qualities in a man, and I truly love you for it. However, these honorable traits may be exploited outside the marriage by individuals and politicians."

Father Tibor didn't say a word, so she continued. "We the Jewish people cannot forget. Therefore, we cannot forgive. Anything bad that happens to us will be exaggerated, reported, and repaid many times over. We expect and want mercy for our wrong deeds, but we never give it. We don't believe the Bible about an eye for an eye— we believe in an eye for a tooth. This is hard for you to understand, but this is going on now and will be done as long as we can have the upper hand. We believe our hurts are worse than anybody else's, and we believe it wholeheartedly.

"Of course, we complain about our sufferings louder than anybody else does. We, more than others, can justify our actions, not only for ourselves, but for the entire world, and it is relatively easy to do when we control the media. Look at the massacre in Ukraine. Stalin starved at least ten times as many people to death than those who died in the concentration camps. However, if we keep the spotlight on our sufferings in Germany and blame everything on Hitler, we bear no responsibility for our evil deeds against our own people. We will proclaim Hitler was the most evil man in the world, even though he was far surpassed by the wickedness of Stalin— another Jew. The truth is, Stalin is Satan himself, and Hitler was only one of his low-ranking officers who could never hope to be on the same level."

She paused, and Father Tibor just said, "Go on."

"We are less gullible than any other ethnic group and can see through schemes that most likely will fool other people. We crave power and control, and these things include money, knowledge, title, recognition, politics, and wealth— in whatever forms they come. We are willing to do almost anything for power and control without developing any guilt complexes.

This is contrary to Father Tibor's teaching, 'The wealth of the individual is determined based on the work he invested in eternity.'

"Attaining power is the easiest in communism, then socialism. We don't believe the New Testament, so we don't feel obliged to always tell the truth when the Bible is used to swear on. We're also willing to stay out of sight and many times want to be away from any limelight, as it may be more advantageous to work behind the scenes, undercover or incognito. These qualities also make us excellent spies, and we feel no allegiance to any country, only to our own kind. Did you know thousands of Jewish spies worked and are still working for the communists in the USA alone? Also, the American NSA can keep secrets from the public, but not from us.

Even the OSS is a joke, as far as we are concerned. We have our people or influence in every government office worldwide."

"I disagree, as most people, regardless of ethnicity, are also power-hungry," I claimed.

She responded, "We have a larger percent of people with undesirable traits than other ethnic groups. For example, it only takes a few Germans in leadership positions to ruin the entire group image, or it takes a very low percentage of other nations' bad behavior to spoil their clout. However, in our case, I estimate about half of us have highly noticeable undesirable traits and characteristics, such as conniving. Take me, you cannot imagine the pleasure I get from having almost limitless power in dealing with the working public or any politically or socially lower ranked persons. My desire for feeling important is just about fulfilled, but I want the thrill of climbing even higher, with the fulfillment of even more power."

I interrupted again, "How come I know many more good Jews than bad Jews?"

She responded, "You may be the fortunate few, but think about encountering a bad one; he or she is really bad, as we want to excel regardless of the direction we are going." She paused and returned to her monologue.

"The German has the 'über alles' [above all] attitude, but we believe and perpetrated the belief that we are the chosen people of God. That alone gives us an edge as the most powerful vision over everybody else, and it also gives us a superior attitude toward the rest of the world. Basically, every Gentile is a second-class citizen in our eyes."

"What is your belief in this matter?" I asked.

"Almighty God is not a Jew, his Son wasn't a Jew, and Jesus's earthly mother, Mary, wasn't a Jew, either, but we claim otherwise. The Holy Ghost wasn't a Jew, so God is for all people, and we should treat and love everyone equally. I believe God chose our race to help spread Christianity and its values all around the world, not to hybridize it with old and outdated Jewish beliefs or mores. I also know from my grandfather, and I believe him, that many parts of the current Bibles contain a lot of insertion from men. The old rabbis not only served as religious leaders but as medicine men and financial advisers for business. They inserted much wisdom in the Bible with good intentions. Some examples of the medical aspects are the circumcision, keeping contagious diseases from the healthy population, or the kosher way of slaughtering animals.

"The rabbis knew about and encountered the genetic flaws in Jewish boys often enough. Their foreskin growth does not keep pace with their sexual maturity, so in an excited state, the foreskin can limit the fresh supply of blood to the head, increasing the possibility of infection and inducing a lot of pain for teenage boys, hence the circumcision. Ordering the lepers to identify themselves and keeping them from others was the best way to prevent spreading the disease. In the hot climate, it is the blood that spoils first, hence the exsanguinations of animals before using their meat. And pigs spread trichinosis.

"Parts of the Bible representing God's words are coded with special messages, which could be read and interpreted by old rabbis. The rabbis made up the entire Judeo-Christian concept in the late third and early fourth century when the Jews recognized the fact that they cannot defeat

Christianity. So they joined and influenced the cause and direction. In fact, they took an active role and leadership even in setting up the hierarchical church empire, and we all know Jesus didn't want that. Jesus taught peace, love, and he asked for the evangelization process to continue.

"But we had the 'if you cannot beat it, join it' attitude and changed Christianity to our favor to Judeo-Christianity. Christianity, in its pure form, and as Jesus had taught it, represented a real and present danger for Judaism, and the rabbis worked very hard to stamp it out. Besides being instigators for and instrumental in the execution of Christ, we destroyed all the original New Testament records we could find written in Aramaic and many Coptic scrolls, and we added a lot of our own versions to them, which were typically written in Greek, not Hebrew. The documents that were successfully hidden from the Jews were labeled as evil to discredit the Gnostic [meaning 'knowledge-based'] writings that closer represent Christianity and maybe more of what Jesus taught.

"When the Greek Orthodox Church discovered some of our evildoings, they tried to separate the Old part and called the New Testament the true Bible. In response to their efforts, the Jews worked very hard and succeeded in canonizing the modified Bibles. The entire sacrifice part of Jesus had to be sold and included in the Bible to gain forgiveness for the Jews' actions against Christ, destruction of records and the Aramaic writings from Jesus's time.

"We even claimed Jesus was a Jew, and people believed it, even though we know Mary, the mother of Jesus, was not a Jew, as she was regularly attending the church. Jewish girls were not allowed in the temple. Jesus was perceived by the rabbis as an enemy from Galilee [meaning foreign] and had to be destroyed, not sacrificed for our sins, as advertised. Sacrifice is a pagan custom kept up by the Jews but totally discarded by Jesus.

"Furthermore, the Jews will do anything to discredit Jesus, his mission, and resurrection. My grandfather told me they, the rabbis, worked very hard and invested much money to destroy the image of Christ as the Messiah and Savior by falsifying records, and they went as far as trying to recreate the tomb of Jesus with a fake skeleton. The rabbis demanded crucifixion to remove the memory of Christ, as the Roman law forbade mentioning the names of people dying on the cross."

She paused, we stayed quiet, and then she continued. "If we'd gain power and military strength, we would be more dangerous than any other army, as we have a longing for power and revenge. When my people gain a permanent foothold in any country, you should feel sorry for all the people there, as they'll be considered second or third-class citizens, just as they are in current Hungary or Palestine. Any resistance to this system will be punished tenfold. Remember, we want mercy, but we don't give it.

"The big threats of Christianity to Judaism were that Jesus treated everybody equally, Jews and Gentiles, women and men. A Jewish woman could not attend the church, and she was deprived of a lot of rights. Jesus selected Mary of Magdala as one of the apostles, but we cleverly removed her stature and importance from the Bible by labeling her an ex-prostitute.

According to my grandfather's research, it is a made-up story. Now her apostolic writings were found in Egypt, Nag Hamadi, but since we had the current Bible canonized, all the original apostles' writings will stay as independent literature and will never be added to be part of the New Testament, and worse yet, they will be referred to as undesirable or Gnostic gospels.

However, we also succeeded in assuring the Roman Catholic popes, unlike Jesus, will not let women be priests or church leaders."

All the information she threw at me was too much to digest at that time, but Father Tibor followed it and seemed to understand or agree with most of what Lara had to say.

She continued. "We know education for the next generation is the most important function for parents, Judaism, and our future. Therefore, we do everything possible to create the best schools for our own children and systematically weaken the public or other sector schools for the general public. There will be a plan to internationalize the Hungarian language to lose its uniqueness and superiority, and cover up the facts that over fifty percent of your language can be directly traced to the Sumerians. We will do our utmost to establish a second Israel in Hungary, as the people here are trustworthy, civilized, and humane. This effort from our part is also justified by predictions from the Bible and the writings of Nostradamus. Very few people know Nostradamus wrote predictions about the entire world, and mostly about Europe, but he wrote an additional and separate book on Hungary alone. We believe his vision that most countries will be destroyed by God, including Israel, except for Hungary. Therefore, the Jews must have a strong foothold in this country."

I remembered my brother Bende's vision of God saving Hungary and looked at Father Tibor for a sign of disagreement, but none was given.

Lara said, "We will do everything in every country to gain sufficient influence to control the people, not only by inferior schools, but through media, reporters, newspapers, entertainment, sport events, pornography, politics, religion, and dope."

"How do we know when this worldwide control and influence will come to pass?" I asked.

"I cannot tell yet, but you'll know when it's close, as we'll find the tomb and skeleton of Jesus, whether it exists or not." She paused to let it sink in and then continued.

"We have no moral deterrent, whether selling drugs, prostitution, secrets, justice, or anything else to the highest bidder. We like to make a profit on everything we do, and recognizing the human weaknesses is the best way to achieve it through such things as drugs, sex, love, survival, fashion, and cosmetics. We thrive on feeling important, survival, and being different, but to gain the love of others is secondary. To make them feel sorry for us is more to our liking. However, not all Jews are like that."

She was cool and collected when she relayed her perspective, and it stayed with me for the rest of my life; therefore, if I encounter a Jewish person, I always try to evaluate if he is one of the good ones and can be trusted.

Lara presented ideas that were totally foreign to me, but her message got through and gave me a new perspective in dealing with any ethnic group. Now I believe that most of the ethnic hatred is due to a misunderstanding of the race, the religion, genetics, or the background they have.

If we only tried to understand and find common traits in other races, religions, and ethnic differences, we could easily adjust and accommodate it instead of fighting it. It is like the feminist movement in the USA; instead of celebrating the differences between women and men, they try to make everybody the same. Just like the teaching of communism. Instead, let's start looking for good in people, individuals, and forget about race, religion, skin color, or other differences.

It became dark by the time Lara finished her dissertation, and we all were emotionally exhausted. Father Tibor asked us to join him for a glass of wine with salami and cheese. Since I was always hungry, I looked at Lara's face, hoping she would accept, but I could only see a sad, dejected look on her, without smile or color. She looked at me and said, "I'm just like the rest of us, even selling my own people short."

I didn't know what to say, but finally Father Tibor spoke up. "We love you, regardless of what you think of us or the many disappointments you may have had in your own life. That entire heavy burden you have carried in your young life had to be loosened and come out one day. I'm glad, and we feel honored, that you shared it with us."

Before I could say anything, she stuck her hand out to me and said, "God be with you."

I just stood up in a daze, could not think of a word to say, but grabbed her hand, pulled her close, and gave her a hug. The warmth of my hug was not returned, but she whispered in my ear, "I have to go and finish my work without you."

I knew what she meant, and that really spoiled it for me, and I was afraid to let her go. I just kept my arm around her for a long, long time until she squirmed out of it and left immediately without saying a word to Father Tibor. I could see on Father Tibor's face that he was very unhappy about the situation, but he knew he also had to let her go. I felt like somebody had hit me with a two-by-four, but instead of physical pain in my head, I had the emotional hurt in my heart.

Father Tibor persuaded me to stay and offered me a portable military type cot. Feeling alone, dejected, and wanting to be physically close to Lara, I accepted the invitation and stayed, thinking tomorrow might be a better day. I asked Father Tibor if Lara's comment about his weakness was correct. He responded he was surprised, as he never mentioned to her either why he became a priest or his second thoughts about priesthood. I asked him to share with me, as I didn't have the seventh sense like Lara.

He obliged and started up while swirling his half a glass of red wine, spinning the glass on the table.

"I was one of the youngest captains assigned to protect one of the narrow, seldom used passes through the Carpathian Mountains in 1917 in the Northeast. I had about one hundred light cavalrymen without any cannons, as the pass wasn't wide enough for heavy guns, artillery, large tanks, or equipment. I had my sentinels posted on the crest, and they had a good view to the east to give ample warning if the Russians would use the narrow trail to come up. Hungarians and Polish people who lived on the east side of the pass did come over one by one, and some of them, with their own horses, even joined my company when the Russians got close.

However, the Russians decided not to take a chance on the narrow pass, but instead they blocked it off on the east side.

"We stayed there, looking at each other for a few weeks in a standoff, when one night I woke up with a crazy dream. I saw a large unit of the enemy breaking through the Austrian line and crossing the big pass just north of us, thousands of troops totally encircling us, without any hope of escape. All of a sudden, an inner voice told me if I promised to serve my God better, he would show me the way out. In my dream, I promised I would, and a vision came to me to charge in a single file at the center of the enemy line and just keep charging forward, riding our horses, and keep running.

"That next morning, my guard woke me, saying we were

totally encircled on our west side, no place to go, and we must give up, as we are outnumbered at least ten to one. I called my officers for a quick conference and told them that there is a way out if they follow my strict instructions.

They all agreed to follow my recommendation of attacking the Russians head on in a single file, right in the middle of their line. These types of moves or tactics were unknown to my soldiers, but they trusted me. I led the charge. The Russians were so surprised by the counterattack with a single file that we could split the line in the middle, and when they fired their cannons, which were lined up parallel to each other along the front line, nobody got hit in between.

"We all jumped over the center of the enemy line and headed straight between two deep creek banks dropping ten meters or more on both sides. In some cases, the banks came so close together, only a single column of horses and hussars could pass. In full gallop, they all made it out and the enemy could not follow, as after the last man cleared the narrow gap between the two banks, the walls collapsed, leaving a huge hole the Russians could not negotiate with the heavy equipment.

"All my men and the top brass bragged about our cleverness and heroism, so when they pinned the medals on my chest, I resigned my commission and reported to the nearest seminary. And the rest is history."

"What are the regrets?" I demanded.

"Since I was the only living male left in our family, I often thought that I should have joined the Greek Catholic seminary, and then I could have a family of my own."

I could not fall asleep for a long time, but eventually I did.

Father Tibor's loud voice saying "Something is wrong" awakened me about one in the morning. I remember seeing him grab his old beat up umbrella, flash light, put a dark robe on, lifted up the entry flap on the tent, and left. I sat up, stayed, and listened. I could hear his quiet footsteps leading away from our tent toward Lara's. I had a bad feeling, so I got up, put my trousers on, and stepped outside to look.

There was no moonlight, but a faint beam coming from the cracks of the restrooms, and it was just enough to make out his silhouette as Father Tibor opened the flap and stepped inside Lara's tent. With bare feet, I ran to the same tent. It took only a few seconds to cover the twenty-meter distance, but I was too late.

I first saw Father Tibor's figure from the back as his flashlight scanned the inside of the tent. Then I heard a terrible scream right in front of him and saw a naked man standing up, grabbing his right arm with his left. A naked man turned toward us. His face in the light clearly showed Sasha, the young Russian officer, with an angry and painful look. Sasha yelled, "Yoebt foye mutch!" and ran out. On the bed was Lara, lying with closed eyes, a fearful and painful face, her long yellow nightgown cleanly cut in the center from top to bottom, and her naked body totally exposed from the front. Immediately to her left side was a large pool of blood that had squirted past the bed.

Father Tibor turned off his flashlight, and with the most loving and tender voice, he asked, "Lara, you are safe now. But are you okay?"

I could see her no more, but her response was, "Sasha tried to rape me, holding a big knife to my neck, then he cut my gown and was on top of me when I sensed the beam of light, followed by a horrible scream in my ear."

Father Tibor said, "Cover your body, and let's get out of here before they return."

She responded, "You can now put on the light. I'm covered."

I went closer next to her bed and saw the deed. Father Tibor's umbrella was lying right next to me, without the handle. The handle with a sword was still in his right hand. I moved even closer to help Lara, but I tripped on something. I spoke up for the first time, asking Father Tibor to shine the light by my foot. There it was— a bayonet and a lifeless hand next to it, still oozing blood.

"I call this a success. My dear child is safe, and there is a madman running around without his right hand," muttered Father Tibor. Lara sat up, holding her cover up to look at the crime scene. She saw the lifeless hand and a big knife on the floor.

Lara dressed in the dark, and all three of us slowly walked

over to our tent. She was holding Father Tibor's left arm while he still had the sword in his right hand. I brought along the rest of the umbrella while walking behind them. None of us could sleep or talk; we just sat together, waiting for reprisal.

Finally, I broke the silence when Father Tibor walked over to the table where I put the other half of the umbrella. While inserting the thin, sharp blade that locked together with a snap, I said, "I would have never guessed a priest could carry a weapon."

He responded, "Whether I'm a priest or a civilian, I swore to protect the weaker and the innocent."

Father Tibor asked me to leave, just as a precaution so I wouldn't beimplicated in any way. Lara also thought it would be a good idea for me to leave, as they had enough explaining to do, especially if the Russian officer bleeds to death. Thinking of my recent previous experience and the prison time, I got dressed and left on foot in the pitch dark toward my barracks more than five kilometers away.

That was the last time I saw Father Tibor.

Deception and Reality - Living Through the Missing Pages of History

Glimpse of The Traitor

While walking back to the barracks, my mind was full of pictures, like individual photographs of the events just having transpired. Father Tibor's flashlight created these images in my mind, like strobe lights in the dark.

Once I rehashed the events, my thoughts turned to what if Sasha survived and implicated me? Did he see me? This thought really scared me. I kept hoping he hadn't noticed me, and he may not able to identify Father Tibor either. Reviewing each step chronologically, there was a good chance Sasha didn't see anybody but Lara. It was pitch dark in the tent, except for the short burst of light coming from Father Tibor's flashlight, and both of us were behind the light source. I wondered how the young officer would explain his missing hand, the very sharp bayonet, and his clothing left behind in the commissar's tent.

It was close to three a.m. when I arrived at the barracks, and to my surprise, the small gate was slightly ajar and no guards could be seen anywhere.

I became suspicious and stopped to listen. A few seconds later, I heard a girl giggle on my right, so not wanting to interrupt the young couple, I sneaked through the slightly opened gate without being noticed by the second guard sitting, and most likely snoozing, in the dark inside the small guard house. It was still dark when I got to my room, so I climbed into bed but could not sleep at all.

It wasn't the snoring of Ben next door that kept me awake, but the potential ramifications for Lara, Father Tibor, and possibly me. My feelings for Lara were still strong, but deep down, I knew the romance was over and the real concerns should be for Father Tibor. He'll not lie if asked, and that Saturday night only four of us were there— Sasha, Lara, Father Tibor, and me. The border guards were stationed quite a distance from the tents, and if they heard something, they probably didn't care, as the noise came from behind them, not from the other side of the border.

It must have been around five-thirty a.m., right after the reveille should have sounded on a week day, but I received the unusual wake-up call on Sunday early morning when someone knocked on my door very loudly. I knew it was a man. Here comes my second arrest, I thought.

Kele D. Gabor

The Communists' ruling by fear had left its mark, made me jumpy, and started to wear on me.

I never wanted to give in, but in reality, it made me a nervous wreck. I jumped up from bed, and just in my undershirt and shorts, I opened the door before asking who it was.

Right in front of me stood the tall captain whom I met on my arrival at the compound, with his smiling face looking at me. I noticed he was alone, and the smile grew to the point where his ears had to move back to give room for his ever-widening mouth. I asked, "What's the problem?"

"You're here," was the response. "I was told you went to the digging site Saturday late afternoon and nobody saw you return. I guess you must have returned before nightfall."

I again asked, "What's up?"

"There was a horrible accident last night in the political officer's tent."

"What happened?" I asked innocently. "The young Serbian officer attacked the party commissar, that really sexy Jewish girl, but she was able to defend herself and cut off his hand with the same sharp bayonet used against her, and I wish she would have cut off only his eleventh 'finger' instead. The officer must have been drunk and will be in a lot of trouble."

"What is so funny about this terrible event?" I asked.

"Oh, I was just glad to see you here, so you don't need to be a witness for anyone."

I started to smile, as it occurred to me an alibi like the captain himself would be enough to keep me in the clear. The captain made an about-face in a military fashion and walked away, I presumed, still smiling. I thanked him, but he didn't hear me.

I was tired, but my mind was racing. Finally, I'd be finished here the next day and then be heading back to my regional office, where my boss could send me to the main cartographic office in Budapest so Zoli and I could finish our job of tracking down the double agent.

For the first time in my life, I didn't feel like breakfast, even though the company cook often provided me with free meals, saving me a lot of money, which we needed to purchase photographic equipment and cover other expenses associated with tracking down the double agents. I went down to the chow line, both for being seen by others and hoping my appetite would return.

It was a good move, as the guard who had seen me leave the compound was there and inquired about my return. "How did you come back without being seen by any of the guards?"

Not thinking straight, I just said the truth, "I sneaked back through the open gate."

He thought out loud and said it must have been before eleven p.m., as we lock the gate then on Saturday nights. He continued, "I have to go back and correct my report to the officer of the guards."

"Never mind, the officer already knew, as he rudely woke me up very early this morning, and he was happy to see me here."

I did end up having a small breakfast of cold cuts and real coffee, which was only available for the commanding and political officers on weekdays, and for all officers on Sundays. For the most part, Ben and I were treated as one of the officers, and to our surprise many of them would often seek out our company during the meals. Invariably, they wanted to know about the civilians and professional work available on the outside. We definitely got the impression they wanted out of the military life under the Russian command and control.

Ben didn't show up for breakfast, so I went up to check on him. He didn't feel well after trying some very spicy Southern dishes for supper last night in the nearby town. I went back down and got him a cup of milk.

After he wiped off the white line from his upper lip, he asked me if I could double-check all the measurements with the help of some volunteers and mark the entire site on the already finished map tomorrow so we could head back Tuesday morning.

Seizing the opportunity and excuse to go back to the site to find out what was going on and get back to finish our urgent detective work, I suggested that we do all the remaining work today and head back as soon as possible, like tonight. Ben approved my plan and started to pack. I went to see the officer of the day and asked for two volunteers who could carry the chains for me and have a driver of the vehicle take us to the site. I got two interesting border guards, two friends recently transferred to the unit who already had seen the only movie playing in the nearby town.

During the measuring process, their intelligence and unique friendship commissioned or noncommissioned officers, and they only had the rank of corporal. Both grew up in the same area, but one was from a Romanian family and the other from a Croatian family. Being relatively close to the border of both of these new countries, I asked them why they stayed in Hungary. The Croatian guy disliked the Serbs, and the Romanian preferred the better educated Hungarians over his compatriots. I wished I had more time to chat with them and find out more details about their choices, but I was in a hurry to finish up. I needed to check out the situation with Lara and Father Tibor and get home at the latest early Monday morning.

It only took a couple of hours to double-check the measurements around the marked parameters while keeping an eye on Father Tibor's tent, as Lara's tent was not visible from the site, except for the red flag on the top. I asked the two "gentlemen," as I called my volunteers, which they liked, to double-check my measurements while I went to the toilet.

I hurried up the small hill to get a view of Lara's tent, as I had not seen any activities in front of Father Tibor's tent. Once I reached close to the top of the small sand hill, it was easy to make out the Russian major standing by Lara's tent giving instructions to two of his soldiers. I passed by Father Tibor's tent, lifted the cover, and found it totally empty except for the two cots, a table, and two wooden benches. I walked up to the major and asked him where comrade Lara was. He asked me to step back, as he had to take some pictures of the crime scene.

As I waited outside, I could see several flashes of light, as he must have taken at least twenty pictures. When he came out, he instructed the soldiers to clean up and turned toward me. He asked in perfect Hungarian what I was doing there. I told him I was finishing some last-minute measurements before we concluded our work here and head back to our office but wanted to say good-bye to the chief archeologist and the great Communist Party representative. He smiled with a dismissing gesture and a grin while playing with his beautiful Leica camera, fully equipped with flash attachment on the top and a small, thin tripod still screwed in on the bottom.

This was the exact equipment Zoli and I needed to get photographic evidence of the traitors.

The major obviously did not realize how much I wanted to have his camera or I was an unwilling witness to the incident he called a crime, and I knew now he was really Russian, not Serbian. These facts gave me the courage to insist on finding out what had transpired since I left the scene just around two a.m. this morning. I said, "You referred to this place as a crime scene, but I'm only interested about the whereabouts and the wellbeing of the comrades."

He was visibly taken back by my firmness to the point of looking at me with deep suspicion, but he did respond to my inquiry. I could tell he was thinking on what to tell me and how to verbalize it in Hungarian.

After a short pause, the major said, "In summary, there was a lover's quarrel between the comrade and one of my officers, who was injured in the ensuing fight, and the comrade is fine and is being escorted home by the old archeologist." He obviously could see my relief and commented, "You must have also noticed the shapely comrade— every young man liked her, so I understand your concerns."

He turned around to see the content of a small suitcase being shown to him by one of his men just exiting the tent. I could not see what was in it, but I assumed the officer's shirt, pants, the bloody bayonet, and maybe a lifeless hand.

I did go to the outhouse to relieve myself and remove other possible suspicions by my temporary, but very intelligent, assistants. When I walked back, only about a hundred meters, they already had loaded all the equipment into the vehicle and, with a smile, announced all measurements checked out and that they would like to go back the long way to pick up a couple of beers I had promised them earlier. I agreed, as it was not more than a few extra kilometers and we would still arrive at the base before the noon meal.

We stopped at the still closed pub and knocked very loud for a long time. Finally, someone came out to help, and I bought four cool bottles of beer and we headed back. The chow line was pretty long, as Sunday meal was usually the most popular; even soldiers on short leave would come back early for the better meal. I had my two assistants hold my place while I went to deposit all the new marked maps equipment and one cool beer for Ben.

Coming up the steps, I could make out Ben talking to the Russian major, not suspecting anything. I just headed straight up to Ben's door, which was already partially ajar and walked in, greeting Ben first, then the major. To my surprise, there were two other lower-ranking officers standing behind the wall next to the door. I could not see them until I entered.

Kele D. Gabor

Ben looked agitated, and instead of the gray, pale look that he had from the spicy meal from last night, he was totally red in the face. He turned toward me and asked me to leave. The two officers grabbed me from behind, took the rolled up maps from under my arms and the cool beer for Ben from my hand.

"What is going on?" I protested.

The major turned toward Ben and said, "You explain it to your assistant during your noon meal and go now."

Ben reached for his jacket lying on his bed, but the major grabbed him and pushed both of us out the door. Ben's face became even redder and, with shaking knees and voice, started to tell the story while walking down the steps. Ben's opening remarks were the worst language I ever heard from a distinguished, professional gentleman.

Transcribing from the rude language he used, the actual message was this: "The so-and-so Serb-loving officer confiscated all of our works without required paper or authority. I have never been insulted and embarrassed as much in my whole life, and he will have to answer to the highest level for the insults and stealing our official maps and notes."

Walking to the chow line, I didn't want to say the Serb officer was really a high-ranking Russian officer who was assigned the job of destroying all evidence relating to the archaeological digs and finds. I just listened and let him blow off some steam. Luckily, we didn't have to wait long, as my two new assistants held our position, which was now right by the entry door.

Ben had to stop while I introduced my newfound friends and assistants and was able to change the subject so Ben could at least temporarily forget his troubles.

The four of us had a great dinner, pörkölt (beef stew with a lot of red paprika) with potato and salad. Even Ben was amazed at the knowledge base these two low-ranking border guards had. We talked about music, chess, aerial and color photography, the universe, ancient civilizations, and of course women. We finished our dinner by one p.m., but we were still talking at two-thirty p.m.

We had to hurry to make our Sunday evening express train from the nearby town, which would take us home in a few hours. When we arrived back to our room, we had to repack, as everything was thrown around and every piece of map was taken, along with our notes and sketches.

When I finally arrived home late that night, my mother waited up for me with open arms and said, "I felt it in my heart you would come home tonight." I was too exhausted to do the usual summary report to my mother, who always listened with great interest. The tiredness must have shown on my face after not getting much sleep for the previous forty-eight hours, so my mother asked me to postpone the report.

The next day I woke up late, and my mother was waiting for me with a hot cup of tea and toast. She told me I tossed, turned, and fought in my dream I must have had a rough assignment. She knew nothing of my ordeal, but she suspected that not all was well. For obvious reasons, I didn't tell her about the arrest, short prison stay, the difficult interrogation, meeting Father Tibor and Lara, or the incident that happened and I witnessed on Saturday night.

I was late going to the office and stopped by my boss's office to apologize, but he didn't want to hear anything of that sort. He just said, "I have high-ranking visitors coming, we'll talk later. Ben stopped by my home late last night and already gave me a short report."

Before noon, I felt a gentle tap on my shoulder. It was Julie, the office sweetheart. Everybody liked her positive attitude, team spirit, warm smile, melodious songs, and funny jokes. She was married to an engineer for over ten years, but they had no children. She went nuts when small children visited the office, so everybody speculated she could not have one of her own. She asked me what was going on, as the entire big brass had come to visit us and now our boss wanted to see me privately.

I tried to return her sweet smile, but there was no way anyone could compete with hers. She was genuinely pretty, with big blue eyes and a wonderful smile, always making one feel good all over. We nicknamed her Angel, and if anybody ever felt down or sad, we just asked Julie to visit that person and cheer him up. Many times, she beat us to having to ask her. I suspect my boss asked her to see me for the same purpose, even though I wasn't down, but I was always preoccupied, deep in thought, and the strain of the last few weeks' events and the worries about the near future might have shown on my face.

I stood up, looked in her eyes, turned around, and left, moving toward the big office. I just made a few steps when Angel jumped in front of me and asked me again what happened. I just said, "Nothing special."

Kele D. Gabor

She put both hands up to my shoulders, looking in my face, and she said, "You have a lot of sadness, and I see great conflicts in your eyes. I must help you out, or it will affect you for the rest of your life."

The passing thought came to me that Angel may want to help me the same way as my landlady, who offered herself after my interrogations and short stay in prison. If Angel were a psychologist, she would have been among the best of the world. I promised her we could talk after I saw my boss, and she let me go. By the time I got to my big boss's office, I already felt better, more relaxed. Just the fact that someone noticed, cared, and was genuinely interested in my troubles was a big help. I now could see why Julie's tall and handsome husband never looked at another girl and truly adored her.

My boss sat me down next to his desk and pulled his chair around to face me so we could talk without anything between us. It felt so good and made me feel at ease when my boss talked to me as an equal and a human being.

Unfortunately, I seldom experienced the same courtesy from other managers or officials. They all hide behind their big desk, set their chairs higher, or stand up to emphasize their higher position, just like the communist hierarchy, lawyers, and politicians. Many a time, one can surmise the management or leadership quality of the person just by looking at the furniture arrangements in the office.

He asked me how I was, the family, and if the recent events dampened my spirit, as he was concerned about me. I set him at ease by saying, and meaning it, that most of the recent unexpected events were taken as experiences to learn from and only a few people in history are given the opportunity or the exposure to learn so much in such a short time. Of course, I did not mention the recent incident involving Father Tibor, Lara, and the young Russian officer, Sasha.

My boss added, "You have the right attitude and approach. Keep it up, and you'll be very successful. You'll survive and recover from any setbacks."

After a long pause, he started to say he would like to add to my recent experiences and wanted to give me the opportunity to learn just a little more. I responded, "I sincerely hope these new experiences you would expose me to will be easier on my body, mind, and soul."

He continued, "The representatives from the ministry of interior, foreign affairs, and the Communist Party came to visit me this morning.

The special envoy arrived about ten o'clock, and they assured me all was well, but I have to change a few things in my books."

I asked, "What kind of things?"

He explained, "Like my office never sent anyone to the archeological site, but you and Ben went to study the meanderings of the Tisza River and how it may affect settlements, structures, and wetlands along the banks."

I smiled and asked if that was all.

"Not quite," he said. "I cannot hire Ben for any work anymore, as he is permanently retired." I was scared about the word permanently, and he could see it on my face. He continued and just said, "There is nothing to worry about concerning Ben. He will be okay, but get the message— the words 'archeological find' cannot be used by you or me in reference to your recent work."

I asked what about the other people involved. He showed me a list of names left by the Communist Party representatives containing the persons' names who need to be warned about not talking about our recent project. The list included only the Hungarian persons associated with the project, including my boss, our secretaries, Mr. Big, his secretary, Rosa, Ben and I, two officers, and three enlisted men, but they left off the two volunteers I hired the previous Sunday morning for a few bottles of beer. I told my boss it was not a complete list. He looked surprised, as he was assured that the Communist Party did not make mistakes, period. We came to the same conclusion: the two volunteers were plants.

We talked a little longer, and he told me Mr. Big's opinion was that "trouble would always find me and I could bring bad luck to any organization."

My boss suggested I take a week's paid vacation just to get back to normal. I took him up on his offer and asked him to transfer me to the main cartographic office for this short week, not to create any suspicion among my colleagues. He liked the idea and added, "Since you were assigned to check the meandering of the Tisza River, I'm adding as assignment the investigation of flood patterns, so bring back copies of all historic maps of the Tisza river into our archives." I was delighted about the new and easy assignment, as it also gave me the chance and freedom to start my job with Zoli in earnest and practically full-time.

After our short and successful meeting, we went our separate ways to lunch. I looked for and found Julie right outside our building, eating her sandwich. As promised, I reported to her, and I got there as she was trying to swallow a large bite of liver pate with pickles. She waved me to hold it until she finished chewing and swallowing it. She smiled; so did I. She looked into my eyes again and said, "Get some rest. You look okay— you must have had a good meeting with our boss." I invited her for an ice cream; she accepted and advised me to be the same kind of boss as ours. I promised, and I have kept that commitment.

I look for abilities, positive attitudes, and then experience before hiring someone, and I treat everyone with dignity and fairness; from the office cleaner to my superiors, no difference, just like I had learned from my ex-boss.

It was Wednesday before I could go up to Budapest, and I immediately headed for our ping-pong club to see if Zoli left me any messages. There were four envelopes with coded notes inside, dropped through the opening of my locker door. I put all four envelopes in my pocket and carried my ping-pong paddle to the shower room, which was not being used at that time. The bathroom stalls were too dark most of the time to read and decode our messages. The first message said, "You must meet me ASAP. I'll check every day." The second message read, "Piri got involved without my permission." The third read, "As soon as you show up, go and say hello to Hodos." And the last one read, "Meeting time changed to nineteen hundred hrs."

All four notes were troubling and very disturbing, as some undesirable events must have happened, forcing Zoli to change our plans while I was away; Piri should have not gotten involved, and finally, Hodos should also be left out. I got very upset and immediately headed to the big office where Hodos worked. On the way, I could not fathom what could have happened in the last three weeks while I was away and out of touch.

It was late afternoon by the time I arrived at the old office building and headed straight for the mapping department, where all the cartographer and draftsmen were working, including Hodos as a low-level supervisor.

As I was passing between the lines of tables, I saw that Sándor's desk was cleaned up— bad sign, but nobody occupied that space yet.

Hodos's desk was closer to the hallway toward the manager's offices, as he was considered a senior cartographer in spite of his young age. He was often left in charge in case his superior was gone, and people preferred him to the typical Communist Party–selected or–approved managers. He wasn't at his desk, but his coworker could see I was looking for him. He said, "Hodos just left, but you could probably still catch him, as he just went to lock up the manager's office."

I quickly opened the door leading to the wide hallway and looked left and right, hoping to see him. His colleague helped me out again and said, "The third office on the right." I turned right and looked left, where all the offices were, and saw most of the lights were still on, including the third door marked high up with number Twenty-three. I knocked on the tall double doors with big panels of opaque glass from the handles up, decorating the old, chipped, off-white painted frames. One could see only the shadow of a person standing next to the glass or close to the door. No answer came to enter, so I was just ready to test the lock when I saw the outline of a person approaching the door. The light source came from the other end of the office, so as the individual got closer to the door, the shadow became smaller and sharper. The right side of the double door opened up, and right in front of me stood Hodos.

He was a fast talker, and as usual, he blurted out some questions that he had to repeat so I could comprehend. When I understood his question, my answer was, "I'm doing fine, and I'm here on official business."

He asked, "How long?"

"As long as it takes, but I hope a week will suffice."

"Well, I have to hurry now, but you must come with me, as I have an important envelope to give you in private." He had his attaché case already in the left hand and the key to the door in the right. He just pushed me back and turned around and locked the door. "Follow me, and I'll make time to retrieve your envelope. Just hurry, please."

"What is the big rush, as I often have seen you burning the midnight oil?"

"I have to pick up my mother at the station and get her home, as her health is failing."

"Why is she traveling when sick?" I asked.

"Her sister just passed away, and she had to go back to take care of family matters."

I expressed my deepest sympathy, as I knew what it was like losing family members.

Hodos moved so fast that I could barely keep up. We already passed the guards in gray uniforms under the Russian style officer's hat as we were exiting the building running down the steps. He turned to the left, and I told him the station was the other way. He looked back at me, smiled, and waved to follow him. We went across the street. The building on the corner was a big public library. He went in, and I followed. He headed to the librarian's desk and asked for someone by name. He was still talking fast and probably quietly, so I could not hear what he said.

The middle-aged librarian left, and a few seconds later a beautiful tall young lady with a big smile headed directly toward Hodos. I whispered, "Who is that?"

He slightly turned his head back and said, "Dora, my girlfriend."

I wanted to say he had excellent taste in women, but Dora was already standing in front of him. He whispered something in her ear; she stepped back and looked at me, nodded, turned around, and left as fast as she had come. I could not help watching her light walk, with the feminine sway of the hips that was tantalizing. She had a dark skirt on, with an eggshell blouse that showed her great figure and narrow waistline. Hodos looked at me, and seeing my reaction, he said, "Don't get any ideas, I want to marry her." I guess I closed my mouth and was left speechless.

Before I gathered my thoughts, Dora was back with a book with a rusty brown cover and handed it to Hodos. "I believe this is the book you wanted us to hold for you," said Dora, with the nicest voice I ever heard.

Her voice was more pleasant and had more ring to it than the best wind chime I had ever heard.

He slipped the book into his attaché case and said, "Thank you." Hodos turned around and said, "Let's go."

I just stood there smiling at Dora and asking him, "Aren't you going to introduce me?"

Hodos responded, "I wouldn't know which of your names I should use."

I was dumbfounded by his response. He grabbed my arm and pulled me away. I felt embarrassed, and as soon as we stepped outside, he turned right to go toward the station.

Deception and Reality - Living Through the Missing Pages of History

The next few minutes, his response to my request to be introduced became clear. Hodos pulled me in the next dark entryway and said, "I promised that I would give you this." He opened his case, took out the book, removed a sealed, blank envelope from it, and handed it to me.

I asked, "What is this?"

He said, "Your friend from the embassy gave it to me to pass it on to Lxxxx, Sándor's friend, as soon as possible, and I had to think about whom that may be. So what name should I have used while introducing you to my sweetheart, Kele or Lxxxx?"

I was shocked that Al would give my code name away, but of course, that was the only name he knew me by, and he didn't know any better. I asked Hodos never to tell anyone about this incident and don't tell any person my other name. His response was music to my ears, but not the comment he made afterward. He said, "You can trust me, as I trust you, and I would never spoil your anonymity by telling him or anybody else your code name. However, if I were you, I would not deal with an amateur."

I didn't say anything, but it was not the first time Al goofed or made a mistake, including the slip he made by originally telling me the name Hodos. I asked him how he came to know Zoli. He said, "He looked me up in the office last week to find out where exactly you were and asked if I wanted to help him, as you didn't show up at the contact place and time."

I thanked him for his help, and we parted company, as I had to make my way to meet Zoli on the Buda side of the city or the west of the Danube by seven p.m., and I had to get a bite to eat before I got there.

I went down to the nearest streetcar stop to catch a ride to Buda, but since I still had some extra time, I stopped off by the small donut shop right inside the station and ordered the biggest donut and the tallest glass of milk. Once I paid for the snack, I moved to a well-lit section having some shelves built into the wall, where one could have some privacy to consume a snack. Before taking a bite of the delicious looking and smelling donut, I took the envelope from the inside of my pocket and gently opened it up, cutting the top end with my pocketknife. There was nothing in it. I became very puzzled and tried to figure out what Al's empty and blank envelope could signify. While eating, my mind imagined so many plausible meanings about the missing letter from the envelope I lost count and decided to get Zoli's input.

Kele D. Gabor

I arrived at the designated point before Zoli. I saw him button his shirt at his neckline while going down at the side of the bridge. After the proper signals, we re-emerged together in the corner espresso cafe. We sat away from the windows as an added precaution in case lip readers had followed one or both of us.

Zoli spoke first. While smiling, he said, "Piri applied and was given a mediocre job close to the embassy and decided to do her own spying by just observing the goings-on— when the ambassador came and left, in what kind of car, and who was driving— making diligent notes on every little thing she could. She worked the second shift in the pub, so the morning was free, but she came in early just to make better and longer observations.

During her shift, the pub became busy only after most of the staff had already left the embassy, so she had the opportunity to observe before the really busy time of the day. Even though she was often caught by her supervisor not tending her post, she made friends with him by getting involved and interested in the boss's hobby— photography."

I interrupted impatiently to shorten up the story to give me the important stuff.

He smiled and continued while nodding his head. "Piri told me that within the first week, a pattern emerged when two young embassy employees came to drink between four and six p.m. but always arrived separately, and they only stayed for a short period, sometimes not even finishing their drinks. Also, always the taller one paid. While at the pub, they kept a lookout for other embassy personnel passing by. If one came in, they parted company. One of them, usually the taller, darker, thinner and the better-looking, would meet the other embassy person by the door and buy him a drink, like he wanted to avoid being seen with the other guy.

"Piri really became suspicious when the other friend would actually try to hide and never left the pub before the others departed. When she passed by their table or delivered the drinks, they lowered their voice but continued talking English. Since Piri only knows how to translate but cannot speak well and has difficulty understanding the spoken words, she could not make out what they were saying. One occasion, when the better looking and taller person came in, Piri approached him and asked if she could take his order. The person responded, 'Köszönöm nem,' or 'No, thank you,' in proper Hungarian and with excellent pronunciation."

I was sitting on pins and needles, as what she observed could be suspicious, but this behavior would also explain homosexual lovers. Zoli ignored my visible impatience and continued.

"Hearing all this, I decided to set bait by calling the embassy with the number you left me. I asked for Mr. White. He responded, and I told him a false code name we agreed on in our plans, the amount of money I wanted, where, and what time. He asked me the code, and I gave the one Al gave you just before you left."

I interrupted, "That code may not be valid, as I just picked up an empty and blank envelope from Al, via Hodos."

Zoli looked at me funny and with question marks in his eyes. I repeated what I had said, but he shook his head and said, "Your empty and blank envelope must mean something else, as Piri took off the next day from work and followed the taller guy to the Obuda cemetery."

"So what?"

"She was afraid to follow him inside, but she called me, describing the particular bouquet of flowers he purchased and the amount of time he spent in the cemetery before returning to the entry gate empty-handed."

I was starting to get agitated about the long story, which most likely led to nowhere, so I interrupted again. "How does it help us?"

Zoli said, "Just wait till the end."

I showed calmness, but I was burning up inside to have him get to the point, and he continued. "I arrived about an hour later, my sister waiting for me, and we walked while Piri answered all my questions." I nodded approvingly that finally he got my message and wouldn't repeat all the questions he had asked Piri.

He went on. "Then I went inside the cemetery, looking for the flowers. I had to proceed slowly, in case I entered the drop zone and someone else was also observing. So I decided to zigzag slowly through every second row of cemetery plots. About the fifth row, on my left I noticed the yellow roses, with one red one sticking out of the middle. The name on the headstone was invisible, like someone purposely rubbed it out. However, the stone was about a meter tall and gray. Since Piri didn't say anything about the red rose, I walked back to the flower shop by the gate and asked for a bouquet of yellow roses. After I paid for it, I asked the old lady if she had sold a bouquet like this an hour ago. She responded, 'Yes, but he wanted a red one placed in the middle. Odd, isn't it? He also had a dialect that I never heard before.' I shrugged my shoulders, thanked her, and left with the roses.

"It started to get dark, which I didn't mind, as I wanted to sneak back and exchange the flowers without being noticed. I had to take out the red and insert it in mine in case it signified something. The red rose hung up, so I had to lift up the whole bouquet from the vase, which had no water in it. To my surprise, the red rose had a white ribbon with some interesting decorations. Taking a closer look, I could make out my made-up code name I left for Mr. White, but it was written with the Cyrillic alphabet."

"We got him!" I yelled out loud enough that everyone looked at us.

Zoli just smiled, and I was angry at myself for bringing attention to us. "You better smile too," said Zoli in a quiet manner. So I did, and Zoli would not continue until we left the place a few minutes later. Then he said, "I'll continue the story after we arrive at the park."

In the meantime, I showed him the blank and empty envelope again. Zoli took it from me and, under a lamp post, started to examine it. When he turned it inside out, there were visible writings with small letters along and right on top of the sealed section, running down and up in a V shape, following the glue line. Zoli gave it back to me, saying we should wait until we get better lighting at the ping-pong club. "By the way, Al must have not trusted Hodos completely, as he wrote the note so it's only visible when holding it against a strong light source or after steaming open the glue." I interrupted Zoli's deliberation by telling him what Hodos said about Al and the other Western agents— "amateurs."

Zoli started another long story about why Western agents deserved the adjective of amateurs when it came to espionage. Until we arrived at the park, Zoli poured it on about the ignorant ambassadors, untrained, high maintenance, undedicated, spoiled, money-hungry Western agents.

At that time, I took his outrage as a way of venting his frustration and pain in losing his brother. However, later I realized Zoli knew things about English and American agents and their failures in protecting military secrets from the KGB and the total infiltration of Russian agents or Communist sympathizers in both governments. The two top issues for Zoli were (1) the giving away of the secrets associated with the atomic bomb (implosion) and (2) the Western sellout of Central Europe to communist Russia.

He went on about the Roosevelt administration being run by

Deception and Reality - Living Through the Missing Pages of History

Communists or Russian spies: Theodore Hall, Seville Sax, Alger Hiss, Charlie Gold, Green, Rosenberg, William Wishman, and Gus, to mention some. All these Communist Party members or KGB agents in America were really working for Russia and Stalin. According to Zoli, almost none of them were caught, even after the American code-breakers found out who some of them were. However, Zoli's idol was an American code breaker Meredith Gardner, who had a good command of twelve languages.

The American code-breakers impressed Zoli, as they could crack all codes, but nobody could crack theirs.

Later, Lara told me that the top five hundred and most successful spies for Communist Russia in America were all Jewish because they do most everything better than others and they were dedicated communist sympathizers.

She even listed some of the high positions and government agencies in the USA, which were controlled or infiltrated by communists. For example, senior assistant to the president, others in the departments of state, defense, justice, and transportation. The KGB also infiltrated the British and French governments in similar manner.

I had to interrupt the litany and venting of frustration by Zoli when he didn't stop after getting to the designated place.

Zoli took a few deep breaths and continued. "I wasn't sure what to do with the bouquet I had. I knew I could not exchange them as mine didn't have a red rose or the white ribbon on with the writing, but eventually I decided to put it on a lone not maintained plot a few rows up and away, but definitely out of site from the drop zone. By the time I left the cemetery, Piri was really concerned as I spent over twenty minutes there while the embassy employee less than ten."

I interrupted again. "Did you set up a watch with a camera to take a picture of whoever picked up the yellow roses with the white ribbon?"

"Yes and no. Since it was already dark, we decided to go home our separate ways and meet early the next day." Zoli explained, "We didn't have a camera, color film, or the money to buy them. We decided we should find out what was going on and then decide on the course of action after you returned, with what we hoped, enough money. However, in the meantime, Piri befriended her boss enough to get basic training in photography and, later, to be able to borrow the camera, as long as she could provide the color film."

Kele D. Gabor

I reached in my rear pocket and counted out all the cash I had saved for this occasion, and it was a little over a thousand forint. Zoli took the money but gave half of it back, saying, "Whoever sees Piri first, give her the five hundred. That should be enough for the particular color film she needs for the camera. By the way, Piri wants to see you right away."

I said, "As soon as you finish the story, you could show me where she lives."

"She has a sublease of a single bedroom, right over the pub where she works."

"Isn't she clever?"

"She is my sister."

I agreed, as she was sweet and smart but a little too emotional. Deep inside, I have cared for her a great deal, and it really bothered me to expose her to these difficult and very dangerous challenges. I now told Zoli he has to finish the story on how far they got.

Zoli continued, "Piri took the first watch early Saturday morning, as she had to work that day, and I took her uneventful watch over around noon. By two p.m., I got anxious and worked my way closer to the headstone.

The roses had opened up, and the bouquet looked fuller. However, the red rose was gone. I looked around and went closer. Then I saw a white one replaced the red rose, and it was hidden among the yellow ones, like it had a shorter stem. I just reached in to pull up the white rose to be level with the rest of them. I noticed the bouquet looked much fuller because the stems were no longer tied together. The white ribbon with my made-up code name was gone.

"I didn't first understand why the white rose was so hard to pull until I separated the yellows by pushing them aside, and then I noticed a round box was tied to its stem. I carefully looked around, pulled the white rose out, and looked into the round, elongated metal box. It looked like an old .50-caliber ammo shell filled with green paper. It was so tightly rolled it took a long time to pull them out and even longer to put them back with shaking hands after checking it out. They were almost new twenty-dollar bills, but I was afraid to count them. I became nervous for some reason, put the money back, reattached the string to the stem, and placed the white rose back to the vase as close to the same way as I could make them. I stepped back, looked around, and hurried away.

"I was already close to the exit when I saw the same embassy employee described by Piri coming in. He was tall, thin, dark hair, dark eyes, and kind of an attractive young Jewish man. I turned my head and stopped after he passed me. I turned around and watched. He headed straight to the unknown person's headstone, and all of a sudden, his head disappeared from my view. Obviously, he'd bent down to pick out the white rose and took the shell casing with him, as I knew he would not take the time to take the money out and count it. I waited until he stood up, came around, and headed toward the exit sign."

Zoli turned toward me and said, "You don't know how I missed a camera and a handgun then, as now we have to repeat the whole scenario and expose all of us to a possible mishap. I still don't know if Piri or I missed the exchange of the red with the white rose. However, you are here now, and the extra set of eyes will be a big help this weekend."

It was very late, in fact closing time at the club, when we arrived. We had to beg the porter to let us in, making the story up that I left my wallet and personal papers in my locker. We headed to a well-lit area, took my wallet and the reversed envelope out, and examined the small, hand-printed words. I must have gotten red in the face because Zoli asked, "What's wrong?"

"It is in English, and I know almost nothing in this language," I answered.

Zoli's response was, "You'd better go and see Piri about translating it."

We parted company, as we would be meeting again the next day. He already had turned around when I asked him why he changed the meeting time. He said, "We have to wait until dark, as we can only monitor those dirty people in the daytime."

I stopped and hugged him, whispering in his ear, "You and Piri are great people, and I feel honored to help you anytime, and thanks again."

Zoli said, "We're doing it for our brother, and we should thank you for sticking your head out for your friend."

I told him I also liked Piri and him, and we parted again. However, I stopped again and asked Zoli how Hodos got involved.

"I had to do it, as you indicated that come hell or high water, you had to register on a designated date for military service, so you were supposed to be back over a week ago, and when we didn't hear from you, we got concerned.

I discussed it with Piri, and we decided to finish our job, regardless of what happens to you, and the only trustworthy contact at the cartography office I knew was Hodos. Therefore, I just went up to the second floor and asked for comrade Hodos. I convinced him I was legitimate and trustworthy, and the rest is history."

It was close to quitting time for Piri, so I just went to the pub and ordered a shot of apricot brandy. I looked around and found no other customers by the bar or at the tables. I didn't want to ask the bartender where Piri was, in case the bartender was her boss, and I knew he liked her, so I just slowly sipped my brandy, waiting for something to happen. He was drying some glasses with a striped towel when he checked his wristwatch and came over to ask if I wanted another shot as they would be closing in five minutes. I just shook my head, indicating no. He walked back to the end of the counter as Piri appeared, coming from the back office. She had not noticed me, as I picked the darkest section of the counter on purpose so if anyone else saw me, they wouldn't be able to recognize me. Somehow, I had become cowardly and jumpy after my incident with the short but scary prison stay a few weeks earlier. I felt I became too careful and may mess up in difficult situations.

The bartender asked Piri why it took so long to count the money. She said, "It didn't. I was just waiting for the last customer," while looking toward me.

He said, "Never mind, as he won't have time for another, and we could always put his money to be counted tomorrow."

Piri smiled and asked, "Isn't that improper and illegal?"

He laughed and said, "The only thing wrong is you want everything done properly, but sometimes a little flexibility goes a long way."

She picked up another towel and started to wipe off the counter, coming toward me. When she got within a meter of me, I lifted my glass and finished my drink. She didn't look up, just said, "You don't have to hurry. It will take a few more minutes to close up."

As she wiped off the counter in front of me, I gently grabbed her hand.

She looked up and immediately recognized me. She didn't say a word but had a big, sweet smile instead. She looked toward the bartender, who was busy rearranging some bottles on the shelf. She whispered, "Can you meet me at the back of the pub right after we close?" I nodded yes, stood up, and headed to the exit door. I didn't see, but I could feel the bartender was right behind me to lock the street side door as soon as I left.

I circled around the building block and found the small alley that led to the back of the pub, with loading facilities for delivering barrels of beer and cases of liquor. I played it safe again, and instead of walking up to the small metal back door, I waited for Piri in the shadows. Piri showed up first, wearing an overcoat, and she looked around for me. I hesitated, making sure the bartender wasn't right behind her.

Sure enough, he ran after her and yelled, "Why don't you wait for me?"

"I'm in a hurry," was her response, but by that time, he was already opening the same back door with keys in hand to lock it from the outside, and he also had a small package under his other arm. The small lights above the door cast a long shadow as they stood next to each other. The bartender was at least a head taller and looked at least ten years older than she did.

Piri said while turning toward him, "Bandi, I told you I cannot let you court me until you let me experiment with your camera so I can be sure what you taught me was good photography."

Bandi responded, "I cannot let you have my Leica, but I got you another brand just for you to experiment and play with."

She acted like he stabbed her in the heart and said, "Your mistrust hurts right here," pointing to her heart and starting to sob.

Bandi responded, "Okay, you can have my camera if I can go along to help you."

She said, "Forget it," and walked away.

Bandi had a hard time closing the iron door, as the lock must have been rusty or un-oiled. While Piri was walking toward me, he yelled after her, "Okay, you can have it either for Saturday or Sunday, but not both."

She didn't respond to Bandi; she just kept looking toward me, and when she saw me, she pointed to go back around the other side of the building. I didn't want to wait, in case Bandi would follow her, so I quickly stepped to the designated area. I could hear Bandi still fighting the rusty lock when Piri caught up with me.

She just came and hugged me like I was her brother and said, "It is so good to see you. We started to worry about you since you indicated you would get out of the assignment in a week and a half, come hell or high water."

I apologized that there were extenuating circumstances for the delay and asked her, as a favor, to translate some English for me.

"Okay, but tell me first if you had a chance to get an update from my brother on our accomplishments?"

I said, "Yes, and congratulations, but you are playing with fire and your life doing it, and I don't like it."

She didn't answer; she just put her index finger on her lips for me to stay quiet. Sure enough, Bandi was making his way out of the alley toward the station to catch the last bus for the night. Once Bandi the bartender was gone, Piri just grabbed my arm and started to pull me back toward the street. As we emerged from the shadows, she asked me to come and see her little apartment, which consisted of a shared kitchen, bathroom, hallway, and one private bedroom.

I asked her if it was okay to visit her so late on a weeknight. She responded, "You're always welcome at my place, and the landlords won't object, as they have already accused me of not liking boys." She added, "You'll be my first male visitor, as even my little brother doesn't want to come up to avoid us being seen together."

Right around the block on the street side was a small entryway. We walked up on the steps, and she unlocked the old door leading to a stairway. It was obvious the elevator hadn't worked for some time. The lift (elevator) cage door was half torn off, and the steel cables were missing. We headed up to the third floor, where she turned toward the first off-white door marked apartment No. One and reached into her purse and pulled out a single key attached to a small chain. She gently inserted the key and had to turn the key counter clockwise twice for the door to unlock and open by the handle. I waved her in first, and I followed.

There was a long, at least two-meter wide hallway. On the left was the shared kitchen, with a door open, followed by three other doors. The first door after the kitchen must have been a very small room or a bathroom, as the spacing between the doors was close. We had to go all the way to the end of the hallway, where facing the entry was her bedroom with double doors. It wasn't locked; she just pressed down the handle and pushed the right side door open while reaching in with her other hand to find the light switch next to the door.

Deception and Reality - Living Through the Missing Pages of History

One would expect a large room with double doors, but it was surprisingly small, about five by five meters. In the center of the room stood an old, beat-up table right under the light, covered with a rusty brown tablecloth with gold fringe and an empty vase in the center. Right across from the table was a double window covered with sheer curtains, facing the street below. To the right of the entry door was a divan bed, with a brown blanket cover. On the left of the door was a washbasin standing on a small but tall table. Right across from the divan bed was an unusually long, tall, and dark wooden armoire, with drawers on the bottom that could easily accommodate a wardrobe for two people. There was one chair by the table. Another, not a matching one, stood just beyond the bed, with some cloths hanging on the top to dry.

She picked up her dry clothes from the chair and put the chair right next to the table opposite the other one. Then she reached up and pulled the light, hanging on an adjustable cord, down closer to the table top so the low power light only covered the top of the table, making everything else barely visible. Piri excused herself and asked if I wanted to use the bathroom, and when I shook my head no, she asked if she could bring me back some milk. I told her I'd be happy to share, but I didn't want a whole glass.

While she was gone, I peeked out the window, but nothing was moving in the street below, just the lamp posts standing guard to the empty street.

I was thinking how pretty she was. I imagined her in the light-blue gown again— poor Piri had to do a lot of observing on the outside, as no embassy area was visible from this or the pub's window. I turned toward the small table, took five hundred forint from my pocket, and placed the envelope with Al's cleverly disguised message across the table in front of her chair.

I sat down to think about tomorrow and the strategy to follow and catch, at least on film, every dirty double agent involved with selling out young Hungarian men for peanuts. I noticed a stack of papers with a green book on top at the chair side of the table. I picked it up and put it back when I noticed a small lock on it— obviously her diary. The stack of papers was full of written words with beautiful calligraphy. I never saw so many font types and size variations, so perfect. No line exceeded the page width, and no line was the same. First I thought it was a special poem, but I could not make out any rhyme or rhythm.

KELE D. GABOR

The door opened, and Piri appeared, looking refreshed, with a tall glass of milk. She asked, "What can I attribute the pleasant surprise of you finally showing up to see me?"

Without thinking, I responded while she was eyeing the money and the blank envelope placed right in front of her. I said, "Dear Piri, I'm sorry I'm late showing up, and I'll tell you why later, but now I need a big favor and special help from you before we talk or do anything else." I smiled and looked at her sensually.

To my surprise, she kept quiet and just looked at the money on the table. She finally looked up to my grinning face and, with some harshness in her voice, stated there was no way she could help me, even for the extra money that she could definitely use and needed, as she planned and wanted to stay a virgin until her honeymoon. I got confused about her comment, but all of a sudden it came to me she might have misunderstood my intentions.

I stood up and said, "There is a big misunderstanding. The money is for the two rolls of color film we'll need in getting evidence of the person or persons exchanging stuff in the drop zone. The envelope contains an important message for all of us, but I need your help translating it."

I must have been too harsh with the delivery of the message, as she got red in the face. She started to apologize that since she had this job at the pub, a lot of young men have offered big tips for sexual favors, and she just naturally jumped to the wrong conclusion. She sat down, and pointing to the envelope, she asked if this contained the message.

I said, "The message is written in English inside along the glue line, following the V shape of the envelope flap."

She looked at it closer and said, "It is a clever way to deliver a message, but I first have to write it out with my hand, as the prints are small, and I barely can make out some of the characters." She got up and took a blank piece of paper from the bottom of the stack I had just looked at and a pen from the bottom drawer then started to write the English message with larger and neater letters.

I stood up, went around the table, and stood right behind her, watching as she worked. She turned back, looked at me, and I asked if it bothered her. She smiled and said, "Usually, when people watch me, it bothers me, but your standing close to me makes me feel comfortable and secure.

Please pull the chair over to my side and sit right next to me."

I did just that, and a warm and comfortable feeling came over me. She smiled when I accidentally bumped her shoulder while putting the chair right beside her. She grabbed my arm and pulled me down right next to her. I really felt good and special working with her so closely. She slowly wrote the meaning of each English word underneath and then proceeded with the transcription to Hungarian.

The message basically said, "I have to leave on a family emergency, but should be back in six to eight weeks. In emergencies, call Roger at the same phone, but there is also a new code word: 'film.'"

My first comment was that the new code word was very appropriate for us, but we'd have to change plans, as I didn't want any more people involved. The more I thought about the unexpected changes, the more worried I became.

I must have shown my displeasure, as Piri put her hand on mine and with her soft and sweet voice said, "We could look at this as a blessing in disguise, as we gain more time and more training to track down and gather evidence to identify all the people involved." She could see and feel I was not satisfied with her soothing words, so she added, "You look very tired. It is after midnight, why don't you just stay here? I can put a mattress on the floor. I have plenty of bedding, and you need a good night's rest."

I thought about her attractive offer for a moment. If the previous misunderstanding about the cash had not happened, I probably would have accepted the enticing invitation. However, I declined the invitation, as I had to get into clean clothes before I went back to the office next morning. She definitely looked sad about my reluctance to accept her invitation to stay.

I asked for a metal container, and we burned both the envelope and the paper with the translated messages in an old bronze candleholder base. As the paper burned, I couldn't help noticing her beautiful printing, just like that of her brother Sándor. I looked up, but Piri wasn't watching the flames but me, with her now sad, big dark-blue eyes.

The tall glass of milk was still standing, almost in the middle the table. I reached for it and offered it to her. She grasped the glass by covering my hand and pushed it to my lips. I resisted and pushed it back to hers. She took a sip and pushed it back to me. After I took my first sip, I looked at her and smiled about the white mustache the milk left above her shapely upper lip. She smiled back, and without any reservation I bent down and kissed her while taking the white line off her face.

She kissed me back, removing the white line from my upper lip, but so sweetly that it beat all previous kisses I had ever had, including Kathy's, Lara's, and a few more.

Our hands still in embrace, we put the glass down on the table, and when she let my hand go, I put my arm around her and kissed her with passion. She didn't melt in my arms; instead, she put her hand on my waist and held me tightly, like she never wanted to let me go. I started to get excited and felt a little guilty but enjoyed every second of it.

When we let go of each other, I started to apologize, but she just smiled and put her index finger on my lips. She said quietly, "Why did it take so long for you to kiss me?"

I couldn't give Piri a meaningful response but avoided a straight answer by passing the buck, saying, "You never gave me the opportunity, and I was afraid of pushing my luck."

I could see she didn't like my words, so I hugged her again and kissed her all over her face, eyes, ears, nose, cheeks, hair, lips, chin, and neck like a madman. I couldn't stop.

Her face and lips got very hot, and her aroma kept pulling me closer and closer. She didn't mind but said, "You're a wild man. I don't know if I should let you kiss me like that again."

I glanced at my watch; it was half past midnight. I thanked her for everything, especially the returned kiss that was hotter than Lara's. I turned around and said, "I must go, but I would very much like to stay."

She walked me to the door, gave me a big hug, and slowly let me go. I heard the double click of the lock as she gently locked the door behind me.

All the way to my temporary official place of stay, I was thinking about her and what she said, "Why did it take you so long to kiss me?"

I didn't have an answer or excuse except for my love for Lara, which was fading fast, especially when I thought of Piri.

Setting The Trap

I arrived very late at my place, but for some reason, I was more happy than tired, in spite of the difficult and long day full of disturbing news. Thanks to Piri and some of the progress report, I felt good. I must have slept well, as I woke up refreshed the next day and only missed the usual Thursday morning office meeting where the communist propaganda was discussed, based on that day's headline from the copy of the Russian Pravda, which was full of lies, innuendoes, and misinformation. I knew that during the morning discussion the party representative would check our presence, looking for individual participation, but since my regional office was elsewhere, she most likely would not have my name on the list. I was wrong.

The insecure and paranoid Communist totalitarian government had to know everybody's whereabouts.

I reached Hodos's desk around nine-fifteen a.m. and inquired about today's topic, in case I'd be quizzed about the party line before obtaining the special permits and properly stamped papers in order to enter the map archival library vault in the middle of the basement. It was kept up as an expensive wine cellar— cool with temperature and humidity controls and special lighting that did not damage the old papers or papyrus.

Hodos told me the topic of discussion was the control of the Suez Canal by the Soviet Union in the name of the peace-loving people of the world, and in concert with other communist nations, they must protect the vital passage from the ugly capitalists.

By this time, I had to hurry to get my permits in order to access the old maps in the library, and my first stop was Hodos's boss's office. As usual, I had to go to several levels of management to get the necessary papers in order to have at least limited access to the map reading rooms. I also had to have a place or office for rescaling all the maps, and I hoped for an expert assistant to help finish my newly assigned task on investigating the meanderings and flood zones of the Tisza River.

I received my first level approval from Hodos's boss, located in Room number Twenty-three, and after he read my assignment papers, he suggested using his secretary's table and sharing his office for privacy. I pointed out I'd need more room. He scratched his head and pointed to a door opening from his office, then handed me a key. I opened it and found myself in a small room with a very small window to the outside and practically no furniture, with a few filing cabinets thrown on top of each other. I told him I'd be happy to take it, but I'd need better lighting and a large drafting table in the middle of the room. He suggested he could provide the drafting table, but only after I got the remaining permits and approvals to go to the building engineers with my lighting request. He handed me two keys, one to his office and one to the small room next to it.

The higher management was less approachable, but their secretaries were a big help in obtaining all the stamps and signatures for the limited access to the map archives library (in government-run organizations, one finds the most red tape, bureaucracy, wasting time, and money).

While waiting for my papers with the many levels of approvals, signatures, and properly stamped documents, I started to wonder what kind of world it would be without secretaries or administrators. I came to the conclusion that without secretaries, it would be close to impossible to get through most of the red tape, especially in a communist system, and probably the entire modern civilized world would grind to a screeching halt, especially in government-run organizations and even at large companies in the private sector.

Later in life, I gained even more respect and admiration for good secretaries. I certainly could not have succeeded without them, as my English spelling remained atrocious. The secretaries' efforts have often served as the glue to keep divisions held together and make them run smoothly, and I appreciated their work more than that of some of my bosses. At one time in a large company, I was named the best business-letter writer and communicator, thanks to my super-secretary Gloria. Prior to that, I was named the best engineering-specification writer, thanks to my boss's secretary, Mimi. And of course, I gave all of them the credit and always treated them with respect (I probably would have learned more about the English language if I could have a meaningful or logical explanation as to why pants have to be plural but bra is singular).

It was past lunch break, so I hurried to get a hot dog, croissant bread, kifli (first made in the shape of the crescent moon in Hungary to celebrate the liberation of Buda from the Turks in 1668, then copied and made popular by the French). I also bought a drink at the nearby bistro and then went back to the maintenance engineers to request the extra overhead light in my new office. Not surprisingly, they laughed at me when I asked for speedy changes by next afternoon.

They should not have made the ridiculing comments because immediately headed to Peter's office, requesting his assistance. His very cute blond secretary wasn't there, so after my knock, he opened his door and stuck his red head out. I asked for his help, as he was a friendly Jewish Communist Party member with special privileges, and he liked me. He grabbed his key and locked his office door. He was in charge of all strategically or politically sensitive maps, such as locations of new bridges, military places, bases for jet fighters, and the planned rocket silos.

We headed down to the maintenance engineers, and without knocking, he opened the manager's door and just walked up to his desk, where he was finishing his lunch with a bottle of beer. As soon as he saw Peter, he jumped up and asked how he could be of service.

Peter pointed behind where I stood and said, "This comrade needs new lighting in his Office number Twenty-three A, and his request was postponed by you indefinitely."

The boss man, visually shaken, started to apologize, saying he didn't know the work was for him, and pointing to me, he said, "The comrade didn't tell us."

Peter, ignoring his comment, asked when he could put it in.

"Tomorrow," came the confident response.

Peter turned around and saw my smiling face, so he asked, "Is it satisfactory?"

I nodded.

He then turned toward the maintenance manager and said, "I want it today!"

We turned around and walked toward the open office entry door to exit.

"Please wait a minute," came a gentle request from behind us, so Peter and I turned around to see what he wanted. "Could you approve some overtime for us, comrade?"

Peter turned around and yelled, "I have provided jobs for all your family members, including a plush one for your young lover— isn't it enough?"

The maintenance manager became red in the face and asked Peter to forget his request.

I thanked Peter for his help and headed down to the map library's archival section.

A pleasant middle-aged lady, elegantly dressed with a simple but striking hairdo, greeted me with a smile and asked how she might help me. I showed my papers to her, and after careful examination of all the papers, permit stamps, and signatures, she looked me over. She said, "This was the first time a non-party-member Hungarian was allowed to conduct any sizable research here since 1948, after the Communist takeover. Whom do you know?"

I asked how she knew that I wasn't a party member. She made a fan of all my permits and pulled out the third card, which on the bottom indicated "non-party member" in small print. Later, it became obvious why we were not supposed to have access to the place.

She asked me where I wanted to start looking for the changes in the Tisza River flow. I said it may be an amateur approach but could I look at all the maps in chronological order and make copies of the areas we would be interested in, redraw the selected maps on the same scale, and finally make a master map coded by year, indicating the river bed, isolated sections, and flooded areas. She nodded approvingly and picked up a small silver bell on her desk. She shook it once and asked me to sit down by her desk.

Looking around, I saw row after row of large file cabinets, huge bookcases with hanging maps, and at the end of the aisles two big walk-in safes, like vaults, in the back. I noticed an interesting smell and asked her to help me identify it. She said salts, which also acted as preserving agents for the old and rare maps, maintained the low humidity. Small fans with fine filters circulated the air to reduce the dust. In fact, the place was ideal for preserving almost any document, regardless of ink or color used. There were even some very sensitive old and rare color photographs. Time capsules were also stored in the great vaults.

Later, I found out the Communists didn't even know what items were stored there. The time capsules from the turn of the nineteenth century were supposed to be opened in the year 2000. I noticed she was wearing a beautiful large brooch, but before I could ask her about it, a very tall, pale young man with a small hunchback appeared from nowhere and introduced himself as Henry (Imre), my new assistant. He bent down to get a closer look at me, and I noticed he had large gray fish-eyes and the palest face I had ever seen, especially it being contrasted with his dark hair. He had either never seen the sun or was sensitive to ultraviolet light. I found out it was the latter.

He asked me to follow him and if I ever had been trained to handle old documents. I stated I had no training whatsoever. Henry led me to one of the two closed small rooms situated about in the middle of the huge archival room and opened the door. In one, there was a large table with two chairs and a small light above them. Inside the room to the left of the door stood a covered cabinet with a key in it. He opened the cabinet and took out two pairs of white silk gloves, handing me the smaller of the two.

Henry turned toward me and said, "Under no circumstance are you allowed to touch any maps made in the 1800s or before without these. In any case, I'll be your assistant, and I would appreciate if you leave all the old map handling to me."

I nodded and said, "I feel honored to get an expert gentleman like you to help me."

He smiled and said, "I haven't been called that since the Communist takeover."

I knew I had made a friend.

The next few days, Henry opened my eyes to a new and interesting field of historical cartography. He introduced me to maps made as early as the ninth century hermetically sealed under glass. He explained the evolution of mapmaking, the standardization of notations, which, for the most part, is still with us. Hand-drawn military maps from the thirteenth century up to today's printed maps have more in common than I had thought. I saw bird's-eye views of cities and settlements, dimensional maps of terrain showing relative heights and proportion to neighboring mountains and rivers. Today's topographical maps are less to scale, especially when it comes to the width of rivers or three-dimensional maps of mountains, as those two are greatly exaggerated. Land grants, territories, and countries were mostly defined by words and often with a primitive map attached.

Some of the documents and maps looked like, and reminded me of, the land grants my ancestors received from Louis the Great, king of Hungary in the fourteenth century, for defending the country from the Tartars. All borders followed natural features of the lay of the land, and the defined borders were rivers, large year-round creeks, or mountain

Kele D. Gabor

crests. I have never seen a straight borderline for a country, territory, or land grants. The borders always followed a natural easily defendable line of high mountains, deep rivers, or sea.

Henry explained and showed plenty of examples of the great ignorance of politicians dividing countries without regard to people and natural defendable borders by drawing straight lines and ignoring the natural features of the land, just out of stupidity. Henry showed me copies of maps carved in clay tablets from the Greek and Roman times of Central Europe. He showed me some English and German maps from the nineteenth century, which typically showed many erroneously renamed places, areas, and cities, such as Cairo for Al Quaidah, Cologne for Köln, Vienna for Wien, changing the real geographical names at will and without regard to correctness.

Henry, well-versed in German and English, made a point about the same people who disregarded or ignored the real names of places having a fit when someone accidentally mispronounced or misspelled their names.

He showed me Latin text from the eleventh century, accompanied with drawings of people and a map indicating the names and titles of the recipients.

To my surprise, most of the people wore trousers instead of togas. Henry pointed out all of the people wearing pants were Hungarians based on their names; they introduced some of today's men's wear in Europe, such as the undergarments, as other Europeans wore togas or skirts without underwear.

Later, I found it interesting that one of the largest and longest lasting countries in all of Europe was the kingdom of Hungary. For over a thousand years, we occupied the entire Carpathian Basin, one watershed as one unit that at times grew some but never shrunk short of the mountain chain until the new political map drawn by the French, with the help of Benes. In 1920, they connected cities with straight lines to draw the new borders.

It just didn't make any sense taking away Hungarian territories over a millennium old and changing borderlines by connecting settlements with straight lines.

Henry was a great admirer of Samuel Mikoviny (1700–1750), drawer of "Hungaria Nova" and one of the best mathematicians, engineers, and a practical and theoretical surveyor of his age. Mikoviny was probably the first true hydrologist and hydraulics engineer. He was the first one in Europe who created a very clear formulation of the basic principles of mapping. He initiated topographical mapmaking based on astronomical and geometrical (triangulation) surveying and checked by magnetic needle alignments. His maps were the most accurate in the entire eighteenth century. To prevent distortions, he assigned a meridian and measured the angular distances between the meridian of Pozsony (Bratislava) and several European observatories so the network could be connected to the international system of geographical degrees. This type of accurate mapmaking work was not done anywhere else until 1793 in France by C. François Cassini, who followed the Mikoviny method.

I wish I could have stayed longer and learned more from a map worm, but I had to at least start my work in earnest before leaving to meet Zoli to set the trap and ensure getting some good photos of the double agent caught red-handed. Also, before quitting time, I had to find Hodos to tie up the loose ends before we swung into action. It made me very nervous that there were too many people involved already, and I still didn't know how Hodos received the envelope from Al.

I thanked Henry for his patience and training and excused myself. He was very gracious about my early departure. I told him, and meant it from the bottom of my heart, that I was looking forward to meeting him the next morning around nine o'clock. Henry could tell that my remarks were sincere and gave me a nice smile. He took off his white gloves and asked me to do the same. We put the gloves on an open shelf.

As we exited the room, I saw Peter entering the next room. Peter didn't notice me as he handed a map to Henry for filing. Once Peter shut the door behind him, I asked Henry what Peter was doing here. Henry showed me a map with small red circles on the south side of the Matra Mountains, close to an air force base, and said Peter often comes here to update new military or other map markings in restricted areas. I asked Henry if Peter and I were the only ones with access to this highly guarded facility.

"No," he responded, "many other people can come here, and often high-ranking Russian military officers and party leaders, as they select or recommend locations for potential military sites. On occasions Slovak, Romanian, Russian, and Serbian surveyors come to find the locations of old Hungarian triangulation points or to help key off from old maps, as they know very little of the new areas given to them by the

French, and Stalin." Henry added, "Anybody having access to this facility can also have access to the big vaults where all the secret maps are stored."

I asked, "Will that include me?"

"Of course, and you now can also qualify to have your own time capsule," came the response.

I was shocked such a gaping hole existed in the KGB-approved and secured facility. Boy, I thought to myself, This could be a gold mine for me or anyone else trying to sell information to the West. I asked him what a time capsule was. He said, "You get a container of specified size and shape where you can put things, then hermetically seal and date mark when you want to have it opened." I didn't think much of using it for a long-term safety deposit box of my own, but I did wonder how many items could have been stored and lost there already. Now with spy satellites and greatly improved optics, the movements of rockets and locations of military facilities are much easier to obtain.

It was close to quitting time, so I hurried upstairs, jumping two or three steps at a time, to find Hodos before he could leave. He was still in the big room, helping someone with problems. I could see he was showing and explaining something to a young cartographer over a big table with several large maps on it. I just moseyed near and waited until he finished. Then I caught up to him just as he got to his desk. I stepped up real close and asked him to meet me after work, as I had some very important things to discuss with him in private.

He nodded and said, "I expected you, and I'm willing to help you. I'll meet Dora in about an hour by the espresso where we went the first time.

I hope a half an hour is enough."

I responded, "I hope it won't take that long."

Hodos smiled, winked, and said, "Good, because I still don't know how to introduce you to my Dora."

I returned his factitious smile and decided to go ahead, select a table, and wait for Hodos there. I hurried down the steps, and the guards stopped me for my ID. I asked what was going on, as they all knew me, as I often visited this facility and they never asked me anything after the first time I came. The shorter of the two guards said anybody having access to the map archival place must be checked before leaving the premises. I thought to myself, That is good to know before trying to smuggle something out. They asked me to open my attaché case. They looked inside and waved me off. I could have brought out at least ten pages of letter-size maps, as they only looked on the top.

I still beat the rush hour and walked over to the espresso cafe. It was getting very cold, so I buttoned my jacket and headed outside where no one was sitting. It took a long time before I was asked by a young, shapely waitress in uniform what I would like to have. I ordered a double espresso, which I changed to two, as I just noticed Hodos coming, crossing the street. The young lady smiled and said, "I guess you're expecting someone soon, but don't forget, girls are always late for a date. I'll have the two espressos here sooner than expected."

I ignored her comment but smiled. I could tell she'd just started her shift, looking fresh and well-rested. By the time the two double espressos arrived, Hodos was sitting right across from me. I asked for the check and paid her, leaving a sizeable tip so she would leave us alone. Unfortunately, the opposite happened; she asked every five minutes if she could bring us anything else.

Hodos started the conversation by saying, "I guess you needed my help in interpreting the envelope with nothing in it."

I said, "No, I want to know how you met my contact." I sat back, sipping my hot coffee, and he started to talk.

"The entire thing started with my boss's secretary coming to my table close to dinner time, saying a person with a heavy German accent had asked to talk with me on the phone. I responded that I didn't know anybody with a German accent, but the curiosity to find out who it was and how he knew my name made me follow her to the office phone.

"When I said hello, he asked to talk to me, and I knew right away it wasn't a German accent. With incorrect Hungarian, he asked me if he could give me a letter to be only handed to Mr. Lxxx, Sándor's friend. I was suspicious, but after using the title of Mr. instead of 'Herr,' the German equivalent, I immediately knew he was an English-speaking person, so I said yes before I even knew for sure who Mr. Lxxx was. He then asked me to meet him at that expensive restaurant none of us could afford, so I figured I would get a free meal, even if at the last moment I changed my mind and declined to be a delivery boy.

"On the way to the restaurant, I put two and two together and concluded that you were the most likely candidate to receive the message.

Kele D. Gabor

When I stepped inside the door, I realized he must have known me, as he didn't describe what he looked like. I stood around, waiting for the contact, when the maitre d' approached me and asked if I'd like to have a table. I told her I was still waiting for someone. 'Oh,' she said, turning around and handing me the same envelope I passed to you while she apologized for the gentleman who was unexpectedly detained and could not meet me at this time. However, he had already paid for any dinner and drink I would select from the menu."

I interrupted, "You mean you never saw my contact?"

He continued, "He could have seen me, but there was no way I could identify him, as several tables inside were occupied by a single person. I found the situation and possible consequences so mysterious and scary I turned around and left, looking for a place to drop off the envelope before a KGB or AVO agent could arrest me while in possession of the article.

I kept on walking in the opposite direction from which I came, looking for a trash can that I could not find. I dropped the envelope at a busy station, right in front of a tobacco store, hoping it dropped into the drainage system. However, a little girl behind me picked it up, ran after me, and handed it back to me while saying she saw me drop it. I thanked her and turned around to leave, but the little girl insisted that I put it into my pocket so I wouldn't lose it again. She pointed to a small ball in her pocket and said, 'Just like this, as my mom taught me.'

"I followed her instructions while turning around and looking for men with leather coats, but no one seemed to follow me. I went by the library, talked the things over with Dora, and she offered to help hide the envelope until I decided what to do with it. Dora loves intrigue and mysterious things."

"You mean you never saw my contact?"

He nodded. "The next day, a skinny man wearing an old, oversized jacket showed up looking for you and asked me to meet him after work.

He told me you trusted me and it was good enough for him to ask for my help. After confirming how well he knew you, I agreed to help him in case you were caught or delayed or had disappeared. I also told him about the envelope. He said he would notify you in case you reappeared."

"What did my friend tell you?"

"Nothing, but I knew something big was going down if you had your own agent and contact, not Mr. White, and probably you all had code names. By the way, Dora could help. She can be trusted completely. She is the one who stores the maps and sketches I pass on to Mr. White, and sometimes she makes the drop. Dora loves the excitement that comes with some elements of danger."

I sat there across from Hodos, thinking to myself how well Al handled the message and its delivery, indicating that he might not be an amateur.

The news that neither Hodos nor Dora met or even knew the name of my contact and that they didn't really know what was going on made me feel warm all over. Also, the thought that they could be trusted and wanted to help made me feel good inside and out.

I stood up, thanked Hodos for all his efforts and help, and offered my handshake. To my surprise, he asked what his next assignment would be.

Once again, I was put in a leadership and decision-making role without wanting to be there. I didn't want to turn them on or off about the potential job, as we might need them later. I shook his hand and told Hodos we most likely would need a few very smart and trusted friends' help soon, as our mission was complicated and difficult. It was to conclude in a short period of time with the small team we currently had, and for security reasons, I would like to keep it that way. I could see in his eyes he was ready for any exciting assignment, but how could I tell him that detective work was hard, difficult, boring, expensive, and unexciting? Only books and films glorify it, without doing justice to the danger involved, especially on the amateur level, without sufficient financial backing or the minimum tools required or training.

I asked him if he had a good camera and film. He said, "My sister has an excellent camera with a telephoto lens. I would just have to convince her to let me borrow it again. Film, we could always buy."

I asked, "Do you know how to use it?"

Hodos answered, "Both Dora and I often use the camera when we go to the zoo, as she loves wild animals and takes great pictures of the monkeys."

I promised that he and maybe Dora could be needed soon, so I asked for a contact place and time the next day, Friday. Once we agreed, I asked him about the proper signals and to think of a code name for him and Dora. If he or she touched their face anyplace, the area might not be clear and the meeting place would move to an alternate site, usually at a railroad station. By the time we parted, Dora was coming across the street, so I hurried away, so as not to be seen together. I could not help noticing her, keeping my eyes peeled, looking at her light, feminine sway as she crossed the street with her long, shapely legs. It was exhilarating.

I left happy just seeing Dora approach my side of the street, but I knew I had to get moving and prepare for the meeting with Zoli that evening. I decided to stop off at the club, get a few light table tennis games in, but not to work up a sweat so I wouldn't have to change before meeting Zoli. There was nobody around to play, as everybody was intently listening to the radio about the Olympic competition schedule updates, expected performance, and preliminary results from Melbourne.

I decided to review in my mind today's events and assess our situation. I was thinking to myself about taking a chance and having Hodos help us at least part of the day. It was too hard to cover late Friday afternoon, Saturday, and Sunday with just three of us with one camera. Further assessing our situation, it became obvious that Zoli and I were the only ones who knew about the entire operation. The next person in line was Piri, followed by Al, who was, it was hoped, only temporarily out of the picture.

I kept thinking we needed at least Hodos, and we could include him with only telling him a small part of the complete picture in order to reduce the chance of discovery. We definitely needed his camera to have a chance to succeed with our surveillance and get the proof. Some of my problems were that Zoli knew Piri, Hodos, and me. Hodos knew Zoli, Dora, and me. Dora knew Hodos and me, and I knew everybody else, including Bandi (his indirect involvement with lending his camera).

Our original plan was for only one to two contacts for each participant, but it had gone to pot just because I could not make the promised rendezvous with Zoli two weeks earlier. It also bothered me that Al was gone, and the catching of Zoli or me by the KGB or AVO pretty much guaranteed an agonizing death for about five young persons, and most likely including the same other close friends and relatives. Our next move had to be foolproof, without any slip-ups, and executed with extra attention to alternatives and what-ifs. Zoli and I must do an exceptional job planning out the next few days on short notice. Gee! After a successful operation, we also had a problem storing the films at a safe location without anybody knowing about it until Al returned. Regardless, our main objective of catching the double agents who were responsible for turning in and most likely killing my best friend and the brother of Zoli and Piri might come to a close.

We were definitely close to getting the photographic proof.

When Zoli and I met, his first question was how the translation went and what message it contained. I said, "Al had to leave on an emergency and won't be back for one or two months. The new code word is 'film,' and Al's replacement is 'Roger', in case we have to contact the embassy." He nodded and asked how the envelope was delivered to Hodos. I told him Al professionally did it, as he had done it without giving his identity away to Hodos. Zoli raised an eyebrow and looked surprised. I also updated him on the interesting events of the day. He asked a lot about my newfound "gold mine" with my access to the map archival place and possibly my own safe deposit box. He was surprised about my suggestion that perhaps Hodos and Dora could help relieve the pressure by covering the entire surveillance time. With more eyes, we could have extra assurance that we would not miss a thing with the camera.

It was Zoli's turn to talk, and he pulled out a piece of paper that I found very unusual. He said I had to flowchart all the events we had set into motion in order to avoid any mistakes. The alternatives and backup plans made it so complex I could not keep everything in my head. I told him we needed to go to a better-lit place to review it, and I was very hungry for supper. We needed a large place with food available where we could talk safely. We selected the university 'menza', or cafeteria. It was brightly lit, where two young men could peer over charts, papers, and books and talk without raising any suspicion.

We ordered the only thing on the menu— noodles with cheese— and sat down at a long table where no one was around. It was one of the cheapest places to eat, but the food wasn't necessarily very tasty. We sat almost next to each other on the bench, leaving enough places for his papers, which we started to review one at a time. It was the first time I noticed what orderly and legible writing he had. I guessed it was a family trait.

Like most good plans, they contained the objectives to achieve— who, what, why, when, and where— leaving the how part to contain the

KELE D. GABOR

details.

Each page had boxes and connecting lines, with parallel broken lines for alternatives or what-if's. The objective was, of course, getting undeniable proof of espionage or an exchange of information and money between Western and communist agents.

The final plan looked somewhat like the following, with code names and words, which ended up looking like a regular flow diagram: Z, L, P, H, or D is responsible to complete the tasks.

> Identify with pictures the agents passing information to KGB and the Western agent picking up payments from KGB.
> Stop the arrests and murders of young Hungarians who were helping the West.
> Areas covered: embassy, meeting places, cemetery, and pub.
> Get the proof in the next three days, if possible.
> Call embassy to exchange map for money, using fictitious name.
> Identify caller, drop zone for map, money, and time.
> Watch embassy employees interact and obtain photographs.
> Follow person to the cemetery with flowers and take pictures.
> Get photographic evidence of the ribbon with the name.
> Photograph the pickup and exchange.
> Develop negatives, store films and photos at safe places.
> Provide copies of pictures and names of double agents to Al or 'Roger'.
> Disband the team until the arrest of the double agents, but provide progress reports on a "need to know" basis.

The above highlights of the plan did not cover the what-ifs or alternatives, and it was simplified. The execution of the plan was much harder to do, as we lacked phones, radios, mobile phones, or other signaling devices and especially financial backing. We even had to discuss the possible murders of Western or KGB agents if our team or a key team member was in danger of discovery.

In retrospect, I'll never forgive myself for not killing BT, as our success in identifying him didn't result in the punishment of the guilty due to the failure of the Western justice system, which was more preoccupied with protecting the rights of the guilty than providing justice, protection, or fairness for both witnesses and victims.

The detailed plan had to cover all responsibilities for the entire duration of this operation for each team member, and protection for each individual. Without having enough money, support, or having our own photographic equipment and film developing laboratory, we all faced unbelievable strain and difficulties.

"Amateurs against professionals" was our motto, and "Succeed or die" was our goal.

We could only preserve the one-to-one contacts on a very loose basis, just trying to protect each other in case one got caught. Slowly but surely, most of the team members suffered premature deaths, I believe, at the hand of BT after he went to work full time for the KGB, starting around 1976.

Kele D. Gabor

Getting Some Evidence

Late in the evening when Zoli and I parted company, we had a good master plan on a single page of paper. We agreed the plan was foolproof or as close to it as possible under the circumstances. Considering our handicaps, lack of money and equipment, and no outside support, we covered all the bases. There was a lot to do for all of us individually in a coordinated effort in trying to trick the highly trained and well-financed professional groups, including the AVO (Hungarian secret police), KGB, CIA, and possibly catching diplomats or their staff making grave mistakes. In retrospect, we succeeded because of the inherent weaknesses and the blind belief of superiority or invincibility of these so-called professionals. However, the mistakes we made along the way and the resulting price we paid became the darkest and saddest part of my life.

The Western embassies could not police themselves, as it was easier to blame others. They always ended up in the state of self-denial, and they became nonchalant and careless about their activities. We, as dedicated amateurs, had to succeed where all those professionals had failed. If they could not find the double agents among themselves, we could not just point at the obvious and logical conclusion; we also had to prove it.

Even today, we have many examples of double agents in every Western espionage agency, with unbelievable longevity of operation before discovery, like Mr. Hansen and the Walker family.

We had to notify each team member in time, explain what was expected of them, why, where, when, and how, without showing him our master plan. Minimizing contacts among team members was also critical.

That evening, I had to make a professional-looking map, a copy of what I saw earlier in the archive, entirely from visual memory, with the proper red circles indicating potential Russian rocket silo installations. The location of the rocket silos on the Matra Mountains without a topographical map was almost impossible, and I could not take a chance in requesting one. However, using old geological maps, I was able to create a good facsimile on scratch paper that I could finalize later on vellum paper. I went to the university library, and from the drafting area, I was able to secure three necessary sheets of vellum papers after promising anything to the lady in charge, including telling her that I would fail the drawing course if I didn't turn my project in the next day.

I knew that the Matra mountain chain was about thirty kilometer long, running west to east and northeast, and the approximate size, shape, and location of the four red circles I saw on the south side of the mountain that afternoon on the map in Henry's hands. These planned rocket silos were obviously placed there for a purpose, either to protect us from or to attack the Balkans.

I had to meet Piri to give her assignments, as she also started the next day, to pay particular attention to the two embassy employees visiting the pub. It would be a lot of help to have a photograph of both of them together, just a single picture showing contact, which they obviously tried to hide in front of other embassy workers. Therefore, Piri had two assignments: getting a picture in the pub, covering either Sunday morning or afternoon at the cemetery with the camera, and getting photos of agents involved in either dropping off the ribbon with the informer's name or picking up the money by the embassy worker.,

The next day, I had to talk to Hodos and Dora about covering the area with the camera and where to take photos of the agents involved for all of Saturday. I had to get the map ready in time to make it to the drop zone by five p.m. and meet again with the team members to review their assignments. I hurried to catch Piri before she went upstairs to her flat.

She showed up right after I arrived. Standing in the shadows, I unintentionally scared her a little, but she forgave me after giving her a firm hug. She invited me up with all my paraphernalia, walking ahead of me.

I enjoyed watching her from behind; she had a light walk, and her good figure showed and moved well on her shapely legs.

Once we got to her room, she excused herself, and I put one chair across from the other one after placing my rolled up vellum under the light. Her diary and the stack of papers were still there, but she left her green book unlocked. I now wish I had picked it up and read from it, but the fleeting thought passed quickly, as it would have been a dishonorable deed. Also, my head was full of the timetable and what everybody had to do on time in order to succeed. I took out my scratch paper from my attaché case, placed it on the table, and pushed everything else to the side while reviewing my lines, approximate scale, and possible title to the map, which had to be ready before the drop-off time. I was not really looking for an all-night drawing session in my small temporary flat.

Piri came in so quietly, I barely noticed when she placed a small tray with two shot glasses and a small bottle of 'Kecskeméti' apricot brandy by my left side. She gently picked up the bottle, and while pouring a half-glass, she said, "I know that is your favorite." She raised her glass and wished us success.

I returned the gesture while standing up and said, "God bless us and watch out for us during these dangerous times."

We emptied our glasses while looking at each other. She looked so innocent and sweet with her big blue eyes, lovely smile, full lips, and her long dark hair. I put her head gently between my hands and kissed her lips as gently as I could to make up for last night's wild streak. She now melted in my arms the way I liked, pushing her body against mine while wrapping her arms around my waist. It must have been a new record for me as we embraced and stood together for a very long time while my hand gently moved around her back. It was the first kiss after parting with Kati and Lara that made me forget about them, as she made their memories fade away slowly and surely. Again, as Kati taught me, we exchanged our breath without breathing through our noses. This mouth-to-mouth respiration eventually used up all the oxygen, and we fell into a dizzy state, barely able to keep our balance.

It was Piri who broke up our embrace, taking a big gulp of air and saying, "You take my breath away." I smiled and said, "That was my intent since I first laid eyes on you, when I heard you play the piano and sing, over a year ago." She had a sweet smile, and I felt compelled to say it, "I love you." She stepped back into my outreached arms, and we hugged each other for a long time again.

She again broke the embrace and asked what I had decided and what would be her assignment. I told her that Zoli and I worked out a plan, but we wanted to keep it to ourselves, telling each team member only the individual assignments of what, why, where, and when to do it for security and personal safety in case one of us would get caught. She agreed, and I gave her her assignment, saying how important it was to have a picture of the two embassy employees being together. Later, most likely Sunday if needed, she would document the pickup and exchange with the camera in the cemetery.

She liked her assignment; she showed the two new rolls of films she had purchased for Bandi's camera and asked me if I could be her backup either Sunday morning or afternoon. I agreed for the entire day or until we succeeded if she would make sandwiches for lunch. She thought a moment and said, "Okay, but what will your assignment be?" I told her

I'd rather not tell her. She should concentrate on her job, making sure she gets the camera, as I had to finish a map tonight before going to the office tomorrow.

Piri did what all girls do after the boys tell them "I love you." She started to tell me what and how to do things. She started by saying she had a large table, all the necessary equipment to draw a map, and she could help me with the text printing if I stayed. I told her we both had a busy schedule starting the next day, Friday. "Saturday, and especially Sunday, may take the entire day, so it's better for me to leave right away."

While I made my excuse, she'd already started to clean the tabletop and take out her tools of calligraphy. As she pushed the stack of paper aside, some of the sheets fell to the floor. I picked them up and looked at them— a pattern emerged. I asked if these were practice sheets for calligraphy. She said, "Since my brother was ten years old, we competed to see which one of us writes nicer or prints better. So we started to leave single line messages for each other, waiting for the other to respond in kind."

I asked, "Why are so many fonts and sizes of letters used?" She replied, "Their shapes and sizes also indicate feelings or other meanings we wanted to convey to each other. Then we took the two written lines on the page to our mother to try to interpret our mood and be an impartial judge in selecting the nicer of the two hand printings. My mom was always good at judging. She would say my printing was nicer, but she let Sándor win the expression of mood and meaning or vice versa."

She proceeded to show me an example. "You see this," she said, pointing to a pair of lines on one of the papers. The first line was "I love you," with bold, beautiful large red heart-shaped letters, followed by the second line, "Me too, as much or more," also in bold red square-looking letters.

"You see, my mother said my first line was the nicer calligraphy, but the second was better for reflecting mood, as the square letters were harder to write and expressed that he even loved me more." She laughed and said, "You see, it really doesn't matter, as both lines are beautiful, but my mom had to appear impartial." She bent over the table to reach for the rolled-up vellums, straightened one out on the flat, large drawing board, and using four thumbtacks secured them on all four corners.

As she was helping to prepare for my map drawing session, I could not help commenting on what I saw— a shapely and beautiful derriere. I said, "While we were kissing, I felt how firm your derriere is, and I just wonder what sport you did in high school?"

She answered, "I have been a four-hundred-meter runner since age ten, winning a lot of races. In fact, I was very good, and my derriere will stay firm like my mother's, as we always sit on hard surfaces and never use soft chairs or pillows."

"Are you still running?" "No, I gave it up two years ago when I found out that my boy fans and entourage were following me to all my races and training sessions to watch the movements of my breasts." She continued, "By the way, I really appreciate you looking into my eyes and face and not looking at my boobs."

I said, "Sorry to disappoint you, but every chance I have or you're not looking, I admire your figure, including your beautiful breasts."

She looked up at me with a disapproving glance and said, "I will never understand why men go so crazy about big boobs."

I asked her to change the subject in case she wanted me to stay, as I was already getting excited and wouldn't be able to work. She said not to worry and left. She returned in an old lady's dress, without shape, color, or any open area. She even imitated the slower and shorter strides of old ladies, moving her feet by barely bending her knees. I laughed and said, "I guess I'll stay and start on the map immediately."

I became involved in trying to transpose my updated draft to the clean vellum in front of me. With light pencil marks, I transferred the outlines, approximate crest line, the one-hundred-meter contours, the few close by communities and circles on the south side relatively positioned as I remembered seeing them, but without coordinates. While concentrating, I could hear Piri moving a chair where my attaché case was close to the foot of her bed, and when she saw me turn around, she said, "Please wake me up for the printing part," and she slipped under the cover. I kept looking at her, but she turned her head toward the wall, and I resumed my work.

It was about two o'clock and the second try when I felt somewhat satisfied with my creation, including the scale. I put on my first vellum, which became my last almost-completed draft, all the letters with a red pencil so I could quickly copy them over to the final one. I put in the date of last year to indicate a recently updated map, then titled it "Proposed Rocket Sites for Defending Attacks from the South." I drew in the scales for one, five, and ten kilometers, showed north and west arrows and copied over the estimated coordinates for each circle based on actual geological old maps.

    I became very tired, but I had no heart to wake Piri up; she had passed her REM stage of sleep and lay motionless, so I had to go over to see if she was still breathing. While she was in her deep sleep, I decided to move my things together, including my case, before I sat down to print. When I lifted off my case from the chair by the foot of her bed, she moved, opened her eyes, and said, "You thought you could get away without waking me up." She just sat up, rubbed her eyes, and now without the old lady dress, just in her long silk nightgown, she started uncovering herself and swung her legs out. She untied the broken thin black string from her big toe she had attached to the handle of my case. I was amazed by her dedication.

    She stood up, put her gown and slippers on, and came to the table. She looked at my draft with all the notations, sat down by the final copy, and, using her own tools, started to print all the text. I was tired, but I watched as her eyes scanned the draft and her hand kept an absolute straight line on the map, like a printing machine. All her letters were well-proportioned, with the right spacing that made it look like it was coming fresh off the press. She put down her pen, closed the India ink containers, wiped off all the tools used, put everything in order back in the drawer, then she closed her eyes for a moment.

    I looked at my watch, and it was almost three a.m. She got up, pulled a mattress from underneath the bed, put on two blankets, and said, "Go wash up and come to bed. I'll wake you up at seven o'clock," and she went to her bed and slipped under the covers.

    I had the map ready for the five p.m. drop-off time, so I followed Piri's instructions and fell asleep about two meters from her with some difficulties.

    I felt a gentle tug, followed by a kiss on the forehead, but I was still sleepy and didn't want to wake up. She started to sing, "Early morning, the little man rises from the little bed and quickly gets ready to go to work…"

I had to open my eyes and sit up, then rubbed my eyes to get them moving. She stopped the cute wake-up song and told me I had a restless dream. I saw a lot of beautiful young girls, all wearing light-blue bikinis.

They circled me, and each of them asked me if I loved her, and I had no choice but to say yes. Once all of them heard my answer, they encircled me and asked me to do all kinds of crazy things. If I didn't do it, they would cry, but when I did what they asked, they made fun of me. Piri interrupted by saying, "I guess you are already thinking of marrying me, but subconsciously dread the idea of being a henpecked husband.

Don't worry, I could never control you, and I wouldn't be a nagging wife."

I ignored her statement, and I could see she didn't like my getting up, putting on my trousers, and leaving to go to the restroom without saying a word or smiling. When I came back, there were two cups of hot tea on top of the table, bread, jelly, butter, and a small wheel of cheese waiting. I thanked her and asked which side she wanted me to sit on. She responded that I had to make a decision and she would take the other chair.

We sat down, prayed, and both reached for the teacup first and both took a sip. I sliced the bread, offering it to her first, and she took it and I carved one for myself. I waited while she put some butter and a slice of cheese on her bread, then proceeded to help myself. She looked up at me with some concerns and said, "Sorry, I ran out of sugar, so you have to drink your tea with honey, but I did iron your shirt, as it was too wrinkled to go to the office.

I looked up to her, smiled, and said, "Thank you." I stood up, went around the table, bent down, and kissed the back of her neck, right cheek, and lips— in that order.

She stood up and also asked for a hug and said, "It is okay if you don't want to talk in the morning, but please give me a hug any time, any place, whether you come or go."

I gave her a firm hug, she put her arm around my neck so I could feel her front pressing against mine, and then I let her go, but she stayed clinging on my neck. I ran both hands down on her back, feeling all her curves, from the back of her head to back of her thighs. She stayed that way until she felt I was getting excited before she pulled away. I was no longer hungry; I just wanted to make love to her.

Deception and Reality - Living Through the Missing Pages of History

She noticed my frustration and said, "Calm down, as it is hard on me too. God knows how much I need you and have wanted you since we first went swimming together last year, but I'll keep my promises to wait till our honeymoon." Looking at me with her beautiful, big blue eyes into mine, she said it so sincerely with a sorrowful smile that I did calm down and finished my tea with two pieces of bread, butter, cheese, and jelly at the end.

It was just past eight a.m., so I grabbed my shirt, put it on, gave a quick kiss to Piri, and headed out with my jacket in one hand and the attaché case in the other. She jumped in front of me, smiling, and said, "Hold on, don't forget your new map."

I put on my jacket and reached out to grab the rolled up vellum, but stopped halfway, saying I couldn't take the chance of walking into the office with that, as I would most likely be searched before I left. I asked if she could take it instead and I would come to the pub to pick it up around three p.m.

She said, "Today I have to start earlier, but you could come by the pub, order a beer, and I'll hand it to you wrapped in today's newspaper."

I arrived in my little temporary office next to Hodos's boss's office just before nine a.m. I dropped my attaché case and hurried to meet Henry by nine, as promised, but going through the big office, I asked the boss if Hodos could help me today for up to an hour.

He said, "Okay, but check with him first, as people have started distrusting you since Peter became your friend and sponsor."

I said, "Don't worry about it. Asking for help from Peter to get my job done does not mean that I'm a Marxist or Communist."

He waved, and I headed down the steps to see Henry. Both Henry and the lady seemed to be busy talking with high-ranking uniformed Russian officers. She acted as a translator for Henry to get maps for the officers. When I stepped close to the desk, both of them noticed me and waved me to stop. I stood next to the desk, but only for a short time, as Henry came over to tell me they would be busy for the next hour and I could stay and look or come back. This was exactly the break I needed to talk to Hodos about his and Dora's assignments. Again, I rushed up the stairs and headed to the big cartographers' drafting room.

Hodos was at his desk, reading something. As I approached, he noticed me, put his magazine down, and asked, "What's new?"

I noticed he was reading a photographic journal on the proper uses of telephoto lenses. I asked him to come to my office but to first make sure his boss was out of his office for at least fifteen minutes. He said, "Follow me."

We went straight to his boss's office, knocked on the door, and I stepped in right behind him. Hodos said, "Kele needs some help with his project, but I can only do it with your permission. Also, while I'm here, please go to my desk, as the new draftsman is very insecure and needs to have his hand held."

Hodos's boss said, "No problem, just let me make a phone call." He picked up the phone, called the switchboard, and asked them to transfer his wife's call to his secretary, who was on special assignment helping out in Gergely's office in the bridge division.

Hodos asked, "What is Gabriella, your secretary, doing helping the bridge division?"

He got up, smiled, and said, "You two hurry up, and come and get me when you finish."

We walked into my little office, and Hodos was impressed with the large new drafting table with an adjustable new light hanging above it, with one high and two low chairs neatly lined up in front of the table.

Hodos immediately asked what his assignment was. I put my index finger up to my lips, indicating to stay quiet, and looked around for potential listening devices, which were typically put under the telephone receiver or into the new hanging lamp. I could not find even an old telephone in the room or any particular indicators on the newly installed wirings, light, or light switch.

We sat down face-to-face, and I started talking. "I need your and Dora's help all this Saturday as long as it is light enough to take pictures secretly and preferably with the telephoto lens so you both can stand far enough and out of sight."

He seemed excited about the job and quickly agreed and asked where. I said, "Before I tell you, can you make sure I can also talk to Dora during lunchtime?"

Hodos said, "I don't understand your approach, as we work together and we make a good team."

"The success of our work will largely depend on anonymity and limited contacts. Ideally, we like to keep it to two per person in order to maximize success and protect the team, even if one of us gets caught. You already know me, Dora, and Zoli, which is one more than I like to have."

"I can still pass on all the information to Dora, as we will stay as a team, regardless of what you think."

"It is too much to cover an entire day, so I'd like to have you and Dora work in alternate shifts when possible to improve alertness, notice the person or persons in time to take several pictures, and to ensure success."

Hodos argued they would have divided the tasks between themselves anyway, but not necessarily one in the morning and the other covering the afternoon.

I had no time to argue, so I agreed to let them work out the shift coverage between themselves, and I only gave the assignments to Hodos.

I trusted his intelligence, but not necessarily his alertness when the two lovers were close together or just side by side, especially after seeing how sexy Dora looked. I said, "I accept your argument, but if you fail, I cannot trust you in the future."

"You mean this is just a test?"

"No way, it is serious, dangerous, and can be deadly for one or for all of us. We cannot fail, in spite of our handicaps."

"What handicaps?"

Thinking quickly, and to impress him, I said, "You two will have to substitute for three highly trained professional foreign agents who all were badly hurt in a car accident during a run-in with the KGB. The only reason I asked Dora and you to fill in is because the embassy and I trust you, and we know we can depend on you."

"Of course," he said with gusto and a twinkle in his eyes.

I explained the details while he listened intently. I said, "Saturday morning, this cemetery opens at eight-thirty a.m. and closes at seven p.m. During this time, the following may occur, and one of you must take photos of the following significant events. A young man with a narrow, long face, but good looking with black hair, about the same height as I am, will come to this cemetery and buy a bouquet of flowers. He'll take the wrapping off, tie a ribbon on to hold the flowers together, and place the bouquet on the plot located on the left in the fifth row. The forth obelisk-shaped head stone is without a name on it. We could not make out the name on it, except a barely visible gold letter Z, for the beginning of the family name, with a Star of David on the top. A bouquet of flowers will be placed in a simple metal vase, but no water added.

"Soon after, but maybe during his stay in the cemetery, another person will come untie the ribbon, take it off, and replace the center flower with another stem and color, with a small metal roll attached. After the exchange, the person who originally put the bouquet in will return and take the newly replaced flower with the metal roll away. If you can get each event recorded before the cemetery closes, your job is finished right after you hand me the roll of negatives."

Hodos started up, "What is the significance of the ribbon, who is the guy, what is in the metal container, and who is the other person?"

I said, "I cannot tell you that, but before you go now, you must repeat what and how many pictures you will need to take to complete your assignment."

Hodos scratched his head and said, "First of all, I always take two pictures just to make sure. Dora and I have already picked up a fast German Agfa film, and if I were you, the following events are those I would consider critical to record on film to show 'continuation' and the 'actions' to prove our points. A, the guy entering the cemetery. That means one of us has to stay outside and signal the one with the camera. B, record the purchase of the bouquet at the time the individual exits the flower shop. C, watch and record the placement of the ribbon in the bouquet. D, also take pictures of him placing the flowers on or below the headstone. Therefore, if not the described person but some substitute person delivers, someone must be close to the headstone site to signal the photographer to at least record that particular event."

I said, "Good thinking, as I have not considered that possibility because we know that he is the only person who speaks Hungarian well enough to take public transport, buy flowers, avoid detection, and look European."

He continued, "Keep an eye peeled on the activities near the grave and signal the partner if someone approaches or turns into the fifth row. That way, two pictures can be taken for identification, then wait and be ready to get pictures of the removal and keeping of the ribbon, followed by the replacement of the central flower with a small metal cylinder attached. As soon as all that takes place, we can go home and not wait till closing time of the cemetery."

I told him I was happy we picked him and Dora, and if his mission was accomplished, we'd save a lot of young Hungarians from KGB torture and certain death.

Hodos perked up and asked, "Do you really mean that?"

I said, "Yes."

The only thing left was to agree on a made-up story we could tell his boss about what we had done together while he was away, and then we could part company.

It was close to ten a.m., and I headed back down to see Henry, but he was still busy with the Russian high brass. However, the lady came to help, and I told her I needed to leave before three p.m., so all I needed to get was the most recent map of the river region. Once I got one, I could transfer the area of the south part of the Tisza River, mark all relevant lines, and put the date and the scale on it. When I'd finish copying the first map, I'd return it, then I'd ask for a map made even earlier. She hurried away and returned with a map dated 1951. I thanked her, took it to one of the rooms we had used before, and laid out the relatively new and latest map we had based on aerial photography. I fastened the vellum over the region, put the date and scale on, and started marking the flood plain, cut off loops and the riverbed itself, including a few lakes created by the last flood.

I wasn't quite done when I heard the knock on the door and Henry appeared, apologizing for being late. I said, "The lady in charge already gave me the latest and one dated earlier maps, and I'm just about finished with the second one. Please wait a few minutes, and I'll return this one, to be exchanged with the next older one."

He was watching me as I double-checked my copy and asked why I wore my white gloves working with such a recent map. I told him I loved maps, as I appreciate their importance, the amount of field and office work and printing that finally produced the most accurate description of any area. "There are not enough words that can describe as well on a single page what a simple map can show."

Henry nodded approvingly and said, "Too bad you are not assigned here permanently, as I definitely could use a friend like you. It is lonely down here without people who really appreciate maps and the associated work with it, including the proper storage and preservation of these important historical documents."

"You're right. I didn't mention the last important work relating to maps is the proper storage and preservation to give us a different view of history and geology/geography." I also told him I needed to take off early that afternoon.

"I understand if you have a hot date and need to get away."

"You got the idea, but I'll return Saturday morning to make up some of the lost time."

Henry brought the older map that was on a different scale, so I took vellum and marked the important points, still using my white gloves every time I touched the older maps. Henry was really impressed, but I did it for the love and joy I got out of reading maps, especially old ones. We even found a city map of Kassa, showing population statistics of different minorities. I was amazed at the small number of Slovaks, less than seventeen percent, but now the city and surrounding areas belong to the Slovak Republic.

Henry knew I was handling all the maps the right way, so he excused himself and returned about an hour later, just as I was removing the vellum from the top of the map. Henry said, "I timed it right. Are you ready for the next older map?"

I looked at my watch and said, "Why don't we wait till after lunch?"

"It is a good idea. I will set up the next older map for you by the time you return. Also, you seemed to be interested in the time capsules. Would you like to have one of your own?"

"I don't have anything worth storing for some generation ahead."

"That is not the way it works. You specify a container, put in your name or code and the length of time you would like to keep it, unless you want it sooner. I put in an old Doxa pocket watch that belonged to my grandfather before the past war, and the date to open is 1965. I'll be interested if twenty-five years later, the watches will be better."

"We lost everything during the war. The Romanians, Russians, Serbs, and Slovaks robbed us blind, leaving nothing valuable behind."

Henry corrected my line of reasoning, "The time capsules are set up for preserving technological steps for historical records, not for storing valuables.

I added a lighter, a necktie, the terrible speech from our Communist Party leader, maps of the actual and the mutilated Hungary to see how unbelievable these items will be a generation from now."

I told him, "I'll think about something and let you know."

I wanted to be alone for lunch, just to rethink and go over again all the steps and the timing of each of the actions I must complete today and

Sunday. So I asked Henry to let me stay in the office after he took the map and brought me the new one. I was hungry, but I'd rather skip this important meal than mess something up today, tomorrow, or Sunday. I had to pick up the newly created map from Piri at the pub around three p.m. and make the call to our contact at about four p.m., just to give him enough time to secure the necessary cash. I had to give him the new code name for myself, which is difficult to pronounce or write in Russian, to help identify the rat, put the map in the new drop zone in the church before five p.m., check the receipt of the money by six p.m., meet Zoli at seven p.m., and update and assign him for Saturday backup for Hodos and Dora without Dora knowing about it. I also had to wash, shave, and change clothes at my temporary place by ten p.m. and meet Piri by eleven p.m. to find out about the picture taking of the two suspects involved in the crime and find out if she secured the camera for Sunday.

I was secretly hoping she would invite me again and I could spend the night with her and go to the office in the morning from there. I figured I had a good excuse to stay to rehash our planned activities for Sunday, but without telling her, Zoli would also be there for backup for Hodos and Dora.

I looked at my watch, and it was almost one p.m., ready to start or at least pretend to work. A knock on the door, and Henry came in with a neatly wrapped sandwich in his hand. He put it on the chair and said, "Shari and I decided to get you lunch, and here it is. Enjoy it."

I asked who Shari was.

"Shari is the lady who checks everyone before they can have access to this place, and she is also my stepmother, but no one else knows it."

I said this was the first time I heard her name, as everyone else called her comrade. Henry said she hated to be called that, but under this sick Communist Russian puppet government, which he hoped wouldn't last much longer, she put up with it.

I immediately asked, "Is that what you wish for, or do you know something I don't?"

Henry said, "Shari and I have been watching, listening to the sick economy, the inefficiencies in production, the big government, injustices committed, and the brute force they use to keep communism going. The bubble must burst pretty soon."

"I like to believe that, and we already expected it after Stalin died, and nothing really improved much."

"The West must know this, and they could put real economic pressure on Russia. They must also know by now that communism and its leaders are much worse than Hitler ever was. In the Russian concentration camps, over fifty million died, unlike in Germany, where less than a million Jewish people lost their life. The West is for freedom, and they are against the communist/socialist regime."

I didn't want to discourage Henry by telling him the Communists, in large part, live off the West, either through industrial, technological, or political espionage. The KGB is much more successful than the CIA, and the Western communist sympathizers, including the liberals, prevent any harsh actions against the Soviets. I also didn't want to tell him that, in my opinion, the West is getting too soft, full of communists or communist sympathizers, socialists, and liberals, and many of their agents are traitors, selling out people such as you and me. In addition, their world and history knowledge is limited. Therefore, their foreign policy does not have the right direction and is without vision for the future. Money has more clout than personal responsibility, commitments, honor, and country. They refer to us as "informants" and think nothing of selling us out to the KGB for about two hundred dollars per head, without blinking an eye. I also didn't want to tell him that most likely Russia, using the old American plates, makes the dollars they receive, and it is pure forgery.

Henry interrupted my thinking with the comment, "I see this news made you think."

I responded, "Yes, and I want to pay for the sandwich."

He wouldn't accept. I reached over, grabbed the sandwich, and went out to eat it in the hallway.

I came back ten minutes later and started to work on the last map for the day, thinking I should get an earlier start just in case. Hodos's boss wouldn't look for me there, as he could not enter the reading room anyway. I wanted to drop by Hodos's desk to tell him Zoli would be the backup and Dora should not know about it.

At two p.m., Henry showed up with another older map, dated 1910, that included a lot of statistics about the regional populations, but I was not finished yet with the 1938 one. I asked him to put it on the shelf, and I would get it after I'm done.

Henry said, "I took care of all my work for today. Can I stay, assist you or just watch what you're doing?"

I welcomed his suggestion and asked Henry to stay, watch me, and keep me company. Henry commented that after I set up the 1910 map on the table with the vellum trace paper, he would take me to show the big vaults. I agreed, and in about fifteen minutes, we headed down the middle aisle to the two big doors.

Henry asked, "Which one first?"

I pointed to the right, as the door was already ajar. We went in, and Henry switched the light on. The red bulbs painted everything pink but were strong enough to see well.

He pointed to rows of shelf units with wide, deep, thin metal drawers.

He opened one of them and said, "These are the ones I just had copied for the Russian general. In fact, it is the same as what I showed you yesterday."

I thought this was a God-given chance to look and see again and compare it to what I had come up with last night. "Can I see it again?" I asked. Henry reached in and gently took out about a forty-by-sixty-centimeter map and showed it to me again. I said, "This is a copy. Where is the master?"

Henry said, "The master is not marked up with red circles."

I kept looking at it, and it seemed like I put in more features, and my circles were a few millimeters off but close enough and should suffice for the title of "Proposed Map…" I kept reviewing it, and Henry wondered what was so interesting about it. I said, "Nothing, really. I just think I should not look at this map."

Henry said, "Don't worry, I won't tell anybody, and if you want me to cover for you while you're gone this afternoon, I'll be happy to do so."

"Thank you, but I cannot ask for that."

"Why not? Every person having access to this library often uses me for covering for him, including Peter when he wants to leave early. Never mind, I will cover for you whether you ask for it or not. You see, my father was a professor at the language school, speaking seven languages. My mother died, so he married one of his pupils, my stepmother. That is why we get along so well, and it helps that every needed language I don't know, she handles very well. We make a good team, and we both like you. You are a breath of fresh air for us here."

Kele D. Gabor

I thanked him for trusting me, and I also excused myself to get an early start. I didn't know then that he would be my protector and instrumental in saving all the evidence we collected.

I looked at my watch, and it was too close to three, so I told Henry I must take off, but I would meet him tomorrow morning about nine o'clock.

He told me not to worry about today, and he would be here to help me (Saturday was a working day under the Communist system).

I went up to Hodos and pulled him aside and told him Zoli would be there for backup if something went wrong, but he would be the silent third helper without Dora knowing about it. Hodos nodded and said, "I really understand the limited contact concept, and I agree. You must have had some formal training in espionage." I didn't have the heart to tell him we were total amateurs and the only person who was smart enough to keep us from tripping over ourselves was Zoli.

I also told Hodos that Zoli would be inside the cemetery in view of both the headstone and the outside gate. "If he takes off his cap, you must hightail it to the headstone to take pictures, as you and Dora either missed the guy or someone else is doing the drop." I just left him thinking about their mission for tomorrow and took off.

Going out the main entrance, the guards stopped me and apologized for it, as they heard I was working for comrade Peter. The maintenance manager probably told the security guards that I was a very important person. I didn't want to disagree, but after opening my attaché case, they only lifted my empty thermos to look underneath. They smiled, closed my case, and I received a very smart salute from both of them.

I hurried to catch a bus to the pub to pick up my map from Piri. I went inside, and only a very few patrons were present. I walked by the counter to see if Piri was around, and before I could order a beer from Bandi, she appeared in the sexiest outfit I ever saw, smiled, and asked for my order.

She had on black nylon stockings, with black high heels, short red skirt, a white blouse, a small red vest with black ribbon decorations, and a small bra that only lifted her breasts up like she was offering them on a silver platter for anyone to see. I was offended by her overly inviting, sexy look.

She came real close while taking my order, and for the first time I saw makeup on her that made her look even cheaper.

Deception and Reality - Living Through the Missing Pages of History

She said, "I will put your beer on that table," pointing to the dark far corner of the pub. I was confused, jealous, angry, mad, and very upset seeing all her feminine curves accentuated and exposed. I ran into a chair trying to get to the table, as I could not take my eyes off her while she walked away from me with an exaggerated wiggle of her hips.

I got to my table and could not think what to say to her, but for sure, I must let her know I was greatly disappointed in her appearance. When she showed up with my beer on a tray, I just let her have it. "You look terrible, especially with that ugly lipstick on, just like a cheap night club dancer."

Instead of her getting hurt, she said while smiling, "There are at least two men here who really care about me, as Bandi pretty much told me the same thing. However, I told him why I dressed this way, but in your case, you have to figure it out yourself." She put the beer on my small table and a rolled-up used newspaper, where she already had put my map, as we agreed earlier. She bent toward me, exposing the centerline and curves of those beautiful breasts, smiled, and said, "I love you."

I didn't respond. I felt stupid. I asked her to do a difficult and potentially very dangerous job obtaining photographs of the traitors, and then I scolded her for using her feminine charm to succeed. She obviously wanted to complete her mission, regardless of what was required of her to help catch the guys responsible for the disappearance of her beloved brother.

I emptied the glass to quench the thirst I had built up after eating my late lunch. I looked on the table for the newspaper, then slowly and carefully picked it up and looked inside for my map. The map was folded twice, easily fitting inside the rolled-up newspaper holding the map in one of the folded creases. I noticed the newspaper was titled Népszava, translated "people's voice." This was another big lie under a communist system, as they rule by fear and absolute power, destroying everything in the process that is human, including freedom of speech. The socialists demolish truth, justice, fairness, freedom, families, democratic ideas, and religion, especially Christianity, equal rights, or anything good for a healthy society.

I looked at my watch again, and I had a few minutes before I had to get back close to the drop zone. I started to think again about why she would dress like that, as Piri was a very proper lady with a proper upbringing.

Kele D. Gabor

Even though I had partially figured it out, when she reappeared with a bill, I was still offended by her looks. She said, "You can pay as you go out, but I want to know first what you think of my outfit."

I responded, "It is in bad taste and too sexy, or do you want to get something from a man, like a camera from Bandi?"

"Bandi will provide it for us for the entire Sunday, and he also brought it with him today to take a picture of the two agents whom we expect here this evening. However, I have to look very sexy for the guys to be willing to take a picture with me standing between them."

She was right. I told her, "While you were talking, I figured out your tactics, and I'm sorry to be so rough on you."

"I'm glad you were upset— now I know you really care. Come up to my room when you finish your work, and we'll exchange notes on how we each accomplished our tasks."

I got up, leaving a good tip for her.

She said, "So far, every young guy and a couple of older gentlemen who came in propositioned me."

I responded, "No wonder."

I left the pub and headed toward the drop site and to be close by public phones in the post office. I knew I must make the call as close to four p.m. as possible and give them only an hour to pick up the map to squeeze them for time and delay the exchange of the name for money between the double agent and the KGB until tomorrow or Sunday. I got a private phone booth at the post office, took the thermos out from my attaché case, screwed off the metal cup cover, and put the cup on the shelf in front of me to be close at hand when I needed it. I put the thermos and the folded newspaper back in the attaché case, closed it, and pulled my note out, which we made up with Zoli last night. The note had a new "informer" name and outline of what I had to say, and possible extra enticements and excuses in case I would need them.

My watch showed exactly five minutes to four when the call went through with a loud ring. After the third ring, it was picked up as usual, and the response came back in English. I knew I had to wait without a sound until the operator switched to Hungarian. For some reason, it took longer instead of the usual ten-second delay, I almost had to wait for a half a minute. I was already planning to notify my team members to cancel our evidence-gathering for Saturday and Sunday when finally the "Hallo" came through. I asked to talk to Mr. White, and she asked in what regard. My response was "about the film." She immediately connected me to Mr. White.

I picked up the metal cup, placing it by my mouth so everything I would say sounded untraceable to my voice. I knew from Al that the embassy usually recorded the informers' messages for later review, identification by matching the voice and correct understanding.

Mr. White came on the line and said, "How can I help you?" With the thin aluminum cup by my mouth, I introduced myself as "Hiteles Ödön."

Zoli and I made up this code name to find out about the Western double agent. The h and the o with umlauts in Hungarian can be difficult to write with the Cyrillic alphabet and also hard to pronounce. The Hungarian ö is pronounced similarly to the last three vowels in the French adieu or the u in church. Even the h is often pronounced as (Hitler=Gitler). A person who learned Russian in school would transcribe it differently than someone who knows the language, as these pure sounds are not present in their language.

Mr. White said, "I cannot believe you, as you have already sent me for a wild goose chase last week."

I said, "I apologize, but last week, I saw a man with a brown leather coat tracking me. I'm in a very sensitive position in the government, with access to secret vaults, and I could not take a chance of discovery, but I need money fast."

"What do you have for us, and how can you avoid detection this time?"

"I have disguised my look and have a new drop-off and pickup sites.

However, because of the sensitive nature of the map and the important secret information it contains, I demand four hundred dollars cash in twenty-dollar bills." - We had decided earlier with Zoli that we should ask for twice the money the double agents get from the KGB for putting our lives on the line and, at the same time, force him to contact the embassy financial officer for the extra money, as Mr. White was not likely to have that much cash on him.

Mr. White started to laugh and said, "Under no circumstance do we pay over one hundred dollars to any informer, regardless of the nature of the document." I said, "I'll make you a deal. You pick up the stuff at five p.m., and if you don't think the information was worth the money, you don't pay me anything.

Kele D. Gabor

If you are satisfied, leave me the four hundred dollars, and we might do business again."

"Where and when is the drop?"

I could hear the tape recorder making a noise running in the background, and I started, "At St. Joseph Church, you should enter through the main door, and then you can see both sides of the foyer. Turn right.

On the right, there is an almost life-sized figure of the Virgin Mary, on the left side a little taller figure of St Joseph. The choir loft overhangs the entry foyer, so no one can observe you as I place or you pick up a folded newspaper, Nepszava, on the kneeler in the back row. [Communist agents typically used the choir loft to spy on people, and if one is recognized, he usually loses his job.] Pick up the paper, and inside you'll find a map you'll be very happy with."

Mr. White interrupted, "What if I cannot get the cash in time?"

"You have an extra hour to examine the new map, and if you like it, put the money into the left side of the foyer, into the locked bronze collection box by St. Joseph's feet, next to the row of candles. You must clear out of the area right after six p.m., as the evening litany begins at six thirty. Do you have any questions?"

"What if I like the map but I cannot get the cash?"

"No more top-secret information for you. I'll find another interested party." I didn't want to answer any more questions, so I hung up the phone.

The phone conversation took almost exactly four minutes, leaving him over fifty minutes to get the cash and take the ten-minute automobile ride to the church. I figured if he had that much cash on him, we wouldn't have a chance to get the necessary evidence this coming weekend, so praying for an official transaction in the embassy, I headed for the church. I was there before four thirty, so I just went inside, turned right, and kneeled down behind the last pew in front of the Virgin Mary's statue. There were a mother and a teenage daughter praying quietly, only the young girl turned around and looked at me. I smiled, and she turned her head back and made like she was praying too. I opened my attaché case and very quietly lifted out the newspaper with the map and placed it under my knees. I prayed again to succeed in our noble effort to catch the double agents.

A few minutes later, the mother and young girl left, leaving behind another old, folded up newspaper. I immediately got up, picked up the other paper, and placed it in my case. I stayed until four-fifty p.m., then got up, walked out to meet Zoli across the triangular-shaped plaza, where he was already waiting for me by a big, round metal post used for posters next to the street. When I got close, I opened my shirt button and he closed his to indicate the coast was clear, no one had followed us. He was reading the advertisements about a new movie on the large metal post, and I read the next poster about a show in the cabaret theatre.

Very few people, and even fewer cars, were around. When I got within arm's length of Zoli, I tipped my hat to start a conversation. He, like most Hungarian young people, wore the cheap but handy beret-type cap.

I said, "I think I'm in love with your sister."

He responded, "Did you tell her?"

"I'm pretty sure I let her know."

"That is good, as after the first weekend you spent with us in our vineyard two years ago, and right after you left, Piri told my mother she wants you for her husband."

"She never told me that."

Before he responded to my comment, Zoli stood aside and looked toward the church. I followed his movement, but I went to the opposite side of the advertising cylinder and peeked at the church. I didn't see anything, so I went back and asked Zoli, "What's up?"

He pointed to the other side of the plaza. I saw a black car stop, and Zoli said, "That must be an embassy car."

I asked, "How do you know?"

Zoli said, "Piri gave me a list of license plate numbers, but this isn't one of them. However, it has a diplomatic plate, and I can make out the small flags on the front fenders."

They seemed to come too early, so I started to worry. Mr. White couldn't get the cash, so he or his messenger came to pick up the map and drive away. The car parked in the no-parking zone, but that didn't seem to bother the chauffeur. I had to assume they had diplomatic immunity. The car stayed there a long time until a second one pulled up right behind the other one.

Zoli said, "They are ready to pick up. They came in the diplomatic car, with a diplomat and a diplomatic attaché case to make sure they won't get into trouble in case we set them up. Do you know what it means?"

"I responded, "What?"

"You did well and got through to them. They have the cash in case they like what you left them."

A passenger from the first car came out and went to the car behind him. We could not see if he sat inside or just bent down to talk to someone sitting inside. Precisely at four fifty-five p.m., the first car left, driving west behind the church, made a loop, and started to come toward us.

Zoli said, "We better move, as we don't want them to see us."

However, the car slowed down and parked on our side of the plaza, but far enough so we could stay out of sight. Before the car came to a full stop, a person emerged from the second car with an attaché case and walked toward the church. Zoli and I watched as a middle-aged, well-dressed man walked through the church doors and disappeared from our view.

We waited, and Zoli spoke up first, "Why did it take you more than a year to notice my sister Piri?"

"She was too pretty for me. I already had a kind of a girlfriend, and I went through some rejections earlier, so I was not ready to face another likely disappointment." This conversation was going on while keeping our eyes peeled for any sign of success or failure.

"I cannot blame you, all the boys were crazy about her and nicknamed her Gina, after Gina Lollobrigida."

"Piri is much prettier and has beautiful blue eyes."

I noticed the well-dressed man come out of the church and head straight for us. Zoli and I were ready to leave our hiding place behind the advertising post when the individual turned toward the car parked on our side of the plaza and got into the passenger side. The car took off before the passenger door was fully closed. To our surprise, the second car stayed, still in the no parking zone.

I told Zoli, "It looks like they are waiting to confirm the worth of the document, and that means they have the cash."

Zoli said, "Therefore, I can leave and get ready for a long day tomorrow at the cemetery, and I certainly hope we get the photographic evidence to prove our case."

"I can go too."

"Don't you want to know if they are going to make a generous donation to the St. Joseph church?"

"I'm not going to wait another half an hour just to make sure."

"If you don't want to wait, I have to."

"Why?"

"It'll be to our benefit to know the result. Maybe we can pull another one on them in case we fail to take the incriminating photos this weekend and make another poor church rich."

We kept on entertaining each other by exchanging stories about our sisters, but the more we talked, the more I missed Piri. I think it was at that time when I felt total commitment, not like before, but this time in body, mind, and soul to a wonderful girl. Piri, all of a sudden, became the center of my life. While Zoli was talking, I was thinking about her and her alone.

I soon realized I might jeopardize the entire operation and worried about tonight and Sunday with Piri. Would I be able to concentrate on the task at hand or fail because of my love growing for Piri by leaps and bounds, with each passing minute? Now I started to worry about her and was ready to do anything to keep her out of harm's way.

I must have been daydreaming, as I felt someone grabbing my upper arm and asking me to pay attention. Luckily, it was Zoli. He said, "Where have you been? Can you see the man approaching the parked embassy car?"

I looked at my watch; it was close to six p.m. I looked up and saw the man entering the parked car on the far side, and a minute later, another person came out on our side of the car. He hurried toward the church and disappeared through the main door. About two minutes passed before the same person emerged, hurried to the parked car, and they took off. It was exactly one minute past six. Zoli looked at me, and I looked at him. We said in unison, "We did it!" Zoli and I hugged like team members winning the gold at the Olympics.

I said, "The cash collector in the church will have a great and pleasant surprise tonight, as they usually count the donations a half an hour after the litany."

At that time, we had no idea of the headache and grief we created for the local pastor and the monsignor. Having Western currency in anybody's possession was a crime under the paranoid Communist system. The poor church eventually turned over the cash to the local Communist Party, just to make sure they were not in violation of the law.

Kele D. Gabor

This was a shame, and later on, it bugged us a great deal that somehow most of the American money or any aid seemed to go to the Communists instead of the intended needy people.

After hugging, we shook hands and Zoli said, "Let's hope Hodos will do what was asked of him tomorrow."

I said, "I also worry about me."

Zoli disregarded my comment, and we parted company.

I decided to go to my temporary place, wash up, shave, and put clean clothes on before heading back to get the rundown from Piri. I hurried back to my place of stay, but on the way I was thinking about Zoli ignoring my last comment on worrying about myself, as I considered love to be a sickness, and what it might do to me on Sunday working together with Piri, who also reciprocated my love. How would I act? Would I be alert, prepared, and careful not to goof up, or would I lose my composure and my alertness just because I was in love and wanting to be close to her every moment? Every time I had been in love before, it became painful for one reason or another.

I decided to keep thinking about the hurts so as not to get others or myself in trouble. I was thinking of all the young Hungarians, like my close friend Sándor, who lost his life being an "informer." He was sold out by the very people whom he tried to help because of his hatred of communism, socialism, and the occupying Russian forces. I noticed later that I wasn't looking at the girls as I was heading back to my place, not by the bus station, not outside or inside the streetcars. I knew I was in trouble. For the first time in my life, I had to make a concerted effort to look around for pretty faces, long legs, warm eyes, smiling lips, huggable breasts, curly long and dark hairs, attractive voices, and pleasant aromas.

I arrived back at my small place. I cleaned up, took out my last clean shirt and underpants, washed up, brushed my teeth, shaved, and got ready to go to see my sweetheart. It was only eight p.m., and I didn't want to wait three hours for her until she got off work. I decided to review today's events, and all the success started to make me happy, but I really started to miss Piri again. I figured if I walked, it would take over an hour to get there. If I started watching the pretty girls while walking on Friday evening, it might take two hours to get to the pub. So I brushed my shoes and left my place and headed toward the pub. Instead of looking at the pretty girls, I started to worry about Piri and how successful she had been getting the pictures and/or if the embassy guys showed up at all.

After about an hour and a half of walking, I found myself across from the pub. I tried to look in, but the huge wall-sized windows with an arch on the top were already covered about two meters high with mustard-color curtains on a brass rod. Next chance I had, I walked across the street to look in by the double front doors. Being Friday evening, there was surprisingly little traffic through the doors. This is just the opposite on Saturday night, as the number of clients will swell considerably. I could not see inside, and the closer I got to her, the more I missed her. I decided to go in and have a shot of brandy. I figured I'd rather stay in the warm, smoky room looking at my sweetheart than outside in the cold.

I walked up the five steps leading to the front door, pressed the handle down on the right side, pushed in the door, and stepped into the pub. I looked around, as stepping in from the dark gave me the chance to see more, even in the dimly lit part of the huge room. Again, I got perturbed, as I could not see Piri after scanning the entire place, but Bandi the bartender was there by the cash register. I headed toward him, and I was just about at the counter when Piri showed up with her hair pinned up, looking more mature and also showing her beautiful feminine long neckline. She still wore the short red skirt with black stockings, light blouse, and the small red vest. As she moved between the tables, my jealous eyes noticed all the patrons turn toward her as she walked by with her tray, avoiding hitting the chairs or the customers. Walking in the maze of tables accentuated her feminine swing, and it looked very sexy.

I headed to the same table she sent me to earlier in the afternoon and sat down. There were about twenty people total, four at the bar, and the rest sitting by the tables. I kept waiting for her to notice me or come close by, but to no avail. I looked at my watch, and it was close to ten in the evening.

Finally, four tables up from me, somebody yelled for a refill, so she wiggled her beautiful body toward me. She picked up the order and the empty glasses while turning her back to me. As she reached to get the farthest empty glass with her back to me, I could make out the black panties and almost white upper thighs with bare skin showing right above the top part of her stockings. Even though I had seen her in her swimming suit, I got furious. I grabbed the large empty ashtray from the middle of my table and practically threw it to the floor.

She turned around and must have seen me, as she immediately headed toward me with a big smile, picked up the ashtray, and asked, "What may I get for you?" I asked for a shot of apricot brandy, and then she said, "Good thing you came early, as I can get off at ten tonight, but I decided to stay anyway until you showed up." She turned around and left me while I was watching her with pleasant thoughts in my mind.

A few minutes later, she brought the tray with two orders but delivered the other first. When she came to my table, I asked if she was successful in accomplishing her mission. Her response was yes and no. I asked her to elaborate, but she just put the shot glass on my side of the table and came close to me and said, "I have to tell you later, as it is a long story. After you finish your drink, wait for me by the entranceway to my building. The drink is on the house."

"No way!" I responded. She was taken aback by my harsh words.

She did not have any idea how much trouble I got into before just by accepting a few "free" drinks. I forced a smile and emptied my glass while she walked away. I could tell I hurt her feelings, but I just left a big tip and made my way out of the pub. Before I closed the door behind me, I made a quick scan of the entire room and the bar area to make sure I didn't bring attention to myself and nobody was watching me.

I waited in the shadows of her building entry, and I waited. Every few minutes, I thought I looked at my watch. It seemed like my watch either stopped or slowed down incredibly, as what I thought was five minutes, according to my watch, was only one. Finally, about ten after ten, I saw her. She had a long raincoat on and a good-sized bag in her arms. I looked out and didn't see anybody around. I stepped out to greet her and hug her, but she refused, and I could detect no smile on her face. I gathered my thoughts, and I apologized for my rudeness in the pub, adding I had a good excuse for my ungentlemanly behavior and when she would hear my story, she would more than forgive me. I didn't realize then I might not have a chance later to explain the reason for not wanting to accept free drinks. She nodded approvingly and said, "That's okay."

We walked up the steps together without saying a word. She handed me the bag, and she reached into her pocket to get the key. After she opened the door, she put her index finger on her lips to indicate "Be quiet." We walked to the end of the hallway, and I gently opened the door and let her in first. She walked straight to the table and sat down, looking exhausted.

I put the bag on the middle of the table, walked around her, and gently touched her shoulders with both hands. She leaned forward, put her arm on the table and her forehead on her folded arms. I automatically started a gentle massage from the neck down to her waist. She didn't say anything for a minute or two, and then she slowly uttered the words, "Don't stop." I was thrilled and happy to touch her, to give her a gentle, relaxing massage.

It felt like the shortest massage I have given to anybody, but when it was over, my watch showed I was massaging her for at least half an hour.

She finally lifted her head and sat up, turned around, and smiled at me.

She said, "Get the other chair and put it to the other side and sit down.

I got off earlier, as I couldn't take a break all afternoon, and now I'm very hungry." While I went to get the chair, she stood up, pushed the chair back, took her coat off, threw it on the bed, reached into the bag, and started to take out a big loaf of bread, a bottle of milk, and a few small packages with the aroma of cold cuts. Looking at her pale and tired face now without the makeup, I suggested she go refresh, change, and I would set the table.

She smiled at me and said facetiously, "You mean you don't like me in this dress because I don't look pretty enough for you."

I said, "Just the contrary, I can barely hold myself from attacking you."

She smiled again and left. I knew I was forgiven and things would come back to normal once she returned. She was gone a long time, and she returned in her long blue gown, accentuating her eyes and her hips with the tight belt around the waist. I was quite taken aback, as the long blue gown looked very much like what I had seen in my daydreaming at the castle, just before my first arrest. Unfortunately, her eyes were reddish from the smoke and looked tired. She looked at the table and said, "I'm surprised nothing is missing— plates, silverware, napkins, glasses, cold cuts, cheese, bread, and butter."

I walked around the table and said before she sat down, "I love you, and I must hug you now or I die."

I could see she was pleased to hear it and turned toward me while opening her arms. I picked her up, squeezing her against my body while giving a short kiss. In a second or two, she asked to be put down and be let go or she might faint shortly.

I gently let her down, holding her body against mine, and whispered in her right ear, "I told Zoli that I'm in love with you." As she sat down, she asked what Zoli said. I told her, "Zoli indicated you love me too." She said, while smiling, that Zoli often exaggerates. I came around the table, and we both sat down to eat. While she was spreading butter on her bread, I asked her to tell me how it went.

She said, "I think we should be happy how it ended so far, but let's eat first. I know you didn't stay in line when they handed out 'patience' and you like to interrupt, but this time let me tell you my story my way, including what you should know about me, the family, and how it went today."

I said, "I hope you start with today." I saw on her face that she didn't like my comment.

We ate in total silence. We could hear each other breathing, biting, chewing, and cutting pieces of meat, cheese, and bread. I was hungry, but I could not eat much, and she took her sweet time eating. She chewed slowly and, with each bite, seemed to savor all the flavors. I was wondering if this was the way she wanted to be in control or maybe there was an alternative motive, but I kept quiet.

When she finished, soon after I put my fork and knife down, she said, "I know what you're thinking, but I'm very tired. I just started my period, and a lot of things happened today, so bear with me and just listen."

I didn't want to believe her comment was the explanation for the concerns I was having on my own mind. Did she read my mind? I relaxed, as I found it impossible that she could read my thoughts since she never slapped my face.

She continued, "I'm sure you sometimes, or should I say often, think about me, not only lovingly, but also as a sex object. That is natural."

Now I got scared and tried not to think about her, especially because she looked so inviting. She got some of her color back to her face and looked more relaxed. While I was wrapping up the leftovers, she closed her eyes and waited until I put the stuff away and returned to the table.

She said, "I have to start at the beginning, and you just listen." I did as she asked, as her story was captivating, but I had to bite my lips a few times to keep myself from interrupting her. Some parts of it reminded me of the monolog I heard from Lara not too long ago.

"I got the picture you wanted, with both embassy employees with me in the middle, but it was much harder than expected.

"As you know, after Sanyi [Sándor], my brother, disappeared, I dedicated myself to find out who was responsible and pay back for my pain somehow. I dropped out from my junior year without telling my mother or grandmother and literally stalked the embassy even before you and Zoli would know about it. I learned a lot from Zoli and went on my own spy mission. I changed my look every day so no one could recognize me while I watched every move from the other side of the embassy." She went to her huge wardrobe, opened the door, and she showed me dresses of every kind, from girly dresses to grandmother outfits. Inside the doors were large mirrors where she pointed and said, "This is where I practiced to be good and have my movements match the outfit I was wearing to avoid detection.

"I was fortunate to be born into a good family, but it was still difficult to make ends meet. My father was an army officer, and he was never home.

He was either on the front, a POW, or in prison. The only male figures we had were my older brother and my grandfather. My grandfather was the head of the Hungarian anti-espionage agency. He practically raised Zoli, as they became real friends, beyond just a grandchild-grandfather relationship.

My grandfather taught everything to Zoli and trained him. That is why he is so knowledgeable about this business."

I thought, No wonder he knows so much.

"My grandfather was able to sneak out to the West in 1947 and worked in Switzerland, training security people. He returned home in 1948 with a new identity as the person who helped the Jews escape to Hungary from the Slovak Nazi Tisso government. He was welcomed as a hero but was able to disappear in Eger, where he returned to his wife, my grandmother.

The Communist government never tied the two together, as my grandmother, being the only child of the family, kept her maiden name to keep the family lineage alive, and their son became my father. They lived in our spacious home until he died, leaving his wife behind. If you decide, we can get married, we could go there and live with her, as there are lots of rooms, even for a large family.

"After my observations of hundreds of hours of watching the embassy, I came to realize the pub where I work might be used as a place to trip up the Russian agent. However, after they hired me, and making further observations, I realized that both suspects worked in the embassy, and there was no Russian agent contact or involvement there. Then I started to follow the better-looking, dark-haired, thin-faced young man, as he was very mobile, took public transportation, and spoke fluent Hungarian. Later I found out that very few people spoke Hungarian in Western embassies. "Once I observed that the dark-haired young person was responsible for selling out Hungarian informers, I made a promise to kill him myself with help from Zoli, but now you're back and we could use your help. Zoli and I were very concerned that something bad had happened to you, as it did to my brother. Once you returned and came to visit me, I knew I wanted to stay alive as long as you do. Therefore, we must find a way to get rid of the rat without us being implicated in any way. With your and Zoli's help, we could make it look like an accident.

"Ever since I was working in the pub, this guy always had an eye for me, and I did nothing to discourage him. I even let him hug me and touch me once just to get him to fall for me all the way. Today was a special day, so I went in early right after my lunch. Bandi was also there, so I reviewed with him what I expected him to do about taking the photograph of both agents together, of course, without telling him why. He took me outside, and we went on a walk, as he wanted me to take the four remaining pictures on the roll he had inside the camera and see how I handled his expensive tool.

I had to take pictures of both people and objects standing and moving instances so he could give me further training in using his camera.

"Once we finished the roll, he made me take it out and put the new one into the camera. He took the roll of film and the camera back until tomorrow, Saturday night. I'll have the camera all day Sunday, with the new roll of film in it and the picture you requested of those evil guys. I had promised Bandi to go out on a date with him at a time and place of my choice. I'll ask for a ballet matinee. I'm sure he will be a little disappointed, but I don't want to lead him on like the dirty, filthy

Deception and Reality - Living Through the Missing Pages of History

Communist double agents from the embassy.

"When the agent showed up around five p.m., I told him I dressed up for him to notice me. He was very pleased until his friend came in close to half an hour later. He drank beer, and every time I delivered a new glass, he would reach up behind my skirt and pinch me. I told him he couldn't pinch me until he tells me his name. He said Berry, but I should call him Béla. I hated his pinching me, but I was able to force a smile every time."

She turned around, pulled the robe to the side, exposing her beautiful, shapely legs, and then pulled up her panties on her right cheek, which was covered with black and blue marks.

My blood was ready to boil, and I wanted to kill that guy now.

"I told him I wanted a picture with him while holding me. He said to wait till his friend is gone. I already got Bandi to commit to taking the picture once I got between the two. So I signaled Bandi, went over to their table, put my arm around each one of them, asked them to smile, and Bandi took the picture. Of course, the great flash gave him away, and both of them got very mad. I tried to smile and hang on to the darker-hair's neck, trying to tell him the picture I wanted and he should not bother Bandi. Finally, they calmed down if we sell him the negative for twenty dollars. Bandi agreed, but they wanted to have it right away. In fact, they fought for the camera and wanted to open it up to ruin the negative.

"I screamed, hit him in the face with my elbow, and he let go of the camera for Bandi to take out the film. Bandi took out the roll and handed it to Béla. He took it, with his pocketknife opened the roll, and pulled the film out, ruining the shots. I was furious, but Bandi smiled and took the twenty-dollar bill. Later I found out that when I screamed and hit Béla on his nose, Bandi just reached into his pocket and gave him the films we took earlier. So thanks to Bandi's quick thinking and hands, we have the film in the camera, which I will have on Saturday evening and all day Sunday. Now I have to go to bed and rest while you tell me your story."

I didn't have the heart to keep her up anymore. She was very tired and pale. I told her we would have enough time for that on Sunday. I picked up my coat and waited for Piri to escort me out and lock the outside door.

She said, "What is wrong? I thought you wanted to spend the time

Kele D. Gabor

with me?"

"You're exhausted. Let me just go."

She pulled out the mattress from underneath her bed, gave me two blankets, a pillow, and with the sweetest voice asked me to stay, as she felt more comfortable, slept better, and was more relaxed when I was close to her. I kicked off my shoes and went to the bathroom only in my socks. I returned, took off my coat, shirt, and trousers, and went to bed. By the time I turned toward her, she was visibly sleeping with the bright lights on. I turned off the lights, and slipped under the blankets. It took me a long time to fall asleep. I was worried about how the film turned out and the fact that we didn't have the film in our possession bothered me, but eventually I let myself go to the dream world.

DECEPTION AND REALITY- LIVING THROUGH THE MISSING PAGES OF HISTORY

The Evidence

I woke up before Piri. I went out to wash up and wondered about the rest of the people who had subleased the room to Piri. How come I have never seen them? I decided to clarify this point with Piri the next time I saw her awake.

When I returned to her room, she had not moved and was still asleep.

I was able to gather all my belongings without waking her up and sneaked out the door. The problem was, if I left the apartment, I could not lock the outside door without a key. I put on my clothes in the hallway, picked up a scratch paper, and wrote a note for Piri to the fact that I had to leave. I left the apartment door unlocked, but I would come by during lunchtime to check on her. I folded the sheet of paper and placed it between the cracks of her door at eye level. I knew as soon as she woke up, she would head to the restroom and see my note before she opened her bedroom door.

I headed toward my office, but I missed, as my mother used to say, "the most important meal of the day." I was really getting low on money; the last few days, I had used up all my daily allowance by buying and spending it on things which in my frugal situation were considered luxury. However, I had to get something in my stomach. I passed by a dairy goods shop, went in, bought the cheapest cheese, a small glass of milk, and a piece of moon-shaped bread (kifli). No other customer was in the shop, so I asked the young girl with rosy-red cheeks behind the counter if I could have my milk warmed. She could not help me, but she offered some of her own hot tea from her thermos. It made me feel good that on an early Saturday morning, a young girl working for the state would offer part of her own breakfast to a complete stranger.

I complimented her; she smiled and said, "Today is my first day alone in this job, my parents had a photo shop before, and there I learned the importance of happy customers." I asked if her parents still had the shop.

She smiled and said, "There is no more private business in Hungary, and you should know that."

"What are they doing to earn their living?" I asked.

Kele D. Gabor

"The Communists didn't know about it, so they didn't confiscate the small lab we had at home, and they still do some photo enlargements and copies."

Over the next few days, we became good friends, as I made a point to drop by whenever I visited our main office.

It was before eight in the morning, but the security guards in gray uniforms were already standing in the open doorway. I passed by them, and both saluted me. I returned their greetings by tipping my hat and slightly nodding my head. I was thinking about how fast news travels about somebody's perceived importance or his potential threat. This is the first time I realized how powerful a mid-level young manager could be just being a Jew and card-carrying, active Communist Party member. Just by mere association with him, I had more clout than I needed.

I went up to my little office, but I could not get in because I had forgotten my key to Hodos's boss's office. I must have left it in my pocket when I changed clothes the previous evening, as I was preoccupied thinking about our very dangerous job ahead. I didn't want to wait for the boss's return, so I decided to test the clout I had just by knowing Peter.

I went down to the maintenance office, knocked, entered, and asked if they could open one of the manager's offices for me. "There is no problem," was the response, and the guy was already reaching for the master keys in his desk. He did ask me which office. I told him I was in Room Twenty-three A, but I had to first get through Room Twenty-three. He walked up with me, opened the door, and let me in while asking if he could be of further assistance to me.

I said, "No, thanks."

"What if the manager in Room Twenty-three does not come in today?"

"You could lock it for me when I leave."

He incredulously repeated, "When you leave?"

"Yes."

However, he had a better solution for me by providing a master key, against all regulations from the front office.

I settled in and laid out the three map copies I had made of the same areas around the lower Tisza River from different dates. The last two were on the same scale, so I decided to keep the identical scale and expand the third one to match so I could overlay the three maps and see the meandering, and the changing flood or cut-off branches, of the river in the last forty-six years. When I rescaled the third map to match the first two, it was already nine fifteen, so I hurriedly put them on top of each other and held them up against the light to take a quick look. I didn't want to be late in meeting Henry in the map library.

I hurried down and apologized to Henry, as he was already waiting for me. Henry said, "You're the first person having access to our place who ever expressed an apology for missing an appointment or thanks for our extra efforts."

"Do you mean other people don't care?"

"They may care, but don't show it."

I was thinking of my big boss in the regional office— how polite he was in expressing thanks for extra work, apologizing for being late, and giving praise when deserved. I was lucky to be trained by him, as I also became an effective manager just by voicing appreciation when deserved and thereby encouraging professional work and behaviors.

We went to my reading room, where Henry already laid out the fourth older map and placed clear vellum over it, so I just had to trace the required lines and put in the scale— so it went very fast. The setup time probably took longer than copying or tracing the few lines, which defined the riverbed, flood zones, and a few small settlements. Henry, on his own initiative, made the next setup in the other office. Ping-ponging back and forth in the side-by-side reading rooms, I must have retraced seven to eight older maps by noon.

Unfortunately, I had to rescale most of them, as none of the older ones had the metric scale. There remained five older maps reaching back to the beginning of the thirteenth century, but it was obvious they were not to scale. From the lines drawn and the nearby settlements, we could tell the floods were quite extensive before the engineers started to regulate the river flow. The engineers cut off large loops of the meandering river, deepened the riverbed, and removed large piles of debris. They might have also eliminated the large beaver population.

There were many fishing villages, beaver colonies, and bison ranges. These settlements no longer existed, but we could tell their functions by the names of the villages indicated on the map. A few examples were Beaver, Bison-crossing, Salmon-run, Sturgeon-many, and Pelt-market. These Hungarian settlement names extended all the way to the city of Nádor Fehér (meaning "white Palatine" in Hungarian), which is now renamed Belgrade (meaning "white city") by the Serbs.

All city maps south of the current borders had original Hungarian names, some of which translated to Latin or German, but I could never find any foreign settlement names until after the seventeenth century, after the Turks were pushed out of Hungary, and then only German or Croatian. Only maps made after 1925 had new names, like Romania, Czechoslovakia, or Yugoslavia. I found a map of Romania from 1850, but all their territories were south or east of the Carpathian Mountains, and it was called Walachia. Going back to the maps and the old description of borders and countries, only Poland and Hungary existed for a thousand years. Germany, Austria, Italy, much of Britain were nowhere or were small parts of the Roman and, later, the Holy Roman Empire. None of the formidable Eastern countries existed besides China, India, Tatar lands, Tibet, and the Mongol territories.

Henry and I took a break around twelve fifteen. He went over to the city library not far from us, where Dora worked, but I knew she and Hodos were away, as they had some more important work to do. I decided to go early and see Piri right away. When I wasn't concentrating on the work, I was thinking of Piri, and by this time, I must have been totally infatuated by her. I knocked on the apartment door, but no answer came, so I tried the door handle, but it was locked. I figured she had to go to work earlier, so with the saddest heart and face, I went down the steps. As I was exiting the main entry, I looked to the left, hoping to see her coming back. I stood there awhile, trying to see the young girls hurrying from lunch, shopping, or for an early date on this sunny Saturday afternoon. I decided to wait ten more minutes and head back to the office around one.

Just as I put my pocket watch back, a young, beautiful lady with a big smile greeted me on the step right below me. I bent down and kissed her on the cheek, but she puckered and pointed to her lips. I gave her a short, noisy kiss, and while straightening my hunched back, I lifted her up on my step. She said, "Let's go inside. I have a few questions about tomorrow."

We walked up together holding hands, and I helped her carry her shopping bag with my other arm. As soon as we stepped inside, I put my arm around her and gave her a firm hug, followed by a nice kiss.

She wiggled out of my arm and said, "I guess you like me and want me."

"I'm really worried about tomorrow and concentrating on the important job at hand."

While walking to her room, she said, "Don't worry, I won't let you lose your composure."

"How will you do that?"

"Never mind. Let's eat first." She put her bag on the table.

"I have to get back to finish my work and get ready for tomorrow."

"No, no, no, you must stay with me tonight, even though I probably have to work till midnight." She reached into her bag and gave me a newly made key to the apartment. "I just had it made for you, as I need you here. I sleep much better with you at my side."

"This reminds me. I keep wondering about the apartment owners. How come we never see them?"

"They are older people and work six days a week, from six in the morning till three, in the afternoon on an assembly line. They go to bed early, and they are sound sleepers. On Saturdays after work, they go to the outskirts of the city and stay with the grandchildren either at their son's or daughter's place. They won't be back till late Monday afternoon. The daughter used to have this room until she got married, and she really needs her mother's help, with two little babies eleven months apart. I hope we can wait more than a year between our children."

I said, "Whatever you like or want, as motherhood is the most important, honorable, rewarding, and difficult job, but it is also the most challenging." I could tell she was happy with my remarks. I took a few bites to eat, drank a glass of milk, excused myself, and after a big hug and kiss I left for the office.

When I got to the office building, I went straight down to the map room, as I knew Henry would be already there waiting for me. Two older maps were already set up for me, but these were really inaccurate as far as scale and proportions were concerned. One was from the end of the fifteenth century and was made during the reign of King Mathias and the other after the Turks were pushed out of Hungary, around the year 1700.

These two maps were very interesting to see and compare because they showed the big difference in population. Where the earlier map showed thriving Hungarian communities, the newer map was blank. It was obvious much of the Hungarian population in the Turkish-occupied territories disappeared. We knew the young boys were sent to Turkey for military training to be ferocious-fighting men called "janicsar" (janissaries) and young girls to harems to boost the Turkish birth rate.

Since the proportion of the older maps seemed to be off, I decided not to include them in the three maps I had collected and copied. I thanked Henry for his superior and invaluable help and bid goodbye to the map archival room. I headed up to my little office and started to bring all my map copies to the same scale, or to a common denominator. This time, I started on the oldest one and decided to work my way back up to the present. I had only finished one when a knock on the door broke my concentration. I said, "Come in."

Hodos's boss stuck his head in and asked, "I'm leaving, and don't you want to do the same?"

"I have been thinking about it, but I have to make up some time, as I left earlier yesterday."

"You don't have to worry about it, let's go."

I put my stuff together, turned off the light, picked up my coat, and walked out with him. The guards saluted me again and very courteously asked to check my briefcase, emphasizing it was only a formality. I opened it, and without looking into my case, they closed it, and while bending down, I heard a phrase that was totally foreign in a communist system, "Thank you."

Hodos's boss didn't want to believe his eyes and ears. He asked me, "Whom do you know or who did you kill?"

I said, "Somehow they got the impression I work with Peter G."

"Enjoy the royal treatment while you can, but most of us resent him, so you may lose a lot of good friends. The only reason I still support you is that Hodos assured me you're more than okay, but I'm afraid to spread the good news about you being trustworthy, as you may lose a lot of privileges among the subservient groups."

I went back to my temporary flat, looked over my laundry, and decided to wash some shirts, underpants, and socks in case I had to stay until next Wednesday. I hung them out to dry on the community line in the courtyard.

Many lines were full, as Saturday afternoon must be the primary wash day for most people, especially on a late fall sunny afternoon. Just for fun, I counted the ladies clothes outnumbering the men's by almost ten to one. Of course, they change everything more often, including their minds.

All of a sudden, I had a great urge to go to the cemetery and check on the team. I figured Piri wouldn't get home until late, and I might as well do something useful outside while my clothes dried. It was almost closing time at the cemetery. Many older people were still going in to pay respect to their loved ones, as Saturday late afternoon or Sunday were the only times working people could spare their precious time. I stayed outside just to assess the situation and find each team member before I interrupted something or possibly botched things up.

I first saw Dora about five rows back from the drop and pickup point by the headstone, leaning against a large black locust tree, watching a squirrel. It looked like all she was interested in were animals. She had a casual outfit on, and the camera with telephoto lens hanging on her side. For me, she was too obviously open, but it took me some time to find Hodos and Zoli.

I had to be careful about being seen by Dora while talking to Zoli, as she was not supposed to know about the third set of eyes. I made a big circle far enough around the drop zone so I would not interfere with the operation and, at the same time, avoid detection by the team, except for Zoli.

I just about completed the circle when I spotted Hodos at the far end of the fifth row, standing by a big headstone with a small hoe, looking alert while seeming to attend to a stranger's burial site. He had a dark-blue beret on, so I presumed he was using it to signal Dora. I knew Zoli had to be in sight of Hodos for signaling, so I approached Hodos very carefully, but quite a distance away. There was a huge weeping willow just east of the drop zone. I decided to go around and use it for cover while approaching him. As I was passing the willow tree, I noticed most of the leaves were gone except on the west side facing the drop zone. I decided to go closer, as it had a clear line of sight to the back of the headstone.

As I approached the tree, I kept looking at Hodos, as he often looked up toward the drop zone and toward the willow, so I had to presume Zoli was hiding behind the natural curtain of the hanging branches from the willow tree. I was right on, but as I was closing in, I could not see Zoli. I stood right behind the tree when I heard but could not see Zoli. There was a big crack on the north side of the trunk that was all black inside, and he was leaning against the crack in dark clothes, so he was hard to see until I was right next to him.

Zoli asked me to step back, and I did. I asked why. Zoli responded, "I don't want Hodos or Dora to see you, as I want them to concentrate on the job." I asked how it had gone so far. Zoli, while keeping his eyes on the back part of the headstone where the gold letters had almost totally faded, said, "One down, two to go." I asked for an explanation. He said, "The thin-faced, dark-haired guy was here placing a bouquet of chrysanthemums in the metal vase, and if you step to the right a bit, you should be able to make out the flower standing right in front of the headstone.

I moved to the right, and sure enough I could see a bouquet of light lilac chrysanthemums."

I said, "I don't see a different colored flower in the middle."

"There is a dark purple one and wider white ribbon tying those together, with your new code name written in Cyrillic letters on the ribbon."

I was eager to find out if the embassy employee learned the Russian in school or at home. I asked how the guy spelled it.

Zoli said, "If you first tell me how Piri did yesterday, I will tell you."

I said, "She was successful with some difficulties, and she found out the guy's name to be Berry, but he preferred to be called Béla here. The other guy, his partner in crime, left when a fight ensued after the picture taking."

"Is Piri okay? And where is the negative?"

"Piri has a few blue spots on her behind, and the picture is inside the camera, which we will use tomorrow. Now it is your turn to update me."

Zoli said, "We almost missed the first shot because they were looking at each other, not necessarily the entryway. I can't really blame Hodos, as Dora looked like, dressed like, and walked like a beauty queen— that is what ballet can do for a good-looking tall girl. I hope none of the agents will notice her sexy shape. When I took off my cap, I had to wave it to Hodos to be noticed. On top of it, Dora's hands were shaking because of the excitement, so I didn't think the first picture came out when this traitor bought his bouquet. I had to have a talk with Hodos to keep himself separate and have Dora concentrate on steady hands, as is required with a one hundred and fifty mm telephoto lens. I think we got two good sets of pictures when this crappy guy tied the ribbon on and placed the bouquets in the metal vase without being noticed. Dora was taking a few extra shots just to make sure, but either the double agent was expecting someone or just very suspicious, as he kept looking around and behind himself. I don't know how we will handle the situation tomorrow without a telephoto lens."

I said, "Zoli you have not told me how he spelled my code name."

"In my opinion, he is Russian, probably a Russian Jew whose parents migrated to America and didn't learn the language in school, as he used both spellings. The code name, Hiteles Ödön, was transcribed two ways, the Russian h and g in parenthesis. Ödön was again written with the Russian u with umlaut [bl] and the simple o also in parentheses. We should kill the rat that turned in my brother and let the embassy find out afterward that they were employing a Russian spy. I think next time I see him, I'll kill him," he said and pointed to his pocket, where he kept his pocketknife with a ten-centimeter blade.

I suggested to Zoli not to meet today, as we already updated each other, and there was less than half an hour to closing. Zoli said, "It is fine with me, as we'll see each other tomorrow when they open the gate."

There was a gray stone bench north of the willow, so I walked over and sat down. We were still talking a distance from each other, but I had a more secure cover from Hodos and Dora. I was looking at the setting sun, and I wasn't there five minutes when Zoli made a particular hissing sound. I looked at Hodos. He already had his cap down and momentarily stopped leaning forward, like he was pulling some weeds. He looked at Dora, who was leaning on the backside of the black locust tree, holding the camera with the telephoto touching the bark, I suppose, to steady the picture-taking process. From my vantage point, I could see she was actively taking a picture about every ten seconds.

When I tried to look in the direction where the telephoto was pointing, I noticed a well-dressed young lady walking straight toward the headstone, carrying a single strand of white flowers. I pulled closer to Zoli and said, "She is a Russian barishna. Look at her tits, boots, walk, and dress. She looks like a military officer in civilian clothes and probably smells like an overpowering cheap perfume."

Zoli said, "I also noticed the Russian pointed bra that makes the breasts look like torpedo heads. The Russian military lady boots, her walk, it all adds up. Once she picks up the bouquet, takes the ribbon off, switches the flower, Hodos will have to follow her, with Dora right in front of him to find out where she takes the ribbon."

"I would also like to follow."

"Only behind me, as I don't want Dora, or even Hodos to notice you."

I stayed and watched as the tall, shapely Russian lady picked up the flowers, took off the ribbon, exchanged the center flower with the white one, put the bouquet back into the vase, and rearranged the flowers.

Without looking, she turned around and walked back as she came in. I watched as she made it to the same open gates and turned right. I was thinking Béla and the shapely Russian woman might be lovers on the side.

I saw Dora following and taking a picture as she passed through the gates.

I saw Hodos and Zoli a good distance away.

By the time I reached the gate, they were closing it, as the sun had gone down. As soon as I stepped out of the gates, I turned left, cut over to the other side, and headed to some bushes where I could wait for Zoli. I kept looking toward where the three of them had been, but it took a long time to see a young couple hand in hand, smiling and talking while they headed toward me to the bus stop. The two of them passed me without noticing me, but I could have stood in front of them, and they would have run into me before they would have noticed. I pinched myself and told myself, "Kele, you have to do better tomorrow than these young lovers."

As Dora and Hodos passed me, I heard and later saw a Russian Pobeda ("Victory") automobile passing all three of us. Surprisingly, Dora took her camera off her shoulder and snapped a picture just as the car was passing them. I knew then that the person or persons doing the exchange were inside the vehicle. I must have waited for fifteen minutes, and it was getting dark, but there was no sign of Zoli. I was really concerned when he finally showed up almost an hour later. I jumped out of the bushes, grabbed him, and asked him what had happened.

Zoli said, "I'm glad you waited for me, as I have no more cash to buy a bus fare home. I had to follow the lady who handed the ribbon to the guy in the car, who looked like the KGB agent with a partially missing eyebrow you described to me originally when you worked at the canning factory. By the way, the young lady must be his lover because I saw them kissing before parting company."

"Where were you gone for an hour?"

"I had to follow the Russian woman. She headed across the open field and disappeared right after reaching the first block of buildings. We walked at least two kilometers to make sure she had gone inside one of those structures, as I could not follow her close enough because of the open field."

"Did you find where she lived?"

"I have to assume she lived in the particular building where the other Russian military officer's family stayed. I know these relatively new buildings with spacious apartments located outside or close to the city limit, and everyone nearby spoke Russian."

We headed back to the bus stop, and we didn't have to wait long. After giving him all my leftover money, he asked me to wait for the next bus, as he didn't want to be seen with me. I asked him that before he would pick up the negatives tonight from Hodos, he should try to borrow the camera, as I was really concerned about getting close enough to that crazy son of a bitch. Zoli said, "They just about shot all the pictures, and I doubt if they had two left." It really bothered me, and I felt uneasy about Piri having to approach the pickup place so closely without a telephoto lens to get meaningful pictures. I decided I would take the pictures to ensure Piri wouldn't get into any trouble.

I had a long wait for the next bus, but I didn't care, as I thought about what they accomplished without exposing themselves to too much danger, and of course the telephoto lens was a big help. Dora never had to be close enough to the objects to hear the click from the camera. I stopped off at my temporary pad, headed to the courtyard, collected my dry clothes from the line, and walked up to my room. I folded my dry clothes, put them by my small suitcase, washed myself in warm water, and headed out to see my love.

It was past ten in the evening, so I took the trolley and transferred by the bridge to get close to Piri's workplace. I went up the steps to the pub,

but I didn't want go in, as I had no money left for a drink. The little I got was from milking all my pockets at my place. Every time someone came out or went in the pub, I acted like I was waiting for someone and peeked in just to get a glimpse of Piri, but without luck. I badly needed a shot of brandy, so I headed to Piri's place, hoping to find the fine apricot brandy she served me a few days ago. I got up the steps, but I had a hard time opening the apartment door. The new key wasn't ground close enough, and the fine tolerance required by the lock mechanism didn't want to accept my diamond in the rough. Probably the lock itself needed some oiling. I had to go down and look for a place where I could find a small amount of oil, preferably without having to pay for it. Late Saturday evening, only pubs or drug stores were open.

I returned to the pub where Piri worked and walked in like I had some money. I walked straight to where Bandi was standing behind the counter listening to a tipsy customer's joke. I had to wait until he finished. Bandi made a big smile like he appreciated the joke, and then turned toward me.

This was the first time I was eye to eye with my potential rival for Piri. He was slightly taller than I was, broad shouldered, round faced, with a little funny smile under his small nose and above a miniscule chin. Overall, he was a pleasant looking chap, but with no distinguishing features making him look special or masculine. In fact, he had more of a feminine look, with a hairless, pale face and wide, thin, long lines for eyebrows, and small eyes. After the first impression, I decided not to be jealous of him taking Piri next week to the ballet matinee.

My made-up story line to Bandi was, "My zipper is stuck on my leather jacket, and it is too cool to ride my motorcycle with my open jacket. Could you give me a thimble full of oil?"

He said that they had no oil around the bar, but if he did, he would first put it on the back door of the store, as it was getting very hard to open and close.

The tipsy guy sitting next to me said, "Hey, I had my zipper stuck before, and the best thing for it was paraffin."

Bandi said, "We have some old candlesticks for emergency, when the lights go out."

I said, "If you can spare one, I would like to try."

While Bandi was looking for the candles, I looked around very hard, trying to find Piri. No sign of her. The place was full of smoke, but not more than ten middle-aged guys were around. I thought Bandi might have let Piri go earlier, so I was ready to leave when Bandi showed up with several candles and gave me the shortest one. I thanked him, offered to pay for it, but he waved it off. I was happy about his generosity.

I hurried back to the apartment, knocked, but no answer. I lit up the candle, dropped some hot wax on the key, inserted it fast while the wax was soft, and it worked. The lock did move, so I blew the candle out, opened the door, and took the key out and hurried to Piri's room. Her door was unlocked, and it was pitch dark when I stepped in. I groped around for the light switch, and once I found it, I turned the light on.

The room was clean; the middle of the table had something on top covered with a big kitchen towel. I carefully lifted the towel off. There was my favorite brandy with two shot glasses, a round loaf of bread (buci), butter, a large slice of cured smoked ham, two plates, and silverware. I even found a note under the brandy saying, I should be back by midnight. Drink, eat, and enjoy. Love, Piri.

I inhaled, took a sip of the brandy, held it in my mouth, and slowly let it trickle down my throat, warming me up all the way down while exhaling the entire fresh apricot aroma settling into my palate, and fully enjoyed it.

I sat down and looked around. The place was spotless except the inside clothesline stretching from the upper corner of the armoire to the door full of Piri's undies. She must have cleaned up and washed after I left, leaving everything clean and fresh. It was close to midnight, so I really started to worry about her because I didn't see her in the pub and we had a hard day tomorrow. I had to make an alternate plan in case something happened to Piri or we couldn't get the camera. I decided to backtrack to the pub, go in, and confront Bandi. I put my jacket back on, had another but smaller shot of apricot brandy, covered up the food and the drinks, turned out the light, and walked out to the hallway.

I was opening the front apartment door when I heard someone coming up on the steps slowly. I thought it must have been an old lady, but it was Piri, pale and carrying a big bag. I ran down to meet her, grabbed her bag, and took it away from her. I asked what happened to her; she looked pale and tired.

She stopped on the steps, took a big breath, and said, "I slept too much.

It happens often when I have my period."

I asked where she slept, as I was in the pub looking for her and could not find her.

She said, "When I took my break late around eight o'clock, I told Bandi I didn't feel well, and instead of taking a supper break, I just wanted to lie down and rest. Bandi told me I was pale and could lie down on the cot in the storage room and he would wake me up after my break. I fell asleep, and Bandi didn't wake me up until about half an hour ago. Now I'm all rested and probably won't be able to sleep, but I'm glad you're here."

She sat down by the table, and I uncovered the drink and food. I put the big, heavy bag down on her bed and poured a shot of brandy for her.

She didn't want to drink until I poured myself one. We raised our glasses, and then she took a gulp while I took a small sip. She was still pale as a whitewashed wall but looked relaxed.

She turned toward me and asked, "Could we eat? I'm very hungry."

I sliced the bread, ham, and pushed all the food toward her. After making the sign of the cross, she started to eat ravenously. After the fourth piece of bread, butter, and ham, she took a big breath and said, "I'd better slow down and let my stomach catch up with digesting before I can take another bite." Her color started to return; so did her smile.

I went around the table, lifted her hair in the back, and gave her a long kiss on the back of her neck. I felt her whole body shiver when I touched her spine with my tongue. She turned toward me and said, "You can do that to me any time."

I said, "If I can hug you, I'll give you a great massage."

"Let me take out the camera, lay out my clothes, pack up the food, get ready for early morning tomorrow, and set the alarm for seven."

I agreed and helped her with each task. When we were done, she went out and returned with her nightgown on. She pulled out the mattress, put a pillow and blankets on, and slipped into her bed. Turning around, facing her pillow, she said, "I could use your massage now."

I sat on her bed right next to her and started the relaxing massage at the back of her head and slowly worked my way down to her waist. When I was ready to move my hands back up on her back, she said, "Lower." I even started to massage her enticing round derrière, and I asked if the black and blue marks were still there. She said, "Probably, but why don't you take a look." I lifted up the long nightgown skirt over her fanny, but her panties covered the spot. I started to get excited, so I let her skirt back down and continued massaging the area between her kidneys and her derrière. In ten minutes, she was asleep. I covered her up, and I also went to sleep. It felt good to be near her, and soon the dreams took over.

Piri got up before I did, and the hot tea was already waiting when I opened my eyes. I woke up about six thirty, before the alarm would go off. I went to the bathroom, put my shirt and pants on, and returned with a refreshed look. Piri looked better, not as pale as last night, and she had a big smile on her face. I went and hugged her. She just melted onto me. It felt good to have her body and soul touching me as we caressed each other.

She said, "You slept soundly I have tried to wake you up since six fifteen.

Even kissing your face didn't do the trick. I had to tickle your foot to get you up, and you too have a nice fanny and good-looking legs. When I tickled your feet, you kicked off the blanket, totally exposing yourself. I didn't know you slept without anything on."

I didn't blush, but I said, "I'll try the same trick on you next time and see if you would kick the cover off."

"It wouldn't help you, as I wear a nightgown."

I agreed and told her every time she got up, her gown was rolled up to her waist.

She did blush and asked, "How do you know?"

"I saw you last night when I woke up. You were uncovered, showing your derriere all the way to your feet, with the exception of the contraption you wear when having your period."

Now she really blushed and invited me to the table to have a hearty breakfast. I told her I was totally out of money and hoped she had some to spare. She said, "I still have your five hundred forint, as I asked Zoli to buy the films and leave them with Bandi."

"You mean Bandi knows Zoli?"

"Not really, he just left a small bag for me at the pub with two rolls of film, but they don't know he is my brother."

I thought out aloud, "God, no wonder Zoli didn't have a penny on him last night." I told Piri that I would share half the five hundred with Zoli.

While we ate our breakfast, we discussed the strategy of arriving separately at the cemetery, but we must be in visual signal range. She pulled out a brown beret and said, "You better wear this, as your hat will be too formal if you intend to wear your sporty brown jacket." The beret didn't quite match my jacket, as it was slightly lighter in color, but when I put it on, she pulled me to the mirror to show that it looked better than the hat with my leather jacket. It was her turn to dress up, and she chose to look old. This way, she could avoid recognition by Béla when taking a picture at close range.

She opened her wardrobe and started looking from left to right, as the older dresses were to the right. Her hand stopped momentarily at a gray costume, but I shook my head. She would have looked good but not old enough not to be recognized. Finally, I agreed to try a dark-brown heavy long skirt with a slightly lighter colored cardigan. She held it up to her front and shook her head. I said, "It doesn't look good because underneath you have the long medium blue gown matching your eyes." She took off her gown. I saw her beautiful figure, with just her panties and a bra on. I commented that her bikini was much smaller than her underwear. She laughed and continued looking.

The only other choice was a black dress, but neither one of us liked it. We ended up with the original brown outfit. She put on heavy dark-gray stockings, which I would have liked to put on her, but we were running out of time. She turned around, put a heavy padding between her panties and crotch. When she put on the heavy brown mohair skirt, she needed some padding. She took one of her soft small pillows, put on heavy-duty, old fashioned long underwear and pressed the pillow between her waistline and the heavy underwear. She still had to use a belt to make sure the skirt wouldn't fall down. When she put the cardigan on and flat old lady's shoes, she looked quite old as long as I didn't see her face. She put on an old dark gray scarf; even tying the scarf under her neck didn't hide her pretty young face. The dark material made her even paler, but she had to retrace all her soft lines on her face with an eyebrow pencil and kind of rub it in. While I admired her old lady look, she commented that probably the hardest thing for a young woman was to make herself look older. But we have to get that rat at the embassy.

She took a large black purse, put the camera in, along with three sandwiches, and we were ready to go at seven forty-five a.m. Since we had plenty of time for the less than an hour long public transportation trip, we started to fool around like an aunt and nephew. She was amazing how she walked, slightly bent forward, making her look at least fifty-five years old. She started to have fun with her looks, as people were very courteous to the old lady, letting her on the bus ahead of others and offering their seats. I grabbed her arm like she needed support, and we smiled all the way to the cemetery, seldom talking in public, as her voice imitation of an old lady was not up to par. In fact, a middle-aged lady scooted over to leave more space for the "old" Piri, who automatically thanked her for her kindness.

The lady commented that Piri had the voice of a twenty-year-old. I got off just one stop before the station by the cemetery, as we had plenty of time before the gates opened. We didn't want to arrive at the same time, and it was easier for an older person to get there before the opening than a young one early Sunday morning. I noticed Zoli was already positioned in the bushes where I waited for him last night, just diagonally across from the main gate of the cemetery. We let Piri go in first. I would follow, and then Zoli, most likely taking a big circle, would go under the huge weeping willow. I followed Hodos's steps, as the end of the row by the big, almost black, and tall headstone provided not only a hiding place but also fresh flowers, most likely placed there by Hodos.

I could not find any gardening tools, so I went to the northern fence consisting of a high and heavy hedge, cut a meter long dry branch, and sharpened one end just in case I need a tool. When I was walking back to the big stone, I could see Piri in the sixth row diagonally from the grave, where the pickup point was located. As far as I was concerned, it was dangerously close for Piri, not more than four to five meters from where the money roll was waiting in the vase by the foot of the headstone.

After I saw Zoli taking his position, I worked myself within two rows behind Piri, and when I was in line with her, I whistled like a bird and got her attention. I told her everything was in place, but I wanted to double check that the money was still there. She nodded, and I slowly worked myself to the pickup grave while looking around, and I had to bend down to check. The loose bouquet was still there, but the middle light-purple flower slipped down, possibly because of the heavy metal box on a drying stem. I had to reach in and find it, and the box was still attached. I decided to push the flower even deeper in the vase, giving more time for Piri to get into position and possibly take two shots while Béla was looking for the money box. As soon as she would take one shot, she must turn the opposite way and take another photo, like she was photographing the huge willow tree. We rehearsed it well ahead of time, so I was not worried about Piri's action in this regard.

I was really getting hungry around lunchtime, so I signaled Zoli, approached Piri, and asked for two sandwiches. She said, "I left my bag right by the second grave from me toward the escape route. There are three sandwiches on the top, take two of them and enjoy." On top of her dress, she was only wearing the scarf and the camera, as I found her folded raincoat also in the bag. I took two sandwiches and slowly circled the big willow, putting Zoli's sandwich on the stone bench where I was sitting last night. I put two hundred and fifty forint inside the sandwich bag, turned around, and went back to my observation spot. I waited in position until Zoli walked over to the bench, picked up his sandwich, and returned to his post.

Very few people came and went this semi-warm early fall Sunday morning and early afternoon. Last evening, I saw more people in an hour than all morning long. I looked for a spot where I could sit down and still see Piri and Zoli. I had to go one row back toward the main gate to find a high-enough stone monument to sit on while in sight of Piri and Zoli.

Piri was already sitting, and I saw her getting the last sandwich. She kept an eye on the entry of the fourth row while slowly eating her sandwich. We didn't take any drinks, so after eating, we went one by one over to the faucet, about twenty-five meters away, and we had to drink out of our hands.

We started to get discouraged, as the entire afternoon was gone and we didn't see a single soul coming our way except an old lady. She stopped by Piri to see if she was okay, as she was sitting there motionless for a long time. Both Zoli and I had an easy time to take care of our needs; Zoli could easily use the trunk of the tree to relieve himself, and I used the hedges behind me. Poor Piri had to go real bad around two p.m. When she signaled me, I thought the guy showed up, but the danger sign meant a bathroom break. I took over the camera with a very short training lecture, like point it and press the button.

I was nervous, as I felt uncomfortable with a beautiful, practically new, and very expensive camera. On top of it, we couldn't afford to buy one, nor could I afford to pay for professional training of any sort. Those days, taking pictures was more complicated, adjusting for different films, having to estimate distance, light conditions, manually setting the aperture, and advancing the film. I was praying Béla did not show up while I was handling the camera. I was too nervous to take such an important shot. It seemed like an hour, but she was back in less than ten minutes. She came back a different way, but I could not tell why.

At twenty minutes to closing time, I was ready to give up, signaling both Piri and Zoli to cut, but they shook their heads. A cold wind came up, and a cloud covered the setting sun. I could see Piri adjusting the camera to handle the lower light condition. She stood up, and in the corner of my eyes, I noticed some movements from where Zoli stood. His whole body was visible, and his cap was off. He had a direct view of the front gate, so I took off my cap for Piri. Piri stayed sitting down, and she had the same angle Dora had yesterday, but much closer to the headstone.

I finally saw Béla, neatly dressed in a light-gray suit tailored in a European style. It was double-breasted jacket with a light gray, almost white, shirt underneath and a bright silver necktie around the collar. He was hurrying toward the vase. Emotions and an urge to jump out took over me. I wanted to grab and torture him to death for killing my best friend and the brother of my sweetheart and the many others we lost, but that wasn't our mission.

As soon as he passed Piri, she stood up, lined up the camera, and waited until Béla bent down, picked up the flower stem with the metal box attached, and took the picture, the final evidence showing Béla's profile with his hand in the cookie jar. I was standing behind the high headstone, invisible to anybody looking toward me in the fourth row, but I could still see Zoli and partially Piri. I took a peek down the row, and my finger moved to push the button on the camera when Béla pulled out the stem with the money box.

Béla lifted it closer to his face like he wanted to smell it, and that was when I heard the click. I could see Béla freezing and slowly looking around, first toward me, and then I heard the second click, with Piri standing up holding the camera in the direction of the willow. Béla eased off, took the metal box, and as he was putting the money in his side pocket, I heard the third click. I looked, and Piri was turning toward the willow when Béla took a hard look at her.

Béla dropped the small round metal box in his side pocket, then headed toward Piri. My heart was pumping as never before as I ran toward both of them. I saw Béla reaching for Piri's head and grabbing the scarf and pulling it back. Piri automatically turned around and faced Béla, and right behind him, I was running toward them. I could see the forced smile on Piri's face as Béla took a second to examine her face. I could not hear what Béla said, but I could see his left arm swing to grab the camera.

Piri stepped back, and Béla missed catching the leather strap and case.

He raised his right hand to hit Piri, but I was already there to grab his hand by his wrist. He tried to pull his arm out while backing away, but I swung to his side, putting my other arm under his elbow, bending it backward.

He was ready to scream because of the pain, but instead, he hissed like a snake and tried to hit me with his left fist. I pulled him to the ground, and when we both ended up sitting in the dirt, I pushed his head into the soft dirt on top of the next grave and kicked his face with my knee. I shifted my position and put my knee on his throat when Zoli arrived. I asked Zoli to get my sharp stick to kill him. Béla was just hissing, but louder, like a huge python. I was amazed how much stronger I was, both in holding him down and tripping him earlier. There was no way Béla was trained as a spy, just experiencing his soft and weak muscles.

I looked up, and Piri's still and motionless body was standing about two meters from us; only her head was turning left and right, indicating disapproval of our current plan. Zoli showed up with my sharp stick, and I was ready to thrust it in his throat when Béla shook his head, obviously wanting to say something. I eased up with my knees so he was able to talk.

While waiting for him to get some air to his lungs, Zoli said, "Why make him bleed? Just put your weight on his throat and let him suffocate."

The dirty rat wanted to buy his way out by saying he had a lot of money on him and could get us more if we would let him go. There was no way we would take Judas's money from this miserable lowdown character. Without waiting for Zoli's response, I started to put pressure on his Adam's apple, but he quickly turned his neck and said, "I'm a Jew, so you cannot kill me."

I automatically asked, "Why?"

His answer was, "We pay back every crime against us tenfold."

I remembered what Lara said about her own kind, "eye for a tooth," but I was ready to break his spine when Piri spoke up, "Maybe we just need to teach him a Christian lesson."

I asked, "What, just let him go?"

"He won't do us any more harm," said Piri.

Béla seemed very pleased about Piri's comment and said, "She is right.
Just let me go. Christians teach tolerance and forgiveness."
I thought again about what Lara said, We cannot forgive, as we cannot forget. We heard the main gate closing, and I eased up on Béla's neck.
We three stayed there motionless for a few seconds. Béla showed no sign of wanting to get up and run. Finally, Piri said, "We did the right thing."
Zoli turned toward Béla and said, "Run, as we will be after you all night. If we catch you, we'll kill you."
Béla got up sheepishly and ran toward the main gates. We knew it was already locked, and we also knew how to get out. While heading back, we wondered how Béla spent the night in the cemetery, but we felt proud of not killing him. We hated him from the bottom of our hearts for selling out many Hungarians to the Russian KGB or the Hungarian secret police (AVH), including my good friend and the brother of Piri and Zoli, Sándor.
We knew the embassy would take care of him for good once we turned over all the evidence and our hands would stay clean.
Piri bent down, picked up her scarf, and put it on. I noticed the difference.
Even in the twilight, I could see her face getting much older looking with the scarf on. Did Béla recognize her without the scarf? I wondered and worried.

In retrospect, I consider my inaction to be my greatest failure in my entire life not to have killed him right then and there. I know I'll feel this way for the remainder of my life, but I don't know how I would feel if I had killed him.

Kele D. Gabor

Dangerous Game

Zoli got off at the bus station and pocketed the second roll of film. Piri and I went toward the bridge so we could go across and escort her home.

An uneasy feeling came over me, and Piri asked, "What is wrong?"

I said, "I have to meet Zoli tomorrow and discuss a lot of things before I can tell you my concerns."

Piri insisted that there was nothing left to worry about. I said, "I sincerely hope you are right, but wait until we have the films developed and make copies. What if some of the pictures didn't turn out to be the caliber required by the Western justice system? Zoli has both rolls, but no pictures yet." As soon as I uttered those words, Lara appeared again in my memory, and I saw her as she said, "People seeking truth and justice are dreamers, like you. We have to acquire power, money, and force— that is what's real."

When we were close to the pub, she suggested turning back the empty camera to Bandi before going back to her room. I suggested she change before we do it.

She said, "I forgot how old I look now."

I said, "I noticed you don't drag your feet or hunch your back anymore.

You're starting to look and move like a young lady in old people's clothes."

She ran up the stairs, and I after her. She headed for her wardrobe, started to strip all her old-looking clothes off. When she finished, she asked what to wear. I said, "Stay the way you are, as you look very good, especially if you wash your face." She put her gown on and left me standing by her armoire. I opened both doors and looked at myself in both mirrors.

I looked okay from the front, as I had pretty much cleaned the dust off after rolling in the dirt, but my khaki-colored pants were green and black in the back. I must have rubbed against some vegetation, so I took off my trousers and started to rub the dirt out with a small towel when Piri appeared.

She said, "You also look good without your pants on, so let's celebrate our intermediate success." She poured a full glass of brandy for both of us, lifted her glass, and said, "Now this is for us, our happiness, and may God grant our wish."

I responded with, "Health, money, love, and a long life to enjoy it." We both took our time sipping the brandy and admiring each other until we emptied the snifters. She took my pants to the restroom to wash them. I asked her to wait until we returned the camera. She responded, "The camera can wait till tomorrow, and you have to stay until your pants dry." I said, "It may take all night."

"That is the idea. We are finally paying back the evil ones for their terrible deeds. We have the proof to lock them up for a lifetime, and now we can forget our sorrows and think about our future and happiness." She could see I was not in the mood for anything, so she said, "After we eat, your smiling face may return." She then started to put food on the table.

My recurring thoughts were on what Lara had said. What if Béla, the double agent, recognized her with the scarf down, as she had only changed her hairdo to a bun?

As soon as she set the table, she left the room, returning with two bottles of fine beer. "I found out from Zoli you really appreciate good stuff, and that may be the reason you love me too," she said. I smiled and opened the bottles, as it went very well with the soft cheeses and salty ham. She finished before I did, so she came around to my end of the table and gave me an even better massage than I did for her last night. Her hand touched all my pressure points, from the face, across my forehead, scalp, my neck, my shoulders, my spine, and my back. When she finished, she thanked me for protecting her from that evil man, and I felt like I lost all my worries and the weight off my back.

After the relaxing massage, Piri asked to go to bed and rest up for next day. I followed her lead.

I had the best sleep of my life and woke up more refreshed than I could ever remember before. She apologized for putting a stop to a fully pleasurable night, but she promised to make it up on our honeymoon. I said, "I cannot get married yet, as I still help my family until my younger siblings can also help out."

Piri said, "I understand, but in the meantime you and I have to be satisfied with the limited intimacy we had last night."

I smiled and said, "I'm willing to make the same sacrifices every night or any time until we marry."

"I'm happy to hear that, but what happens if I lose my head and get pregnant?"

I assured her I loved her too much to let her down. She continued, "What if we both lose it?"

I suggested slowing down, and also the fact that I cannot come up to the city as much as I want to should help a great deal. I added, "You can tell your mother and brother I plan to marry you, and I'll come and ask your mother's permission before the engagement."

She was visibly happy to hear my comments and said, "I know my mother will be happy to hear that, as she likes you very much."

I mentioned that mature women like me more than young girls, and I asked her not to say anything to any friends outside of her mother and Zoli until I finished getting rid of the embassy employee and his helper working for the KGB.

We finished all the remaining food we found. I had an unusually good appetite.

I arrived at the office just about ten minutes after eight in the morning. I hurried up to my small temporary office. This time I had both keys, which was a good thing, as Hodos's manager was not in yet. I sorted all thirteen map copies made and found three on the same scale among them and two other pairs with matching scales. I decided to work on the easiest first and rescale the two pairs to match the latest ones I found in metrics.

By ten o'clock, I had seven maps on the same metric scale. I decided to take a break and see Hodos. However, just as I was opening my door,

Hodos was coming in through his manager's door. I invited him to my office, asking him for an update.

He said, "You know everything. You should be updating me." I asked what he wanted to know. Hodos asked, "How did the shots turn out, and were you happy with our performance? Did we get all the evidence we want?"

I responded, "You and Dora did an outstanding job, and it will result in catching the persons responsible for turning in informers like us, and as you know, with dire consequences.

"The films are being developed as we speak. Zoli is handling it."

"No wonder you are in love with Dora, and we cannot blame you for being jealous and protective of her, as she is a strikingly beautiful and attractive lady."

Hodos's lips almost reached his ears as he smiled and asked what their next assignment would be. I told him we had to lie low and wait until the guilty parties were behind bars. He got up, saying, "I can't wait for that," and we parted company.

I ran down to the map archival place to talk to Henry. He welcomed me, so did Shari. It was a slow Monday morning, so we sat down in one of the vaults and talked. Shari told me about her Armenian ancestry and how her parents escaped the Turkish extermination, how the Kurds fought to preserve their freedom, and how the Western big powers divided their countries, as they divided most of Hungary. When I thought the ten minute break was over, I looked at my watch and was surprised to see that almost a half an hour had gone by.

I excused myself and ran up the stairs. Both Hodos's boss and my office doors were half-ajar. I hurried in, and Peter was looking over the maps I was working on. Peter had the habit of walking in unannounced or without knocking and just appearing out of thin air. He always wore soft-soled shoes so one could not hear him coming. Peter said as I walked in, "You do a good job. Why don't you transfer to my department? I could double your salary."

I said, "I sure appreciate the offer, but my family is down south, and I still have to help them financially."

"I can just about solve any difficult problems, and so far what you mentioned are all minor issues for me."

"What would you need me for?" He said, "I'm not sure, but everybody seems to like you. You have a good rapport with everyone, but I'm always fighting an uphill battle with many of them."

"I don't believe you, as I've depended on you since you have more clout and power than most of us combined."

"I know I have political power, but not necessarily respect. You have a lot of respect, but very little or no political clout, so we would make a good team."

"I will definitely think about your attractive offer, but you could get the same things accomplished with some management and sensitivity training."

He responded the training he was getting from the party was all he needed. I appealed that if he wanted me to work with him, we would have to listen to each other and be in accord.

Peter responded, "We can work together better if one of us is the boss, and it has to be me."

I tried to argue with him that teamwork is different from authority over a servant, but he claimed the best teams have a leader. I agreed and said, "It is true, but that leader has to be selected by the members, not appointed by upper management or delegated by the party.

Peter said, "That is democracy, and I prefer socialism or communism."

I was thinking again about Lara's comments, how good it feels to be important, and having power over others, thanks to the Communist Party.

I told Peter I would get back to him, and if I didn't, he was welcome to call me any time. I turned toward my newly drawn maps as Peter was leaving.

I rescaled two more maps, leaving four for Tuesday. The way I figured it, I could head back with my consolidated map on Thursday. However, it would be nice to delay my return as late as Sunday so I could be with Piri over the weekend. It was late afternoon when I called my branch office and asked to talk to my boss. He was away from his desk, so I left the message with his secretary to pass on that I could be finished on late Thursday, but I would like to delay my return to Saturday or Sunday so I would report to our regional office on Monday morning. She was a very efficient secretary, and when I would compliment her, she would say, "It's your director's fault, as I'm a mean woman, but my boss keeps me in line." Most of us knew that wasn't the case. He was the best boss I ever had; his staff and the entire organization felt the same way and would fight to keep him.

I was heading out of my office just past quitting time when the secretary came back to tell me my boss was on the line for me. She stayed in my little office looking at the maps I was working on while I went to answer the phone on her desk. My boss called me back, wanting to know if I had run into difficulties or just wanted to stay a few extra days. I told him that the latter was the case. He said, "If you hang loose, enjoy yourself, and don't go near the office, I will authorize your stay to return next Monday." I thanked him, and then he asked if I had a new girlfriend or was it still the same one. I responded I had met two exceptionally attractive ladies and I wouldn't mind spending some time with them. He said, "You should have a third one for backup." I thanked him for the advice, as it reminded me of my grandfather's motto: "Always keep three lovers until you marry."

I had to hurry in order to meet Zoli at an earlier time. He advised me that a change was in order, just in case. Zoli was already there, looking very somber, and I asked him why.

He said, "We have to rescue my sister. The more I thought about last night, the more I believe that rotten guy recognized Piri."

I said, "I got the same impression." I asked for the films and pictures.

"This is another complication. My friend who has a photo lab cannot work with color films. On top of it, we don't know when Al returns, and I don't want to involve the new guy, Roger, from the embassy. They have not found a traitor among themselves for over three years." He added, "We must get Piri to safety ASAP." I agreed.

We set in motion a new plan to get Piri out of harm's way. The plan was simple, with only the three of us involved. Piri, Zoli, and I would find a hiding place for Piri and tell her boss, Bandi, she was terminally ill (we picked leukemia as her illness since it would be quite believable because of her paleness and weakness recently). Zoli, as the brother, would tell Bandi, and I would transport her to the hiding place no later than tomorrow.

Zoli felt strongly that transporting her back to Eger in their old home where their grandfather used to live would be the best, as she seldom had gone there and she could be introduced to the neighbors as someone taking care of the old lady, her grandmother. If push came to shove, I knew of a walled-up place in the cellar no one could find. It was the hiding place for my grandfather and his important papers. She could come out at night, as the courtyard was totally enclosed, and I could supply her with all the necessities, as I would often visit her, and I was no stranger in the neighborhood.

Zoli added, "Ideally, I alone can handle her, but this time to persuade her to go, I may also need you, as she can be stubborn."

I said, "Let's not wait any longer. Go now and get started."

We took separate buses, and I went ahead, as I had the key in case she wasn't at home on her day off, Monday. The knocking didn't help, so I had to unlock the door. The extra wax I put in the lock mechanism before helped, and it took little effort to move the tumblers. The apartment owners were still up, so I carefully walked to her room and looked around. Everything seemed to be in place.

I started to search for suitcases where we could put her stuff. I found two large suitcases under and behind her clothes collection inside the huge wardrobe. I started packing the stuff I knew was hers. I carefully folded her dresses and placed them in the smallest suitcase, as she had a limited number of formfitting clothes. I also found a place for her high heel shoes, she only had two pairs, but I left out her tennis shoes. They would serve her best on the long trip with heavy suitcases. Her sets of underwear easily fitted on top.

I was on the second suitcase when Piri appeared and was happy to see me until she saw what I had been doing. She said, "It looks like you want to get rid of me."

I responded, "If that's what it takes to keep you safe, yes."

Her big blue eyes seemed to get bigger, and she asked, "Is Zoli okay?"

I told her why Zoli and I had agreed on this course of action. "We know the son of a bitch recognized you when he pulled down your scarf, and we have to move you tonight." She got pale, worried, and then asked, "How about you"? I responded that we were fine, only she was in danger. "Béla knows you and who you are and where you work." I told her Zoli was at the station getting her ticket for the midnight express.

She said, "We have to leave some of the things behind. I won't be able to carry more than two suitcases and my big personal bag." She took over the packing and pointed to the small bag on the table and said, "We might as well finish eating it, as I cannot take it with me. By the way, where am I going?"

I told her what Zoli and I had agreed on earlier. "He didn't want to tell me, but you'll find out once he gives you the ticket at the station."

While she packed, I asked her if I could return the camera. She said, "I already did and told him I would go out for a date with him, but he didn't believe me, as I was too beautiful and sophisticated for him. I told him that I will keep my word and we'll have an enjoyable date together." She then asked how the film turned out.

I told her Zoli's contact could not develop color films or make color prints. "And he gave me the two rolls, as he wants to accompany you to a safe place."

"I understand all the good intention, but I'd prefer you come with me."

"I cannot, I have to finish my work here, but I'll visit you very soon."

By eight thirty, she had everything mostly packed except the food on the table and her brown outfit she had worn the previous day. I had already put the brown outfit into a paper bag, and I volunteered to dispose of it.

We heard a quiet knock. I knew it was Zoli, so I went to greet him after opening the apartment door for him. He said, "I only got one ticket, as I didn't have enough money." I asked how much he needed while reaching for my wallet. He said, "At least one hundred, but would be better to have two hundred." I took out one hundred and fifty forint and said, "It is all I can spare until I pick up my pay tomorrow or get a cash advance."

Piri was already by the open door and hugged her younger brother while asking why Kele could not come with us. Zoli said, "I wish I could get rid of him," while winking at me. "He has a tendency to screw things up unless somebody holds his hand."

I told Zoli right there, "I agree with you as long as not you but Piri holds my hand."

She turned toward me, gave me a brotherly hug, and then kissed me on my lips.

Zoli objected, "What is going on behind my back? Have you become kissing cousins? Wait until I tell my mother on you two." Zoli was a big teaser, so we just went along with his funny remarks. He looked around and said, "I have a few things to pack, and I'll meet you by track four about eleven forty-five.

She said, "Not until we eat all the food I picked up for us," pointing to the table. Zoli said, "I have to go down and take care of one more thing.

I'll return and eat all the food you two leave me."

From the sad expression on his face, I knew he went to talk to Bandi, telling about his sister's deadly disease.

While we ate, Piri started to cry.

How terrible it would be until I could come to see her, and if I didn't show up soon, her heart would stop beating. I reassured her I would do my utmost to see her every time I had an opportunity. She was still sobbing when Zoli returned. Zoli pushed me aside and started to eat.

Piri went out and brought back two more bottles of beer and said,

Kele D. Gabor

"These are the last two, you guys might as well finish it." I opened the bottles, and we obliged her by drinking it all after she took a sip from mine. While we drank, Piri asked about notifying Bandi.

I responded it was already taken care of, and Zoli commented, "I told Bandi you are very ill, and he said he knew it, as you were very pale, and he saw you when you passed out once in the storage room." Piri responded, "That was very nice of him to say, but I didn't pass out.

I just lay on the cot and immediately fell asleep."

Zoli left only crumbs and took the heaviest, not the largest, suitcase and left after giving me a hug. Piri sat down and wrote a note for the people who subleased the room for her. The note said, Due to family illness, I have to leave immediately. She had enjoyed her stay, and after recovery she would like to return. She looked up and asked, "How long do you think I have to hide?" I said, "The wheels of justice may turn slowly, but I estimate two to three months unless the KGB gets actively involved."

She put a PS on her note that it may be four to six months before recovery so they should feel free to rent the room out.

She picked up her diary from under her pillow and dropped it into her bag. She looked around, lifted all the blankets, checked around the washbasin, and said, "I'm ready," after wrapping the nearly new bar of soap in paper and dropping it into her bag. She looked again in her huge wardrobe. I noticed she left behind the three or four old lady's dresses. I asked her about them, and she said, "They belong to the people here, and I hope never to have to use for them again."

I opined, "We have plenty of time, but the sooner we leave this place, the better off we are."

We arranged so I would carry the two suitcases and she would carry her bag, purse, and the paper bag containing the old clothes she wore the day before. I had already picked up the suitcases when she said, "Wait." She pulled out the middle drawer on the lower side of the wardrobe, and from the back, she lifted out a bottle of my favorite brandy and said, "Put this on the table in your place, and every time you see it, you can remember me."

I said, "You take it with you so when I show up, you can offer it to me, as I would rather have a picture of you instead, as I could keep that in my wallet close to my heart all the time." (Hungarian men carried their wallets in the inside pocket of their jackets).

She put the bottle in her bag, pointed to the door, and said, "I'll send you my favorite picture via Zoli. Let's go."

Before I turned off the light, I looked around just to make sure. The only thing on the table was her letter with beautiful handwriting and a spare key she made for me. When we left the apartment, she locked the door from the outside and slipped her own key under the door. It was only about ten o'clock, so we walked slowly to the nearby bus stop and got on the next one to take us close to the railroad station.

Once we arrived at the waiting room, I had her sit down to watch her suitcases, and I left with the paper bag to find a suitable dumping place for the possible incriminating clothing Piri wore at the cemetery. I left the station and went around an electronics store, where I dropped the skirt into an empty box. I went to the other side of the street, and behind a furniture store, I dumped the cardigan and decided to leave the shoes for someone to use. I placed the nearly new shoes in an empty shoebox

I found behind the shoe store. I checked again that, in fact, I did a good job cleaning them and made them look like new. The shoes were like a new pair that had been tried on often. I left them by the back door in the box without the cover on, looking like somebody accidentally threw out a good pair. The pair of black stockings found their way to the garbage can by the ladies' bathroom door in the station.

The scarf I smelled and carefully folded it and put it between my chest and shirt, buttoned my jacket, and went back to her at the waiting room.

She said, "I was really worried about you, so I hid in the dark side of the waiting room, expecting only Zoli back. I figured out where we are going, as I checked the track assignment. Number 4 track will take me south, but I don't know the final destination."

I said, "You should know Zoli by this time. He never lets us know until the last minute."

We went to the designated track around eleven forty-five, but Zoli wasn't there. It was the last call, but no Zoli. I was concerned he had been arrested, but it didn't seem likely, as he was superb at what to do when it comes to hiding or getting away from KGB or AVH agents. I decided to wait. As soon as another train pulled out, we saw Zoli on the other side by the fifth track previously covered by the train in front of us. I jumped over the tracks and bawled him out. We could have departed on the wrong train.

He said, "I was hoping you would, and I would have brought you back down this side, so it looks like you're taking a train south."

I said, "We're overdoing it."

"I learned from my grandfather you can never be too careful."

We got up on the right train, and I waited to get off until it started moving. I hugged Piri, but I could not tell her anything, as she was crying on my shoulder.

I went back to my official temporary place very late and could not get to sleep for a long time. I was sure Piri was safe, but I was worried about Bandi too. If Béla recognized her, he would tie the two together.

Bandi took the first picture in the pub, and the same camera was used in the cemetery.

I woke up very late Tuesday morning. I was late getting to the office, but nobody said a word except the two security guards who said, "Good morning, comrade," with a salute. I started to work on my maps but could not concentrate. I needed to talk to someone. Before I even started with my work, I had to take a break. I wanted to talk to someone whom I trusted.

I walked by Hodos's desk and waved to him. I went to the hallway and waited. Hodos came out, looked both ways, and came to me asking, "What is up?"

I said, "I need to clarify a few things with you and also want to use you as a sounding board."

"How much time do you need?"

I looked at my watch and said, "At least ten minutes."

He grabbed my arm and said, "Let's go to your cubby hole."

I went ahead, followed by Hodos.

I told him our efforts might have been compromised. He jumped up from the chair where I had him sit before and said, "We had nothing to do with it. You have to look elsewhere."

I corrected myself, indicating I had no intention to implicate him or Dora. I just wanted to make sure everyone involved was safe and stay that way.

Hodos said, "Just tell me what is bothering you."

I said, "I cannot without compromising others. Why don't you tell me who do you know who were involved in this operation."

Thinking, Hodos started to give names. "Dora, you, Zoli and me for sure, and on the enemies' side, the thin black-haired Jewish boy, the Russian lady, and a Russian guy with the missing eyebrow in the car. If your contact Al is involved, I would not have known."

I asked what Dora knew.

"Dora knows me, you, and from the other side the young Jewish boy, the Russian lady, and the guy who took the ribbon from her."

"You mean Dora doesn't know Zoli, Al, or anybody else?"

"Definitely not. I wouldn't expose her to more than I would absolutely need to."

"Dora is safe, and so are you."

Hodos asked who wasn't. I told him no one he knew and we had better leave it that way. I thanked him for his help and told him to take good care of Dora.

Hodos stood up and said, "You were right. I should not have involved Dora. She is constantly pestering me to get new assignments. She really enjoyed the work and wants to do it again, but I'm afraid for her safety.

Could you help me discourage her from dangerous work?"

I replied, "It's probably the danger part that turns her on. She probably enjoys reading spy novels."

"You're right on." He turned around and left without saying a word.

I rehashed in my mind everything that was said and not said, coming to the conclusion that if revenge was what Béla wanted, he could hurt us by doing harm to Piri and Bandi, but Zoli should be okay. The rat never had a good look at either one of us, so the other team members should be safe. In addition, we could have been just protecting a lady but not involved with taking pictures of him.

I went back to working and finished one more scale conversion, leaving only a few for the afternoon. For lunch, I went to the milk bar. My young lady friend with the rosy cheeks was there. She was waiting on many people, so I waited until most of them were gone. It seemed like she attracted all the clients with her sweet smile and helpful attitude. When my turn came, I asked if she could heat me up some milk or offer her hot tea to me. She laughed and said, "I remember you coming in one early morning, looking real hungry."

I asked her what would be a good time to come back when I could talk to her. She told me her shift ended about three p.m. and I could come around the shop waiting for her by the back door. She was too young for me, so I hoped she didn't think I had a date in mind. I asked for a buci, a small round-shaped hard-crusted bread (resembling a shepherd's bread) and a medium-size bottle of plain yogurt. After being served, I sat down in the corner and consumed it. I felt good, and I promised her I would return around her quitting time.

I went back to the office and finished one more map before I headed down to the archives and asked Henry to cover for me for an hour or so.

He said, "Fine," and went to lock up one of the reading rooms where I was supposed to be if anyone was looking for me.

I headed out the door, and as usual, I was saluted, but without the attaché case no checking was necessary. I got to the milk bar a little early, and I saw the second shift of two middle-aged women entering from the back door. I must have waited there fifteen minutes before she showed up. She came up, and I introduced myself and asked her name. She said, "My name is Liz, but my friends call me Zizi."

I was very straight with her so there was no misunderstanding about my intentions. I actually needed to talk to her father. She raised her eyebrow and asked, "Why?"

I told her a story of my younger brother who was an amateur photographer, and he recently died when hit by a streetcar. I would like to see the last few color pictures he took. He liked nature but sometimes made studies of human characters in action.

Zizi felt sorry for me and asked if I had his films. I said, "You told me your father has a photo lab. Why are you asking me for the film?"

She said, "I help him all the time, and I need to see the films to find out if we have the right chemicals to develop them. Some of the color films require special chemicals."

I reached into my pocket, producing two rolls of film, one Agfa and the other Ektachrome. She said, "I guarantee we can do the Agfa, but I'm not sure about the other one."

I asked how much would it cost, and she told me a pretty high price. I told her I could not afford it, so I would wait until the development would be cheaper or have extra money. She looked at me with sad eyes and said, "Why don't you give them to me, and I'll bring them back tomorrow, but only the negatives."

I told her that under no circumstances would I let them out of my hands since they represent something special from my brother. She thought about it and said, "Come by tomorrow about the same time, and by that time, I will find out if my father can help you." I thanked her and headed back to the office.

By Wednesday morning, I only had one map to transcribe, which I finished before noon. I packed my stuff together, cleaned up the office, rolled up the maps, and went to get a cash advance of one thousand forint, as I had authority to stay until next week. I went down to say good-bye to Henry, and I hugged Shari. They were sorry I was leaving but asked me to drop by any time.

I had a large roll of maps the security guards checked thoroughly. They signed and stamped the accompanying permits to take the maps with me while apologizing for doing their job. Each map I made had to have a release paper and a stamp for me to take them out of the building. While they looked at the maps, I wondered what they thought about me, as anybody could tell they were more afraid of me than I was of them.

I went again to check on Zizi. She told me her father would do it for me, and she handed me his address. I ate lunch in the milk bar, and then I went to see the photo expert with my prized possessions. The man was surprisingly trusting toward me, considering he was running an unapproved and unlicensed photo lab in his house. He told me only foreigners or rich Communists used these expensive films, so they all came to him when they wanted something done professionally.

I asked, "You mean you operate a black market shop with the full knowledge of the communists, and it is okay with them since you are the only one who does a professional job?"

He said, "I'm not the only one, but you got the idea. As long as it serves them well, they do tolerate us, even if it is against the party philosophy or rule." He led me into part of his lab, took the films, and disappeared behind a door.

About fifteen minutes later, he came back saying, "One roll is full of pictures, but the other one only has a few, and would I like to see them."

I nodded yes, he turned around, and I followed. He led me into a red-lit room with similar coloring as we had in one of the vaults in the map archival place and then another room that was almost totally dark. It took me minutes to adjust to the much dimmer red light. He put one of the rolls into an enlarger and started to show me the images on the white surface and said to tell him which one I would like to have a print of. I said, "All of them." He said that would cost me ten forint per print. I said it was okay.

Kele D. Gabor

I figured there were less than thirty pictures, so three hundred forint was well worth it. He ended up making duplicates of seventeen prints, but he only charged me one hundred forint.

Some of the shots with the telephoto lens were unclear because of the movement of the camera, but overall, the quality and the details on the prints were a pleasant surprise. The drying time was longer than I had expected, so I had to stay a little longer than I wanted to. I was very happy about the results, so I was eager to show it to Hodos, Zoli, and Piri. Of course, I was upset about Al not being at his post and available to receive the undeniable proofs of illicit activity by one or more of the embassy employees.

I put the pictures in two different envelopes and the two rolls of developed films in my inside pocket. I headed back to the office to find Hodos.

I left my attaché case and the roll of maps with the security guards so I didn't have to put them through another uncomfortable situation in searching my personal stuff. As I handed them my case for safekeeping, a wild idea came to me. I asked them to take out my thermos, as I'd like to take some hot coffee along on my impending trip late this evening. They put my case on the counter; I opened it and took out my empty thermos.

I hurried upstairs and found Hodos reading his photo magazine at his desk. I had to rush by him to get his attention and indicated I wanted to see him. This time, I didn't wait for him in the hallway but slowly made my way to my little Room, Twenty-three A. I waited at the entrance of the boss's room until Hodos saw me opening the door.

Only the secretary was there typing a letter. I welcomed her back, greeted her, and asked about her temporary job with the bridge division.

She said, "I was happy about it. They selected me as the most accurate typist.

You know, those guys go overboard on perfection."

I congratulated her on being the best, and then Hodos showed up. He asked, "Where is the boss?"

The secretary said, "He just stepped out and will be back in a few minutes."

I said, "Hodos, while you wait for him, why don't you come into my office, as I have something to show you."

He opened the door for me. I guess he figured out why and was anxious to see the result. I opened up the conversation quietly and stated that their action and execution of the assigned job was commendable and started to line up the photos in order on my table. I turned the light on, covering all the photos with a map just in case Peter G. walked in unannounced. One by one, Hodos reviewed each picture they took, and I followed his movement, as this was the first time for me to really examine each photo closely.

I could see Hodos's big smile coming on as he said, "We have to show this to Dora."

I replied, "She would be safer if we tell her a lie." Hodos looked at me funny, so I continued, "The sequence of the photographs indicates without a doubt there is an exchange going on among at least three individuals.

If for some reason you, I, Dora, or Zoli gets interrogated with that new Czech-made truth serum, it would help Dora to know that none of the photographs turned out good as a result of faulty film."

He said, "Okay, but she will be upset after all the effort we put into it. I will tell Dora we did a good job, but the film was faulty, and the white lie should work, as it's happened to us before. The only thing we were not sure about was if it was really a faulty film or an error in development."

We heard someone coming in, most likely Hodos's boss returning, so I quickly put the pictures together and into my pocket. I put the map back on the table and was showing something to Hodos when his boss stuck his head in and said, "I thought you were gone, but I'm glad you came back.

Hodos already asked me for your little hideaway once you were gone, but I wanted to check with you first."

I said, "It is fine with me as long as I can have the place back in case I need it."

Hodos said, "Of course, but I would like to have an even larger drawing table."

His boss said, "Okay. When you leave, give Hodos the key." He turned toward Hodos and said, "I still expect you to check on our troops on the floor at least every two hours."

I said, "I already left the key on your table with a thank you note."

He responded, "Fine, Hodos, please stop by to pick it up once Kele clears out."

Kele D. Gabor

I told Hodos to leave. When he was gone, I cleaned my thermos completely, rolled extra toilet paper around the negatives, one set I had made earlier of an old map I ended up not using. I selected and placed the five best and most incriminating photographs in the map, rolled it up all together without the pictures touching each other, and carefully placed them inside my thermos. The inside of the photographs were turned inward, so the shiny surface of the picture never touched the map to avoid sticking. I screwed both caps back on the thermos and headed down to see Henry and Shari again. They were pleasantly surprised to see me.

I pulled Henry aside and told him that after I left, I remembered about the time capsule. It really tickled my mind I could have one, as I'd really like to know in ten years or less how technology would develop. Henry asked what size I needed. I said, "I would like to put my empty thermos, fountain pen, ballpoint pen, and maybe my pocket watch in it."

He went behind the vaults and returned with a shoe-size wooden box.

When he opened it, I saw the top hinged on one side of the box and an almost translucent rubber seal around the top. The inside had a kind of a gray velvety material glued all around. It reminded me of my grandfather's large chess box. He made out a label with my name on it, asked me for a code name, and I gave 'Piroska', the full first name of Piri. After filling out the label, he turned toward me and asked for how long. I asked, "What do you recommend?"

He said, "I or Shari should still be here in ten years." "Okay."

Henry put the label on to be opened in October eighth, Nineteen sixty six. Henry also made out a card and brought it back to Shari. She reviewed all the information that was a duplicate of the label glued on the box. She put the card in a long narrow wooden drawer like in the library. The drawer was labeled Nineteen sixty six, and she placed my card in alphanumeric sequence under P. She said, "If someone comes to claim your box, he must first give us the date to be opened and the password." I felt good about it and made a mental note to pass on the information to Piri and Zoli.

After Shari filed the card, she sent me back to check with Henry. When I arrived, Henry asked me to recheck the contents of the box, and when I nodded, he closed the top, making sure it was properly sealed. He put a wax seal where the closed top met the bottom part, put a ribbon around the box, and also put a wax seal where the two ribbons crossed.

He said, "Now we're ready. In which vault do you want me to put it?"

I said, "The right one, where we usually hang out."

"As long as the box is here, we will remember you, but we hope to see you at least once or twice a year anyway."

I thanked both of them, and I left with a happy face.

It was almost four, and I was hoping to catch the seven o'clock train that would arrive around nine at the town of Piri's hiding place. As I was exiting the office building, I asked for my stuff from the security guards.

They said, "You forgot the tea."

I answered, "Sorry, I dropped my thermos, breaking the glass inside."

They offered their own thermoses, but when I refused, they asked me to wait, as some people left thermoses they never claimed again. I knew it had to have belonged to some of the "informers" before the secret police took them away. I decided to accept one that had an aluminum cup on the top. They were happy that they could give me something, and I felt better equipped with the thermos cup that I often used to change my voice in case I had to make an emergency call to the embassy.

I went back to my flat, looked around, and picked up my already packed small suitcase. I left a note behind saying I wouldn't return, so they could clean the rooms for the next guy coming to the main cartography office.

As I made my way to the station, most of the buses were full, so I barely made the express train to see my love and perhaps Zoli to show them the pictures and update them on where to get the negatives in case something happened to me.

When I arrived in Eger, I had to go to the men's room, as Zoli instructed me. Behind the door, he would write the house number between two number signs in reverse order, and about a meter away, he would put the street name between two uppercase S. The street name was easy to find, but the numbers were so small I could barely make them out. I knew the grandmother's name, but not her husband's. Very few people knew the name of the person who headed up the Hungarian counterespionage during WWII. He was also the mentor, trainer, and stepfather to Zoli.

Kele D. Gabor

After exiting the station, I asked one of the porters standing near the main door where I could find the street. He seemed to be perturbed, so I offered him a ten forint as tip, which helped a great deal. It was in the old town section of the city inside the once strong castle walls and on the hill. With his direction and the help of the nearby church steeple, I found the street.

It was quite dark. Most of the streetlights were burned out, and the Communist government didn't much care about minor issues, like dark streets. The house was located almost on the top of the hill, and it was a good-size home with a tall brick fence around it. There were a few windows facing the street, so I selected one to knock on gently "OS," in Morse code, as agreed on earlier, on the one closest to the huge entry gate. I counted the seconds, like one hundred and one, one hundred and two, one hundred and three, etc. I was up to one hundred and twenty five, but no response was forthcoming. I knocked again the code, but much stronger. I was at one hundred and five when I saw the light come on inside the gate. I recognized Zoli's voice as he asked who it was. I told him as I was instructed earlier; I was a relative and had come to visit my great-aunt.

I heard the big key opening the door and saw Zoli's head emerge between the cracked door and the wall. Zoli looked in both directions and pulled me inside. He said, "My grandmother is already asleep, and Piri is taking a long bath. She had no idea of your early surprise visit."

I asked him not to say anything, to make it a real surprise. Zoli said, "All day long, Piri was talking to her grandmother about you, and she is in love with her future husband."

I didn't respond to his comment. I just asked if they had enough room for me to stay. Zoli jokingly said, "We have no room for you unless Piri is willing to take you in for the night."

I said, "Please, no joking right now. I just want to see Piri and show you the result of our so far successful endeavor."

Zoli wanted to know and see the results of our operation, but it was my turn to give him a hard time. I said, "I first have to go to the toilet."

He escorted me in the long hallway, where the last door to the right was my destination. I knew we passed the bathroom because the light, steam, and noise were filtering through the cracks on the door. I hurried up. After relieving myself, I washed up, combed my hair, and came out refreshed.

DECEPTION AND REALITY- LIVING THROUGH THE MISSING PAGES OF HISTORY

I came back to the room where Zoli had taken me first, and he pointed to the other side where a tray stood with my favorite brandy and two empty glasses. Zoli said, "Piri put it there this morning and said, 'Nobody can touch it, as it is reserved for Kele and Kele only.'"

I said, "Let's play a trick on her. I'll hide in the next room. You pour out two glasses full and set them on the center table." Zoli obliged, and when we heard the bathroom door open, I walked to the next room, taking all my belongings.

I could hear her coming down the hallway with her slippers going by the room but stopped when she saw the bright light and Zoli by the coffee table. She looked in and noticed the bottle in the middle of the table with two glasses full of brandy. She raised her voice, saying she really meant to save that bottle for Kele.

Zoli said, "Come in. We'll have one drink for Kele's health before you go to bed."

She seemed to accept the invitation somewhat reluctantly. I peeked out from the doorway and saw her in the same blue gown she wore when we were together. She looked stunning, the long gown accentuating her shapely figure. Her dark hair, still damp, was hanging on one side of her shoulders, almost reaching her waistline.

She bent down to get the closest glass, raised it up, and said, "God help Kele and bring him to me."

I stepped out and grabbed the other glass, saying, "God granted your wish."

She dropped her glass right on top of a glass tray, shattering both the tray and the glass. She stood there for a few seconds and then started to cry. It took me at least ten minutes to stop her happy tears. I had never seen so many tears in my whole life in celebration of a happy surprise event.

It was close to midnight before things quieted down and I could show the pictures. They were elated. Zoli made a promise we would only do things like that again with a Two hundred mm telephoto lens. "It would have made our job much easier and less dangerous."

I told them I had duplicates made, and both the negatives and the five most incriminating prints were safely stored in a time capsule. They didn't know what a time capsule was, so I gave a quick explanation, but Piri didn't hear it. She was sound asleep on my shoulder. I finished telling Zoli how to retrieve the incriminating photos and the negatives from Henry, using Hodos as the only contact.

The next morning, Piri introduced me to a lovely petite old lady who was about half her size. She had thin, snow-white hair, light-blue eyes, and a round and pale face. When Piri left us, the grandmother asked me some very pointed questions, like why I loved Piri and what I found objectionable about her. After I made a list of both, she said, "You two will make a fine couple. The only problem I see is that Piri could not give me a list of your shortcomings." I asked what she meant. She said, "Piri is in love, and she thinks she found a perfect man. We both know there is no such thing."

I replied, "I'm surprised. She often tells me what to do, indicating I don't think along the same lines." I also told her that my parents taught us to find our weaknesses, as knowing them would give us more self-confidence.

I started to list my shortcomings. "Impatient, judgmental, quick-tempered—" "Stop. Don't worry about it, as she met you over two years ago, but so far she has seen only your good side."

"I'll try to show her my bad side the next time I see her."

She had a wonderful laugh, and I got embarrassed.

According to her grandmother, there are three kinds of people: pessimists, optimists, and realists. The realists usually don't know when to be happy or when to be sad, and they miss a lot in life, as they see the world only in shades of gray and tend to have no close friends. The pessimists are unsophisticated and miserable people. They cannot find all the good and things to be happy about. Healthy and well-balanced human beings are always optimists, especially during hard times, such as under current Russian occupation and Communist rule. She added, "Piri would be the sunshine in your life, as she can see in the ugliest caterpillar the potential to become a beautiful butterfly."

Piri returned with a tray full of goodies for lunch, and we ate and had a wonderful time together. I asked about Zoli and was told he took the morning train back to look over the situation. I said, "I brought some money for him to take care of his travel expenses."

The grandmother said, "Don't worry about it."

Without being asked, she offered half of her big house to us once Piri and I were married. She said, "The house was built in two stages. My husband added two more bedrooms, a bathroom, and kitchens just in case we had to hide people. I'll show you how to get there, as we have to go through a hidden hallway. It has its own entry place, which was walled up when the Gestapo was looking for my dear husband, but we left an emergency exit through a low window to the outside. It is at the back of the house and was used by some nice Jewish friends. Unfortunately, they didn't listen to my husband and panicked and left. They were recognized, arrested, and we never saw them again."

I explained to Piri's grandmother I was not ready to get married, as

I had some serious obligations to my family and I had not asked Piri's mother for her hand. She said, "It is Okay, as I would like Piri to finish college, but I just wanted to let you know that we accept you with open arms, open heart and open home." I thanked her. After her nap, she gave me a tour of the house.

Once Piri's grandmother lay down, she asked me to arrange a meeting with my family. I told her we were very poor and lived under very difficult political oppression. We lost everything during WWI and again during WWII, but once we improved our financial situation or our living conditions, she would be the first one I would invite to our place. I had a long talk with her about my mother's flight from Transylvania in 1921, my father's imprisonment by the Romanians in 1922, how our family escaped from both the Romanians and the Russians during WWII. I also told her about my father's defiance of the Nazi ideology, the German occupation, and the resultant political pressure and our short stay in a concentration holding camp. I also told her of my father's miraculous escape from the execution, the Communist interrogations and beatings by the secret police, our efforts to save our farm and how it was taken from us. I told her we had to sell everything in order to obtain enough food to survive.

As it turned out, she and her family went through similar situations, and only they were better off financially because they could keep the land and live off it. Both of her brothers and her mother worked very hard to stay alive and make ends meet. She considered it a miracle that the Hungarian secret police had not bothered them after Sándor's arrest. According to her, even Zoli could not find the reason unless Sándor died before telling them anything about the family's past. She went on that she and Zoli think her husband destroyed all the records, so the Communists never connected them with the previous government or with our Western contacts.

At about four p.m., we had hot tea with a piece of bread and jelly.

Kele D. Gabor

Then the grandmother took us on a tour. She had to be very trusting as she showed us the back of the pantry, explaining why it was so cool, and where the large shelf unit stood. It was also the entry to a separate basement.

From this basement, one could enter the other now empty apartment. I asked not to be shown everything, as we were still in a difficult, insecure situation. Piri wanted to know the passages regardless, but I talked her out of it.

Right after supper, Zoli appeared, smiling and happy. He said, "I went to each of our previous meeting places, even visited Bandi, and gave him the proof of a serious illness of Piri with appropriate medical forms and forged signatures. I spent a long time with Bandi, but no one seemed to be interested in me. Bandi inquired about Piri's health, and I told him this sickness is on and off until she dies. While I was there, all the patrons expressed their sympathy for Piri. She must have been very popular. They took up a collection for you so you can see your favorite ballet group from Moscow in the opera house before you get too weak from your illness.

Bandi has already reserved the best tickets in around the tenth row. So you may see a live ballet with Bandi after all and also satisfy your obligation for borrowing his camera, sitting with him in very expensive and, by our standards, unaffordable seats."

Piri got real excited and started to worry about what to wear. She wanted to know how much time she had. She wanted to make herself a proper outfit to attend this elegant gala event. I could see her excitement and enthusiasm about seeing her first real ballet from a premium seat. She said, "I hope Bandi can rent or find decent evening wear for this occasion."

Zoli said the tickets were for next Saturday evening, starting at eight in the evening. She yelled, "I still have eight full days to get ready."

I was jealous, but after seeing her genuine excitement and how much she wanted to see an actual performance by world-renowned stars, I gladly agreed when she asked me if it was OK.

While Zoli ate, the grandmother disappeared. I asked Piri and Zoli where she had gone, as I had not bid her good night. They looked at each other, shaking their heads, and then Piri went after her. They both returned smiling, and Piri called me over, as she wanted to show me something.

She pulled me all the way to the kitchen to see what she had in her hand. She flipped the light on, and in the palm of her hand was a very shiny object, like a pure gold coin, it reflected the bright lights right in my eyes. She said, "I got it from my grandmother for a new dress, but I told her that instead I would like to make my own and save this for you and me later."

I asked, "How you can sell this? Owning gold is a crime."

She told me Zoli had a contact where he could get cash for it any time.

When I confronted Zoli, he told me that in emergency they did sell, but not more than a one per year.

I said, "If you have access to them, why did Sándor sacrifice his life, putting all of us in danger, and possibly ruin all of our lives?"

Zoli said, "The place where I get rid of the gold is on the black market, and when he found that it actually goes into the hands of the Communist Party leaders, he would not let us use up our inheritance from our grandfather."

"I understand and hope Piri never has to convert it to money and make our enemy rich in the process."

I started to get uneasy. Selling gold or anything on the black market was very dangerous, and I didn't want to expose Piri, Zoli, or anybody else to serious prison terms. I told Zoli we had already been exposed because Al was gone and if Piri got into trouble, I would not know how to deal with it. I also told him every girl I was ever in love with I lost under very difficult circumstances, and I could not deal with losing Piri.

Zoli set me at ease for the moment by telling me everything looked good, that the coast was clear and that he had checked out everything before returning.

I asked, "How could you check out if these guys work with others? There is no way of telling who besides the two embassy workers are involved."

Zoli said, "I have my ways to find out or I feel if something is going on. It is like a seventh sense, unless…"

I broke the pause, "What do you mean by 'unless'?"

"Unless he has a sick mind and wants revenge. Any normal being would be really scared and would pull back out after an incident like being beat up in the cemetery. I know we scared the hell out of Béla, and he had a long time to think about it spending the entire night there. So the only concern I have is if he is vengeful and just wants to pay back."

I remembered Lara's assessment of her race, "eye for a tooth." I told Zoli I was uncomfortable until I saw the traitors shipped out from Hungary and had some assurance they were all behind bars.

Zoli said, "I even went back to the cemetery and reexamined the site and the particular headstone where the exchange took place. The flowers are still there, as we left them, and I took a translucent piece of paper, and with a soft pencil, I was able to decipher the name on the stone, Zukor, but the first name may be Peter or Petrov. All the Zukor clan migrated out of the country to America, so there is no connection but only a random and convenient location for the drop-off and pickup point."

I said, "I hope your instincts are good and you are right again. So far you have saved us a lot of headache, and if anything, you were too careful and took us through a lot of unnecessary safety procedures. Now, I may be just oversensitive because I'm in love with your sister and I don't want anything to happen to her."

Piri interrupted us. She came in with a dark-purple sweat suit that really looked good on her. With her big blue eyes and very dark hair, she looked like a beauty queen after the contest. She said, "I want to borrow my boyfriend to help me select the dress he wants me to wear to the opera." I asked if we could do that next morning, as it was getting late. She said while grabbing my left hand, "Come, and you'll be glad."

She took me to her bedroom with a large bed. Many family pictures were on the wall, and one of her suitcases was still packed. She pulled me to a covered table with a stack of old magazines. She said, "Let's look through to see what type of dress you like, and I'll make it in such a way you'll fall in love with me again." I argued it was impossible until I fall out of love first.

She sat down, and I stood behind her while she was flipping through the pages. My mind was somewhat clouded by her fragrance and the touch of her hair. I went closer and closer as I was examining the pictures. Finally I knelt down and kissed her on the lips. She then asked me to stop, as we had only looked through half of the magazines. She said that once we found something we both liked, she wanted me to take all her measurements.

I argued, with ulterior motives, that we should take the measurements first and then worry about finding the dress.

She went to the sewing box standing on a small table and retrieved a tape measure, handing it to me. Then she left the room and returned with a sheet of paper and pencil. She put the paper on the table and drew a beautiful girl figure from the front, back, and the side. She said, "Let's start."

I stood in front of her, grabbed her waistline, pulling her close to me, and gave her a long kiss. Once I let up my hold, she wiggled out and said, "No, I really want you to take my measurements."

I said, "Okay, but you have to tell me where."

"We can start on the top." She turned her back to me and said, "Shoulders."

I put the tape across her shoulders and said, "Forty centimeters."

When we finished, I called her my hourglass lady, divisible by ten, as all her measurements were in multiples of ten. Her waist was Seventy, her chest Ninety, her hips Ninety, her height One hundred and sixty, her inseam Seventy, her shoulders Forty, her neck circumference Thirty centimeters. If Zoli hadn't knocked on the door, we would have ended up in her bed in possibly a very compromising position.

However, after saying good night, we controlled ourselves, selected a pink formfitting dress, slightly below the knees, and a simple black belt with a deep cut in the back of the dress, making sure no one else could see more of her breasts than necessary. Unfortunately, I had to leave the next day, but I made sure I took the very last train.

The next day, the rains came and also my time to depart. It was my hardest good-bye, leaving my beauty queen, my soul mate, and now my only love behind. She and Zoli walked me to the station, and we were able to get a few private moments together, which we used to the maximum in touching and kissing each other.

If I could have seen the future, I know I would have changed it, and I would have stayed with her and never left her side. What would come, I will never forget as long as I live. I also had a hard time forgiving myself, and I'm not sure if I really have. I still miss her and often remember her with fond and loving memories.

Kele D. Gabor

Three Is My Limit

My mother was happy to see me after two weeks away from home. She would have fixed me anything for breakfast, dinner, or supper if we had had the means of getting the raw materials. Meat, especially veal and beef, were impossible to get, as the best cuts went to Russia, then to the Communist Party leaders, then export, followed by the occupying Russian Army, and at the end, the people of Hungary were given the morsels.

One way to short-circuit this was butchering your own animal. This was risky business, as penalties were stiff, and if it wasn't a chicken, duck. or a turkey, you ran the risk of being reported. Pigs particularly made a lot of noise before dying. Probably the hardest thing to come by was a young steer or a calf. Even eggs were expensive, so there were months at a time when the only protein we could afford were mushrooms collected by us, chicken or duck blood bought at the slaughterhouse. After living through two World Wars, occupation by primitive armies, political morons, and anti-Hungarian forces, my mother could make any food taste good. She still had some fresh duck blood when I arrived, and she treated me to a tasty midnight snack with a lot of onion and homemade bread.

My mother noticed right away that unlike last time, I had a successful and rewarding trip for a change. It took her a while to guess I was in love. She didn't ask about her until I mentioned I had seen Piri again and she looked good and she was very friendly to me. She asked how she was taking the recent disappearance of her brother. I told her she was working very hard to make peace with herself and could manage her pain, and of course the entire family was also suffering for the lost brother and son.

She said, "I remember when you spent a weekend with the family and you said how nice she looked, but when I asked if you were interested, you said no."

I responded, "Lara and I had a big disagreement and a falling out since that time, and I believe we split up permanently, so it was refreshing to see Piri again."

I could see her noticing the spark in my eyes when I talked about

Piri, but she only commented that she was happy I had found such an attractive and well-brought-up girlfriend. She also mentioned I should have not split with Lara. She thought we were made for each other, and she went on explaining that her strength was my weakness and vice versa; in other words, we complemented each other. I told her that Lara had sold her soul to the devil and she was a big shot in the inner circles of the mighty Communist executive committee.

My mother pulled her eyebrow up and said, "I know Lara has a good reason for joining and participating in the central committee. She would never sell us out."

I responded, "I hope you are right."

I showed her Piri's picture that I received as a going-away present. My mother was impressed and said, "I think you want to bring her to me soon, but my only objection is that she may be too attractive for you." Pointing to me and smiling, she added, "It's a good thing she lives far away from you."

I responded, "Piri and I fit together even better than Lara and I. I have never felt closer connections to anyone else. I feel in my heart that God made Piri for me. I think I could not love anyone else more or find a nicer girl for myself."

On Monday morning, I went to my office with a smile on my face and greeted everyone with a warm good morning. However, it was Julie, our office sweetheart, who noticed I was in love. She pulled me aside and asked, "Who is she?" I played the dummy and asked her what she meant. She smiled and said, "You know whom I am talking about. You don't have to tell me her name, but I have never seen you happier."

My boss came by and wanted to see me, so I excused myself and followed him into the office. As we entered, I smiled and teased our secretary about her new hairdo. She smiled back and let it go, but before I closed the door behind me, she said, "I see you're feeling better." I winked at her and closed the door.

My respected boss asked me how it went, and I told him it was great. I learned a lot, and accomplished even more. He responded, "I can see you are happy with yourself, and I want you to keep it that way."

I figured I would ask why he was so concerned about his people's wellbeing, as none of the other bosses seemed to care.

He said, "Happy people have happy wives, families, and friends and accomplish a lot more in life than people who are miserable. A person who cannot see or find the bright side of life usually ends up complaining a lot and is less productive. Instead of living a productive life, they become a burden to their partners and society. The realists at least accomplish a lot on their own but don't necessarily recognize the power of teamwork and usually do everything by themselves. To accomplish anything of consequence, one needs help.

"I also have some good and bad news for you. The good news is we can pay you a higher per diem due to your experience level. The bad news is I may have to send you out again to some godforsaken place to resolve a dispute between two collective farms."

I asked, "Why don't you send Charlie? He is more experienced."

"Just between us, you are a little better with people. In fact, I guarantee you'll not only make peace between them, but also make them good neighbors, maybe even friends."

My boss was good at delegating; he always added a challenging mission or goal. This way, one would have more freedom and self-confidence to use one's God-given talents for the benefit of all concerned. Most of all, he let us make decisions, trusted, and supported us. He was great in assigning jobs that challenged rather than discouraged us. He could assess our abilities to the fullest and give us encouragement to achieve our best by showing appreciation when we deserved it. He was just about the most perfect boss anybody could have. Even the less talented or difficult employees would just about do anything for him.

I went back to the office I shared with several colleagues, but usually more than half of them were away working in the field. Only two of them were left behind in the office, and one of them was already on his way out to help the forest department with dividing the logged areas for planting different kinds of saplings. I told my departing colleague that our boss should have sent me instead. He teased back by saying he would have liked my assignment last week, as he heard it was a piece of cake.

Julie came back and asked for us to spend the lunchtime together. I happily agreed, as she usually managed to make one feel even better in the process. After I laid out my maps, I was thinking there was no way she could make me feel better, as I was in love with a beautiful, smart young lady with a beautiful voice and a lot of talents from a fine family.

Before I went with Julie for lunch, I transferred half of my copies to a new map, indicating the meandering of the Tisza River and its known flood zones.

It was too cold outside, but we found a private niche in the conference room, where Julie asked me to show her Piri's picture. Since I was so proud of her, I could not wait to show it, especially to someone who really cares.

Surprisingly, she first looked at the note, To Kele with LOVE from Piri. Julie stated, "I have never seen more beautiful calligraphy, and she is even more beautiful than her handwriting."

I said, "You should see her heart, mind, soul, legs, and her figure. You would be amazed."

"I can see all that in her face. The sparkle in her eyes showing her intelligence, her maturity level, her bright spirit, but I cannot see her true complexion on black-and-white picture or the halo that truly reflects her strengths and life force. In any case, she is too beautiful for you. I have to meet her, as I see something very special in her." Every comment she made also made me even happier than before.

I added, "Piri let me touch a piece of heaven. Every time I touch her, I hear heavenly music, like the Grand Polonaise by Chopin."

Julie smiled and said, "It looks like you found the perfect partner for life and wife to be. Don't lose her, but I must meet her to get to know your soul mate."

"You can meet her very soon, I hope. I already know and feel in my heart, in my mind and in my soul that she is the one and only one for me. I have been in love twice before, but this time, it is even more real."

In the afternoon, I finished the map consolidation, but the map ended up looking too busy to clearly see the shape and pattern of the river for the last four hundred years. I tried different colors, but more than seven layers on top of any map made it hard to read. I ended up splitting it into two maps, just to make sure about the clarity, and took it to my boss to review.

He looked at both consolidated maps for a long time, examining them very carefully. He finally said, "Good work. We can file it for the flood control engineers to have a history of the river flow, and it may even be an important document for future generations. Next time somebody goes up to the main cartography office, these two maps should be copied, and your originals should go to the archives for filing and to be cataloged."

I thanked him for the acknowledgement of my efforts. As I turned around, he halted me. "Stop."

I turned back and asked, "What is wrong?"

He said, "Just wait a minute."

He got up from his chair and went to a large map storage unit in the back of his office. The light-gray unit was about one and a half meters square and about chest high, with many drawers. He said, "These contain aerial photographs, and as I remember, there was one or two made of the same region in the early 1940s. Your consolidated map reminded me of having seen it." Sure enough, in a few minutes, he produced a black and white enlarged photo and the negative of the same area, including a large part of the Hungarian territories now given away to Yugoslavia.

He said, "This map was made for the benefit of helping to select archeological sites for potential excavations." He laid both of them out on the large drafting table by the windows. He got a magnifying glass and started to show me how accurate the old maps were, as some of the meandering of the riverbed was clearly traceable on the photographs just by following the lines of vegetation and size of the trees. Even the old floods and mudflows showed its contours, either in the vegetation or geological features.

I said, "I wasted my time, as this map is even better, more accurate than what I created after all that work."

He said, "It is true these two maps even show more details, but photographs are hard to keep for a long time, don't show the history, and to be honest, I forgot about these until your map reminded me of seeing something similar. These photographs are also politically incorrect, as it shows the remnants of old Hungarian settlements all the way to the Vaskapu (Iron Gate) of the Danube, now located between Yugoslavia and Romania."

"How can you tell what the old Hungarian settlements are?"

"I'm not an archeologist, but I remember identifying the sites. These photographs also show the differences between the layout of the settlements among nationalities, like placement of homes, cemeteries, common wells, garbage dumps, shape of dwellings, churches, marketplaces and parks, which were planned exclusively by Hungarians once the size of the settlement exceeded about one hundred homes. Most of these features are even easier to see in the color and shades of vegetation. Those archeologists can usually tell the age of a settlement by the shading shown on the photographs."

He then proceeded to show me with the magnifying glass the sometimes barely visible but always clean geometrical lines on the ground. There were many, and he knew what most of them signified; i.e., well, cemetery, walls, garbage dumps. I told him I knew a knowledgeable archeologist who showed me how much one could tell just by digging in old garbage dumps. The archeologist had shown me broken toys carved out of bones, broken clay vessels with decorations, all indicating the culture and the level of advancements in art, the primary food they consumed, and the general living standards. For example, Hungarian waste sites contain more broken toys than any other nationality, indicating the importance of family and children's education in Hungarian society.

We would have been there all night, but the secretary knocked, saying she was leaving for the day. My new assignment was to make the copies for our files of the maps I just finished and get the originals ready for hand delivery to the map archival place. My other new assignment was to compose a letter in draft form for my boss to approve, making the request to the appropriate ministries for authorizing aerial color photos of most of Hungary and the surrounding areas for aiding archeological explorations.

I was busy most of the week with exploring my newfound interest in relating maps to archeological sites. The earlier challenging assignment never materialized, as one of the feuding collective farm's leaders was arrested for stealing, and peace quickly returned between the collective farms.

I had to work, as most people, on Saturdays, but I waited in great anticipation of Piri's impression of the first live performance by great Russian artists at the opera house by Monday morning. I told our secretary on Saturday I was expecting a very important call from my friend Zoli on family issues, so even though it was not business related, I would like to have her interrupt me regardless of where I was or what I was doing.

She smiled and said, "I have a feeling that after you answer the phone, your friend will hand the phone to a young lady."

I said, "I'm happy to see good news also travels fast."

Kele D. Gabor

"Everybody knows by your exceptionally happy face that love is in the air."

All weekend long, I could not think of anything else except Piri's happy face and beautiful blue eyes as she enjoyed her dreams come true— seeing the live performance of the world famous Bolshoi ballet.

I was upset that we didn't have a phone nor Zoli or Piri's grandmother.

According to the itinerary, Zoli would take Piri to his small flat Friday evening, and then escort her to the pub to pick up Bandi and from there to the opera. Monday morning, they would call me, and that day they would head back to her hiding place until I turned over the incriminating photos to Al and we had his assurance the traitors were out of our country and preferably already behind bars.

I had a restless night both Saturday and Sunday, waking up often, but could not figure out why. In my dreams, I saw a bright light with a voice calling me. It was weird and frightening.

On Monday morning, I hurried to the office just in case Zoli decided to call before eight o'clock. My expectation was that Piri would be eager to share with me her experience. I could not concentrate on my work, as

I kept an ear open for the phone ring, which would bring me great happiness by just hearing her lovely voice. Finally, just after nine o'clock, the secretary called my name. She didn't even have to raise her voice, and I was there in seconds.

I said, "Hello."

Zoli responded, "I need your help immediately. Take the next bus or train, let me know which, and I'll wait for you by the station."

"Is it your idea, or Piri's?" I could hear in his voice he was not well by the shaking and raspy sound, like he was fighting a cold or tears. I said, "I insist you stop joking and put Piri on."

Zoli started to cry. I got the message— something terrible had happened to Piri, like some accident. I said, "There is a ten-ten a.m. express bus heading up, and I should be there before noon." He hung up the phone.

Without suitcase or warm jacket, I headed out of the office while telling

the secretary to notify my boss and my family I had to take an emergency trip to the capital. Before I could leave, my boss stuck his head out and said, "You might as well take the designated maps to the main office for filing and travel on our expense." I ran back, picked up the two originals, which were already rolled up in a carrying case, and left running.

On Mondays the express bus was typically full, and I wanted to be there in time to get a seat close to the door. I ran the two-kilometer distance and got lucky. I was told that because of the expected storms, very few people decided to travel, so a few seats were still available. Luckily, the secretary handed me some cash as an advance just as I was leaving; otherwise, I would have arrived penniless.

I got a seat closest to the exit sign to be first getting off the bus. All the way up, I was wondering about what could have happened to Piri. I was inclined to think the taxi Bandi used to take her had an accident with a streetcar or bus that usually resulted in serious injuries. She must be badly hurt; otherwise, Zoli would have put me at ease. My nerves were shot by the time we arrived at the outskirts of the capital. On the third bus stop, I would get off, find Zoli, and find out what happened.

When we got close, I could see Zoli standing at a nearby lamppost, looking for me. I almost left the maps on the bus until the driver reminded me of my package. I got off first. I hurried toward Zoli by the post. The closer I got, the darkness around his eyes became more visible, and his pale face was showing great grief and exhaustion. He wore a dark-blue suit, but it was totally wrinkled and just hanging on him, as if a rag. He didn't even wave when I stepped in front of him. He just looked past me with very sad eyes and said, "They got Piri." Zoli was ready to spill everything, but this time, I was the one to stop him until we got to a safe place to talk by a sidewalk coffee shop.

I said, "If they got Piri, they will also get us. Did anybody follow you?"

Zoli said, "I don't know, and I don't care."

The double espresso arrived, and I said, "If we have a ghost of a chance to see Piri alive, we need to be extremely careful, so start at the beginning."

Zoli painted the following picture, and I didn't dare interrupt him. I just wanted to hear every word he uttered.

"We started from home, as we agreed, being very careful and always on the lookout, like I usually operate. She brought a small bag for her personal stuff, and I carried a medium-sized suitcase with her new pink dress and Sándor's suit that fits me well. We arrived at the capital in the dark and went straight to my flat. I hung up our clothes, and I gave her the only bed I had, and I slept on the floor. She was up first, as she was very excited about her wonderful night ahead. That is all she talked about, except she wished you had been there to take her to the opera instead of Bandi.

"We had a small breakfast, but a big lunch. She cleaned up and started to get ready at four p.m., even though we had plenty of time. She was meticulous about lining up everything, and all her clothes had to match.

She brought the small silk purse, black high heels, black silk gloves, shawl, her underwear, and a small gold chain she got from grandmother. She spent an hour fixing her hair, she put it up to look older, and I teased her a lot about looking older than you. She didn't mind what I said as long as I was willing to listen and answer questions about you.

"As expected, we were ready way ahead of time, but she wanted to show off, as she looked very, very attractive. In fact, I have never seen a more beautiful woman in my life. Based on our grandmother's advice, I took her down to a small photo shop close to the Margit Bridge. Even the photographer's wife was impressed by my beautiful sister, and they were pleased we selected them over hundreds of other photographers. Instead of one or two shots, they took an entire roll of film, with no extra charge, and even I had to pose on a few occasions standing next to her.

"They called us the perfect couple until we convinced them we are really brother and sister. It took an entire hour to get all the pictures taken with the poses they wanted, and then we took a taxi to the pub where Bandi was waiting.

"We arrived there early also, so we decided to let the taxi go, as we had plenty of time to wave down or call for another one around seven thirty. I opened the pub door for her, and nobody recognized her, not even Bandi. He turned to me and asked what we would like to have. Grant you, the lighting wasn't that great, but we walked all across the front of the bar and sat at the best-lit table. People started to stare at us, but Piri just smiled and absorbed all the attention she got.

"The new girl at the pub came to our table and asked what we would like to have, and even gave an extra wipe on the table. Piri raised her head and asked to see the bartender. She asked which one, as they were in the middle of a shift change. She said like a queen, 'I need to talk to Bandi.'

She disappeared, and a few seconds later, Bandi showed up neatly dressed but without a jacket. I watched him as he approached our table, and I could hear his brand-new lacquered black shiny shoes squeaking. Before he got all the way to our table, he recognized Piri, but not me in my new blue suit. Bandi just knelt down on the floor right next to Piri but could not talk, just admired her. Finally, Bandi found his voice, 'You're the most beautiful woman in this world.'

"Bandi got real nervous and took quite a while to fully admire her and then asked Piri if she minded standing up. When she got up, Bandi lifted her left hand, and facing the entire room full of patrons announced that this was Piri, whom he was taking to the opera to see the famous ballet group from Moscow. One guy in the back started to clap, and the entire pub followed. My sister, like she was the star in the theatre, stepped forward and gave a lovely curtsy. The applause became even louder, and Piri stepped back and sat down before the clapping subsided. I was happy, so was everyone else.

"Bandi excused himself and returned a few minutes later fully dressed, and he looked pretty good, as long as you weren't concentrating on his miniscule chin and long neck. He announced the taxi may be here any minute, so he would escort the lady outside. As the young couple walked out, every eye would follow. Bandi opened the door, turned around, and asked Piri to do the same, then he bent down toward the patrons and belched out a very loud 'Thank you for helping me get the best seats in the opera house.' His smile went around his head.

"I stayed until the front door closed after them; I got up and walked slowly out while watching the crowd. They were still under the spell, but one called out and was followed with loud agreements and toasts, 'Piri is our Cinderella,' from a waitress to a ballerina. I closed the door behind me, and I could see the taxi had already pulled away from the curb, heading toward the opera house. Since there was so much time left and I didn't have a ticket, I walked around looking at pretty ladies. Being Saturday night, good-looking and elegantly dressed girls were all around. I figured if I catch a movie starting around eight o'clock, it would finish at the right time, just to walk over to the opera and welcome them as they emerged.

"I just had to see Piri's face when the program ended. I figured that after they took the taxi to my place, I would just take public transportation to give them a few minutes of waiting for me, as I didn't give her my key purposely. I went to see a stupid Russian film, but the scenery was impressive, and afterward I just walked toward the opera house. It was eleven fifteen when I arrived there, and people had just started to spill out on both sides. I positioned myself in front of the main entry, where most of the patrons would come out to catch a taxi. The taxis were lined up, ready to pick up anybody with the slightest hint of arm movement.

More and more people came out, but I guessed they had stayed behind to maximize the full effect of the beautifully decorated inside, looking at the orchestra, meeting some friends, or just showing off. Piri certainly had a lot to show off, and I'm sure was the envy of many ladies attending this gala event. I was concerned about Bandi, how he would handle young, rich— had to be Communist— boys' advances toward Piri during intermissions.

Bandi may have not been educated or sophisticated enough to fully appreciate the ballet or the music."

I just about exploded trying to control my impatience, but I waited out the too much detailed-oriented report by Zoli. I wanted to be sure I caught things he might have not found significant about the disappearance of Piri.

"There were very few private cars, but a few state and embassy cars were either parked by the side or just ready and waiting close by, with chauffeurs inside. I must have waited there for fifteen minutes without seeing any sign of Piri or Bandi. Most people were gone, and even the taxis started to leave, as there was not even a trickle of people coming out. I decided to run across the street and check inside, as members of the orchestra were also leaving in the back. I went inside. Nobody stopped me or checked for identification. The janitor staff had started the cleanup process, and they figured I was a well-dressed young man just returning to pick up something I had accidentally left behind.

"I went and looked on the main floor. I knew they had premier seats in row seven. I went all the way down, but nobody was inside. I ran up the stairs in case they were up there to take one last look of this beautiful place, but the entire theater was empty except the sweeping people and two ticket collectors. I ran to the left, then to the right side, circling around the entire building outside, but found no sign of them.

"Piri promised to signal me before they stepped into the taxi. That is the reason I stayed so long at the front. I knew that kidnapping is a

Western crime. Only the secret police do it here regularly. I started to get desperate and lose control, then I started to investigate the right side of the theater, as their seats were closest to one of the exits there. On the gray stone by the curb, I noticed some fresh tire marks indicating a quick getaway by a vehicle, but it was not enough to go by.

"It was well past midnight, but I decided to walk the path a secret police car would take to the courthouse prison cells. I was very concerned, as something was telling me, and felt it deep inside that it is too little, too late. I remembered your comment about not trusting my report, but I thought you were just jealous about letting Piri go and enjoying herself with another young man. I should have listened to you.

"I went by a police station on Andrássy Street but was afraid to go in and complain, as the first place they call is the secret police headquarters.

I went all the way to the banks of the Danube. It must have taken me over an hour trying to listen and see any movements anyplace. A few times, I had to cross the street where young people were in embrace, kissing and touching each other in the darker side of the street or on benches in the park. I looked very hard for any clues or people who might have seen something. I presumed the secret police car might have taken side streets, so I tried to retrace the shortest way from the headquarters to the opera house, using no major streets.

"I was almost back at the opera house when I noticed a group of young people standing around a spot right by the plaza. I had to cross the street, and there I found about fifteen young people making a circle around a dead or dying animal. Before I got there, one of the guys asked me if I wanted to see a dead man. I hurried there, and right next to the curb was a well-dressed man's lifeless body, totally surrounded by curious onlookers. I asked to borrow a flashlight, which is a luxury item under communism. Instead, I got a box of matches.

"I went real close, and I heard a girl's voice saying, 'Look at the weirdo wanting to look at the dead man's face.' I asked if anybody had reported it to the police, but nobody answered. Then I asked if anybody had seen anything. One of the guys in the middle said he was behind the statue at the plaza when he heard a big thump, a car door shut, and a quick takeoff. I asked how long ago, and the answer was 'about an hour but could have been less.' The girl next to him said that it was only a half an hour ago at the most, and they were the first one here to see what happened. I asked her, 'Did you see the car?' She said yes but could not tell the color or make.

The boyfriend said that it was a dark-colored Pobeda (Russian made automobile used by the military, Communists, and secret police). When I got really close, I recognized Bandi's face, which was totally bashed in and almost unrecognizable, but I could tell by the small chin and the suit he was wearing.

"Surprisingly, his face was not too bloody, in spite of the big blow by a heavy instrument on his face. I lit a match, and I saw a gaping cut on the throat from the left ear, all the way past his Adam's apple. His main artery was cut, and no more blood flow was detectable, but one could see the big black spot underneath. I rolled him to his back, and I noticed something darker as the blood lying in the puddle. I lit a match, and it was one of grandmother's black silk gloves Piri has been wearing that night. I remember her putting them on large cups all night to stretch them to fit her hands. It was about four o'clock in the morning when I saw the police vehicle approaching. I stood back and watched. The police made a faint attempt to find out what happened. There were at least as many onlookers as before, even though half of the original spectators had already left.

"The police inquiry had fallen on deaf ears. Nobody answered. They picked up the dead body without any inspection, rolled him in a dark canvas, and three of them pulled the body inside the van. One of the policemen looked around with a flashlight but either didn't see the black glove or just left it there. I decided to wait to retrieve it. It started to get light before I could go there to take the glove without anybody seeing it. I shook off the coagulated blood and wrapped it in my handkerchief and put it in my pocket. I could not and didn't want to go home in case the secret police were already waiting for me. I also wanted to talk to you before I did anything else. I have not eaten, rested, or slept for over thirty-two hours. I headed straight to meet you."

I told Zoli there was no reason to blame himself because it did no good.

However, putting together our heads, we had done very well so far and we could save Piri. I thought I knew how. Zoli's eyes and ears perked up, and he just looked at me. I said, "Once we were able to save a priest and get him out of prison after long and hard work. Piri is even more important to me." I took Zoli to my temporary official place and asked him to lie down, as when I returned in the evening, I would need all his brainpower.

I headed to the Communist Central Committee to find Lara. Since I was not a member of the party, the guards laughed at me and sent me fishing. I tried the Ministry of Internal Affairs, with similar results. It was close to four in the afternoon, so I hightailed it to the central cartography office, and the guards recognized me, saluted, and I walked up to my little Office, Twenty-three A. It looked like Hodos had moved in, but I could not find either him or his boss.

I walked to the map room, and there was Hodos. He was explaining something to somebody, but I rudely interrupted him, saying I had a very urgent message for him. He saw my concerned look, so he just followed me to his new little hideout without saying hi.

I just told him, "Be on the lookout, as our operation has been compromised, but the agent arrested does not know about you or Dora." He thanked me for warning him.

I asked him to take the maps to be stored in the map archival place and handed him my package. I told him we should stay apart. If he must get in touch with me, he must call me at the regional office with the standard color code. "Red is danger, yellow is alert, green is okay, but instead of saying the color, leave a message or say of the appropriate object having the right color." I turned around, leaving him standing in his room, and hurried to see Peter G.

I knocked and waited for his secretary's response before stepping into the office. From the secretary's desk, one could see enough through the opaque glass to Peter's desk. It looked like he was on the phone. I told his secretary I was here on urgent business, so I would just like to wait until he got off the phone. As soon as he put the phone down, I reminded his secretary, who was busy rearranging her file drawer, that I must see him. Peter had the best-looking redhead in the entire building, and likely the best paid, but I didn't even bother looking at her gorgeous behind in a short and tight skirt when she was looking in her file drawer. She even complained I was too serious and didn't even tease her about the deep cut of her blouse. She even bent forward to accentuate the cleavage pointing just at the bottom of the V. I told her I was preoccupied with a very difficult problem. She commented I came to the right place, as Peter was the best problem-solver around there. She went to Peter's door, knocked, and stuck her head in while saying, "Kele is here to talk to you about some very serious problem."

Peter just yelled out, "Come on in."

I stepped in while unintentionally brushing against her, and she smiled at me, saying, "This is more like it."

Once I was inside, I closed the door behind me and went right in front of Peter's desk. While leaning forward and looking in his eyes, I said, "I need your help, even if you don't want to."

Peter asked if I had changed my mind and was ready to join him in his department. I didn't answer him. I just said, "I need to find and talk to a very big honcho in the Communist Party."

He said, "You are talking to one, and I know most of the big shots, but why don't you join us to get ahead so you don't have to always come to ask me favors? I could make sure, once you join, you would get advanced quickly, as we need some non-Semites we could trust, if nothing else but for show."

"I have to talk to Lara G. ASAP!"

He looked at me and said, "I can't even talk to her, and many a times I wanted to ask for a date."

"You are married and have a little girl."

"Never mind, it is just wishful thinking."

"How can I get to see and talk to Lara as soon as possible?"

He looked down by his feet, and I could see he was thinking. He looked at me real fast and asked, "About what?"

"I have known her for a long time, since she was a little girl, but I lost contact with her, and now I have some important news for her."

"Why didn't you just tell me you have something for her instead of needing to talk to her?"

"It is private, and I'm sure she would prefer it to stay that way."

Peter opined, "You probably have a message from the poor, miserable guy whom she left brokenhearted, but I know she will never go back to him."

"How do you know about that?"

Peter responded that any time someone approached her, she rejected any attempt, and her excuse was that she was already committed. I felt like telling him her commitment was not to a person but to a cause, but I kept my mouth shut. Peter offered a seat for me, and I took it. He took a small notebook from his attaché case and started to look through it. He kept turning the pages while looking at names and phone numbers. He was past the halfway point when he smiled and looked up.

Peter said, "Here is the private number for the minister of Internal Affairs. That should work— he knows Lara and all the right people in the central committee."

I asked, "How about a backup in case he is not there."

"Let's try him first, and we'll look for an alternate in case we need one."

Peter picked up the phone, but before he dialed, he asked what the message was for comrade Lara. I said, "She must talk to Kele about an important message for her at this number."

Peter, still holding the receiver, said, "This number is often monitored, as that is how we keep tabs on each other. The secretary's phone is better if you want to keep it private."

"Yes."

Instead of dialing, he started to explain, "The entire monitoring is meaningless, as we know which phones remain private, but this stupid system is one of the holdovers from the paranoid Stalin era, as he had trusted no one."

I just about screamed with impatience, and he finally noticed, so he dialed. It was a long time with many rings before someone answered the hotline. It was, we assumed, the wife or girlfriend. Later we found out that it was both; she was his girlfriend and someone else's wife.

Peter told her there was an urgent message for Lara G. and I must have her private number. After Peter impressed upon her it was an important and urgent message from Kele, she wrote it down. She took Peter's secretary's number and promised to pass it on to David, the big honcho, soon. Peter hung up the phone and said, "It's close to quitting time. Let me send my secretary home. You can wait by her desk, and I can also leave."

I stopped him. "Wait a minute. I don't know and I don't think I want to know David."

"If anybody calls, it will be Lara, as I know David has a direct line toher, and he owes a lot to her. David will make every effort to pass on your message right away."

"What if no one calls?"

"Then Kele doesn't impress Lara, or she is attending some very important meeting, which is unlikely considering the fact it is late Monday afternoon. Anyway, you will get a call, as Lara is very efficient in handling emergency situations. If nothing else, her secretary will leave you a message where and when she can be reached. If you don't get a message back by seven or eight o'clock tonight, go back to your place and be back here no later than seven in the morning, as Lara takes care of all her urgent business before starting a new work day."

"How do you know all that?"

"My father was a close friend of her father's. They hid together in Slovakia for almost a year. When I found out what happened to Lara's parents, I went to see her and saw how she operates. That is the reason she got ahead so fast, and her sexy looks were also a big help." Peter pushed me out of his door, got his jacket on, and locked his door while I sat down by his secretary's desk with a piece of paper and a pencil to plan out what and how to say my request to her.

Once everybody left, the place became too quiet. There were no ambient noises coming from people walking, talking, typing, or moving furniture pieces around. I felt isolated, as if I were in a crypt, totally blocked from any sound. The outside walls were over a meter thick, and with the double windows, not even the outside street noise filtered into the office.

I felt very alone.

I was praying for Piri and could not concentrate on anything else. I knew the only thing I wanted to accomplish was to free Piri from the hands of the devil. My hope was high, but I could barely hold back my tears when I thought about her situation. How she would act seeing an interrogation room with all the pain-causing instruments, who would be her interrogator, and would they just scare her like me or go beyond. I tried everything to make myself concentrate on finding another way out in case Lara failed me, but I just could not get my mind off Piri. I was thinking about the best scenario of the AVH (Hungarian Secret Police) treating her right at least the first couple of days, like the Gestapo, to get her to talk.

They must know Bandi was not connected; otherwise, he would not have been killed so fast. Or did Bandi start to fight to protect Piri?

Finally, I dreamed up some unrealistic, wild ideas of getting bulletproof clothes, a machine gun, and blowing my way in and out of their headquarters, freeing Piri in the process.

My dream was interrupted with a loud ring in front of me. Halfway into the second ring, I picked it up and said, "Hallo."

I could recognize Lara's voice as she popped the question, "Peter?"

I answered, "No, this is Kele, and I need to talk to you about a life-and death situation as soon as possible."

Lara said, "I could meet you at the Wörösmarty [the best and most expensive pastry shop in the capital; today it is Gerbaud, as it had been before the Communist state expropriated it] in forty minutes."

I asked if we could meet someplace else. She responded, "You know I have a sweet tooth."

I said, "Yes, but I cannot afford it."

"You'll be my guest," she said and hung up.

I arrived in less than thirty minutes, but I didn't want to go in until Lara arrived. Usually one needs to go in right away to reduce waiting time, but this early evening on a weekday, there were not many people around or in the waiting line. In a few moments, she arrived in a very shiny and black (Pobeda) automobile with a chauffeur. As soon as she got out, she sent the driver away.

Once the car was out of sight, I went to greet her and gave her a long hug. She didn't seem to mind, so it was an encouraging sign. She had a dark-blue lightweight custom suit on and said, "Let's go in, I'm cold." In the bright light, she looked tired and older than I expected after not seeing her for a few months. We were shown to a small table right between two large windows. I pulled the chair out for her, and she remarked, "You were born to be a gentleman, not a comrade." I didn't say anything.

Once I was sitting, I reached for the menu, but she reached over the table, grabbing my arm, and said, "Try their new Rigó Jancsi" (Gypsy Johnny chocolate mousse). I said I needed something hot. She said, "They make excellent hot cocoa or coffee au latte." I chose the hot coffee.

We had our order taken by a very thin, tall, masculine looking-lady dressed in a black uniform with white accents. It looked like they knew each other, as she asked if the chocolate mousse would be satisfactory. Lara said, "Bring two, and two hot coffees with cream," then the waiter left.

Lara said, looking at me, "You look terrible and worried, but I meant what I told you last time. I'm hurt too, but you have to deal with it the best you can. If you want to know where Father Tibor is, all I can say is he is safe, and my Russian suitor had to resign his commission. Even though Sasha believed you cut his hand off, he could not admit his failure against an untrained civilian like you at the hearing. You're free and clear."

I said, "I'm running out of luck with beautiful and smart ladies, as every time I meet one, I fall in love and end up losing her."

"You didn't lose me yet, but under the current circumstances we must go our separate ways."

"I accepted that, but it looks like I just lost another one, and I need her back badly."

"I cannot help you winning back her love."

"I didn't lose her love, but I lost her body; she was kidnapped two nights ago by the secret police."

Lara's eyes widened, then narrowed, and she sat quietly for a second.

"I came here to ask you to help me get her back. You were successful freeing Father Tibor. This should be much easier, as she is a small fry for the secret police or for the KGB."

"What does she looks like?"

"She is a little taller than you, dark hair and big blue eyes. She was at the opera last night with another man. They were both kidnapped, but the man's body was found in the gutter with his throat cut and face bashed in."

"This doesn't seem to be our secret police, as they dispose of the body a different way. It looks more like the KGB is involved and they want to send a strong message to someone."

"That is impossible, as this guy or girl was not involved with anything that may arouse suspicion. I knew her for over two years, and I heard her brother was involved with something, so they arrested him about four months ago."

"The girl must know something, or they would have dropped her the same way as the guy."

I think I was quoting Peter's earlier comment when I told Lara this must have been the residual paranoia of the Stalin era; they were suspicious of everybody. She thought about what I said and commented, "If you're right, I can get her back, but if she is involved with some politically illicit activities, it will be hard, if not impossible, to obtain her release."

I was thinking of the last incident in the cemetery, how short of a time Béla had to see Piri's disguise without a scarf. I said, "I'm sure there must be some big mix-up. She either shares her name with someone or she looks like someone else."

Lara said, "Kele, believe it or not, I feel hurt knowing you're already in love with someone else. I didn't realize I still have feelings for you, but if possible I'll make sure she is returned to you. How do I get in touch with you?"

I handed a telephone number to her and said, "This will put you in touch with my boss's secretary, and she always knows where I am."

"I should know something by tomorrow late afternoon or evening."

"I more than appreciate your help, and I cannot wait to hear from you."

"If I do this for you, promise me you'll never come to see me or contact me again."

"Why?"

"It'll be best for both of us."

"I cannot promise that, as you still are a very important person in my life, even though I'm no longer in love with you."

Lara pleaded, "You don't need to know, and I don't want you to know why, but that is the way it must be until I release you from this commitment." I would have never guessed then that she would try very hard in the future to return to me, but that is another story.

I asked her to give me a clue about what was going on. She said, "There is no way I can accomplish my vision, goals, and mission in life unless you totally release me in body, mind, and spirit. Please just follow my request."

I nodded that I would comply as long as I got Piri back.

After she paid, we went out together, and I asked for a last big hug. She didn't mind at all, and I held her until she asked to be released. She kissed me on the cheek, told me she wished the circumstances were different so she could fight to win me back, as she still misses me. We left to go our separate ways. I was relieved and started to relax. I was sure she would get Piri my love back soon.

I decided I should leave early tomorrow to get back in time for Lara's phone call in the late afternoon. I headed to my official state-supplied flat and found Zoli deep asleep with his suit on. I sat on the couch, and I also fell asleep. I woke up early with a kink in my neck that was worse than I had ever experienced. I started to massage it but could not get the pain to subside. While trying to put myself in a more comfortable position, I knocked over an empty vase on the table next to me. The clinking noise woke Zoli, and he was ready to soak up any news with hopes of a big success in bringing Piri back.

I told him a friend of a friend promised to look into Piri's disappearance or kidnapping and she believed she could win her release. As always, Zoli asked what the alternative plan was. I said we'd have to think about it fast, as I expected a call as early as this afternoon about the whereabouts of Piri. Zoli was smiling but still wanted to know what other options we may have. I told him he and I should think about another plan and exchange ideas ASAP. Since it was unlikely that I could come up to the main office for a while, I asked him if he could come down and visit me. He liked the idea, but he wanted to stick around to help Piri in case we won her release soon. Since I was already up, I told Zoli to stay here at my temporary place for a few more days and keep the room clean. Find a friend who could check out his little apartment in case the secret police were already watching it, and I would take the early-bird special home.

Zoli said, "I already figured out how to handle my apartment, but how long can I stay here?"

I said, "Until someone else needs the place, but if you keep the room clean, the janitor will definitely leave you alone."

"What will I say to my grandmother, as I promised her to be back no later than Thursday or Friday?"

"Let's hope Piri will be released before that time."

Zoli promised to keep in touch with me by calling the secretary as often as he could in order to provide information of any sort.

I was back in my office around lunchtime. I reported to my boss the maps were filed in the archival library under the category of Tisza River.

I was very anxiously waiting for Lara's call, and I was praying for Piri's safe return. I had an easy job to copy some maps for guides when the next land redistribution would come around. I hinted to my boss it was a very painful job of taking away land from the owners who had it in their families in some cases for over eight hundred years. Worse yet, it also took away their livelihood. I learned firsthand the Communist or Socialist approach to wealth redistribution like the land reform— taking from the hard working people and giving it to the lazy ones. When I complained to my boss, he said, "Just because you are more sensitive about justice than others doesn't give you the right not to pull your own weight." Sure enough, I was assigned to another "land reform" program in the Communist style the following week for redistributing wealth, but not to the poor, but for the Socialist government and their officials. I was happy I would know Piri's situation before I had to leave the office. However, I heard nothing from Lara on Tuesday, not even Wednesday. I was just ready to ask for a leave of absence again when Thursday afternoon the call came through from Lara.

She asked me not to respond, just listen. She told me it took a long time to trace the whereabouts of Piri because she was right the first time, as the KGB took her first, but they already released her in the custody of the local Communist State Secret Police. It was good news, as she either was found to be innocent, didn't know anything important, or she refused to talk. Once she found her, it would be easier to get some kind of solution such as an early release, as she had more clout at home than with the Russians. She promised to call me early next week. I responded I might be in the field, so I asked if she could give me a number where I could reach her. She declined and asked to have the secretary give her the new number where I could be reached. It was some encouraging news, but I still had not heard from Zoli. He was supposed to call me no later than Wednesday for an update.

I decided to go up to the capital and find Zoli over the weekend. Finally Friday morning, Zoli called, and I gave him an update. Zoli indicated his apartment was not being watched, but he was still staying at the state supplied flat for civil engineers. Zoli's biggest concern was about what to say to his grandmother and their mother, who didn't know anything about their ill-fated adventures. I suggested sending her a note that he had decided to stay for a few more weeks. I also asked him to retrieve all the photos that they took at the photo shop just before the opera, and if possible get the roll of the negatives, too. Zoli promised to take care of it and would also call me again soon.

My trip to the field was postponed. I received a draft telegram from the Hungarian military again, and I had to report the following Wednesday for testing.

Tuesday morning, I got a call from Lara that something was wrong.

The secret police did not want to release Piri, so she would have to go in person to talk with the head of the justice ministry. I tried to postpone my military-testing date so I could be in the office to receive

Kele D. Gabor

Lara's update. No excuse, true or not, could get me off the hook this time. I wished I were at the land-redistribution assignment, as that would have been the only way to postpone my military-induction testing.

After I passed the physical, they started the written tests, followed by the political interviews. Because of my profession, they assigned me to the artillery. I was to report for basic training and active duty starting in late November, about six weeks away. After the testing was over and I had my assignment, I went back late to the office to see if Lara had called. At my desk was a note from the secretary: A young lady called again, and I told her you could not be reached till tomorrow.

I was in the office the next day before seven in the morning, based on what I had heard about Lara's work habit. Before our secretary came in, the phone rang and I answered it. Lara said, "I failed you, and I don't know if I could ever make it up to you."

"What is going on?" I asked while my heart stopped beating.

"This is all I can say at this time, but if you come up and meet me this coming Saturday evening about seven o'clock at the same place, I'll take you to see her."

I thanked her, but she didn't respond. I figured that either someone was listening in or the line was disconnected. I started to worry and became very uneasy about these complications.

I was preoccupied about seeing Piri this coming weekend and could not concentrate or do any work. It was Julie who noticed my distress and came to help me. Regardless of how she approached me, I rejected her attempts. She gave up, saying, "I understand what bothers you must be resolved by you and you alone. I'll stay out of the way, but I'll be available when you change your mind or need me."

I didn't feel like doing anything, I just wanted to have my love back.

I skipped lunch, and it was a good thing, as Zoli called for an update. I told him I would be going up to see Piri this Saturday evening. I would be taking off from work early to make the two p.m. express to avoid the Saturday rush, and we could meet at the railroad station about three-fifteen p.m.

Zoli wanted to know more details, which I could not give.

I knew I'd need more cash, so I went to see another friend to borrow some money. He said, "You don't need to, as I have to get some trustworthy people together to help deliver sacks of corn around midnight tonight. They will pay us three hundred forint per sack, and we can divide the profit." I knew a lot of that was going on— stealing back from the Communist government what they squeezed out of hard working farmers and reselling it on the black market. Most people justified their actions because they were also victims of Communists taking most of what they had.

We met at ten p.m. and boarded a state-owned truck with a driver who worked for the state. He had stolen enough gas from the government to make the deliveries. We drove to the state-owned mill, where we loaded many sacks of corn with the help of the security guard who was hired by the state to prevent stealing while being watched by the state employees of the night shift, and we drove off to make the deliveries. Therefore, if anybody ever tells me that a state-run business can be an efficient, effective, or profitable operation, I would call them less than naïve.

We delivered to places where there was a large-enough courtyard to drive the truck in to unload. We finished before midnight, and I made more money in two hours than my monthly salary. I even bought myself a new raincoat with a removable warm lining for the upcoming winter, pretty earrings from a private party (black market) for Piri to show off her lovely long neckline when she pins up her hair. I even had some extra cash left over to give my mother. She promptly used it to buy suits and shoes for my poor brothers. Those new suits and shoes were the first they had received in the past seven years. Until that time, we only had hand-me downs and used clothing and shoes to cover our bodies and feet.

Saturday morning, I put on my best dark-blue jacket, cream-colored shirt, silver necktie, light-gray trousers, and black shoes to look neat when I saw Piri again. Everybody teased me in the office, but I ignored their well-meaning, facetious remarks.

At one p.m., I excused myself and headed to the station to catch the express to the capital city. Nobody tried to stop me from leaving three hours early, and nobody dared say a word. On the train, I could not sit still, so I walked around impatiently. I could not help noticing the young ladies' eyes, as at that time I was still a handsome man. They looked at me with both envy and disgust. I could tell some of them were thinking, Too bad, here is another young Hungarian guy who sold out to the Communists, having the money to travel in such a pricey outfit on a workday.' I could feel any approach by me to those young ladies would be rejected, regardless of how charming my attempts might be. I wish I could have yelled out, "I'm not a Communist and not a Socialist. I just want to look my best for the lady I love."

Zoli was waiting for me outside the station to avoid any unwanted eyes, and he was dressed up as he was when he took Piri to the pub. When we were sure no one was following us, we went into a coffee shop but stayed inside, as the cold October winds made it uncomfortable to sit on the patio.

Zoli said, "I picked up the pictures which were ready, but I didn't have enough money to get the negatives. They asked my permission to put some of Piri's pictures out for public view as advertisement. I agreed, as long as I get the negatives and the copy of the same size pictures they display.

They would not agree to the release of the negatives. They thought that at least some of the pictures taken could be entered in a photo contest." He opened his raincoat top and pulled out a flat paper bag full of the pictures and proofs.

I was more than impressed, and my chest swelled with pride, as Piri really looked stunning in most of the pictures. For some reason, Zoli was not as photogenic. One particular picture was just about perfect, showing her beautiful complexion, rosy cheeks, almost black long hair pushed to one side of her shoulder. Her big blue eyes, long neck, cute nose and part of the pink dress framed and showed off all her colors, including her beautifully shaped bosoms and her thick red lips. Zoli said, "I never knew or appreciated how beautiful she is." I took that photo and put it into my attaché case before Zoli could object.

Zoli looked at me and said, "As soon as I get more money, I'll get the same one in a gold frame. We agreed that was most likely the picture the photographers want to send to the photo fair and display in their shop.

I updated Zoli on Lara's report, and he wanted to come with me to see Piri, come hell or high water. It took me another hour to convince him to wait until the next day, Sunday, when we would meet in the church during the ten o'clock mass, unless I could see him late tonight. Since he still stayed at my official flat, I escorted him back, put my case down, and pocketed a few more proofs of Piri to show her off to Lara. I put the earrings I just bought for Piri in my jacket's inside pocket.

I again arrived early at the pastry shop, and Lara also came early with the same shiny black automobile. This time, she had an attractive medium gray warm custom suit on, with a light-yellow blouse. She headed straight to the main door, thinking I would arrive later. I waited until the car disappeared, and then I followed her. I caught up with her, and she was surprised to see me. I smiled, but she stayed very cool and serious. I told her she had sneaked in before I could hug her. She didn't say a word, but we got a suitable place in the back of the large eating area. This time, a young, attractive waitress showed up, and she also asked if Lara would like the chocolate mousse. Lara ordered two with two coffees with cream.

She told me right away we wouldn't be able to see Piri tonight, but for sure early tomorrow morning. She could see my disappointment, but I smiled and told her if we couldn't see her in person, we could admire her anyway. I pulled out the photograph from my pocket. I put Piri's picture right in front of her. She looked at the picture for a long time and then turned it face down and handed it back to me. I was eager to hear her opinion about my love, but she said nothing. I attributed her demeanor to her jealousy or hurt of losing me to a more attractive girl. The order arrived, and instead of her digging in the plateful of chocolate, she looked at me real hard. I asked what she was thinking. She very quietly stated Piri was absolutely beautiful and gorgeous. I was half-finished with my plate, but she hadn't touched her chocolate. She was only sipping her coffee slowly.

I asked her why the delay in seeing Piri. "Could we get her released soon, and could I bring her brother along, as he is also dying to see her?"

She looked confused about the three simple and expectable questions, so I asked what the matter was. She said she had to start from the beginning.

"Let's go to a more private place, as this one is filling up fast with the Saturday crowd."

A bad feeling came over me, and I asked, "Where would you like to go?"

She replied, "I want to take you and show you where I live." I asked her if she was alone. She said, "Yes." I responded that it might not be a good idea, as I really loved Piri and there was no way she could win me back. She said, "That should be least of your worry, just come along."

I picked up the tab, but she literally tore it out of my hand. I said, "Now I have the money. I insist paying for the treat which you so well deserve."

"But I don't want you to," she said while raising her voice.

I argued, "I have not seen you this angry since our night together in Father Tibor's tent."

She just walked to the cashier, left a one hundred forint on the table, twice the amount on the bill, and turned around. "We must go now."

She went ahead, and I followed. As soon as we got outside, she called a taxi, waving her hand. I saw the taxi pull up in line where we were walking to the edge of the plaza. I opened the door, she climbed in, and I followed.

I commented, "I find your behavior very peculiar, what is wrong with you?"

She started to cry. I was confused. I hugged her and pulled her close to me, but she pushed me away. I was not paying attention to the address she left for the driver, but I could see we passed the St. Margaret Bridge, heading toward the Hill of the Roses, an exclusive section of the capital that had been taken over by a lot of Communist leaders. I tried to break the ice and commented she had good taste for picking a place to live. I got no verbal response, but she stopped crying.

The taxi pulled up to a three-level building, not counting the basement.

She insisted on paying, and then I got suspicious. I jumped out and opened the car door for her, offering my hand for assistance. She accepted. I could see a faint smile of thanks on her face as her body brushed against mine while getting out of the taxi. She went to the main door, where a guard in a civilian suit jumped from the side and opened the door with gusto, saying, "Good evening, comrade."

As we entered on the main floor, she turned right and pushed the elevator button. I started to laugh. There was no elevator working in this city since the Communists took over, especially on a three-story building. Before I finished my comment, the elevator came down, the doors opened, and the light came on inside. I was amazed. She pushed No. 3 on the display, and up went the elevator. Inside the elevator, she stated we could not talk while in transport, as all taxi drivers were working for the secret police and they communicate with radio to headquarters as soon as they noticed or heard something suspicious. I showed surprise. "I didn't know that." I let her out first, and she opened her purse, took out a key, and inserted it in her front door, right across from the elevator. When she opened her door, I insisted she go in first. She flipped the light switch on, and I found myself in a good-sized entryway festooned with coat hooks, decorated with mirrors, lights, arrayed with a small armoire, umbrella holder, and a shoe rack. All pieces were made of hard wood resembling cherry or mahogany.

On the left was a well-equipped kitchen, and on the right the toilet. In front of us was a glass door leading to a living room.

I hung up her raincoat along with mine in the hallway, and we entered almost together into the living room. The living room was exquisitely furnished with dark walnut furniture, which included a lot of hand carved decorations. The couch was deep, dark reddish-brown fine leather, with matching love seat and chair around a large marble coffee table. There was one door on each side, and I had to presume one of them led to her bedroom.

She offered the leather chair to me. She went to the liquor cabinet, took out two brandy snifters made of lead crystal with fine cuts and decorations, and took a bottle down from the shelf and poured two doubles. I could smell my favorite brandy— apricot.

She brought over both, handed me one, and said, "We both need this."

I responded, "I won't drink until you tell me what is up with Piri and why you were so evasive answering my questions."

She said, "As you wish." and she emptied the entire glass, hinting that I had gotten her started on this brandy. I drank about half of it.

She sat down right in front of me. She looked at me and started. "I didn't have the heart to tell you, but I did get her released, unfortunately too late." I dared not interrupt when she talked about Piri.

"Starting from the beginning, I inquired about her locally, but our AVH had no knowledge of her. I went to see my friend at the KGB, but it took some time, as he was out of town. He is a colonel, but a reasonable guy, especially with me. When I told him about Piri, he said yes, one of his men believed she was somehow involved in passing secret information to the West. The agent told us where she worked, and we sent over two of our agents to find out as much as they can about her. Our guy at the Western embassy recognized her, so we set a trap by getting her and her boyfriend the best seats in the opera, and from there, we brought her in for interrogation, but we think there was a mix-up, as she knew nothing.

Kele D. Gabor

"We didn't want to release her until she had recovered from our interrogation, but also we didn't want to keep her here any longer. I signed the transfer for her to be taken to the Hungarian prison for a temporary stay. We seldom do it that way, but after looking at her, she impressed me as innocent and an exceptionally attractive young lady. The actual transfer took place late Saturday afternoon. She was received by one of the Hungarian guards, as the captain was not there at that time."

I interrupted, "What did the KGB do to her that she needed recovery time?"

"The colonel showed me the signed copy of the acceptance of the prisoner.

I can only assume the KGB used the 'under the nail poking' to get her to talk, and those nails do get bloody and infected most of the time."

I shivered just hearing about and imagining her pain. I remembered when I was interrogated and shown the contraption of finger holders so your nails are exposed to a needle or other sharp instrument insertion. I also remembered the pain when just a small splinter got right under my nail.

"I called the AVH, and they had no knowledge of such a girl. I got suspicious and went down to the headquarters. They respect me, and they're afraid of me, as I know almost the entire brass because most of the high ranking officers are also Jewish. It was Wednesday night by the time they dug up the paperwork and the guards who received the prisoner from the KGB. I talked to the guards myself."

Lara got up, brought the brandy bottle to the table, and refilled our glasses.

I asked, "What did the guards say?"

"They took the beautiful lady, read the Russian release paper, and since neither the captain nor the official translator was around, they asked one of the guards to translate the instructions. They showed me the paper that basically said, 'Custody for temporary handling of the prisoner.' Since many of our prison guards are from the bottom of our society and often brutal thugs without education, with tendencies for masochism and sadistic behavior, they made a grave error in translation.

"These particular guards originally came from the failed Greek communist revolution in 1951, and the only job they were good for—prison guards. They purposely, or out of ignorance, translated the

DECEPTION AND REALITY- LIVING THROUGH THE MISSING PAGES OF HISTORY

Russian word vremenuy [temporary] as svodnuy [free]. So instead of temporary handling, where the prisoner usually recovers, they took her to mean 'free to handle' as they wished. The five Greek guards had their way with her all Saturday night and continued with the shift changes all the way through Sunday.

When they realized what they done with her, they killed her to avoid any possibility of reprimand."

I jumped up and yelled, "This is another trick! You told me that I could see her tomorrow!"

She indicated I should sit down, and she continued. "As I promised, you will see her tomorrow if you wish. I made arrangements to keep her until you could see her and before her body disappears."

"Where is she now!" I yelled.

Lara responded, "Her body was delivered to the medical university to be used for research and training of students. This is the standard way to dispose of bodies if they are not overly mutilated. There are interns for pathology and coroners who are responsible for accepting or rejecting the cadavers. Their functions also include checking and accepting the reason for the individual's death. The cause of death for these bodies typically sent there is suicide. As you know, Hungary has the highest suicide rate in the world, and these corpses help to achieve this dubious record.

"It is better this way, as the Serbs just mass-murder people, burying them in mass graves. With their methods, they could inflict serious bodily damage, including mutilation and acid burns, since they do not have to supply the dead corpse to medical schools. We think our ways of disposing bodies are considered more civilized. We have intimate knowledge of Hungarians being mass-murdered, mistreated, starved, discriminated against as much or more than the Jews had been right outside of our current borders, but to maintain good relations with these newly created countries, we keep quiet about these atrocities.

"Stalin approved the deliberate extermination of Hungarians by our neighbors, and most of the Allies just keep their eyes closed for the sake of peace. By the year 2000, the Hungarians living outside our borders will be reduced from five to two and a half million, according to the Communist leadership, in order to avoid border conflicts or readjustments.

"For example, in Romania, mixed marriages are encouraged, as all children will automatically become Romanians and lose all right to claim their Hungarian ancestry."

I interrupted, "I know these genocides are going on all around Hungary, but I want to talk about Piri, as I need and want to know everything about her, including the true cause of death and who disgraced or mistreated her."

"You may know about what is going on in Transylvania, as half or more of your family is already dead or imprisoned, and about the closing of Hungarian schools and universities. But you really don't know about the Slovak Benes decrees designed to kill off Hungarian and German minorities, with the full knowledge of the Allies. The Benes decrees will allow them to confiscate all of their properties, denying them any privileges, jobs, retirement income, close all Hungarian schools and deport or imprison them.

"However, returning to Piri's sufferings and death, I cannot find out, and if I could, I would not tell you the individuals responsible for the crime. Piri's body will be added to our suicide statistics. Tomorrow early morning, we'll talk to the admitting intern who subsequently examined the body and can tell you a lot more that you and her family is entitled to know, according to the communist system we live in. You must not talk about me, my friend at the medical school, or what has been said and discussed.

"I'd also like for you to stay with me tonight so I can take you early in the morning to see Piri."

I responded with a painful voice, "Lara, I know telling me all about the suffering of other Hungarians is a diversion tactic on your part to reduce my pain of losing my love. I remember Father Tibor used a similar method easing your pain of losing your loved ones. However, you'll do anything to repay the Nazis for the pain and suffering they caused. But whom do I have to hate and repay for the pain and suffering— the Communists, the Socialists, the Russians, the Jews, the Allies? I need to know the responsible person and persons, as I do not believe in hurting or blaming groups when there are individuals responsible for the actual crime that might go unpunished."

Lara agreed with my arguments and said, "I'll definitely look into that, and I will keep you posted on my progress."

I could not sleep. I stayed in the living room, drinking the apricot brandy, going half-crazy over Piri's death. How would I explain her sacrifice to the Western embassy, the pain and death they cause us because of the lack of self-policing and hurting the very people who try to help them? How will I make peace with myself? What can I say to her mother, grandmother, and to the last remaining son, Zoli in the family?

I had already gone through the denial phase, and I was still in middle of the blame and anger cycles when Lara shook my shoulders. It was already six o'clock. The last time I had looked was three thirty. I must have fallen into a dreamless sleep. Hot coffee, butter, bread, jam, cheese, and cold cuts were waiting for me after I came out of the bathroom. I could not eat, look at Lara or myself. I must have had an empty and crazy look on my face. I was just staring into space when Lara handed me the coffee.

She ordered, "Drink it, as I've already called the taxi to pick us up by the corner, not in front of the building." I remember taking a sip or two and then Lara pulling me out and toward the next street. We were already in the basement where the cadavers were stored when I realized where I was and why.

Lara's friend, the intern, was another pretty Jewish girl with an exceptionally pleasant and soothing voice and just a few years older than I. She led us into a long hallway to the end of a huge room with a heavy formaldehyde aroma. She offered me a mask, but I declined. In the room, there were three or four long tables, like gurneys, situated in the middle. The first table had a partially carved-up body covered by a whitish but heavily stained sheet. The second was empty. She led us to the farthest one from the door. This table had a clean sheet to cover a body, the forehead shape, the chest and the feet clearly identifiable. When we got close, she asked me if I wanted to see her. I nodded, and she lifted the cover, folding it back at the shoulder.

I saw Piri's face— all white, like it was carved from white stone, dressed with a black hairpiece with moon-shaped dark eyebrows and big black, curved long eyelashes. I never had seen a more beautiful statue. She had no color to her skin, but her thick lips were dark bluish purple, as if someone had painted them with ink. I stared at her and cried. I bent down to kiss her, but the young doctor prevented me from actually touching her. She asked if I wanted to know her findings after examining the body. I didn't say a word, but Lara said, "Yes."

I intently listened as she went through a show-and-tell. Pointing to her neckline, she showed us the slight impression of a cord that pointed to the cause of death, suicide. She spoke matter-of-factly, as if she were teaching a class. "The rope around her neck was applied after death, as there is no bruising. Also, prisoners have neither access to ropes nor any place to hang themselves. The neck was not broken. I kept the body for myself to examine before Lara called me because she was the most beautiful cadaver I have ever seen. In fact, I took a picture of her, as she reminded me of the image of Mary, the mother of Jesus."

I interrupted her to say Jews don't believe in Jesus. She responded, "We know Jesus was a living person. Jesus's mother was an exceptionally beautiful lady, and many Jewish boys were courting her, but I believe Jesus was a son of God, as we are all God's children."

I didn't say anything, and she just continued.

"I believe her death was caused by an accident of giving too much juice for the electric shock treatment, or she died of will." She folded down the cover all the way to Piri's waist and pointed to her breasts. She showed the damaged nipples; they were totally cauterized almost black and parts of them missing. "The powerful current flowing between her nipples must have stopped her heart, or she was already dead, and the revival attempt failed."

I asked what she meant by being already dead. She responded that her professor pointed it out most of the cadavers received from the prisons had their eyes open, as nobody would bother holding their eyes closed while rigor mortis sets in, but some of the young girls like her come in with closed eyes and lips. "Our theory is that under extreme duress and pain, they have the power to will themselves to die. We believe this is what happened to her."

I asked what they had done to her in order for her to want to die. She flipped the sheet over her left side and showed her right hand that was already stiff. Her three middle fingers had the nails totally separated and were totally black. All her fingers, except the thumbs, showed the black and blue markings of the finger vise. She tried to turn her arm out, but it was very stiff, so she pointed inside her wrist with a flashlight to see a wide ribbon of black markings. She said, "We often see these on young girls, as it seems like they like to tie and stretch them in the desired sexual position to take full advantage of them."

Then she flipped up the sheet by her feet, where we could clearly see the heavy blue-black markings of restraint by the ankles. Like a flash, it came to me, and I recalled the machine I saw that was on top of my interrogation table with T-shaped metal bars on both ends and with equal length of chain connected on top of the Ts. She turned toward me and asked if I wanted to know what sexual torture she had to go through. While Lara shook her head, I demanded to know. She continued, "After examination of the vagina and surrounding area, I found this person recently lost her virginity, which is shown by the state of her relatively freshly broken hymen. The vulva and the region of the labia minora were excessively swollen, black and blue. I could still recover some semen, even after she was flushed out by some liquid that looked like dark tea [Greek iodine]."

I asked for a pair of gloves from the young intern and put them on. I reached over to cover all her body except her head. I put a cross on her head with my thumb and on my chest and loudly prayed an Our Father, followed by Hail Mary.

I started my monologue like I was talking to my love Piri. "I have fallen in love three times in my life, and I lost them all. You are the last one my heart could endure to lose."

I could barely finish the prayers with a shaking voice, hanging my head low, but without crying. My last few sentences came out loud and clear. I covered Piri's head and asked for her body. Both women froze and looked at me, scared.

After a long pause, Lara spoke first, "This event never took place. We all exposed ourselves to grave danger bringing you here. Under no circumstances could we part with her body, as she is logged into the books and reserved for use in a lecture first thing tomorrow morning."

I yelled, "What will I say to her mother, brother, and grandmother?"

They both stayed quiet.

"What would you do if she were your sister?"

No response was coming from either one of them.

"Who will help me to find out the person and persons responsible for her horrible death?"

Lara finally spoke up. "I will."

I thanked them both, turned around, and left in great sorrow, with great guilt for not killing Béla (Berry) when I had a chance.

Since Piri's death, I have loved many ladies, but I could never truly fall in love again, at least not until I hear the beautiful music again, just like when I touched her.

I know and feel that regardless of the size of my heart, my limit is only three for falling in deep love, and I hope no one will experience such a hurt and sorrow as I did. I have also seen many dead bodies during WWII and the Hungarian Revolution, but none other had the horrifying impact of Piri's. For decades, I could not attend funerals. I lost army buddies, friends, and professors, but I could never go to their funerals. I could not even express my sympathy to a young colleague's wife when he died in an accident. It was just too hard not to think about Piri, who didn't even have a funeral. It took me over thirty years to be able to attend one.

I'll never forget Piri, her smiling face, her lovely eyes, her sweet voice, and her birthday, August 19. It has been and shall always be a special day for me as long as I live and maybe even beyond.

Aftermath

After the confidential coroner's report in the basement of the medical university, I stayed in a state of shock for many days. Every time I closed my eyes, I saw the white marble statue of Piri, partially covered with a white sheet on the gurney. The only things strange about her white statue were the long black eyelashes, hair, eyebrows, faint bluish purple lips, and the dark gray and dark coloring around the burned nipples. I guess I was still in denial. I could not believe it was her, instead of an almost perfect reproduction of her body from white marble with hair and makeup.

When I met Zoli after the ten o'clock mass, I was able to gather myself and show some strength in recounting the early morning events passing on the terrible news about the death of his sister. We could see and feel each other's agony and pain. I remembered to ask permission from Zoli to keep the scarf she wore on that ill-fated mission in the cemetery where Béla, the double agent, must have recognized her.

We even reviewed our mistakes. In spite of Zoli's training by his grandfather, we were not even rookies but true amateurs in starting and concluding such a dangerous mission with the worst possible ending, we thought. Zoli could not hold back his tears, and once he started, I lost it too. Walking in the park on this cool October Sunday, we felt no wind, we saw no one, we could not remember the path we took that late afternoon.

A cold drizzle made us aware of our surroundings, but not before we got soaking wet. We headed to the cover of the sport club and stood there, almost without uttering a sentence. I knew we were thinking about how to let the relatives know, what we could tell them, and what we could not in order to protect the rest of the team. The fact that the KGB colonel let Piri go as a mistaken identity might have been a setup.

Zoli stayed a few days to gather his thoughts before reporting back to the family. I had no choice but to return to the office.

After my boss saw me, he conferred with someone and ordered an immediate change of venue for me. My boss sent me again to the field to help consolidate the land for another collective farm in the Southern region. My boss acted faster than usual in the case of personal distress, so I guessed our office angel, Julie, feeling my loss, was instrumental in expediting my speedy departure.

On Tuesday morning, I reported to my new office of land redistribution to a young engineer heading up this operation. He did not notice my sadness and grief, as he had not known me before, but I was able to function in measuring plots along old roads, but often I had to go back and recheck my figures. I guess my new boss thought I was just a slowpoke who was assigned to him, as no one else wanted the job.

My deep and relentless torment eased for a few weeks as the Hungarian uprising started the following Wednesday, October 23 1956. A week later, I heard the news and the following report at the place where I started this dirty land redistribution work for the Communist government, southeast of the city Csaba. The head of the party, who turned me in to the secret police, was hung by the local farmers. Within a day of the news about the revolution, the entire land-distribution project ended by popular demand across the entire country, and every one of us hurried back to our respective home bases.

We were elated to learn the first revolution in the world against both Communist and Russian oppression succeeded over and beyond our wildest expectations. The Russian military outnumbered ours about two hundred to one. Our weapons were outdated— small caliber rifles and a few machine guns— against the well-equipped occupying Russian forces with tanks and high explosives. Since our military and the occupying Russian forces refused to fire on us, we succeeded. We all knew that was the beginning of the end for communism, and now it was up to the West to expedite its final collapse.[14]

Unfortunately, the West, as usual, was caught sleeping and failed to recognize the great opportunity at hand. The United Nations was even worse and proved to be totally inept and ineffective in handling conflicts, not only then, but even today. The UN was originally set up to solve world conflicts, but looking at the world problems, they are getting worse under their watch. The sad part is that some die-hard liberals still want to leave conflict resolutions for the UN to solve.

---

[14] The fact that the Hungarian uprising against the Soviet occupation and communism was successful and our country became independent in 1956 was not reported in Western news. We hear more about the unsuccessful Czech uprising in 1968. -There is an excellent DVD using original film clips about the first successful revolution against Soviet occupation and communism, titled "Torn from the Flag" by Klaudia Kovacs.

DECEPTION AND REALITY- LIVING THROUGH THE MISSING PAGES OF HISTORY

A new Hungarian government was put in place, which cared about people, family, economic conditions, independence, justice, and freedom on every level. Our military committed to protect the country and its people. Even the occupying Russian forces stayed out of our way. Some of them even asked for political asylum, as they didn't want to return to their own even-poorer country of totalitarian communist dictatorship. I know of at least one young Russian officer, with wife and two small children who wanted to stay permanently in free Hungary. Even two Chinese foreign students at the Technical University asked for asylum, and when the Russian communists squelched our freedom again, they escaped to the West.

The Russian Communist government started their negotiation for removing the occupying forces from Hungary. The agreement was just about completed and included a show of respect during the removal of the Russian troops and bringing some fresh ones just to protect the withdrawal. It even included a musical selection for the departing Russian military for a graceful exit. Once the agreement was reached, the final papers were to be signed by General Maleter and the newly selected prime minister, Imre Nagy, in the Serbian/Yugoslav embassy. As soon as our general showed up, he was promptly arrested and soon after executed. It was November 4, 1956, when the new Russian forces mechanized division invaded us the day after the arrest of General Maleter.

Some of the new invading Russian units believed they were at the Suez Canal, as that was what they had been training for. Their desert outfits were not warm enough, and they often took warm clothing from the civilians to augment theirs. That was how I lost my warm leather gloves.

The new invading Russian Army came in two ways, from the Czech side on the north and the Romanian side on the east. Russian diplomats negotiated earlier a seemingly very peaceful deal to ensure the now free Hungarian Air Force wouldn't stop them at the narrow Carpathian Mountain passes.

The West ignored the repeated pleas from our government for help. I remember praying with watery eyes not to be ignored while our request for help was repeated in many languages on the airwaves daily around the clock. Neither the UN nor the freedom loving countries of the West wanted to hear our plea for help!

KELE D. GABOR

We called on our own UN representative in New York to stand up for our freedom fighters, but we couldn't believe what we found. Our delegates were all Russians who didn't even speak Hungarian. Some of the Western radio stations urged us on to fight the occupying Russian force, which outnumbered us at least twenty to one. Our highest caliber weapon was the fifty mm machine gun. The Russians came in with tanks and artillery, which made any resistance futile.

Most people don't realize how hard it is to disable a tank with Molotov cocktails. The burning gasoline has to be poured inside the engine to do any damage. Putting frying pans upside-down on bridges was safer and better temporary deterrents against the Russian mechanized divisions, as they resembled land mines. Tens of thousands of my young countrymen were killed, injured, or taken to prison, to Russia, thanks to the ineffective United Nations and the selfish Western powers.[15]

I still wonder sometimes about the politicians in the UN, and around the free world, if they feel guilty about their pathetic behavior, which resulted in huge numbers of deaths, imprisonment, torture, loss of freedom, sufferings beyond comprehension, loss of the homeland for hundreds of thousands Hungarian refugees. Later, I saw the CIA instigated an uprising by the Kurds against Saddam Hussein, but all of us watched it collapse without the promised support. The West, with the excuse of not getting involved because of incorrect timing, just watched the brutalities committed by the Communists.

The UN is still a corrupt organization without clout. Zoli and I learned a new lesson that the Western politicians cannot be trusted, and they don't care about human rights, communist slavery, and foreign oppression unless they see a direct benefit for themselves. In fact, I recalled my uncle Álmos's philosophy about the Western civilization and its gross failure of vision for the future without wisdom and compassion.

Our uprising was again an invaluable and unique opportunity that the West missed to defeat Communism and stop the Cold War, as the Russians were afraid to reinvade Hungary until they had assurance by the inept and impotent Western politicians and the UN that they wouldn't get actively involved. Zoli and I also came to the conclusion that a visionary politician is an oxymoron, and visionary leaders can no

---

[15] An excellent and accurate account of the Hungarian uprising is told in the book, "The Testament of Revolution (1956) by Bela Liptak.

longer be elected in Western democracies.

On November 17, 1956, when returning from the office, a neatly dressed and well-built young man about the same age as I stepped next to me as I was walking home. He said without introducing himself that he had met me at one of the swimming competitions and we belonged to the same sports club a few years back. He recognized me and said he had a special message from Lara G. I told him I didn't remember ever swimming against him, nor did I know a Lara G., but I would like to know what kind of message he had for me.

He said, "Lara wants you to leave the country immediately."

Of course, I remembered the messenger, but I could not admit it. We did belong to the same swimming club, and I was avoiding him, as I knew he was also a member of the dreaded secret police. I thanked him, and when he left me and was out of sight, I turned around and went back to my office to ask my boss for advice. I just didn't want to leave my country again, like escaping from the Romanians.

I already had to escape once before from my homeland, Transylvania, and I didn't want to end up even more homesick. Also, I wanted to give my life as Piri did for freedom and independence of my small and mutilated country and help fight and defeat the cancer of society— liberalism, socialism, Marxism and then communism. I also wanted to see Al's face when I showed the pictures proving the double agent selling us out to KGB were from the embassy. I wanted to hear what excuse he would use for not finding the mole under their noses for many years. I wanted to see his reaction when I told him about the brutal murder of Piri. But Al was not in Hungary, and no one could tell me his return date for sure. Now I know I would have stayed, regardless of the consequences, if Piri had been alive.

My boss was wise and very helpful. He told me he had received requests for engineers from the ministry just before the revolution to help build bridges in Egypt and some roads in Albania. He could send me to either one. I elected Egypt, as I knew Albania was under the heavy influence of the Russian-style Communism. With paper in hand, I started out to leave my country on November 21, 1956. I felt relatively safe having the official paper to exit the country, as by that time, most of the Iron Curtain was closed again, and borders to the West were patrolled by Russian troops to reduce the number of fleeing Hungarians.

I made a slight modification or forgery in my paperwork by inserting "via Vienna" to indicate the route I wanted to take. Since public transportation was not yet safe and dependable after the failed revolution, I hitchhiked on the road to Vienna. This road also paralleled the cemetery where we took the pictures of the Western agent selling us out to the KGB.

The truck that picked us up was already half full of young men, all waiting to escape the Communist terror following the failed Hungarian uprising. During the trip, I was torn between having to leave my country and wanting to stay. When the truck was stopped by Russian troops near the border, I was relieved of not having to leave my country again.

Soon the Russians turned us over to the Hungarian border guards, who also served as an arm of the secret police. We were escorted to Csorna, one of the nearby headquarters of the AVH, and promptly arrested. The interrogating officer picked me out first from the crowd of about thirty men to be questioned. As usual, I was picked as the perceived leader of the group of young people trying to escape the Communist slavery.

In the hallway leading to rooms, the offices were full of people who had failed to leave the country in an effort to escape the inevitable Communist and Russian terror. The officer led me to his office, where interrupted by a higher-ranking officer and asked to find another room, the officer took me to the stairs, where we went down about a floor and a half below ground level. On the right, at the bottom of the stairs, was an elevator that even went deeper. However, we went past it and took over a guardroom right next to the elevator shaft. Nobody was inside the small room, and what little space was left over was occupied by a desk, two chairs and a gray metal wardrobe stacked full of folders. There were folders on top of every elevated surface, including one of the two chairs.

The captain went around the desk, sat down, and asked me for my identification book. I politely handed it over, and after a short glance at my name, he asked me what I was doing in the border zone heading west. He claimed he knew I was the leader of those young men on the truck, and he wanted me to tell him where we hid the atom pistols and all the other weapons received from the Western fascists and capitalist countries.

I almost laughed about his ridiculous allegations, and I told him I was heading to Vienna without any weapons. He looked at me, smiled, and said, "You're the first one to admit to the fact you want to escape the country."

I said, "I didn't say that I'm trying to escape."

The officer looked perturbed, impatiently banged on the desk, and asked me to explain. I told him, "I'm ordered by the ministry to go to Egypt on a foreign-work assignment."

He immediately picked up a rubber stick and angrily swiped the nearby metal filing cabinet, making a dent and a loud bang. "You're lying, you dirty so and so."

I wanted to reach inside my coat pocket to produce my official paper, but he jumped up, hitting my lower arm with the stick, hurting me quite badly, and yelled, "No tricks," as he unbuttoned his side arm.

I said, "I just wanted to show you my official exit paper and visa."

"Don't move." He came around the desk behind me, pulling down my overcoat all the way to the elbows so I could not move my arms, then came in front of me while resting the rubber stick on my right shoulder. He asked, "Where is it?"

I told him it was in my coat's left inside pocket. He moved to my right, put the stick in his left hand, and with his right hand reached into my pocket over my right shoulder and pulled out an envelope. I said, "The envelope contains my papers."

He was obviously angry. I spoke without being asked, and he let me know it by banging his stick on another metal filing cabinet right behind me. He went back to the other side of the desk, pulled his sidearm out, and put it on the desk right in front of him with the safety off and the muzzle pointing to my groin. He sat down with his finger on the trigger.

With his left hand, he carefully opened the unsealed envelope and shook out the contents on top of the desk. He then asked me to step back as far as I could go. I was able to make half a step before I found my back against a filing cabinet. The double-folded letter containing my mission to Egypt was almost impossible to unfold without using both hands. Instead of his finger, he used the muzzle of the pistol to help open the folded letter. With one glance, he could see my earlier claim was legitimate with the official heading, stamps and signatures on the paper.

He immediately put me at ease by saying they could never be overly cautious, as many Western agents had infiltrated Hungary with dangerous weapons. The small number of Fascist elements and the enemies of the state were helping overthrow this beautiful Socialist and Communist government, and now they were trying to escape, taking the atom pistols with them.

His advice was I turn back and return to my office, as it was extremely dangerous and definitely risky to try to cross the border at this time. I asked why, acting ignorant. He responded the capitalist paid mercenary units were killing anybody leaving Hungary. "As soon as you step over the border, they shoot you down like an animal, and sometimes they use atom pistols like the ones used to blow up our tanks."

I said, "I cannot just turn back, return to my office, and say I was afraid to do my duty to the great Communist state without a legitimate excuse. I must have an official paper to excuse me of not completing my assignment."

The captain agreed with me. He escorted me one more floor down on the elevator to another large room. This room, for all practical aspects, resembled the one I already encountered during my first arrest by the secret police. The room was larger, had more equipment along the walls, but the bloody floor, bloody walls, table in the middle with opposing chairs and paraphernalia were the same or similar. This particular room had more lights in it, so the official chief interrogator must have not been an albino.

The captain said, "This is the place we find out all the evils the Western capitalists are planning and doing against us. You won't believe some of our findings."

I was thinking that so far most of the Western agents I had encountered were working for the KGB, but I kept quiet. He gave me back all my papers, pointed to a chair in the dark corner of the room and asked me to wait there until he asked his superiors about drafting an official paper for me, and left. It was less than a minute before the door was kicked opened and a young redheaded man with long hair and cuffs on was thrown into the room by two guards. They didn't notice me, so they just chained the person to the table in a similar manner as I had been before. The two guards were talking in a foreign tongue I didn't understand. Once the young man was securely tied down, they put the finger lock on both hands. The finger lock looked like a long, narrow cigar case, with screws on the sides to tighten depending on the size of fingers the person had. They turned the screws until there was no way for the prisoner to move his hands or fingers. The two guards left without noticing me in the dark corner.

As soon as they shut the padded door behind them, I got up, went to the table, and loosened the "cigar" box on his fingers. The three middle fingers on each hand had the nails missing, and one of the fingers had a nasty infection, oozing puss and blood all over the table because of the tightly screwed on gadget. The prisoner didn't say a word but looked at me real hard. I looked back at him without blinking. He had light greenish eyes and reddish curly hair with freckles really showing up on his pale face.

With the quietest voice I have ever heard, he said, "Turn off the microphone," pointing his nose to the other end of the table. I went around and found a black dial. When I pointed at it, he nodded. I turned it counterclockwise until I heard a click. Soon after the click, he raised his voice and said, "That is the dial controlling the intensity of sound. The interrogators use it to broadcast the screams of people being tortured to induce more fear. It is often more effective than watching someone suffer, as our imagination maybe worse than what they're actually doing to the individual in the torture room. When the screams start, even the atheist starts praying aloud. However, their prayer is different than ours. They ask God to save themselves from such a torture while we pray for the suffering victims."

He continued, "I know you are not one of them, as you can look into my eyes. The rest, the interrogators and the Greek Communist guards, are on the bottom of humanity, and they cannot keep eye contact with me.

"My name is JJ, and I'm a priest. We prisoners know something is going on the outside, as more and more the regularly scheduled interrogation sessions are missed or postponed."

I interrupted, telling him we had a revolution and had successfully overthrown the Communist puppet government, freed a lot of political prisoners. "But the Russians overran us again and whoever can will flee the country to find freedom and justice outside our borders."

JJ said, "Too bad no one knew here we were deep underground."

I nodded in agreement, and then he asked me how I ended up here in civilian clothes, being well-dressed and a well-mannered young man. I told him I was waiting for a release paper from the captain and they put me here temporarily because they had too many young people to process without enough space.

He said, "These dumb and brutal guards have been here since 1951 but have not learned enough Russian or Hungarian to communicate.

Kele D. Gabor

They were told several times to suspend the regularly scheduled interrogations, but they still bring us here for our weekly torture sessions, return an hour later, and take us back to the cell."

I told JJ that I was sure they would let me go, as I had well-forged papers to keep me in the clear, and if he had any messages, I could relay them to the outside. JJ said he had a younger brother but didn't know where he was hiding now or how to get in touch with him, as he had not seen him since escaping from Serbia. However, people on the outside should know the secret police are accelerating all the executions here to make more room for new prisoners. Once they obtain a confession, they brutally kill the person, and if it is a young girl, they let the guards have fun with her first— many times, right in front of us. I told him I just lost my true girlfriend and that was one of the reasons I was leaving my homeland behind.

He said, "I'll pray for both of you. Please go back to your chair and sit down, as they'll be back any moment. If they notice we are talking, they will most likely keep you here. It is important the truth gets out of here, so don't do anything that would prevent my message going to human rights organizations in the West. By the way, when I finish telling you what is going on here, if there is a chance, you must turn back on the microphone again without being noticed. If they hear no sound on the tapes or the guards agree that it was quiet, you will be free to go for sure."

I said, "I'll do my best, just tell me what you want me to pass on to the outside."

He said, "They weed out the weak first by having them sign incriminating documents either by fear or by inducing pain. Some of the charges are totally ridiculous, but the fear and pain makes many of us give up the fight. These sadistic interrogators have to produce x number of confessions per week to keep their 'pleasurable' job. I believe the signed confessions are safety measures in case the government changes, so no one can be blamed for the atrocities and executions committed.

"Those of us who can resist are marched down weekly to the execution hall, which is below all the cells. They line us up against the wall about one arm distance from it, tie our hands behind us, and push us against the wall. Our head hits, but not too hard so we can keep our balance on our feet with our foreheads against the wall. Typically, seven or eight naked prisoners are taken down to the lowest underground floor.

Deception and Reality- Living Through the Missing Pages of History

The first one collapsing is shot in the back of the head and left there. The rest of us are marched back to our cell, but our agony will start as soon as they pull us back from the wall. Our forehead gets used to the constant pressure against the wall, and as soon as we are pulled back, our head feels like it will blow up. We can't sleep, stand up, bend down, or any other quick movement will reawaken the pain. Nowadays, one of us will sacrifice oneself after a few minutes to reduce the pain for the others. Initially, we kept this position as long as possible and often for over forty minutes. The longer we stay against the wall with our forehead, the worse and longer the pain lasts.

"The other favorite game for the Russian interrogators, especially during the cold months, we call the icicle. We are not given any warm or replacement clothes, even if they are worn out. When it gets cold, we sleep close together to keep warm. When they catch us keeping each other warm, they separate us and put us into the coldest cells. After a day or two of shivering, they offer a warm blanket. Some will accept, and that will be their death sentence. The blankets are warmed up with hot steam, and it feels wonderful when one snuggles into one. In a few hours, it will cool off, and by the morning, it freezes to your body. That is the end.

"We had a cruel dental assistant last year who drilled across our incisors, tied our hands behind us, plugged up our noses, and then made us run in the snow. The cold air coming through our mouth, the only opening to our lungs, created excruciating pain." JJ smiled and showed his missing front teeth. "When this sadist was replaced, the new officer just pulled out our front teeth without anesthetics to stop the constant screaming."

He told me terrible methods of causing pain and later went into some details to make sure I at least knew what they must endure to survive. I asked him what had kept him alive and going. He said, "People with a strong faith can survive almost anything and resist the worst interrogators.

I have to stay alive also because I'm one of the very few people who was an eyewitness and survived the partisan massacre and death march of over thirty thousand Hungarians and one hundred thousand Germans in Serbia. They took away all the young men, and then the remaining people, almost exclusively women and children, from Hungarian and German villages were murdered en masse. They are now in mass graves in the new Yugoslavia. I have to tell the world about the holocaust following WWII nobody wants to speak or write about. Most who were eyewitness to those horrible historical events will disappear, but I must survive.

"It was typically the atheists, egotists, and agnostics who buckle first and sign their own death warrant. They do not want to go through painful interrogations. They may not have a strong conviction or spiritual strength to hold on to, and the body is weak. Some of them even were given temporary clemency to squeal on others."

I asked for a short pause until I partially recovered from hearing about the horrors of the Communist prison system. I kept thinking about Piri's ordeal.

When JJ passed on these messages to me to relay them to human rights organizations, I started to ask about the equipment against the wall. I pointed to one of the objects, and then he told me about its use. My first selection was an old, dirty, and beat-up birthing table right across from me. JJ explained there were only a few women prisoners who were brought here, so they took advantage of them as much as possible. They were kept alive longer if they were attractive, but sometimes they used the unattractive ones for oral sex.

I started to get sick, as in my imagination, I saw Piri having to go through similar horrors, so I held up my hand again for a break. It was during one of those pauses that the door opened and the captain stepped in holding a piece of paper. I got up, walked toward him, and conveniently tripped, having to grab the tabletop for support. While I was standing there, I asked him to read the excuse letter to permit me to go back to my office without finishing my assignment.

While he was reading the short note, I turned on the microphone, probably louder than I should have, as the guards came in and wanted to know what was wrong, as they didn't hear the prisoner cry while the captain was yelling. The captain asked if I had talked to the prisoner. I gave an evasive answer that I don't talk to criminals. The captain, however, checked with the guards to see if they heard any talking between us before they would let me go. I didn't have a watch, but I would estimate I was there for over half an hour when I was escorted back onto the main floor and let go.

As I was going through the jam-packed hallways toward the exit signs, people in the long hallway, waiting to be processed, grabbed my arm, usually the painful one, as I passed them asking what happened. I lied and said I was free, but I knew I wasn't. What had just transpired had a lasting impression on me. Now I felt obligated to escape to tell my stories to the proper authorities. I was also wondering how many more times I would be arrested before escaping through the border and wondering if I could pull the same trick on the next secret police with my forged official documents.

I was released with a few very young men under the age of seventeen and two young women. Taking the advice of the secret police, most of us went to the railroad station to catch a train back home. Some of them headed east, most likely to return home, but a few of us caught the train to the north, where connections could be made to the western border to Austria.

While on the train traveling west, a middle-aged man in farmer's clothing approached me, saying he knew I was the leader of the small group and he could take all of us to the border, as he knew what sections were still open to Austria. I agreed, as he seemed to be genuine. I had my papers to wiggle out in case of a similar arrest. However, more and more people around us also wanted to join in, promising anything to me if I accepted them into my group.

The farmer assured me he knew a safe crossing point. We disembarked at the designated point, the farmer asked for quiet, and we followed him for a long walk. We walked all night, at least six hours, and I estimate the distance of about fifteen kilometers. The farmer asked for any cash we might have, as we couldn't spend the Communist money in the West. We all obliged.

The farmer made us wait until the dawn and, in a single file, walked us up to the barbed wire fences along a creek. We proceeded parallel with the fences and often stopped when hearing Russian guards talking. Every time we heard the Russian words, we shivered and became afraid of a possible trap.

Eventually, we arrived at the place where the wires had been cut and there were obvious signs of recent landmine removal. He led us through this man-made hole in the Iron Curtain in a single file and led us down to the creek. It was now getting light enough to make out guard towers nearby, but without any sign of guards in them. The farmer pointed to the other side of the creek and said, "That is Austria. If you make it to the other side, you're free." I asked him why he didn't want to join us instead of staying behind. He responded, "There are still many young people who need to escape, and they need a good, reliable guide."

We started down slowly to the bank in single file, and our guide had thrown a plank across the creek that was hidden in the nearby bush.

First, the women and children crossed, followed by the men. When we all crossed, the farmer pulled back the plank and hid it again. After a few steps toward the west, we saw a few Austrian border patrols approaching us in gray uniforms. Only one of them spoke Hungarian, and he asked if there were others behind us. I said no and turned around. The farmer, our guide, could not be seen; he had disappeared.

I asked the border guard what happened to the farmer. He responded, "He is not a farmer. He is an officer in your secret police, and he will come again until this last safe crossing point is discovered by the Russians and closed."

We were taken to a collection point, where we were asked if we had any plans. I told them I needed to talk to someone who was a member of a human rights organization. The Red Cross came by, and I tried to tell them about the human-rights violations that were going on behind the Iron Curtain. They listened for a while and left.

Later that evening, two young men came to see me about my complaints. They were Norwegians. They, of course, needed a translator, but we could not find one who spoke Hungarian and Norwegian. They finally compromised, with German as a common language. As I was talking, they often stopped me so they could catch up with their handwritten notes. It took two hours or even longer to pass on all the messages. They told me they would most likely come back with someone from Brussels or Strasbourg to hear and tape my stories again. They bid good day and left.

I have never seen or heard from them or any other human rights organization again. When I inquired, they said since I was not really an eyewitness to the events, just a courier of the report; I would have to go back and get JJ. I told them, "What a great idea, just prepare a diplomatic visa for me and provide a release paper for JJ from the Ministry of Interior and Justice, and I'll do as you requested."

There was a very long pause, and a different person came on the line and said, "If we could do that, we would have rescued him."

After we crossed the border, the Austrian border patrol led us to a temporary housing place at a nearby farmer's home. The family welcomed us and fed us. There were usually two persons assigned to a farmhouse. I was surprised to find that at every home there was someone who spoke Hungarian, usually the older ladies. After just spending one day with the family, the lady of the house took a liking to me and asked if I would consider staying there. I thanked her for her kindness and gave her a big hug for asking. The next day, we were picked up and taken to a large facility where we were processed, which included a quick medical checkup and provision of clean clothing piled up in a large room.

Most of us needed a change, as we came with only the clothes on our backs. I had a small attaché case with my papers, a change of underwear, a small towel, soap, and extra socks. I picked up a nice shirt, a better pair of gloves than I had, and a pair of good shoes in case I needed to be more presentable. When we left, they also gave us a small package in a carrying bag containing a razor, shaving soap, shampoo, two towels and a small flashlight.

Our German knowledge was almost nonexistent, as in the Communist system, we were forced to study Russian. Learning English was a crime.

Later, they permitted private lessons to learn German, but it was not part of the curriculum.

At the processing facility, I requested a chance to continue my higher education, so I was slated to go to a city with universities. First, they took us to Imst, from where I commuted to Innsbruck University, but after a month, I ended up in Vienna (Wien) and studied chemical engineering.

This university provided space in a dormitory; the Americans picked up the tuition fees and other organizations the food tickets. Therefore, we just had to learn German fast and study. We even had a better opportunity in getting extra clothing from the Catholic Relief organization. We were able to spend an entire morning picking what we liked to look more presentable, unlike the run-of-the-mill flüchtling (refugee).

One Friday evening, while eating my supper at the university cafeteria, someone covered my eyes from the back and asked, "Who do you think I am?"

It was obviously a young lady with soft hands, but the voice was unfamiliar.

After thinking a while, I responded, "I give up." She insisted I try again. "Should I know you?" I asked.

She laughed.

I jumped up, and even before turning around, I blurted out, "Lara!" and then embraced her. It was good to hear a familiar and sweet laughter. I was shocked and pleasantly surprised.

It just came out, "I thought you loved the power the Communist system provided? You're the last person I expected to see in here."

She didn't get upset, just sat down across the big round table and started to talk. I noticed she was very well dressed, wearing a beautiful sable fur coat with matching hat. Even her dark-gray suit under the coat was elegant and made of fine material. I figured she had brought the fur coat from Russia.

"It is true I enjoyed all the privileges that came with my position, including the power, but I have a mission to accomplish, which includes studying Jewish and non-Semite relations everywhere else."

"You mean, you don't see problems between Jews and Arabs?" I asked.

"You're right, I used the wrong term, as the Semites include both the Arabs and us, and I do expect and know there are and will be problems between us. I'm sure it will be our doing if the conflicts escalate, knowing how we operate from a superior position and being the most prejudiced people on Earth," she added.

Since I didn't want to talk about her mission, as it had been a big thorn between us from my perspective, I asked her what would be her next move.

She responded, "I was hoping we could work together. You could be my right hand when we needed to interview non-Jewish philosophers, statesmen, and famous thinkers, as some may not want to share their true feelings about us when I'm asking the questions."

"I may be able to get their true feelings, but I have strong convictions about the Jewish people's arrogance because they think they're superior, the only chosen people of God. The Jews cannot see their shortcomings, and the non-Jews generalize and judge the Jews under one umbrella."

"Believe me, there is more to it than your simplified view."

I asked her how she found me; her answer was through the Red Cross. I wanted her to join me to eat, but she already had had a big supper, so she watched me while I had my first fried octopus. I enjoyed it.

While watching me eat, she said, "I must thank you and take you somewhere tomorrow."

"What are you thanking me for, and where do you want to take me?"

"The place I'll take you tomorrow morning is a surprise, and the thanks are for you not forgetting about me."

"How do you know?"

"You have kept your sideburns long, the way I liked them."

I had to admit she was right, and it felt good that she had noticed.

Lara wanted to spend the entire Saturday with me, but I had lab work at the university from ten to twelve o'clock. We agreed to meet at six thirty in the morning, close to the Ring in front of the city hall, across from the Habsburg Palace within the Ring.

Every time I passed the palace, now serving as a museum of the old Austrian empire, I felt pain, as I knew that at least half, if not more, of all the gold and jewels was either forcibly taken from Hungary or just simply stolen from our people or goldmines.

The next morning was very cold, but most of the snow had been cleared on the sidewalk and on the street. In a few places on the pavement, the frozen ice was slippery, but the surface for the most part was covered with sawdust or ashes in front of each house that I passed. Lara was already waiting at the designated spot. I knew she was going to take me out for breakfast, as she knew I liked to start my day with a good portion of energy-rich food, but I was wrong. She got a taxi and took me to a large old gray building. When we got out, she opened her purse, and I could not help noticing it was practically full of large denomination shillings.

However, she only left a small tip for the driver.

We went to the main door that had a big half-moon shaped window on the top, and all its wood components were made of fine hardwood. The door was at least four meters wide, with a small entry door on the side. She rang the bell, and a lady's voice asked what we wanted. She just said it was Lara. The small door opened, Lara went in, and I followed. The petite lady who opened the door led us to a huge dimly lit room. Once we were inside, she put on the bright lights. I was amazed at what I saw. The finest clothing, shoes, coats, boots, underwear, skirts, pants, trousers, belts, leather and fur coats of every size, all arranged in groups. In the back, there was even fine jewelry of every kind, from watches to necklaces.

Lara said, "All that I'm wearing is from here, and this is the least I can do for you now. Just pick whatever you want, and they will wrap it up and we can take it along. Once you're done, we will have a good breakfast nearby before I take you to the university.

I selected a new attaché case, new boots, a sweater and fine angora socks. What I picked would fit into my new case, except for the boots.

I was tempted to take an expensive watch and a new coat, but they were all so elegant I would have been uncomfortable wearing them at the university, especially in the poor students' dormitory. Lara was disappointed.

She insisted on peeling off my clothes and replacing them with the new stuff, but I declined. She did pick a nice silk shawl for me, and I added it to my collection.

We walked to a small pastry shop nearby and had a good breakfast— cheeses, bread, butter, hot chocolate, a piece of marzipan, and we concluded the feast with poppy-seed strudels. While eating, I asked her from where those beautiful things in the warehouse had come. She said, "America, and more specifically, the Jewish Relief organization." I told her I didn't qualify. She laughed for a long time, and then we had to leave for my lab work.

We took a taxi, and she told me she was heading for Israel, as America most likely would refuse her because of her high-level position in the Communist Party. I was surprised. I just found out days before one of the high-ranking secret-police chiefs responsible for killing hundreds of Hungarians had been received with red carpet treatment in America.

When I shared the news report with her, she said, "It did happen, but now they check the person out before issuing visas." She added, "Many communists left initially, being afraid of reprisals when they saw the revolution succeed. Most of them who came out early were welcomed in America as freedom fighters."

After the taxi let us out, I gave her a big hug and kissed her on the cheek. She also squeezed me tight and said, "I will see you again."

I said, "I hope so. You know my address, but I don't know yours."

A few days later, she came by the dormitory and left a message she was leaving the country the next day. Unfortunately, I wasn't there, and I didn't get the message in time.

I saw Lara again eight years later in Berkeley, California. We had dinner together at the Pot-Luck restaurant. She looked nice but serious, and that was how our meeting started, continued, and ended. She again found me, and when I asked how, she said, "We know everything. You are married, have a son and a new baby is on the way." I was impressed.

She continued, "You have not forgotten me."

"Of course, but how do you know?"

"Your sideburns."

Lara was on a nine-month sabbatical, spending her time in California with an official assignment. I asked her what the assignment was. She said, "We have to keep up the propaganda, the exaggerations, and the lies."

I asked her to explain, and she went on, "If Stalin's terror and Mao's massacre would get ten percent of the media coverage of what the Holocaust gets, we could not milk the world for so much sympathy and money."

I understood the exaggeration part but asked about the lies. She explained, "For example, the gas chambers— there was no building in any of the concentration camps that could be used for gassing people to death. None of them was built airtight."

She was working in her country in connection with human rights. I suspect also spying, as she knew things about the KGB and the master spies of Cambridge, and the European Spy Ring like— Scot, the Romeo from Scotland Yard, Kim Philby, and Melita Norwood.

Lara did share some concerns about how the Israelis treated the Arabs and Palestinians. According to her, successful Arabs or Palestinians in Israel were for window-dressing.

She maintained a dual citizenship, retaining her Hungarian citizenship, and as she put it, she never knew when she might have to escape from Israel to a safer place. She even voted in the Hungarian elections and received a pension for her work while working for the Communist Party. I found that odd and unfair.

She had had a lot of suitors, but she never got married.

When I asked why she didn't seem happy to see me, she said, "Every time I see you, I think of our homeland and feel sorry for Hungary and for all the Hungarians."

"Why?"

"Hungary is completely under our thumbs," she answered.

It is better if I don't elaborate on many personal topics we discussed or her opinion of the United Nations, but she definitely indicated Israel and the Jews slowly and steadily were increasing their sphere of influence all around the world, with the exception of some prominent Arab countries.

She believed once they controlled some of these Arab states and the rest of the Semites, they would be very close to dominating the world, except for China. "We even changed the meaning of Semites, making it to refer to the Jews exclusively. Yet, every intelligent person should know it includes the Arabs also."

"You'll never control the Muslim countries."

"We already have a lot of good Jewish men converting to Islam as we speak. We have to be prepared for the time the Muslims take over the Middle East and Europe."

When I asked if she wanted to dominate the world, she responded, "I don't care, and it's too late to stop them."

"Who are 'they'?" I asked.

"I have a lot of connections. I know a lot of important people. I have retained some of my powers, but I don't know or want to know," she responded.

"Why don't you want to know?" I was probing deeper.

"I might have met some of them, but there is no one person who has this secret and privileged information. The members are extremely well organized and powerful in every regard— politics, wealth, influence, media, business, arts, science, law, military, education, media, spying and religion.

It doesn't work as a conspiracy or as described in the Protocol of the Elders of Zion."

"I don't know about those stories, so please tell me how it really works.

Will the influence include America?"

"Both books deal with theories about a Jewish conspiracy for world domination. Instead, it works somewhat like Darwin's theory of evolution, survival of the fittest and natural selection, but we have to be prepared and ready when the time is right. Just look at the contributions the Jewish people gave to the world in every field— art, sciences, statesmen, advisors, medicine, or any other field."

Then she put on a sarcastic smile and said, "America is easy to influence, and from now on, you won't be able to elect any high-ranking politician who does not support Israel. We'll make sure that no one with anti-Zionist sentiment will be appointed by the president or approved by the Senate. Just look at the support we get from America. It is more than you can imagine or is reported and probably more than the rest of the world combined gets in foreign aid. The only problem we have is the rest of the Semites, but if we don't succeed on our own, we will get America involved to help defeat them."

"Tell me more about this power and control evolution by the Jews," and I added sarcastically, "Have you found the nonexistent skeleton in the tomb of Jesus Christ?".

"We know we'll inherit the world. We have superior intellect, we crave power, and most world leaders are already dependent on our advice in economics, finance, arts, politics, media, banking, science, intelligence gathering, law, you name it. The only concern I have is we tend to abuse power, as we do not subscribe to Jesus's teaching of love and mercy. As I mentioned before, we are not conspiring but looking for opportunities. We keep our fingers on the world's pulse and keep in contact with all who are already in power, either as a respected advisor or otherwise influential person.

Christ's tomb will be found when the time is right."

One last question from me, "What forms will this world domination take?"

"I'm not sure. It'll probably be presented as a benevolent dictatorship, ensuring peace and tranquility on the world. You know as I do— peace, love, and tranquility come from God, not from government. The new world government will take a lot from liberal democrats, and we will need theirs and other socialists' support. But in reality, it will be closer to the communist system where one party rules all facets of life. Most people will buy into the new order, as it'll appeal to masses who think with their hearts and not with their brains. There will be a lot of suffering for those who don't buy into the new world government.

"To be successful in domination, the government must be either totalitarian in nature, requiring a strict belief system, or rule by fear. Therefore, the process has already begun to discredit faith-based organizations, to minimize the church's role, as religion of any kind will be in direct competition with the new world Order. There will be no prayers, displays of religious symbols in public places. In public schools, the children won't be able to learn about Christian religion or pray to a God. All this will be done legally, as there will be a reinterpretation of your Constitution by the highest courts. This world order, in order to succeed, must embrace or hold you three ways— body, mind, and spirit."

In 1966, I did not believe this part of her predictions. Now I know a high school student in public schools must go to prison before he can have unlimited access to the Bible or practice any religion in school.

We parted company very late that night. I escorted her to the plush apartment she had nearby. We had a coffee but didn't talk much. She gave me two books, The Predictions of Nostradamus about Hungary and Henoch Apocalypses. At that time, I didn't know the existence of such writings.

Around midnight, I bid her farewell, wished her good luck, and gave her a big hug. For some yet unknown reason, she cried when I left. I intend to find out the reason.

About twenty-three years later, she contacted me again and left a message that my oldest son and his wife may be in danger while working in Hungary, as the paranoid Communists were still around and believed that the couple spied for Western agencies.

I tried every method known to me to warn my son confidentially and without exposing myself, but being brought up in the free America, he was too naïve to take it seriously. Luckily, Lara intervened and was able to save him and his wife from unpleasant and embarrassing situations. Thank you, Lara!

After reading Nostradamus's visions of Hungary, which I received from Lara, I understood why the Israelis want to retain our land as their second home. As seen in my brother's vision, Nostradamus predicted a safe place within the Carpathian Basin while the rest of the world burns.

Nostradamus (1503–1566) was born Michel de Notredame in St. Remy, studied philosophy in Avignon, and later became a physician. His visions and predictions were first published in 1555 in the poetic book Centuries.

He also wrote Les Oracles de Nostradamus sur la Hongrie (Predictions about Hungary by Nostradamus), containing ninety-nine prophecies covering little over one thousand years and starting with the sixteenth century.

Henoch Apocalypse also deals with predictions and visions of the future.

It has many dire predictions but still contains a lot of fascinating prophecies worth reading about.

Kele D. Gabor

Conclusions

Half of my family and half of my friends are lucky survivors of WWII and the Communist oppression. Living under these conditions was challenging and difficult. The constant fear, hardship, the many life-threatening moments, bombings, explosions, death and suffering, starving, and discrimination had a long-lasting effect on our lives.

Yes, we could have given in, joined the Nazi or Communist Parties, stopped going to church, as many others had done, and had a much easier life. However, none of us could live with such a betrayal of our loved ones, beliefs, country, people, freedom, liberty and justice. We also identified with and felt responsibility for our people in the entire Carpathian basin. We knew that we had to resist and fight back the best way we could during the Nazi-controlled German occupation and the Russian Army– enforced communism dictated by Stalin and his puppet governments. We just wanted to gain back our independence and freedom for our nation and the many Hungarians who were forced to live under foreign governments as the new borders were drawn around them.

There is no claim made here that others didn't suffer as much or more than we did. The fact remains that there are many Hungarians who had to pay the ultimate price, which, in my mind, was not death but suffering under the yoke of foreign powers for decades, like millions of Hungarians under Serbian, Russian, Romanian, and Slovakian ultra nationalistic rules.

One has to experience any combination of humiliation, death marches, forced labor camps, prisons, tortures, beatings, displacements of families, deportation of the young, prejudices and injustices, which was the lot of my people, in order to appreciate the plight of the Hungarians.

In order to really comprehend the extent of our recent past and current sufferings, one needs to be an American Indian, an Armenian, a Kurd, a Pole or a Jew who survived the concentration camps, or an ex-slave. Only the aforementioned groups can fully identify with the Hungarians still suffering under ultra-nationalistic foreign governments. They were robbed of their lands and freedom, their families massacred

Deception and Reality - Living Through the Missing Pages of History

or dispersed, their children scattered, their schools and universities closed, their possessions stolen, and their freedom of speech denied. The use of our mother tongue is still discouraged. In Romania, there are many Hungarian churches, but in most of them, they are not allowed to have the mass or the sermon given in their native tongue. Unlike the Indians, we only lost seventy one percent of our land and over forty percent of our population, but similarly we lost the prime and best part of our territories, rich in natural resources.

The Western diplomats cannot even fathom the suffering, the cost in human lives, and slavery they had created for my people when they subdivided Central Europe, and thereby destabilized the entire region.

Western nations who did not reject the French- or Stalin-dictated peace treaties and the subdivision of Central Europe are still paying the price for their shortsighted policies. This includes, but is not limited to, the huge costs of WWII, the cold and civil wars, and the animosities among different nationalities that are forced to live together, separated from their native country.

In spite of all the suffering and pain, I feel fortunate to have survived and have experienced so much that gives me a better perspective on historical events, and sometimes helps me predict the future. My views, therefore, are different from the average person's and more in focus than those of most political commentators or views expressed by politicians, journalists, editors, newspapers, or the general media. I think I can see things behind the biased views of commentators, and the lies or half-truths from people asking for your vote. For example, good leaders don't point fingers or have the time to blame; they work on solutions.

Ten years after the Hungarian Revolution, my wife, my ten-month old son, and I returned to see my country again. I was able to retrieve my time capsule, the thermos from the map library with the negatives, which showed the exchange of information between the embassy worker and the KGB. The color prints were in bad shape, which I attribute to the imperfect development methods at that early age of color photography.

I smuggled the two rolls of negatives out of the Communist-controlled Hungarian border. A week after the return to our free country, I passed on the film to Al, who by that time enjoyed a high management position in the agency. It took him almost two years to initiate some kind of legal action against the ex-embassy employees working for the KGB.

The Western double agents we identified were eventually called back with the bait of potential promotion, and an official hearing was conducted.

As the judge presiding over the hearing stated, "We are not here to find scapegoats, but to find remedies for avoiding similar mishaps or misunderstandings in the future." The defense for the individuals who were accused of turning names of informers over to the KGB was that their prime directive was to establish contact with KGB agents and subsequently recruit them in any way possible. The two embassy workers also claimed that while using us as bait to lure KGB agents over, they did not realize what harsh, deadly, and painful methods were used to deal with informers for the West.

Both double agents were released on their own cognizance until the next session, thanks to their energetic defense lawyers. The double agents disappeared without a trace before the next hearing. A few years later, they resurfaced in Central Europe, and I'm convinced they started to work for the KGB in earnest. However, the KGB or the secret police still doesn't know how the list of MIG's identifications and military serial numbers or the location of planned silos for rockets found their way to the West.

After the two agents, BT and PZ, left the USA, they both found their way to Europe and started to tie up all the loose ends. They worked hard to track down the persons involved with exposing them and subsequently eliminate them. Since they'd already killed Piri and Bandi, and many other young people indirectly, they were looking for Zoli and me in earnest.

Fortunately, they did not know about Dora and Hodos.

The revenge I was promised after our fight in the cemetery showed its ugly head in 1988. Twenty years after the initial hearing, Zoli was found tossed by the side of the road with similar injuries like Bandi had suffered the night he was kidnapped with Piri at the opera house. The last witness living in the USA believed he was safe. However, thanks to Al, in 1995, I was warned. I received a concealed weapon license and a note: Your code name is compromised. BT knows who you are, and we may not be able to protect you.

BT followed me and made it all the way to Mexico, where he died of lung cancer in 1999. Now I'm safe, I hope.

Deception and Reality - Living Through the Missing Pages of History

Living, dying or just existing in those difficult times meant we had to develop a survival strategy and a special life philosophy. Looking back, with thanks to our parents, families, teachers, faith and learning to be responsible for our own actions, I can look at life as if I were flying a plane as the pilot. Unfortunately, the pilots have no control over weather, time of departures, roughness of the runways, the knowledge of the air controllers, the calibration of the instruments or the condition of the engine and the fuselage.

My friend and I certainly had our share of stormy weather, bumpy flights, wrong landing instructions, engine troubles and having to take off along with the undesired political winds and whims. But we stayed our course as much as humanly possible. Fate gave us the parachute for security and was our instrument panel when sand and thunderstorms reduced our vision.

Our faith provided the courage and power also to pull the cord after jumping out from a burning plane. I have seen other people jumping from damaged planes, but some did not have enough faith to pull the cord.

Later in life, you find a partner as the co-pilot. Take good care of her/him, as when you're down, sick or disabled, she/he can take you to your original destination or help you to a safe landing.

Remember that you always have some passengers— your children, relatives, friends, teammates or others, and just like a ship's captain, you're responsible for all of them. You have to provide the parachutes and show them how to use them. It will be up to them to wear the parachutes during dangerous times and have the faith to pull the cord when needed.

Nowadays, most parents provide a safe car seat, use seat belts for their young ones, and provide other training, but forget to give them the most important survival tool— spiritual education. Most parents do protect their children from bodily harm, but the young ones often are not given the opportunity to also fully develop their mental and spiritual strengths.

Faith gives you strengths far beyond your imagination!

Pilots with vision will keep to the flight plan and get help along the way to ensure landing at the right place. Others are flying aimlessly and without purpose, never knowing where they are or where they are going.

Prayer gives you the extra lift and acts like an extra pair of wings. When the engine fails, it can help you glide to a safe landing, regardless of how high up you were.

Be a good pilot with vision and compassion. Stay on course, regardless of the weather, and have faith when the events or circumstances force you to bail out. Remember that you haven't lived until you experience being close to death.

Living under many forms of governments, one acquires knowledge based on experience. I agree with Winston Churchill: "The inherent vice of capitalism is the unequal sharing of the blessings. The inherent blessing of socialism is the equal sharing of misery."

Less government, fewer taxes, less control equals more freedom and more prosperity. More government, more taxes, more control equals socialism.

If you picked the first option, you most likely take pride in your work and have ambitions. The government cannot give to anybody anything that the government does not first take from somebody else.

"A liberal is someone who feels a great debt to his fellow man, which debt he proposes to pay off with your money" (G. Gordon Liddy). What one person receives without working for it, another person must work for without receiving compensation.

I also found Mark Twain's comment about the media still true today: "If you don't read the newspaper, you're uninformed; if you do read the newspaper, you're misinformed."

"Making a difference" is a wonderful expression with some caveats, as every one of us makes a difference. However, in my experience the easiest way to make a positive difference is just to smile at one another. Regardless of how small your smile may be, you are making a big and positive difference for someone else.

It was very hard and painful to recall many of my unwanted experiences.

One of the benefits of writing about these events is that it freed me from most of my nightmares. Now I seldom wake up yelling or screaming at nights seeing, torture, prisons, or bombing attacks. Most of my nights are now peaceful, but on occasion, I still have painful dreams about my countrymen governed by non-Hungarians and those who are being enslaved and mistreated by neighboring nationalistic states, especially the Serbs, Romanians, Slovaks, and Russians.

Here I'm passing on the best advice I have ever received, "Work hard to find all your talents and abilities, find the right people to help you develop them, and write a vision statement that ensures you use most of your God-given gifts." Then you'll have an advantage over most people, as you'll know what should be the purpose of your life!

I pray that God will take my soul, but my spirit will stay here in the wilderness. Friends and family can look for me here. When you see an unspoiled, beautiful sight, you might find me there.

Kele D. Gabor

Journaling & Notes

Journaling & Notes (Cont.)

Kele D. Gabor

Book Reviews

Deception & Reality, by K. D. Gabor is a courageous and riveting account of a young man's survival and maturation through the 20th century. Inferno of occupation by foreign armies, displacements and the dehumanizing process of becoming and reduced into a refugee in his own country.

His story is more than an expose; it is an indictment of all the conquering powers and their inhumane henchmen, who so callously carved up the old Europe disregarding history, cultures, nationalities, and basic Human rights.

In the end, the reader experiences a soul-searching identification with the author. He is right, deception, lies and cover up is the name of the game of international imperialism.

All powers dictating unfair treaties have blood on their hands, but no one is held responsible, and reality does not include truth or justice for the victims, the dead, the tortured and the dispossessed.

These are indeed those missing pages of history.

I give top ratings of 5 stars to this book.

J. D.

Just finished reading the extraordinary book, DECEPTION & REALITY", by Kele D. Gabor. This volume chronicles the beginning in the tranquil Transylvania, Hungary, – now occupied by Romania, followed by the short Nazi occupation, the persecution of Jews and the enemies of the Nazis, spiraling into the horrible turmoil of WWII, followed to quick succession by the Communist Terror and life in the "Workers Paradise". He talks about the brainwashing activities by having to learn the Communist ideology that is alien to the Hungarian spirit and the defeat of the 1956 revolution. These true stories of starvation, torture, imprisonment, class warfare, execution, and a great detective work all were the author's experiences at a young age. This is a kind of biography registering the extraordinary circumstances leading to the 21st century.

Mr. Gabor's work should be read by all, who are interested in

DECEPTION AND REALITY- LIVING THROUGH THE MISSING PAGES OF HISTORY

humanity and history. Let me quote Alexander Solzhenitsyn's words, "Anyone not hopelessly blinded by his own illusions must recognize that the West today find itself in crisis, perhaps even in mortal danger". The Russian's prophetic words convey a sense of even greater urgency today, because we live in the illusion superseding the past, as revealed by the author, Mr. Gabor in his memoirs. A must read and learn from."
I. D.

> *"The young man tells his story so that we can experience it and feel it through his eyes and ears and fears— and not only does it come alive, it tells a larger story omitted from history as written by the victors, which is never the whole story, or necessarily true story."*
> A. G.

"It is a special eye-opener for those who thought they knew the history of this region. Read and experience the immediacy of a life lived under peace and war, love and courage, fear and oppression— Here in the West we still teach and learn Central and Eastern European history based on what was written by the Communists in the Stalin era."
C. P. V.

> *"History is often revised over time, as the oppressed overcome, as the persecuted escape, and as the occupied are liberated. With passage of time comes a story of life and love, deception and reality, which could not previously be told."*
> C. B.

"For most of us August 6th, 1946 was VE Day in Western Europe the end of WWII. Unfortunately, this was not the case for people living in Central Europe. At the end of the conflict the victors redrew boarders, just like after WWI which played an important part in starting WWII. Most of the indigenous Hungarian population in the Carpathian basin ended up in newly formed countries and they had to adopt the new language, citizenship, and treated worse than 2nd class citizens. For these people being foreigners in their own homeland and the ones under the communist dictatorship the peace time was worse than the wars.

I was fortunate to read his account of events in the book titled,

Kele D. Gabor

Deception & Reality as more exciting stories had never been my opportunity to read. Strictly speaking it would be called an autobiography but that is an inadequate description of these thrilling episodes of living under difficult circumstances.

The stories unfold from a storyteller from chapter 1 on. These are stories within stories. The book is full of unreported historical events, intrigue, passion, and daring love. Many sections are gripping as anything you have read so far, but please don't read ahead!

We should all be thankful for the opportunity to absorb his accounts of how to survive the hardship and appreciate our freedom in the West."
Dr. C. N. T.

> "Deception & Reality" by Mr. Gabor is written for all people; young, old and in between. Especially for those who seek the truth, for those who can gain deeper appreciation of the freedom they enjoy, and for those who still suffer but will find solace in knowing they're not alone and not forgotten.
>
> The readers should find these original stories unique, enlightening, and an entertaining learning experience."

C. G. G.

"Kele's story is set in the time when the threat of discovery requires extraordinary courage to do the right thing"
D. S.

I pray that this book will reach the hearts of our world leaders and policy makers...

                                 - Floreza Alpuerto, editor

www.ingramcontent.com/pod-product-compliance
Lightning Source LLC
Chambersburg PA
CBHW070945160426
43193CB00012B/1808